Violence and the City in the Modern Middle East

Violence and the City
in the Modern Middle East

Edited by Nelida Fuccaro

Stanford University Press
Stanford, California

Stanford University Press
Stanford, California

Printed in the United States of America on acid-free, archival-quality paper

Library of Congress Cataloging-in-Publication Data

Violence and the city in the modern Middle East / edited by Nelida Fuccaro.
    pages cm
  Includes bibliographical references and index.
    ISBN 978-0-8047-9584-5 (cloth : alk. paper) — ISBN 978-0-8047-9752-8 (pbk. : alk. paper) — ISBN 978-0-8047-9776-4 (electronic)
    1. Urban violence—Middle East—History. 2. Political violence—Middle East—History. 3. City and town life—Middle East—History. I. Fuccaro, Nelida, editor.
    HN656.Z9V589 2016
    303.60956—dc23
                                2015021950

Typeset by Bruce Lundquist in 10/14 Minion

CONTENTS

FIGURES AND MAPS

FIGURES

MAPS

CONTRIBUTORS

NELIDA FUCCARO is Reader in Modern History of the Middle East at the School of Oriental and African Studies, University of London. She is the author of *The Other Kurds: Yazidis in Modern Iraq* (I. B. Tauris, 1999) and *Histories of City and State in the Persian Gulf: Manama since 1800* (Cambridge University Press, 2009, 2011), and co-editor, with Ulrike Freitag, Claudia Ghrawi, and Nora Lafi, of *Urban Violence in the Middle East: Changing Cityscapes in the Transition from Empire to Nation State* (Berghahn, 2015).

JAMES E. BALDWIN is Assistant Professor in the Department of History, University of Warwick (UK). He held a Leverhulme Trust Early Career Fellowship from 2011 to 2014. He specializes in the social history of law in the Ottoman Empire, in particular in Egypt. His current research explores the relationship between violence and law in Ottoman-Egyptian political life.

LAUREN BANKO is Research Associate in the Department of Middle Eastern Studies, University of Manchester (UK). Her research interests include Mandate Palestine, the interwar Middle East, citizenship and nationality in the Arab world, and Arab emigrants in the early twentieth century.

ORIT BASHKIN is Professor of Arab History and Culture at the Department of Near Eastern Languages and Civilization, University of Chicago. She is the author of *The Other Iraq: Pluralism and Culture in Hashemite Iraq* (2008) and *New Babylonians: A History of Jews in Modern Iraq* (2012), both published by Stanford University Press.

RASMUS CHRISTIAN ELLING is Assistant Professor in the Department of Cross-Cultural and Regional Studies, University of Copenhagen. He teaches the sociology and history of Iran and the Middle East as well as urban theory. He recently published *Minorities in Iran: Nationalism and Ethnicity after Khomeini* (Palgrave Macmillan, 2013).

YASSER ELSHESHTAWY is Associate Professor of Architecture at the United Arab Emirates University, where he runs the Urban Research Lab. He is the author of *Dubai: Behind an Urban Spectacle* (Routledge, 2010) and editor of *The Evolving Arab City* (Routledge, 2008) and *Planning Middle Eastern Cities* (Routledge, 2004). *The Evolving Arab City* received a best book award by the International Planning History Society (IPHS) in 2010.

ULRIKE FREITAG is Director of Zentrum Moderner Orient (Center for Modern Oriental Studies) and Professor of Islamic Studies at the Freie Universität, both in Berlin. She is the author of *Indian Ocean Migrants and State Formation in Hadhramaut* (Brill, 2003) and co-editor, with Nelida Fuccaro, Claudia Ghrawi, and Nora Lafi, of *Urban Violence in the Middle East: Changing Cityscapes in the Transition from Empire to Nation State* (Berghahn, 2015).

CLAUDIA GHRAWI is Research Fellow at the Zentrum Moderner Orient (Center for Modern Oriental Studies) and a PhD candidate at the Freie Universität in Berlin. She is the co-editor, with Ulrike Freitag, Nelida Fuccaro, and Nora Lafi, of *Urban Violence in the Middle East: Changing Cityscapes in the Transition from Empire to Nation State* (Berghahn, 2015).

DINA RIZK KHOURY is Professor of History and International Affairs at George Washington University and a Guggenheim Fellow. She is author of *State and Provincial Society in the Ottoman Empire: Mosul 1519–1834* (Cambridge University Press, 1997, 2002) and *Iraq in Wartime: Soldiering Martyrdom and Remembrance* (Cambridge University Press, 2013).

NORA LAFI is Senior Research Fellow at the Zentrum Moderner Orient, Berlin (Center for Modern Oriental Studies) and teaches at the Graduate School of Muslim Cultures and Societies of the Freie Universität in Berlin. She is co-editor with Ulrike Freitag of *Urban Governance under the Ottomans: Between Cosmopolitanism and Conflict* (Routledge, 2014) and co-editor with Ulrike Freitag, Malte Fuhrmann, and Florian Riedler of *The City in the Ottoman Empire: Migration and the Making of Urban Modernity* (Routledge, 2011).

PREFACE

Despite the centrality of cities in the modern history and contemporary politics of the Middle East, urban violence has received little academic attention in Europe and North America. Awareness of this gap in the scholarship sets the intellectual and ethical agenda of this volume, which also draws inspiration from a long tradition of studies on violence that have added critical depth to academic practice and to our understanding of social and political life. Building on a three-year international research project, this collection of essays explores the theme of violence and the city in order to uncover new facets of urban life and experience in the last two centuries or so, a period of momentous changes in the urban and political map of the Middle East. The majority of the chapters deal with the twentieth century, particularly with the period after the demise of the Ottoman and Qajar Empires. This choice reflects the urgent need to start unveiling more systematically this neglected era of urban upheaval under colonial, revolutionary, and authoritarian regimes in the post–World War I international system. The short- and long-term reverberations of this upheaval are particularly useful to trace the roots of today's urban age, an age that increasingly projects images of fractured Middle Eastern cities positioned on the front line of local, national, and global political and social struggles.

At the heart of this volume is the recognition that cities and violence—particularly in combination—have been repeatedly taken for granted in Middle Eastern historical scholarship. While cities have been usually approached as central places of government and as the playground of state administrations, the violence taking place in them has been almost inevitably regarded as subsidiary to other social and political processes and outside historical forces. As a result of this association, there has been little recognition of the mutually constitutive relation between violence and the city. By placing emphasis on this reciprocity, this collection of essays foregrounds urban violence as a specific object of study that makes an empirical and theoretical contribution to the growing field of urban history and urban studies as a cross-disciplinary area of research and teaching on the modern and contemporary Middle East. Moreover, reconstructing the violent pasts of cities can open up new vistas on modern Middle Eastern history, offering alternative and complementary perspectives to the making and unmaking of empires, nations, and states, the analytical categories that have dominated regional and subregional historiographies.

To this end the first two chapters have been written with the scholarly and student community in mind as an introduction to and critical synthesis of key themes and debates that have informed discussions of urban violence: those specifically on the Middle East that have inspired this collection and that took place over a number of years among the international group of scholars who have contributed to this volume, and those of other researchers who have studied violence and cities in different historical and geographical contexts. It is hoped that newcomers either to urban studies or violence—or to both—will find plenty of food for thought, while readers already versed in these topics will identify opportunities to develop their work in new directions. The case studies included in the chapters that follow tackle some of these debates and undertake the task of penetrating deep into the turbulent nature of the associational life of towns and cities across the region.

In order to nuance the complexity of their violent experiences, authors move beyond the domain of contentious politics and social movement theory.[1] While concentrating on a variety of performers, including collectivities and state actors, they explore the nexus between order and disorder, conflict and solidarity, and discourse and action as embedded in particular urban milieus. Using examples from the eighteenth to the late twentieth centuries, the authors scrutinize forms of popular and elite activism and resistance and places of encounters, confrontation, and collusion with state discipline. They also unveil the multiple logics and legacies of violent events as moments of both rupture and reconstruction of sociopolitical and spatial orders. Readers will be exposed to violent deeds and words and recognize their power to transform sociopolitical experience and the meaning of urban sites.

This volume has a regional focus but ambitions of connectivity. One of its aims is to tackle the "riddle" of violence—a notoriously contentious and multifaceted topic—in order to link up with interdisciplinary discussions of the roots, nature, and manifestation of conflict and unrest in cities and societies across the world. This comparative approach is not intended to be one-sided but a process of cross-fertilization that exposes Middle Eastern scholars and students to a rich body of work produced outside their region of inter-est while bringing the Middle East to the attention of specialists of Europe, Asia, Africa, and Latin America. The desirability and urgency of this cross-regional approach go beyond the realm of academic research. In an age domi-nated by disturbing images of political turmoil, social unrest, and bloodshed, there is an urgent need to counter representations of the Middle East and its peoples as intrinsically violent. Only by situating the region and its actors within broader debates on the interplay between state and social power in cities across space and time can we dispel a myth that has gained consider-able currency in popular and media discourse—violence as a peculiar Middle Eastern condition. This myth, which has been nurtured by media analysts, politicians, and policy advisers, has made it increasingly difficult to debate and write about violence.

As the editor of this volume and her fellow researchers have experienced firsthand, studying violence often raises eyebrows: the implication is that the topic can be ethically dubious, sexy at best. Some of the blame can certainly be apportioned to the flourishing cottage industry on terrorism, sectarianism, and Islamism that has surreptitiously made inroads into academic and public dis-course since 9/11. The Arab Spring has also added a degree of skepticism and critical scrutiny concerning scholarly efforts at capturing multi-angled snap-shots of Middle Eastern towns and cities as "violence regimes." Retrieving the violent lives of Middle Eastern cities—no matter how far back in time—could be construed as undermining the euphoric images of liberation and peace-ful emancipation from authoritarian rule associated with events in Cairo and Tunis in early 2011. At the time of writing, these images have sadly faded, mak-ing the study of urban violence increasingly relevant to make sense of what might seem an irrational and self-destructive streak in Middle Eastern politi-cal and social life.

The fact remains, however, that we all feel some uneasiness about the sensa-tional and ethical aspects of violence. As voiced by a colleague who has a long track record on researching Southeast Asia, "We can build academic careers studying violence, but do we pay respect to the victims?" While gruesome cases of violence that unfold before our eyes shock us, when somebody has been killed a century ago, the fact becomes "historical evidence." Does this histori-cal evidence inevitably take away something of the horror? These are extremely important issues to keep in mind. This volume does not aspire to offer answers to these vexed questions, or to be the last word on urban violence, but part of a new intellectually, politically, and ethically engaged conversation on this topic that will hopefully inspire students, researchers, and all those individuals who by profession or personal circumstances have an interest and desire to explore the troubled lives of cities, in the Middle East or elsewhere.

London, February 2015

ACKNOWLEDGMENTS

This book is the outcome of a three-year international research project, "Urban Violence in the Middle East: Between Empire and Nation State," sponsored by the Arts and Humanities Research Council (AHRC) and the Deutsche Forschungemeinschaft (DFG). I am very grateful for the generous support of the AHRC, which has funded the British side of the project (ref. AH/I500553/1) and the production of this volume. This collection of essays builds on the collaborative work of an international team of scholars from the School of Oriental and African Studies (SOAS) at the University of London and the Zentrum Moderner Orient in Berlin. I have had the great privilege to be in a fruitful intellectual conversation with Rasmus Elling, Ulrike Freitag, Claudia Ghrawi, Nora Lafi, and Fatemeh Masjedi. In both London and Berlin, we exchanged ideas, discussed issues, and organized group meetings. We also shared enjoyable lunches, dinners, and social events. My very special thanks go to Rasmus Elling, who was part of the research cluster of the project based at SOAS investigating the theme of oil and urban violence and has been closely involved with the planning and execution of this volume. His has been a very generous helping hand, which has brought a great deal of detailed insight, creative thinking, and conceptual rigor to this edited collection. Without him and contributions from many talented and dedicated scholars, this book would have not been possible.

Many other people have enlightened us with their breadth and depth of scholarship. I am indebted to the non–Middle Eastern specialists who participated at a conference on urban violence organized at SOAS in February 2013. Nandini Gooptu, Stephen Legg, Freek Colombijn, and John Parker in particular guided us through some of the intricacies of different regional historiographies of violence. A group of scholars working on the Middle East and based at the University of London have also contributed to this book in different ways. My gratitude goes to Charles Tripp, who delivered the conference keynote and continues to inspire many with his thoughtful work on the politics of resistance, and to Dina Matar, Salwa Ismail, Madawi al-Rasheed, and Sami Zubaida. This remarkable London "crowd" has continuously been a source of inspiration, both as colleagues and friends. So have my postgraduate students with whom I have shared some of the insights developed in Chapter 1, particularly Lauren Banko, Fadi Dawood, and Roberto Mazza.

I have also benefited from the intellectual generosity and hospitality of Oliver Dinius and Vivian Ibrahim, who invited me to give a seminar at the University of Mississippi in October 2013. I would also like to thank the two anonymous reviewers for having read and commented on the manuscript so thoroughly. The SOAS London Middle East Institute has provided invaluable logistic and organizational support to the research project that has inspired this book. I am greatly indebted to the Institute director Hassan Hakimian and to Louse Hosking, Vincenzo Paci, and Valentina Zanardi, who have been great fun to work with. Charles Peyton and Glenn Ratcliffe from SOAS have done an excellent job with language editing and photos, respectively. Finally, I am immensely grateful to Stanford University Press editor Kate Wahl, whose vision, professionalism, and dedication have been a great source of encouragement throughout the different stages of publication. As usual, Shaalan and Paola have always been there when I needed the extra injection of energy, as have been Lia and Aleks from Brixton. Although no longer with us, Clinio and Ida have also been a reassuring hidden presence. Grazie!

Violence and the City in the Modern Middle East

RETHINKING VIOLENCE IN URBAN HISTORY   **Part 1**

1 URBAN LIFE AND QUESTIONS OF VIOLENCE

Nelida Fuccaro

To see like a city is to focus on what happens between people, what enables urban life, what questions arise within it, what solutions are developed, what conduct develops, and to what effect. To see the political in these terms is to refer back to these practices rather than to the ones by which the people are ostensibly "ruled."

Warren Magnusson, *Seeing like a City*[1]

SINCE 2011, Middle Eastern and North African cities have been at the center of political unrest and popular uprisings leading to the fall of dictators, protracted civil wars, and in some cases authoritarian revival. The Arab Spring and its aftermath have pushed the predicament of the city to the forefront of Middle Eastern politics. Yet, until recently, media coverage and academic analysis have often overlooked the urban nature of these uprisings. While it was recognized that violent disorder was performed *in cities*, popular mobilization was presented as part of national and transnational spheres of public contention. Media analysts and academics tended to treat the cities of the Arab Spring as stage sets—parade grounds for popular anger and state repression—depicting mass protests as a new twist in the ongoing struggle between governments and people. The result was that spaces and places of conflict, the stakes associated with them, and the specifically urban dynamics of crowd mobilization were often taken for granted, not analyzed as constitutive of social and political struggles.

Although recent studies of the Arab Spring have started to fill this "urban" gap,[2] the general lack of attention to cities as localities able to shape patterns, ideas, institutions, and practices of social and political life (including conflict) is symptomatic of a broader trend affecting our understanding of past and present landscapes of violence in the Middle East: the tendency to simply consider violence as located *in* cities (often through the prism of states) rather than being *of* cities.[3] It is in this spirit that we should take up Warren Magnusson's invitation to "see like a city," which, in his understanding, refers to a new reading of contemporary politics not as the exclusive domain of sovereign authority but as the result of the cumulative practices of urban life. Seeking solutions to current urban problems at a global scale, Magnusson also reminds us that latent urban tension and unrest are not confined to the Middle East or to the Arab Spring but are a worldwide phenomenon that demands urgent attention, precipitated by sprawling urbanization and the relentless expansion of transnational capital and social inequality.

WRITING, DEBATING, AND NORMALIZING VIOLENCE

While Magnusson singles out the city as an identifiable field of action and organization, violence is a slippery concept and a category of academic knowledge with a contested ethical profile. There is still no consensus among historians and social scientists on how to define and theorize violence, what counts as violence, or how (and why) it should be conceptualized. Adding further controversy, recent interdisciplinary debates have even questioned the usefulness of taxonomies of violence, advocating the adoption of more flexible concepts that can accommodate its protean nature.[4] At a basic level, the great variations in the manifestations, actors, intensity, and visibility of violence add to the predicament. Violence can burst out episodically as conflict, be chronic or intermittent, unfold unnoticed as a pattern of inequality, and be performed as a symbolic threat. Individual or collective, organized or spontaneous, physical and/or structural,[5] violent acts are not only a preserve of power holders but are also deployed as a strategy of resistance. While there is some consensus on the instrumental nature of violence—on how it ultimately serves particular ends—the reasons why violence occurs and the correct way to interpret it are matters of extensive debate.[6]

How, then, as historians, should we write the violence *of* Middle Eastern cities? The multiple angles from which we can read the city and urban life, and the path set by literature in other parts of the world, suggest that traversing disciplinary and regional boundaries is essential in order to tackle this complex and value-laden subject. Writing about violence requires engagement with literature that varies in scope and theoretical orientation—from historical sociology, anthropology, and political geography to urban and post-colonial studies. This scholarship has made great strides in broadening the methodological and conceptual horizons of the historiography of violence. Historians, usually concerned with events, have been particularly concerned with easing the tension between "eventful" histories of violence and long-term political change.[7] Anthropologists have brought to bear on violence an attention to meaning, symbolism, and ritual and a consideration for discursive and cultural representations as subjective and collective conditions of violence. Political scientists have looked at violent lives as forms of politics and elaborated on the crucial distinction between violence and force in the actions of states—a theme also cherished by historical sociologists, from Max Weber to Charles Tilly. Urban specialists have explored acts of violence in relation to urban spaces and experience as particular moments in the material and cognitive production of the city as a space of social and political engagement.[8]

The prolific literature on South Asian communalism in the colonial and post-colonial periods illustrates the interdisciplinary breadth that has characterized the study of collective violence, prompting Middle Eastern specialists to use a comparative approach to think "outside the box" and to use violence as a tool to study different aspects of political and social life. The interpretations of civilian and religious riots that have emerged from this literature are diverse— depicting communal violence as anything from the creation of state discourses to a reflection of either forms of institutionalized grassroots politics central to the preservation of the state or ritualized moments of subaltern action structured by particular symbols, temporal and spatial settings, or affective ties.[9]

The elusiveness of violence clearly has a flip side, which makes it a flexible and effective analytical concept, particularly in combination with categories such as power, space/place, language, and modernity.[10] The violence-power nexus, in particular, introduces an important ethical dimension to the study of social life. This nexus has served as a tool to explore the limits of—and interstices between— acceptable and unacceptable, moral and immoral. Critical studies of the violent profile of the liberal state, for instance, have served to denounce its illegitimate nature and that of colonial domination exercised by European regimes overseas and to underscore how state collusion with violence has tarnished the civilizational project of modernity.[11] Writing about violence has also acted as a means to denounce oppression, inequality, and murder; to disclose the communicative and symbolic worlds of human interaction; and to add nuance to strategies of coercion and resistance. Since the 1960s, struggles against domination, dispossession, and poverty have informed a strand of critical thinking about violence as resistance to oppression: from Hannah Arendt's impassioned advocacy for the powerless and Frantz Fanon's liberating violence of the "wretched of the earth," to the concerns with the socially deprived and with the powerlessness of individuals articulated by Ted Gurr and James C. Scott, respectively.[12]

In the Middle East and North Africa, academic debates about violence have started to create new spheres of civic and public engagement. Recent studies on the memorializing and mnemonic function of monuments, cemeteries, and commemorative spaces have shed light on urban narratives of war in order to foster dialogue and reconciliation. Samir Khalaf's discussion of Sahat al-Burj (Tower Square) in downtown Beirut, for instance, has emphasized its role as an open museum of tolerance, evocative of both the horrors of the Lebanese civil war and of the more recent assassination of Prime Minister Rafiq Hariri.[13] In retelling public histories of war, revolutions, massacres, and uprisings, the central squares of Middle Eastern capital cities stand as the simulacra of nations. Tahrir Square in Cairo, Marjeh Square in Damascus, Place de Martyrs in Algiers, and Azadi Square in Tehran evoke to viewers the violent making of citizens as modern subjects and embody a nineteenth- and twentieth-century legacy of colonial and imperialist oppression, economic exploitation, and revolutionary heroism.[14] Studies that revisit key violent episodes in the history of the French colonial empire in Algeria have prompted broader reflections on society and politics in contemporary France. In Algeria, where national history has inscribed violence "not as strategy but as structure," memories of colonial and post-colonial brutality have engendered rich and varied public debate.[15]

Exposure of the violence of authoritarian regimes has raised ethical issues about representations of suffering and of the many forms of violence produced in the Middle East. As Kanan Makiya (a.k.a. Samir al-Khalil), faced with the daunting prospect of the futility of unveiling the horrors of the Ba'thist regime in Saddam Hussein's Iraq, puts it, "Description is the first and fundamental act of resolution: ruthless, relentless, unforgiving description. Even when their condition seems to utterly disintegrate . . . human beings are able to exercise a degree of control through the power of description. Telling horror stories is the first step towards dealing with the rule of violence."[16]

Makiya's use of description as a cathartic device to make sense of violence brings into sharp focus the ethical imperative of normalizing violence, particularly when dealing with its seemingly "senseless" and intense manifestations, such as war, torture, and mass murder. Labeling violence as "senseless" is what the anthropologist Anton Blok has called "avoidance behavior"—a refusal to engage meaningfully with the concept.[17] Some historians of violence have recently pointed out the shortcomings of this behavior on the grounds that it disguises agency and individual responsibility. Mark Mazower has highlighted the apologetic stance and essentialist nature of studies of mass violence in Nazi Germany and the Soviet Union under Stalin. Proposing a similar line of argu-

ment, the African historian Jonathon Glassman has recently questioned interpretations of South Asian riots as premeditated and engineered by politicians
or agitators. Adopting a subaltern perspective in reverse, he contends that this
reading fails to account for the hideous acts committed by the crowds. Revisit-
ing some of the prevailing assumptions on terrorism as a self-sacrificial form of
violence, Hamit Bozarslan has noted how in the Middle Eastern context it has
been used as a normative concept that obscures "the aims, motives, and minds
of the people who have embraced violence."[18]

Far from being separate from social life, violence creates intimate, albeit un-
comfortable, bonds that elude the simplistic logics of victim versus perpetrator,
ruler versus ruled. As a form of association that defines everyday encounters
in the city, violence can be read as a building block of community. This is one
of the main arguments transpiring from studies on South Asian communalism
and from the seminal work on medieval Spain by David Nirenberg, who has
shown how *convivencia* (the living together of Christians, Muslims, and Jews)
was predicated on intolerance, hostility, competition, and bloodshed.[19] Treating violence as ordinary, however, does not justify the presence of cultures of
violence in societies with a high incidence of bloodshed. Gerard Martin's in-
sightful discussion of twentieth-century Colombia proposes that violence be
thought of as a "tradition" expressed in a variety of ways but situated in specific
historical contexts and taxonomies of social order. A similar argument emerges
from Ussama Makdisi's discussion of sectarian violence in nineteenth-century
Mount Lebanon as a grassroots and multifaceted expression of modernization
rather than the by-product of innate sectarian hatred.[20] Writing about violence
with an awareness of its embeddedness in a specific historical time and place
purges it of the primordialist and primitive aura that has surrounded it—an
aura that has long tarnished our understanding of the Middle East.

VIOLENCE AND THE CITY

As a distinctive type of human, political, and spatial association, the city is an
excellent vantage point from which to observe and make sense of violence. The
distinctiveness of cities has long been recognized in the academic literature:
from the medieval European commune and Mamluk cities studied by Max
Weber and Ira Lapidus, respectively, to the modern nineteenth-century metropolis dissected by Georg Simmel and imagined by Walter Benjamin. In the
fast-developing world of cities of the 1970s, Henri Lefebvre viewed urbanism as
the motive force for historical change, with the city holding the key to future

liberation from repression and exploitation.[21] Arguably, the days of Lefebvre's redemptive and optimistic vision of the city as the exclusive site of freedom are over—particularly when one thinks of the "cities of fear" created world-wide by the imposition of increasingly sophisticated systems of control and surveillance.[22] The fact remains, however, that cities have never functioned as mere appendixes to empires, states, and nations; rather, they have, to varying degrees, shaped their histories, as sites of government, economic centers, and dense conglomerations of people characterized by proximity, mixing, and intense affects and relationships.

The historiography on the Middle East has recognized the individuality of cities and their intimate relationship with violent processes of empire and state building, from the early Islamic period up to the present.[23] Particularly in studies on the modern era, however, regional historians have traditionally treated violence as the elephant in the room, in contrast with their counterparts working on South Asia, Africa, and Europe. Many histories of rebellion, protests, and revolutions in imperial, colonial, and post-colonial cities and towns have dealt with violence in a disguised way. So have accounts of elites, militaries, and crowds and reflections on subaltern and social movements.[24] For instance, the rich literature on urban notables in Ottoman and Arab cities from the eighteenth to the middle of the twentieth century has provided a comprehensive and fascinating view of the political organization of urban society from local, imperial, and national perspectives but has offered only occasional glimpses of the violent social worlds of local leaders and their followers.[25] This lack of interest in violence may have been accidental but is arguably the outcome of particular trends that, until recently, have dominated historical scholarship on cities within the field of area studies.

While building on a rich thematic repertoire, this scholarship was seldom comparative: even urban historians of the Arab and Ottoman world, Turkey, and Iran have tended to work in isolation from one another. Moreover, there has been a general reluctance to open up the historical study of urban public life to new interdisciplinary approaches, as attested by the enduring importance of research paradigms such as that focusing on the politics of notables and the network analysis pioneered by Ira Lapidus in the 1960s.[26] Only recently has the question of urban violence begun to be tackled in depth, in a number of studies that have taken a comparative approach and drawn on insights from classical historiography on contentious politics, European crowds, and Indian communalism and made use of reflections on colonial discipline and urban space.[27]

As a violent actor, the state has cast a long shadow over the history of modern Middle Eastern cities. The organization and fragmentation of state authority are central to any discussion of the interplay between order and disorder, the political infrastructure of cities, and the use of violence as a strategy of rule and resistance. For much of the twentieth century, the profile of many urban entrepreneurs of violence has been delineated by the ebbs and flows of central government. In the colonial period, French and British officials held sway, as they were often able to use counterinsurgency tools such as militarization, planning, and health provisions to great effect in taming the seemingly fractured, conflict-ridden, and chaotic "Oriental" urban societies of Egypt, Algeria, Palestine, Syria, and Iraq.[28] Similarly, the *mukhabarat* personnel who, from the 1960s, epitomized the culture of fear and repression of Ba'thist Syria and Iraq speak volumes about the brutal face of authoritarian rule and its ability to penetrate the dense texture of urban life through military and civilian organizations, party membership, and informers.[29]

Yet, while colonial and authoritarian regimes were undoubtedly efficient ruling machines, plenty of evidence suggests that political crises, civil wars, collapsing regimes, and alternative forms of colonial occupation slowed and limited the power of the violent hand of public authority. In conflict and postconflict cities such as Beirut during the Lebanese civil war, Jerusalem during the Arab-Israeli conflict, and Baghdad after the 2003 US invasion, local leaders and paramilitary forces have often taken on the mantle of enforcers of order while fighting bitter turf wars that had very traumatic effects on residents.[30] After 1967, Israeli rule in the West Bank and the Gaza Strip was advanced "by design," in collusion with architects, capitalist corporations, and even Palestinian militants who participated in the unregulated destruction and reconstruction of natural landscapes and built environments.[31]

State-centered accounts of violence gloss over, or at best reveal only partially, the forms of activism and resistance produced by the city as an organic "social order of parts" with a complex and multiform associational life that in itself constitutes a potential arena of violent conflict.[32] In this respect, urban societies have always been implicated in the definition of forms, expressions, and meanings of violence, partly as a result of the deeply entrenched urban roots of competition over territory, resources, and security. Residents have often taken matters into their own hands. Since the 1940s, spontaneous and unregulated suburbanization on the margins of expanding urban centers has often led to the reemergence of traditional forms of community protection in shantytowns:

armed patrols by residents, strongmen, and youth gangs. The advance of the security state in late twentieth-century Cairo and Tehran forced the urban poor and the informal communities living at the fringes of these two Middle Eastern megalopolises to adopt nonviolent forms of activism as tactics of "quiet encroachment."[33]

The grounding of acts of violence and violent events in the city—making them *of* the city—entails a shift in emphasis from the macrolevel of the institutional setting of the state to the microlevel of its spaces of encounter with residents: streets and neighborhoods, workplace and home, urban peripheries and public buildings. Spatially grounded analyses of collective violence reveal the urban face of everyday practices of government while also zooming in on the substance of ordinary lives, in spite of the often seemingly exceptional nature of violent events.[34] Premodern and early modern neighborhoods (*mahallas/haras*), and religious and legal institutions such as mosques, Shia houses of mourning (*husayniyyahs*), and courthouses were the centers of what Ira Lapidus has called "lumpenproletariat violence" and Edmund Burke has dubbed the "Islamic moral economy": the former ignited by intra-quarter factionalism, military leaders (*zuʿar*), and strongmen (*qabadayis, ʿayyarun, futuwwa, lutis*); the latter defined by Islamic symbols of justice that provided the vocabulary for violent urban protest.[35]

Using place, proximity, and activism to "see like a city" entails recognizing the power of urban locations to form and reproduce social and political relations and experience.[36] Close encounters in these locations have been the catalysts of violent social and political transformations that have reverberated beyond the city—from the revolutionary bazaars of Tehran, teeming with clerics, students, and protesters, to the squares of colonial Cairo crowded with demonstrators and soldiers; from the schools, mosques, and industrial sites that propelled the insurrectional waves of post-colonial Baghdad, to the barracks of late Ottoman Istanbul and Salonika, where the Young Turk Revolution was planned and executed. The ability to control, visualize, and manipulate urban spaces also contributed to their transformation into places of material and symbolic value. An understanding of the geographies of risk faced by urban and state administrations was an important tool of government. The collection of topographical and cartographical data made streets, alleys, squares, and neighborhoods visible and accessible to police and military forces.[37] Intimate knowledge of the built environment was not only the prerogative of surveyors, bureaucrats, and police but also a tool in the hands of rioters, protesters, and urban gangs.

In short, treating violence as contingent on place and the rhythms of urban life can reveal how the physical, material, and immaterial qualities of the city become enmeshed with various forms of state and social power. At a basic level, it problematizes simplistic binary understandings of the relations between state and society, between rulers and ruled, and between citizens and the government. More specifically, given the centrality of the city in shaping the Middle East as we know it today, reading sovereign authority through the prism of the city helps fine-tune the violent contours of the states that ruled urban society. This reading exposes the interface between urban activism and state repression; between street violence and security regimes; between urban norms and institution building; and between civic identity, nationality, and citizenship.[38] The nexus between city and state also poses the question of the analytical and physical boundaries of modern Middle Eastern cities, reminding us that their social and political histories can be read at different scales as simultaneously separating, connective, and disruptive.[39]

Famously, twentieth-century Iranian cities served as the economic and political linchpins of late Qajar and Pahlavi rule, the nodes that joined together royal power, dynastic authority, and European encroachment in Iranian life into a network of forces. At the same time, they were the powerhouses of the Constitutional and Islamic Revolutions—the violent popular movements that obliterated these regimes. While it is evident that towns and cities of the Middle East have constituted distinctive historical formations, it is nonetheless clear that the frontiers of urban life have been open-ended. What constitutes the "urban" and where it stops are questions that continue to be debated. Interdependency has provided a popular conceptual framework in exploring urban-rural relations in the Middle East, in order to explain the variation and frequency of popular protest, food riots, and elite factionalism inside early modern and modern urban centers. Contemporary urbanism is predicated upon the idea of the networked or global city—a city that is losing its boundaries, whose materiality is submerged by global flows.[40] "Seeing like a city" thus becomes a process of zooming in and out, with an awareness of the often invisible and fluid boundaries between city and state.

SKETCHING URBAN GEOGRAPHIES AND EXPERIENCES OF VIOLENCE

Violence in the Middle East and North Africa, as elsewhere, has been both a structural feature and an outcome of the often traumatic historical processes that, from the nineteenth century, have contributed to the transformation of modern cities-in-the-making into experiential and physical spaces that have come increasingly to share the "global urban culture" of the modern world.[41] The incessant redrawing of spatial and sociopolitical boundaries through urbanization, imperial modernization, colonial intervention, capitalism, nation building, and industrialization has engendered stimuli that have contributed to both the fragmentation and unification of collective experiences of urban living. Shaken by aftershocks of the penetration of European, Western, and global capital, urbanization, colonialism, and decolonization, many of the cities and provincial towns of the region have functioned as amplifiers of economic and political power, social and class inequalities, and political turmoil.

Coupled with new strategies of state control, the increasingly intimate, swift, and diverse interactions between people have shaped what Georg Simmel at the turn of the twentieth century called the "mental life" of the modern metropolis—a life that conceived the city as a place both of liberation from the constrains of traditional communities and of social alienation and resistance.[42] Yet the impact of these processes differed considerably throughout the region, reflecting its long and varied history of city life, political fragmentation, and geographical diversity. The main urban centers of French North Africa and British Egypt bore the full brunt of the acute phase of the global expansion of European capitalism and colonialism in the late nineteenth century. The spatial politics of discrimination that characterized colonial urbanism worldwide materialized in the creation of European and native towns and in the empty land of the *cordon sanitaire* that divided many Algerian and Moroccan settlements.[43] After the 1870s, in particular, the development of Cairo and Algiers as dual cities conjures up disturbing images of abuse associated with the European cities of the Industrial Revolution—economic exploitation, environmental degradation, surging crowds of angry humanity.

Like the "negro village" in Africa and the "native town" in India, the Arab "casbah" of Algiers and the *beledi* (popular) quarters of Cairo were perceived by French and British administrations as disorderly and dangerous. While using military force to discipline indigenous populations, colonial governments construed the threat of violence as an irrational force that represented a transgression of urban civic order. The lower-class residents of Cairo's *beledi* quarters were despised by the British administration as riff-raff, and their actions dismissed as illogical and senseless, particularly when they threatened the pristine bourgeois space of the European colonial city.[44] The threat of violence was often used to justify the existence of segregation and to stigmatize, criminalize, and brutalize the city's residents. During the Algerian War of Independence (1954–62), which terminated the country's harsh and long-lasting colonial experience, the medina of Algiers became the paradigmatic breeding ground of colonial brutality and violent anti-colonial insurgency—a combat zone brilliantly captured by Gillo Pontecorvo in his 1966 film *The Battle of Algiers*.

Some of the structural inequalities and harsh experiences of colonial cities were reproduced in the oil towns of Iran, Iraq, Saudi Arabia, and the other Persian Gulf states, which developed in the first half of the twentieth century under the shadow of oil capitalism. British-owned oil companies designed Abadan in Iran and Ahmadi in Kuwait following the model of colonial New Delhi, enforcing the principle of strict segregation between their native employees and Europeans and Americans. Until the 1960s, the life of the workers who populated the shantytowns that mushroomed around modern company towns was not dissimilar from that of their counterparts in the Arab medina or African village. Poor living conditions, harsh regimes of surveillance and industrial discipline enforced by the oil companies, and policies of divide and rule led to occasional violent protests.[45] Similar landscapes of urban segregation emerged from the colonization of Palestine's rural frontier by the Israeli authorities after the Arab-Israeli wars of 1948 and 1967. After the creation of Israel, the construction of settlement towns such as Karmiel, Kyriat Gat, Dimona, and Sderot marked a forced separation between Arabs and Jews and the demise of the relatively peaceful coexistence that had characterized urban life in Ottoman and colonial Palestine.[46]

The slower pace of modernization and capital penetration in the Ottoman Empire and Qajar Iran before World War I partly explains the less troubled urban existence of imperial subjects. In the second half of the nineteenth century, however, the increasing influence of Europe, Ottoman, and Qajar reform, together with the emergence of nationalism, created new ideological, economic, and political fissures in urban societies. These fault lines became manifest in new forms of violent mobilization driven by political and ideological motives. For instance, the 1860 massacres of Christians in Damascus and the actions of Armenian revolutionary groups in Istanbul in the 1890s signaled the emergence of new sectarian conflicts and "terrorist" strategies. Colonial Egypt also witnessed the politicization of urban riots between the 1870s and 1880s—a phenomenon closely connected to British imperial and capitalist expansion in the Middle East and South Asia.[47] The penetration of foreign capital also affected the port cities of the coastal areas of the Eastern Mediterranean. Imperial policies and French capital, for instance, created new spaces of struggle in late Ottoman Beirut, whose fast-developing port became an arena of labor conflict.[48]

By the end of the nineteenth century, a global culture of urban reform inspired by the liberal ideas of Europe had also started to transform the face of Ottoman cities, bringing in new norms and forms of social containment. As in Boston, imperial Tokyo, and colonial Algiers, Cairo, and Bombay, the establishment of municipal administrations recognized the principle of representative local government. Yet it also underpinned the creation of modern police forces and gendarmeries as new instruments for taming social unrest. As elsewhere in the colonial world, the institution of modern policing in late imperial Istanbul popularized new definitions of criminality and public order and marked the beginning of a new era of state control over public security and legislation.[49]

But it was in the context of the post-imperial nation-states that emerged after World War I that urban experiences of modernization took a more violent turn, nurtured by a shared public consciousness of state oppression and resistance and anchored in specific places of dissent. As sites of nationalist politics, streets and public spaces incrementally redefined the "mental lives" of Middle Eastern cities by connecting protesters, revolutionaries, and activists to their counterparts across the region. The path was set by Cairo immediately before and after the British occupation. Violent contestation in and over streets was the hallmark of both the 'Urabi Revolt of 1880–81 and the 1919 Revolution. By the 1930s, conflicts for the control of streets, squares, and public buildings involving nationalist and paramilitary activists, students, workers, and police forces posed exacting challenges to the security regime imposed by colonial administrations. In Mandatory Damascus, for instance, street violence challenged the spatial, legal, and political restrictions imposed by the French regime, triggering a series of gender conflicts between female protesters and paramilitary groups.

As in the townships of Africa, public spaces were also appropriated by new forms of youth violence and gang cultures in which class, ethnic, and anticolonial solidarities often intermingled.[50] While male physical strength and aggressive masculinity became the urban symbols of anti-colonial resistance in Cairo, Aleppo, and Baghdad, they also expressed shifting communal and class loyalties, often nurtured by Arab nationalism and an ideology of "total" violence inspired by Nazi Germany and Fascist Italy. The activism of youth gangs was also underpinned by more traditional notions of honor and masculinity, as in Tehran during the 1953 CIA-sponsored coup against Prime Minister

Mosaddeq, when young followers of quarter leaders became directly involved in the overthrow of the government.[51]

During mass protests, nationalist upheavals, and more localized conflicts, knowledge of the city and its hidden corners guided the spatial tactics of the military, police, and protesters alike. The violent behavior of rioters also showed familiarity with the commodities and services that came to exemplify modern ways of life and instruments of oppression. In 1919, protesters set ablaze and destroyed public buildings throughout central Cairo in a dramatic rehearsal of the Great Fire that engulfed the city soon before the 1952 Revolution. In 1919 the protesters vandalized the tramcars built and run by French and Belgian companies—the hated symbol of foreign capital. As during the 1952 Revolution, they also used the classroom as a new battleground through the mobilization of young students from the modern state schools.[52]

As the oil industry came to represent a powerful nationalist symbol of foreign exploitation in the 1950s, antigovernment protesters in Tehran, Baghdad, Manama, and Dhahran attacked the private residences of foreigners, British and American official buildings, and cars and gas stations—those ubiquitous symbols of modern urban life and oil capitalism.[53] The relentless advance of urbanization after the 1950s transformed the growing peripheries of capital cities and provincial centers into the new front lines of urban radical movements. The making of these front lines that joined together industrial areas, prisons, clubs, and political organizations reflected growing class, economic, and religious conflict, increasingly efficient security systems often modeled on colonial precedents, the beginning of state-led industrial development in Egypt and Turkey, and the growth of the oil industry. The new agglomerations of humanity living in shantytowns across the region added a suburban dimension to street violence, as a result of the participation of rural migrants, industrial workers, and squatters in new political and social struggles. Revolutionary Tehran offers a paradigmatic example of the correlation between unregulated urbanization and political violence. By 1978–79, Iran's capital was a city divided between north and south, separating the wealthy and Westernized middle and upper classes from the urban poor.[54]

Global processes such as colonialism and capital penetration produced discernible patterns of violent unrest in Middle Eastern cities, but less is known about the influence of local dynamics and of the differential rhythms of indigenous modernization since the mid-nineteenth century. We are so far able to dwell only on the broad contours of changing experiences and geographies of violence, mostly in relation to nationalist struggles, state coercion, large urban centers, and episodes of mass mobilization. Particularly for the twentieth century, many local histories of violence and of less flamboyant episodes of bloodshed have yet to be written. In spite of these limitations, it is clear that violence has become manifest as an urban phenomenon in response to the reshuffling of orders of difference: those defining architectures of state and social power, urban geographies of communities and interest groups, and the spatial boundaries of the city.

The latent violent condition and the state of suppressed violence characterizing colonial Cairo and Algiers, as well as twentieth-century oil towns before the nationalization of the industry, can be readily explained by the sociopolitical, economic, and spatial segregation enforced and maintained by foreign powers, often through legal and military means. Similarly, the ethnic, religious, and nationalist conflict that beset late Ottoman cities can be read as reflecting a counterbalancing impulse against new socioeconomic and legal divisions enforced by the penetration of European capital and imperial reform. The more uniform character of collective violence, including shared norms of action and mobilization, that developed after World War I emerged organically from recognizable old colonial ingredients transplanted to the cities of new Mandatory, post-colonial, and authoritarian states: structural inequalities, state discipline, and urbanization. Violent tactics of control and resistance, such as the use of secret police and increasingly sophisticated weaponry, industrial unrest, youth and gang violence, and popular revolution, increasingly took the shape of turf wars that centered on the physical, material, and symbolic control of the city. These wars showcase the intimate connection between urban environments, political and social claims, and the urban experience of violence, and they are a reminder of the increasingly urban bias gradually assumed by Middle Eastern unrest in the twentieth century.

OUTLINE OF THE BOOK

The following chapters elaborate on some of the themes, debates, and evidence presented in this introduction. In Chapter 2, Rasmus Christian Elling explores further some of the methodological, interpretive, and ethical issues faced by Middle Eastern historians. Using the case studies included in the book to illustrate some of his discussion, Elling delves into the relevance of language and space in the writing of urban histories of violence. For him, this is an exercise in translation that requires an acute attention to linguistic registers and to different vocabularies of violence that often make dissonant semantics. Parts 2, 3, and 4 consist of chapters based on original research, written as historical ethnographies of violent events. Reflecting the diversity of Middle Eastern urbanism from the eighteenth to the late twentieth centuries, the case studies cover a broad range of urban centers: Cairo, Tunis, and Baghdad as imperial and national capitals; provincial towns such as Jeddah, Nablus, and Basra; and oil settlements such as Dhahran and Abadan. While the choice of a diverse range of urban locations and historical settings allows a close reading of local specificities, it also helps us "see like a city"—to single out common elements, processes, spaces, and power dynamics that conspired to produce violence as a social and political experience of urban life. With this agenda in mind, and in the spirit of some of the arguments presented in the introduction, the chapters are organized thematically rather than according to geographical region, chronological sequence, urban typology, or any particular taxonomy of violence.

Taken together, the case studies analyze violence through the lens of the dense and subversive associational life of cities, as both a systemic and an experiential feature of urban life. Violence is regarded as a potent ingredient in the mix of group strategies, aspirations, and objectives that have driven the actions of both the powerful and the powerless: elites and ordinary residents, state authorities and crowds, political activists and social outcasts. The focus is on the dynamics of group violence and its actors—not only performers but also narrators and interpreters of violent events, from military elites to oil workers, and from local chroniclers and bureaucrats to eyewitnesses. Taking into consideration the specific calendars of the individuals and groups involved, the authors examine episodes of collective violence varying in intensity, nature, and duration—from brawls to warfare, from interfactional fighting to rioting, and from strikes to large-scale urban upheavals.

Yet they use damage inflicted on individuals, property, and urban spaces as the starting point of their analyses. This common denominator offers them a platform to explore discursive, structural, and systemic factors that have underpinned acts of physical violence and to uncover the local and translocal roots and reverberations—both short and long term—of violent events. In tracing the multiple logics of these events, the authors tackle the question of violence as a "circular" practice and as a language of power whose domino effect involves both those who claim a monopoly of the use of force and those who challenge such claims by violent means. In approaching violence as a form of association rooted in specific histories of competition over urban spaces and resources, the essays make a strong case for violence as constitutive of urban sociopolitical change. At the same time, they tease out its creative and transformative powers—its ability to redraw the boundaries of urban life and experience; to subvert urban landscapes and built environments; to create and divide communities; and to affect the ruling strategies of local elites, governments, and transnational political players.

While they are separated into three parts, the case studies nonetheless remain in dialogue with one other. Some of the chapters could have been included in different sections but have been arranged to draw out particular themes. Part 2 deals with the question of urban networks as distinctive arenas of public violence structured by political and legal norms and social practices, as well as by close encounters between residents, elites, and public authorities. By focusing on the intricate architectures of power that have underpinned civic conflict, the chapters reveal the intimate bonds connecting—and the often fine lines separating—violent actions, social and political routines, and various manifestations of elite, social, and state power.

In Chapter 3, James Baldwin's analysis of early eighteenth-century Cairo highlights the consensual and systemic nature of elite violence in a highly militarized and factionalized political society. As actors and witnesses, military elites and contemporary narrators of events regarded assassinations, invasions of private homes, and battles between military factions as an integral part of the city's political culture and martial tradition. Yet Baldwin also makes a case for the eclectic nature of political violence as an urban norm by discussing how ideas of legitimate or illegitimate, just or unjust, and proper or improper conduct framed the chroniclers' accounts of violent transgressions of elite mansions, streets, and mosques. His close reading of private and public spaces as the physical and ideological sites, and material objects, of power struggles reveals the ethical world of Cairo's elites, as well as popular perceptions on the bloody factional infighting that plagued the city.

Ulrike Freitag's discussion of late Ottoman and early Saudi Jeddah in Chapter 4 explores another facet of the martial tradition in public life. In contrast to Baldwin's narrative approach to elite violence, she discusses the potential for the escalation of conflict during the performance of the *mizmar* dance as a subaltern expression of masculinity. Using the socio-spatial unit of the neighborhood as a frame of reference, she analyzes how the *mizmar* as routine entertainment staged by group of young men (*futuwwa*) from the urban quarters fashioned Jeddah's popular culture, the patron-client organization of its quarters, and the city's public ceremonial. Like Baldwin, Freitag depicts an urban scenario of latent conflict. Yet she also shows how such everyday practices could achieve wider popular mobilization resulting in crowd violence. In doing so, Freitag develops a comparative reflection on male organizations, ceremonial occasions, and crowd violence by using examples from the Middle East and Europe.

In Chapter 5, on Palestine during the British Mandate, Lauren Banko opens up the discussion on the urban nature of the politics of civil rights and citizenship that were the bitterly contested political and legal norms of the interwar period. Concentrating on the towns of Jaffa, Haifa, and Nablus as interconnected civic and colonial spaces, Banko maps networks and forms of Palestinian resistance before and during the 1933 riots in Jaffa in order to trace the escalation of urban violence. In parallel with this, the chapter takes a discursive turn to analyze the interplay between violence and nonviolence in the language of citizenship rights, political action, and colonial repression. Ultimately, Banko's disturbing account of the emergency regulations enforced after the 1933 riots in Jaffa affirms the power of military coercion in stifling civic coexistence in Palestinian towns and cities.

Broadening the geographical and political horizons of the city, Part 3 disentangles the interface between the local and its "others" in the manifestations of violent dissent. Urban violence is treated as a particularly urban condition of interdependence binding actors and spaces of violent upheaval to hinterlands, as well as to imperial, state, regional, and global forces. These case studies situate this condition at the heart of the sociopolitical and spatial transformation of urban environments as the nodes connecting centers and peripheries. Critical attention is devoted to the dynamic and creative nature of urban life as a frontline arena of conflict, always positioned in the vanguard of social activism and repression.

In Chapter 6, examining late Ottoman Tunis, Nora Lafi revisits the classic theme of imperial reform, foreign consuls, and intercommunal violence against the backdrop of the city's rapid integration into the aggressive arena of European and Ottoman power politics. Focusing on the 1857 riots against the Jewish community, Lafi turns the dynamics of urban contention inside out. She situates the attacks against Tunis's Jews within the complex mosaic of urban tensions triggered by the realignment of local military and political factions that was precipitated by Ottoman reform and European influence. Lafi shows how the flagrant violation of the Ottoman *pax urbana* in 1857, and the "situation of fear" that it engendered, was rooted in the demise of traditional institutions of social and legal mediation, most notably that of the petition.

Claudia Ghrawi's examination of the oil conurbation of the Eastern Province of Saudi Arabia in Chapter 7 engages with the violent contours of popular insurgency during the 1967 riots in Dhahran. While placing this insurgency in its local, national, and global contexts, Ghrawi sees it as the climax of an abortive "urban revolution" tamed by a potent combination of American oil interests and Saudi state repression. Contrary to standard interpretations of these events, Ghrawi reads the riots as the cumulative result of routine and structural abuse embedded in almost two decades of oil urbanization and suburbanization. Conceptually located in Henri Lefebvre's idea of "urban revolution," Ghrawi's process-driven and organic understanding of the production of landscapes of urban radical struggle points out the corrosive power of international oil capitalism and the efficiency of Saudi state repression.

The militarization of urban life, the violent state, and the power of national war and popular insurgency to transform and subvert cityscapes are the subject of Chapter 8, by Dina Rizk Khoury, which examines Basra during the Iran-Iraq War, the Iraqi invasion of Kuwait, and the 1991 uprising. Khoury shows how the war mobilization efforts and the line of defense established by the Ba'thist regime around this borderland city blurred the boundary between urban and rural landscapes, contributing to a lingering atmosphere of lawlessness and violence that eventually shaped the 1991 insurrection. The chapter establishes crucial links between the brutal security policies used by the Ba'thist war machine both to protect and discipline war populations, and the ideological inscription of Ba'thist surveillance and propaganda into urban space.

In contrast with the systemic and scalar approaches adopted in Parts 2 and 3, Part 4 tackles violence as a moment and tactic of disruption that both fractures and recomposes the sociopolitical and spatial orders of the city. Concentrating on the interplay between riotous urban crowds and various forms of state and military discipline, the case studies present examples of violent spatial politics that transformed urban sites into icons of communal, national, and class struggle, offering sharply defined images of episodes and places of collective violence as constitutive elements of urban political cultures.

In Chapter 9, examining the situation of the Baghdadi Jews during the 1946 popular insurrection known as the Wathba, Orit Bashkin teases out a key aspect of violence as marking a moment of group cohesion and urban solidarity. Offering a vivid portrayal of experiences of street insurrection and state repression, Bashkin shows how the victimization of the Jews and the blood-shed of street protests erased, albeit temporarily, class, sectarian, ideological, and spatial divisions within the community and between them and the rest of Baghdad's population. Crucially, she argues that bloodshed was a key element in the memorialization of Baghdad as a symbol of a new national and patriotic culture in opposition to Iraq's violent monarchical regime. For Bashkin, popular membership in a new Iraqi nation materialized in inclusive, nonsectarian spaces of mobilization, including mosques, streets, bridges, and schools.

In Chapter 10, Nelida Fuccaro contrasts two momentous episodes of collective violence in colonial and early revolutionary Kirkuk, showing their relevance in structuring the communal, public, and national history of this contested Iraqi city. Reflecting on the dynamics and episodic nature of the traumatic events of 1924 and 1959, Fuccaro recognizes the divisive communal and ethnic dimension of these events in contrast to Bashkin's interpretation of the Wathba. She proposes a more organic reading of Kirkuk's civic conflict based on discipline, place, and language. She stresses the long-term symbiosis between crowd violence and the imposition of public order, the particular spatial routines that imparted meaning to the city as a site of contention, and the importance of violence as a key narrative motif and mnemonic device in the production and re-production of civic strife.

In Chapter 11, Rasmus Christian Elling singles out the spatial unit of the social club as a key site of the violent confrontation between Iranian socialist labor militants and tribal Arabs during the 1946 oil strike in Abadan. Elling explains the 1946 strike as a moment of transgression and reconfiguration of the rigid spatial boundaries of socioeconomic segregation imposed by the Anglo-Iranian Oil Company in Abadan and in the oil conurbation of Khuzestan. Abadan's social clubs in fact constituted outlawed spaces of labor mobilization, having originally been created as elite venues for the white employees of the company. Moreover, Elling shows how the demonization of violent crowd behavior during the strike expressed the intercommunal nature of the class and labor struggle unfolding in Abadan.

Yasser Elsheshtawy's discussion of events in Cairo in Chapter 12 echoes Elling's analysis of spatial politics, offering a vivid reinterpretation of the theme of the dual city. Elsheshtawy narrates an evocative "tale of two hotels," describing crucial incidents of spatial and political upheaval: the burning in 1952 of Shepheard's Hotel—the preeminent symbol of British domination—and the construction in 1959 of the modernist Nile Hilton—the flagship of Egypt's new socialist regime. Drawing on the work of David Harvey, Elsheshtawy fleshes out two complementary modes of "creative destruction": the acts of the violent anti-colonial crowds that set the city ablaze in 1952 and the new urban planning enforced by the military government after the revolution. Elsheshtawy concludes the chapter with a heartfelt reflection on the long-term reverberation of violent ruptures on the spatial, political, and social texture of the city—a reflection whose relevance extends to the volume as a whole.

2 THE SEMANTICS OF VIOLENCE AND SPACE

Rasmus Christian Elling

DURING THE IRANIAN Green Movement of 2009, the global media were suddenly inundated with pictures and video captured on smartphones and uploaded to YouTube from the streets of Tehran. First, the international audience witnessed the awe-inspiring sight of the streets filling up with the color green, as millions marched in peaceful protest against what they considered the rigging of the 12 June 2009 elections. And then, after the Supreme Leader Ayatollah Khamenei announced on 19 June that no more protests would be tolerated, this was taken over by frightening images of black-clad Islamist storm troopers charging on motorbikes, shooting at protesters, and taking control of the streets by brute force. The following day, the image of a young woman, Neda Agha-Soltan, shot to death on a street corner, was imprinted in the minds of millions across the world.

To the Iranian opposition, Neda became an icon of a "surge" (Persian: *mowj*) for "reform" and "change," while in the Western media, the Green Movement was hailed as a "youth uprising" or "Twitter revolution." The Iranian state media responded to both representations by demonizing the movement as a foreign-backed "conspiracy" and "sedition" (Persian: *fetneh*). A worldwide audience had thus caught a glimpse of Tehran's streets as a powerful theater of Middle Eastern politics, of urban life torn apart by the spectacle of violence, and of the conflicting semantics describing contention in the city.

In this volume, historians explore such violence in Middle Eastern cities in the three centuries prior to the rise of social media as a form of global mass communication. This requires an exploration of the intersection between two semantic categories that superficially appear clear-cut and tangible but emerge on closer inspection as ambiguous and elusive: violence and space. In the social context, *violence* is not just about bodily harm, and in the urban setting, *space* designates not only buildings and streets: both categories contain numerous divergent meanings. Violence and space speak in their own languages of power, and power is expressed in the ways we speak about violence and space. "Words are never 'only words,'" Slavoj Žižek reminds us: "they matter because they define the contours of what we can do."[1]

Violence as a physical act appears to speak a clear language. Yet the study of violence as a systemic and experiential feature of urban life also requires attention to what is often communicated in distorted or muted registers. The rich vocabularies with which scholars can describe, qualify, and quantify violence are paradoxically contrasted by the general absence in the historical sources of the word *violence* itself (such as Arabic *'unf*, Persian *khoshunat*, or Turkish *şiddet*). This absence should perhaps not be surprising: after all, even in English, the word *violence* did not convey all the aspects that the popularized and prevalent idiom does today. This underscores the need for scholars to treat their analytical vocabularies as something distinct from the events and sources being analyzed. Yet, while recognizing that a present-day reading will tease out violence that was perhaps not even considered as such in the historical source, the scholar must nonetheless also draw on the semantic world of the source to make sense of urban violence. Translating the "language of violence" into the language of academic research, in other words, entails both normative and practical questions of interpretation and analysis.

This chapter explores such questions by observing language at work on three interlinked levels. First, violence and space each speak their own languages; second, we use a specific language to talk and write about violence in lay or academic terms; and third, the historical sources employ their own vernacular languages of violence, shaped by cultural, geographical, linguistic, and historical factors that are local in each case. I pursue this discussion by posing a series of methodological questions generated by the case studies presented in this volume.[2]

READING AND MAPPING THE LANGUAGE OF URBAN VIOLENCE

Violence can arguably be read as discourse. As a form of communication, it always carries meaning that demands interpretation, whether we evaluate it through our subjective, moral, and ethical lens as blind and mindless or as principled and idealistic. This is, of course, especially true of political violence, as David Apter writes: "[D]iscourse as political violence and political violence as discourse constitute disruptive interventions in the taken-for-granted world of causes, effects, and probabilities. It is then that words can kill. In the beginning is the act not the word. But word follows closely behind."[3]

The case studies included in this volume deal with disruptive interventions in the social and political text of the city—the moments when conflictual relations are reconfigured through violence that simultaneously disorders and reorders established social understandings and arrangements.[4] However, while violence can disrupt dominant structures, as anonymous individuals or marginalized collectives "break through" and enter history in a spectacular manner, it can also constitute or reinforce the structures that oppress and subdue certain groups. Violence is, in other words, constitutive and creative; and in conveying meaningful symbols and choreographed rituals, it is also performative.[5] For these reasons, each interpretation and retelling of a violent event will itself communicate a message.

Many of the same communicative qualities can be ascribed to *space*, even though its role and presence are often barely implied in historical sources and rarely discussed explicitly in historical research. Indeed, the sheer density and taken-for-grantedness of the places and spaces of the city, in particular, tend to obscure the constitutive role of the daily production of space in conflictual social relations and processes.[6] A way of reading the language of space, then, is to focus not simply on the violence that disrupts it but also on that which sustains it:

> What binds violence and space together is not the discrete events which appear to disturb the spaces we occupy but the more subterranean rhythms that already organize those very spaces. . . . In the end, there is no space without violence, and no violence that is not spatial. Violence is the very structure of space. Each discourse maintains a strategic silence about the particular forms of violence which makes both it and what it appears to address possible. This silence is always a silence about space. The most decisive aspect of space is the one that is never discussed.[7]

Addressing this silence will add further meaning to violence as a positive category of historical analysis, with which to study how contention never just *happens in space* but also *relates to space*. While at first glance some words appear to denote static and defined units of urban geography, they often in fact refer to dynamic sites that generate divergent cultural meanings and facilitate diverse social functions. It is thus important to map the way in which the spatial shapes and intersects with the social at the level of language. Ideally, such semantic maps will reveal forms of power and resistance by drawing attention to the relationship between the ideological, symbolic, and historically contingent aspects of place and social action.

Semantic exercises across linguistic boundaries and temporal distances can reveal differences and similarities between cultural imaginaries. They simultaneously illuminate discursive disparities between the languages used by rulers and ruled, and between those employed by historians and their sources. Writing about violence in the past tense inevitably encourages the historian to infer meaning from a message that is dislocated by the passage of time and based on fragmentary knowledge that will inevitably be biased in favor of those who had the power to speak and write. The concern with whether sources are representative is obviously an issue for all historians, but it seems particularly problematic when dealing with events that have cost lives, inflicted pain, and caused misery. Historians of the Middle East must rely on accounts that were often authored by tiny ruling elites or foreign powers. Paradoxically, the archives of former colonial and imperial powers prove more bountiful than national archives inside the region, since materials on the post-colonial era are often censored or have been lost or destroyed during dramatic political transitions.

Another obvious methodological problem with studying urban violence in history is that most sources are textual. Important nontextual evidence that plays into the micro-sociology of violence—such as body language, facial expressions, and sounds—is obviously unavailable.[8] With limited visual documentation at their disposal and no possibility of participant observation, historians cannot easily draw on behavioral, psychological, or anthropological insights. The temporal gulf, not just between source and historian but also between narrator and event, further complicates matters.

In spite of these limitations, the contributors to this volume have employed a wide range of sources, some of which are representative of the alternative or subaltern voices of urban residents, political dissidents, workers, and poets. Written in a variety of languages (from English and French to literary and colloquial Arabic, Ottoman Turkish, and Persian), these sources were produced by individuals and institutions operating at different scales: the urban, the imperial/colonial/national, and the transnational. Scale, time, and authorship defined the semantic worlds within which violence was related and explained. Authors had one or more national, ethnic, or imperial affiliations: British, French, Dutch, Egyptian, Iraqi, Mamluk, Ottoman, Palestinian, Saudi, Turkmen, and so on. Their voices and vocabularies were shaped by their various roles as chroniclers, historians, spies, activists, community leaders, bureaucrats, and diplomats, as well as by the local, regional, and transnational encounters that defined their social and institutional worlds.

Some of them used traditional, localized, or communal vernaculars, while others employed the official terminology of government or the rhetorical language of modern ideology. Their accounts were delivered in various formats: diaries and autobiographies; chronicles (Arabic: *yawmiyat*) and literature on "customs and traditions" (Arabic: *'adat wa taqalid*); public petitions and reports (Arabic/Ottoman Turkish: *tahrirat*); intelligence, military, and diplomatic correspondence; official inquiries and trial transcripts; newspaper articles; speeches and manifestos; fiction, songs, and poetry.

Given the various factors influencing the genre, language, and style of the sources used in this volume, it is no surprise that often divergent and dissonant semantics are at play. Yet the existence of some commonalities points to particular social processes and mechanisms of contention in space that are shared across the region. These commonalities can be explored by examining vocabularies used to describe violence, its perpetrators, and its victims.

THE SEMANTICS OF DEMONIZATION

A methodological problem is posed by the question of how to read official sources beyond the bias that saturates the language of the ruler and stifles the voices of the ruled. The semantics of demonization that justify the violence of the ruler and vilify the violence of the ruled can be seen as a crystallization of asymmetries in power relations. Sometimes these asymmetries run along racial or ethnic lines. From the "hashish-eating assassins" of Hassan Sabah to the "mad mullahs" of revolutionary Iran, the proverbial "East" has for ages delivered the raw materials for Orientalist stereotypes of the irrational violence of the savage, which has in turn justified the violence of the colonizer as preventive.[9] Some of these stereotypes were institutionalized in the languages of the colonial apparatuses that ruled large swathes of the Middle East and North Africa in the nineteenth and early twentieth centuries.

But the obsessive theme of the *savage*, *bandit*, and *fanatic* that permeates the language of demonization is not limited to the context of colonialism. The long history of conflictual relations in Middle Eastern societies generated a toolkit of imagery to describe an enemy.[10] Moreover, since the late nineteenth century, nationalism, socialism, Islamism, and various homegrown ideologies provided a variety of vocabularies of violence and demonization. These vocabularies framed both state power and resistance to it, as Charles Tripp explains:

> For those who inherited the colonial state and then proceeded to claim the exclusive right to rule it, the very languages and practices of power that gave them dominion were eventually turned against them. Idioms that had been used to buttress the power of a restrictive elite were taken up by their opponents and given a very different significance, whilst retaining their potency.[11]

As in the language of imperial and colonial powers, authoritarian post-colonial regimes branded discontented citizens, subversive elements, and marginalized communities as "internal others," and thus as enemies. Typically, certain minorities were condemned as *fifth columns*, *traitors*, and *collaborators*, as in the studies in this volume dealing with Jewish communities in Ottoman Tunis (Lafi) and post-colonial Baghdad (Bashkin). Other minorities, such as the rebellious Arabs of Khuzestan (Elling), were implicitly or explicitly castigated as *backward* and *uncivilized*. In many cases, the exercise of violence against such communities was justified and normalized through the semantics of "otherization" and demonization.

These semantics are reproduced in accounts of violence when negatively laden words are employed to distance the voice of the author from the dreadful shriek of the perpetrator: *animosity*, *bloodshed*, *brutality*, *carnage*, *frenzy*, *hatred*, *outbreak*, and *terror*. Similarly, violent actors are depicted as *belligerents*, *evil-doers*, *hostile*, *notorious*, and *vandals*, and their acts as *barbaric*, *bloodthirsty*, *cold-blooded*, *fierce*, *flagrant*, *horrific*, or *vicious*. Indeed, their actions are sometimes described in gruesome graphic detail: they *beat*, *behead*, *lynch*, *rape*, and *stab* their victims. Violent subjects are inevitably depicted as irrational, whether the violence is reported by a French consular employee in Ottoman Tunis (Lafi), a British oil company manager in post–World War II Abadan (Elling), or the president of Iraq addressing the press and the nation after the 1959 disturbances in Kirkuk (Fuccaro). Violent subalterns are also dismissed by the presentation of them and their actions as rooted in individual pathology and social delinquency: *criminal*, *drunken*, *disorderly*, *drifters*, *hooligans*, *obstinate*, *rude*, *unemployed*. In such cases, the discrepancy between the semantics of the source and the scholar is crucial. What scholars call a "conflict" is often described as a "brawl" in the sources, while a "protest" appears as "lawlessness," a "riot" as "looting and plunder," "slogans" as "swearing," or an "uprising" as a "disruption of order."

The semantics of demonization obviously reduce a complex social conflict to a simple binary opposition and obscure the underlying grievances that motivate the violence.[12] An onslaught of negative descriptors in the sources poses a challenge to the historian, even when circumstantial evidence supports the claim that horrific violence did in fact occur. However, even more challenging than a dismissal of blatant bias is the attempt to draw meaning out of it, usually by teasing out additional information that can throw light on missing voices and aspects of the violent event—not in order to explain the root causes of the violence but rather to understand why they have been left out of the original account.

THE SEMANTICS OF PROFESSIONAL VIOLENCE

The profile and role of professional practitioners of violence in Middle Eastern cities varied significantly in different historical periods. The mapping of professional violence—that is, the violence perpetrated by those in charge of maintaining order—sheds light not only on the increasing state monopolization of the use of violence but also on questions of urban norms and legitimacy (Baldwin, Freitag, and Banko).

In the medieval and early modern eras, military and paramilitary groups—even Ottoman imperial troops such as the Janissaries—were usually aligned with one of a variety of urban elite factions. Those who carried weapons inside the city were often described in generic terms: *armed* (*men*) or *armies* (Arabic: *jund*), and *bodyguards* or *armed retainers* (Arabic, pl.: *khawiyin*). Some worked as *mercenaries*; others were drafted in lieu of tax as *levies* in times of war or unrest. A particularly prominent role was played by local nonstate actors whom scholars often refer to as *strongmen* (Arabic: *futuwwa* or *qabadayat*; Persian: *luti*) but sometimes simply "young men" (Arabic: *shabab*; Persian: *javanmard*). In some cases well into the twentieth century, these actors were connected to particular neighborhoods and had distinct corporate identities and moral codes. When they appear in the sources as elements of disorder in urban life, they are often labeled as "riff-raff" (Arabic/Persian: *owbash*) or "outlaw" (Arabic: *'ayyar*). Sometimes, the *futuwwa* used the occasion of public ceremonies and festivals to fight out inter-quarter rivalries, as in nineteenth-century Jeddah (Freitag). But the role of the violent practitioner was not only confined to inter-quarter, inter-elite, or inter-ethnic rivalries but often transcended the city—as in the case of the military elites of eighteenth-century Cairo, who partook in the factional politics of the Ottoman governor (Baldwin).

As imperial reforms, modernization, and colonialism allowed states increasingly to monopolize violence in Middle Eastern cities, new organized forms of professional violence emerged.[13] Disciplined colonial and post-colonial armies and police forces, and the increasing bureaucratization of public order, established new vocabularies that not only identified new categories of violent practitioners but also legitimized the rulers' use of arbitrary force against the ruled. An example from this vocabulary is the French *razzia*, or "mobile column attack." As Benjamin Brower pointed out in his innovative research on colonial violence in Algeria,[14] the Arabic *ghazw* (raid) moved first into the written language of Orientalism and then into French military vernacular after the conquest of Algiers in 1830. From denoting the savage behavior of the enemy, the term came to identify a particular technique employed by the French army itself. Brower argues that the appropriation of an Arabic word made it seem "as if it was an Algerian or African way of making war." Moral blame for the violence was thus shifted onto the victims themselves.[15]

In the sense of "police raid," *razzia* is today part of the globalized technical vocabulary of modern disciplinary and military systems. In this terminology, adversaries are often described as *agitators, belligerents, combatants, guerrillas, insurgents, rebels, ringleaders,* or *terrorists.*[16] Discontent, resistance, and opposition are routinely clothed in the mystifying language of *conspiracy, disorder, infiltration, rumor,* and *subversion.*[17] The Order in Council issued by the British Mandatory government in 1933 after the outbreak of riots in Jaffa, for example, turned Palestinian *civilians,* in the administrative vernacular, into *enemies,* and *protesters* into *rioters.* This semantic shift reflected a tactical shift and further legitimized a military crackdown on the rebellion (Banko). In the twentieth century, this military/disciplinary vocabulary became part of the everyday language of warfare in many urban areas. During the Iran-Iraq War, for instance, the Ba'thist regime, in pursuit of its military operations against Iran, sought to identify, in Basra and its hinterland, not just *deserters* and *saboteurs* but *insurgent populations* (Khoury).

Through such terminology, the modern state transformed resistant or violent subjects into a depersonalized mass of individuals in the tactical theater of warfare or a generic factor in the calculus of a discourse on *national security.*[18] Outbursts of disorder were countered by violent measures, often backed by legal means, and declarations of *crisis, emergency,* and *exigency* that profoundly disrupted urban life.[19] In this discourse, the imposition of martial law and the deployment of the army were used to *pacify* troublesome cities through *punitive action,* as in Kirkuk after the disturbances of 1959 (Fuccaro), or to *subjugate* and *tame* workers' movements in Iran and Saudi Arabia during the age of labor mobilization in the oil sector (Elling and Ghrawi). The expansion of the disciplinary power of the state introduced new forms of professional violence, both symbolic and physical, clouded in the metaphors of modern bureaucracy.

The rationalization of the use of force and institutionalization of urban professional violence that took shape during the nineteenth and twentieth centuries reflected the processes that shaped the modern nation-state in the Middle East. In analyzing moments of eruption during this age, it is necessary to outline the background on which something was labeled as violence: What constituted a not-violent state, or *normalcy*? Who had the power to label a situation as abnormal? In some cases, it appears that any situation could constitute an exception—hence the continued existence of regimes today that have declared a permanent state of emergency by invoking external enemies and their conspiracies or by referring to the violent crowd as an internal threat.

THE SEMANTICS OF COLLECTIVE VIOLENCE

Since the publication of E. P. Thompson's and George Rudé's classic studies of crowds, scholars have distanced themselves from popular depictions of collective violence as sudden outbursts of irrational anger and of crowds as uncivilized and senseless masses.[20] Historians, including those writing on the Middle East, have pointed out the often rational and sensible motivations driving crowds, as well as how incidents of collective action have been instrumentally exploited by ruling powers to clamp down on dissent and institute far-reaching disciplinary measures (Fuccaro).[21]

The contributors to this volume have therefore been particularly attentive to sources that speak of *congregations, crowds, flocks, masses, mobs*, and *riots*, since such terms often have negative connotations. On the one hand, there are certainly instances in which there is no "politically correct" way to describe a violent crowd and when one needs to call a spade a spade. On the other hand, however, negative descriptors often work to obscure our understanding of the multiple functions of violence. Acts of collective violence can also be read as means of empowerment, as marginalized groups express their feelings of injustice through violent means. In twentieth-century Kirkuk, for example, looting and the destruction of both lives and property served as a subaltern form of communication. Moreover, the retelling of crowd violence has become integral to public memories of resistance against communal discrimination (Fuccaro). In the urban centers of Palestine in the early 1930s, rioting was instrumental in the articulation of formative discourses on indigenous, as opposed to colonial, citizenship (Banko).

In the Middle East, the history of sectarian and ethnic strife has received a great deal of media and academic attention. Indeed, in the early modern and modern periods, certain notions of loyalty, ancestry, and identity became more sharply bordered, loaded with new political meaning, or infused with modern ideologies. But the way in which the present-day researcher seeks to label and understand the violence generated by such contention is not without consequence. Sources that qualify the violence as *primordial* and actors as *zealots* seem to imply that intercommunal contention is a result of unchanging identities or is an inherent cultural trait. Thankfully, the essentialist assumptions underlying such terminology have been challenged by a vast literature on ethnicity, nationalism, and sectarianism.

The excessive attention paid to destructive forces in urban life obscures the fact that the city generates creative spaces for cultural multiplicity, new social identities, and political agency. Thus, the case of the popular uprising in 1940s Baghdad explored in this volume shows that, beyond harm and destruction, the disruptive moment of urban violence can also reshuffle loyalties and reinforce solidarity across the fault lines of a city paralyzed by communal violence—merely by virtue of the participants' being neighbors or of the effect of a cosmopolitan, multiethnic notion of national belonging (Bashkin). Thus, while it cannot be denied that communalism framed the violent mobilization of many crowds in the early modern and modern Middle Eastern city, the fact is that cities also created new communities. This is a process that needs to be drawn out from the sources, in spite of their often simplistic and antagonistic portrayal of the events.

There are also instances in which it is difficult to infer what type of crowd dynamic is at play, as the sources describe the violence in a generic fashion—in terms such as *assault, battle, clash, confrontation, disturbance, quarrel, rivalry, standoff, strife, struggle,* and *tension.* These descriptors convey little information on the performance, symbolism, and framing of violent acts. Furthermore, accounts typically differ on the scope of violence exerted by the crowds, as in the case of the 1967 riots in the oil conurbation of the Eastern Province of Saudi Arabia, analyzed in this volume (Ghrawi).

If violence is not blown out of proportion, not blatantly caricatured, or perhaps not even mentioned in the source, it does not mean that it did not take place. Some words seem to hint at threats or actual harm: they belie the ruler's fear of the rage and violence of the anonymous masses of the ruled. Physical, emotional, and verbal violence can be conjured through descriptions of an *atmosphere* of *anxiety* and *fear* or of *agitation* and *hostility.* In the case of Palestine in the 1930s, the British military-colonial jargon referred to discontent as *seething* (Banko), while labor agitation in 1940s Abadan was considered *sedition talk* by British oil company officials (Elling). Other terms communicate the idea of violence—*abuse, harassment, hurt, intimidation, violation.* Terms for verbal acts, such as *harangue* and *incite,* may convey violent threats and can be considered *injurious*—that is, their utterance can become a violation, an act of symbolic violence.[22]

The question for the scholar becomes, When are historical instances of collective action to be understood as violence? This is as an open-ended question that is pertinent for historians of urban violence. To what degree should collective violence as an analytical category be "read into" a source that is silent or vague about the violent dynamics of an event? To what extent can the historian "read" violence "out of" a source that conveys a caricatured, demonizing description of an event? Some of the same questions pertain to readings of space.

THE SEMANTICS OF SPATIAL VIOLENCE

Studying the historical transformation of cities presents the historian with the task of interpreting violence in relation to spatial practices and transformations, and vice versa. While bringing people together in close proximity and interaction, the city is nonetheless characterized by social, political, and cultural processes that detach and delineate its spaces—city from hinterland, urban from rural, neighborhood from neighborhood, slums from upmarket residential areas, private from public. Yet such norms of demarcation and permanency belie a more promiscuous reality of fluidity and instability. The moments of trespass, violation, dislocation, and contestation over space often narrated by the sources testify that the logic of separation has always been challenged. Again, an attention to the semantics with which the sources describe this challenge can illuminate broader questions of urban life.

Familiar indicators of violated spatial norms are located in the conceptual borderland between threatened violence, actual physical harm inflicted on people, and damage exacted on the built environment or inanimate objects: *block, breach, confiscate, damage, demolish, intrude, occupy, ransack, roam, seize, show* (*of disrespect, strength, power*). Spatial transgression can work on a variety of levels. As can be seen in the case of intra-elite conflicts in eighteenth-century Cairo (Baldwin), the *invasion* and *appropriation* of an enemy's private residence can carry both the symbolic importance of ousting the enemy from his stronghold and the practical purpose of giving soldiers access to booty. Even if the enemy was not at home, this violation was considered a victory by the invader and an insult to the defender, especially when the trespass penetrated the gendered space of the *harem*. Battles over private property therefore also reflected contestation over norms regulating urban public life.

The neighborhood or quarter (*hawma, hara,* or *mahalla*) figures prominently in the stories of violence narrated in this volume. Its enduring importance in urban contention is reflected in its multiple roles as a spatial unit and locus of social solidarity and political loyalties—a role that continued in the twentieth century in spite of often dramatic changes in urban morphology. Episodes of public contention often involved the transgression of quarter boundaries (Arabic: *hudud*), gates, or walls. For example, the ransacking of the historical Turkmen quarters defined the dynamics of the 1924 and 1959 disturbances in Kirkuk (Fuccaro). Quarter rivalries could play out in intricate theatrics and ritualized performances of territorial demarcation and masculinity during the *mizmar* dance ceremonies in early modern Jeddah (Freitag).

Yet space is not only the stage set where violence occurs: the dark sides of the city both threaten with violence and must be contained by means of violence. The modernizing and rapidly expanding cities of the twentieth century, in particular, started to display the fault lines that separated the mushrooming spaces of the urban poor, the unemployed masses, and social delinquents from the pristine residential areas that accommodated the sumptuous, exclusive life style of the elites. In the Middle East and North Africa, examples of real and perceived violent spaces range from sites of dislocation, reordering, or confinement, such as *prisons* or *camps*, to sites of lawlessness, informality, and spontaneity, such as the *ghetto*, *shantytown*, or *slum*. Such "forbidden zones" of the city obviously have a long history. But the modern age brought informal housing on a huge scale and in forms that were reflected in the language, such as the Persian *halabi-abad* (tinplate city) or the Arabic *'ashwaiyat* (haphazard places). Sometimes, only a mere fence or screen kept these squalid areas invisible (Elsheshtawy), but the threat of their violent eruption was never far from the thoughts of those living in the elite areas.

With the far-reaching urban and political transformations of the second half of the twentieth century, spatial violence could sometimes operate on a far wider stage, as state actors engaged in large-scale urban reconfigurations. Beginning in the 1950s, military coups and authoritarian transitions brought tangible change to many cityscapes. The militarization of urban morphology in a city such as Cairo after the Great Fire of 1952 entailed a violent reimagining and replanning of space in both symbolic and functional terms (Elsheshtawy).

Ordinary sites of everyday civil life could suddenly turn into violent spaces. Some chapters in this volume show that some violent encounters occurred in interstitial spaces between the private and the public: in courtyards, on rooftops, in mosques, or in front of shops in the bazaar. At other times, encounters occurred in the square and in the street—spaces that were often monitored by and fully accessible to public authorities. Indeed, some of the case studies in this volume underscore the role of the *maydan*—the historical plaza of Middle Eastern cities that has gained new salience in the recent upheavals of Tahrir Square in Cairo, Pearl Roundabout in Manama, and Taksim Square in Istanbul.[23] Pitched battles between political factions unfolded in the squares on the outskirts of eighteenth-century Cairo, and the violence spread into the center of the city (Baldwin). In a similar fashion, Kirkuk's inner city was routinely used as a parade ground in which the soldiers of the Iraqi army displayed their military prowess (Fuccaro). Urban sites could also turn into popular memorials commemorating those protesters who had lost their lives in urban clashes, such as the bridges of Baghdad during the 1948 Wathba (Bashkin).

More broadly, as urban space rapidly expanded and urban life diversified in the twentieth century, sites of sociability and conflict moved from the coffeehouses, wooden benches (Arabic: *mirkaz*), and traditional meeting places (Arabic: *shilal* or *madhayif*) to the cafés, clubs, labor unions, and headquarters of political parties. At the same time, boiling discontent and organized dissent were often relocated from the bazaars, suqs, and workshops to the factories, offices, and universities. Targets of public outrage shifted from traditional sites of power, such as the amirate, the citadel (Arabic: *qal'ah*), the Islamic court, and the residence of notables to modern sites of governance, education, infrastructure, communications, and leisure, such as the airport, bus terminal, cinema, college, hotel, municipality, police station, post office, radio station, and so on. While functioning as symbols of progress, these sites have also become targets for anti-imperialist and anti-Western rage. Examples in this volume include the Shepheard's Hotel in Cairo, targeted by violent protesters in 1952 (Elsheshtawy), and the oil company installations in Dhahran that were attacked by rioters in 1967 (Ghrawi). To state authorities in cities across the Middle East, novel or reconfigured public spaces became synonymous with the prospect of violent unrest.

Twentieth-century transformations also brought about new repertoires and semantics of urban contention. *Revolts* and *uprisings* (Arabic: *thawra*; Ottoman Turkish: *isyan*; Persian: *enqelab*) obviously have a long history in the Middle East, but in the twentieth century some of these terms were appropriated by new political and ideological forces that transformed their popular meanings into those of *revolution* in its modern sense. Similarly, *demonstrations* (Arabic: *muhadharat*), *civil disobedience*, and *strikes* were novel additions to the vocabulary of public upheaval; and *resistance* (Arabic: *muqawama*) gained new meanings in neologisms such as the Arabic *intifadah* (Banko). The actors multiplied: the civilian, laborer, shopkeeper, trader, and tribesman were now joined by new cadres of civil servants, engineers, factory workers, labor unionists, taxi drivers, the unemployed, and university students, generating new crowds voicing new demands in novel languages of protest. As cities became centers of dense networks of political activism, their residents became *activists*, *dissidents*, and *revolutionaries*. These new actors, sites, networks, and organizations were crucial in disseminating modern notions of citizenship, social action, and political resistance—developments that were reflected in the changing vocabularies of urban violence.

. . .

The ambiguity of the categories *violence* and *space* demands a triangular lexical mapping that engages simultaneously with the symbolic language of violence as a social and political phenomenon, with the vernacular and imaginary vocabularies of the sources narrating it, and with the terminology of the historian analyzing it. The historian must be particularly attentive to the limits of textual sources (missing voices, temporal distance, linguistic differences), as well as to their context (the way in which scale, authorship, and historical contingency frame the text) and to hidden factors (discursive disparity, etymological histories, the necessity to "tease out" violence from silent sources).

The aim of such a critical approach to semantics is to deploy violence and space as positive categories of historical analysis. Identifying the archetypal representations of violence—the savage, the internal other, the irrational mob—serves to uncover languages of demonization, and thus of power. Situating the violent practitioners—the violent subject, the violent crowd, the violent forces of the state—in urban space can reveal dynamics of coercion and resistance and expose the way in which violence is always part of a struggle over how to order society. Interrogating value-laden languages of legitimacy or legality, the historian is able to reveal how norms are challenged, reproduced, and changed over time.

Inevitably, the historian must make normative choices that are reflected in his or her analytical language but must strive not to succumb to simplistic binary oppositions (tradition versus modernity, ethnic strife versus cosmopolitan coexistence, conflict versus solidarity) or to overread either continuity or change. In this endeavor, it is important to remember that the three languages of violence—those of the violence itself, of the source describing it, and of the scholar interpreting it—are in constant dialogue and negotiation.

APPENDIX TO PART 1
Further Readings

Aminzade, Ronald R., Jack A. Goldstone, Doug McAdam, Elizabeth J. Perry, William H. Sewell, Sidney Tarrow, and Charles Tilly, eds. *Silence and Voice in the Study of Contentious Politics*. Cambridge: Cambridge University Press, 2001.

Bonine, Michael E., ed. *Population, Poverty and Politics in Middle Eastern Cities*. Gainesville: University Press of Florida, 1997.

Brubaker, Roger, and David Laitin. "Ethnic and Nationalist Violence." *Annual Review of Sociology* 24 (1998): 423–52.

Burton, Andrew. *African Underclass: Urbanization, Crime and Colonial Order in Dar es Salaam*. Oxford: Currey, 2005.

Christensen, Stephen Turk. *Violence and the Absolutist State: Studies in European and Ottoman History*. Copenhagen: Akademisk Forlag, 1990.

Crang, Mike, and Nigel Thrift. *Thinking Space*. London: Routledge, 2000.

Fawaz, Leila Tarazi. *An Occasion for War: Civil Conflict in Lebanon and Damascus in 1860*. London: Centre for Lebanese Studies and I. B. Tauris, 1994.

Gingeras, Ryan. *Sorrowful Shores: Violence, Ethnicity, and the End of the Ottoman Empire, 1912–1923*. Oxford: Oxford University Press, 2009.

Giustozzi, Antonio. *The Art of Coercion: The Primitive Accumulation and Management of Coercive Power*. New York: Columbia University Press, 2011.

Gorman, Anthony. "Regulation, Reform and Resistance in the Middle East Prison." In Frank Dikötter and Ian Brown, eds., *Cultures of Confinement: A History of the Prison in Africa, Asia and Latin America*, 95–146. London: Hurst, 2007.

Gupte, Jaideep. *What Is Civil about Intergroup Violence? Five Inadequacies of Communal and Ethnic Constructs of Urban Riots*. MICROCON Research Working Paper 62. Brighton, UK: MICROCON, 2012.

Harrison, Mark. "The Ordering of the Urban Environment: Time, Work and the Occurrence of Crowds 1790–1835." *Past & Present* 110 (February 1986): 134–68.

Harvey, David. *Rebel Cities: From the Right to the City to the Urban Revolution*. London: Verso, 2011.

Johnson, Michael. "Political Bosses and Their Gangs: Zu'ama and Qabadayat in the Sunni Muslim Quarters of Beirut." In Ernst Gellner and John Waterbury, eds.,

Patrons and Clients in Mediterranean Societies, 207–24. London: Center for Mediterranean Studies of the American Universities Field Staff, 1977.

Kalyvas, Stathis N., Ian Shapiro, and Tarek Masoud, eds. *Order, Conflict and Violence*. Cambridge: Cambridge University Press, 2008.

Khalaf, Samir. *Civil and Uncivil Violence in Lebanon: A History of the Internationalization of Communal Conflict*. New York: Columbia University Press, 2002.

Khoury, Dina R. *Iraq in Wartime: Soldiering, Martyrdom, and Remembrance*. Cambridge: Cambridge University Press, 2013.

———. "Political Relations between City and State in the Middle East, 1700–1850." In Peter Sluglett, ed., *The Urban Social History of the Middle East, 1750–1950*, 67–103. Syracuse, NY: Syracuse University Press, 2008.

King, Anthony D. "Culture, Space and Representation: Problems of Methodology in Urban Studies." In *Urbanism and Islam Proceedings of the International Conference on Urbanism and Islam (ICUIT)*, Supplement, 339–74. Tokyo: Middle East Culture Centre, 1989.

Koonings, Kees, and Dirk Kruijt, eds. *Megacities: The Politics of Urban Exclusion and Violence in the Global South*. London: Zed, 2009.

Lange, Christian, and Maribel Fierro. *Public Violence in Islamic Societies*. Edinburgh: Edinburgh University Press, 2009.

Lawrence, Bruce B., and Aisha Karim, eds. *On Violence: A Reader*. Durham, NC: Duke University Press, 2007.

Lefebvre, Henri. *The Urban Revolution*. Minneapolis: University of Minnesota Press, 2003.

———. *Writings on Cities*. Trans. Eleonore Kofman and Elizabeth Lebas. London: Blackwell, 2006.

Makdisi, Ussama. "Rethinking Ottoman Imperialism: Modernity, Violence and the Cultural Logic of Ottoman Reform." In Jens Hanssen, Thomas Philipp, and Stefan Weber, eds., *The Empire in the City: Arab Provincial Capitals in the Late Ottoman Empire*, 29–48. Beirut: Ergon Verlag, 2002.

Martin, Deborah G., and Byron Miller. "Space and Contentious Politics." *Mobilization: An International Journal* 8, no. 2 (2003): 143–56.

Merriman, John M. *The Margins of City Life: Explorations on the French Urban Frontier, 1815–1851*. New York: Oxford University Press, 1991.

Ricoeur, Paul. "Violence and Language." *Bulletin de la Société Américaine de Philosophie de Langue Française* 10, no. 2 (1998): 32–41.

Rotbard, Sharon. *White City Black City: Architecture and War in Tel Aviv and Jaffa*. London: Pluto Press, 2015.

Sennett, Richard. *The Uses of Disorder*. New York: Knopf, 1970.

Tilly, Charles. *The Politics of Collective Violence*. Cambridge: Cambridge University Press, 2003.

————. "War Making and State Making as Organized Crime." In Peter Evans, Dietrich Rueschemeyer, and Theda Skocpol, eds., *Bringing the State Back In*, 169–87. Cambridge: Cambridge University Press, 1985.

Van der Veer, Peter. "Riots as Rituals: The Construction of Violence and Public Space in Hindu Nationalism." In Paul R. Brass, ed., *Riots and Pogroms*, 154–76. New York: New York University Press, 1996.

Varshney, Ashutosh R. *Ethnic Conflict and Civic Life: Hindus and Muslims in India*. New Haven, CT: Yale University Press, 2002.

Watenpaugh, Keith. "Steel Shirts, White Badges and the Last Qabaday: Fascism, Urban Violence and Civic Identity in Aleppo under French Rule." In Nadine Méouchy, ed., *France, Syrie, et Liban, 1918–1946: Les ambiguïtés et les dynamiques de la relation mandataire*, 325–47. Damascus: Institute Français d'Études Arabes, 2003.

Wieviorka, Michel. *Violence: A New Approach*. London: Sage, 2009.

Wirth, Louis. "Urbanism as a Way of Life," *The American Journal of Sociology* 44, no. 1 (1938): 1–24.

Wood, Carter J. "Locating Violence: The Spatial Production and Construction of Physical Aggression." In Katherine D. Watson, ed., *Assaulting the Past: Violence and Civilization in Historical Context*, 20–37. Newcastle, UK: Cambridge Scholars Publishing, 2007.

CIVIC STRUGGLES

Norms and Practices of Conflict

Part 2

3 ELITE CONFLICT AND THE URBAN ENVIRONMENT
Eighteenth-Century Cairo

James E. Baldwin

VIOLENCE WAS INTEGRAL to political life in Ottoman Cairo. Egyptian elite society was heavily armed, was factional, and celebrated a martial culture. Moreover,
the rewards to be gained by dominating Egyptian politics, through control of
agricultural revenues or monopolization of the coffee trade, were immense. The
endemic violence of politics in Ottoman Cairo is a major theme of the narrative
sources dating from that period. Consequently, it also appears in the modern
scholarship based on those narrative sources—particularly the works of Peter
Holt, André Raymond, and Jane Hathaway.[1] While descriptions of political violence loom large in the secondary literature on Ottoman Egypt, there have been
few works identifying violence as the category of analysis: more often, violence
appears as a backdrop in studies of political economy, elite household formation, and center-province relations.[2] How should we understand factional violence in eighteenth-century Cairo? Was it anarchic, as it sometimes seems in
the literature? Or was it part of a normative order? If the latter, what were the
norms and where did they come from?

This chapter makes a preliminary attempt to answer these questions by
looking at how political violence was narrated by contemporary Egyptians. I
focus in particular on the norms surrounding the conduct of violence within
the urban environment of Ottoman Cairo. How did chroniclers describe the violent encounters that took place in Cairo's streets and squares and their impact
on the city's fabric and residents? Can we deduce a set of values and norms governing urban violence from their writings? The chronicles written during this
period were generally partisan texts, which makes them particularly valuable
for this purpose. They reveal the values of Cairene society through the narrative
choices they make, the acts they criticize, and the virtues they praise.

The chronicles show that political violence in Cairo, while illegal, was not
anarchic. Violence was constrained by a set of norms broadly recognized by the
members of political society. These norms were loosely connected with religious

beliefs and principles, but they were not derived from Islam. Rather, they were produced in the collision of various cultural factors, including notions of personal honor, courage, and manliness and a conception of justice that prioritized the daily needs of ordinary Cairene civilians. The norms were sometimes ignored, but violations were publicized, and the importance of good reputation provided an incentive to observe them. As well as revealing these norms to us, the stories about violent conflict recorded in the chronicles defined and policed the norms for eighteenth-century Egyptian society.

THE CHRONICLES

The chroniclers of eighteenth-century Egypt were drawn from a range of social strata. One group of chronicles, often known as the "military chronicles," were written in colloquial Arabic by soldiers within the 'Azaban regiment and included anecdotes and legends as well as historical narrative. Others, often called "literary chronicles," were written in formal Arabic by well-educated people who were either scholars or bureaucrats. These two categories represent two ends of a spectrum, and various other chroniclers were somewhere between them.[3]

This chapter is based primarily on three chronicles, each representing different points on this spectrum. The first is Ahmad Katkhuda al-Damurdashi's *Al-Durra al-musana fi akhbar al-Kinana* (The preserved pearl: On the affairs of Egypt), the best known of the military chronicles.[4] The author Damurdashi was a middle-ranking soldier in the 'Azaban regiment.[5] Damurdashi's chronicle is one of a group of related manuscripts by various authors; their similarities suggest that they were drawn from a common model, which may have been a collection of stories passed orally around the 'Azaban barracks.[6]

The second chronicle I have used is Ahmad Shalabi ibn 'Abd al-Ghani's *Awdah al-isharat fi man tawalla Misr al-Qahira min al-wuzara' wa 'l-bashat* (The clearest sign: On the viziers and pashas who governed Cairo), the principal literary chronicle of the early eighteenth century.[7] The author Ahmad Shalabi appears to have been a scholar and a Sufi; he was also connected to the provincial administration, quoting frequently and at length from official documents. He was probably a bureaucrat in the provincial government or in the private service of a political figure.[8]

Third, I have used 'Ali al-Shadhili's chronicle of the 1711 civil war, *Dhikr ma waqa'a bayna 'askar al-mahrusa al-Qahira* (An account of what occurred among the soldiers of the well-protected city of Cairo).[9] This chronicle is written in correct, formal Arabic rather than the inelegant colloquial of the military chronicles. However, Raymond concluded on the basis of Shadhili's sarcastic attitude to the scholarly class that he was not one of them but was an educated member of ordinary Cairene society, perhaps an artisan or merchant.[10]

OTTOMAN CAIRO AND ITS POLITICAL ELITE

Here I give a brief overview of elite political society in Ottoman Cairo in order to make sense of the stories that follow. Ottoman authority was represented in Egypt by the governor, or pasha, who resided in the citadel on the outskirts of Cairo. The governors of Egypt usually served terms of two to four years before being rotated to another post. The governors were outsiders: in contrast to the situation in some other provinces during the same period, local families or groups did not gain control of this office in Egypt. But while the governor was not himself a member of Egypt's elite society, he could govern effectively only through cooperation with it. This provincial elite was arranged into households, headed by powerful men, some of whom were manumitted mamluks (military slaves), and many of whom held the rank of *sancakbeyi*, which was usually shortened to "bey." These households reproduced themselves through both kinship and slavery.[11] Their wealth was based largely on control of rural tax farms and *awqaf* (endowments).[12]

The other key institution in Egyptian political society was the military regiment. The seven regiments of Egypt were institutions that had been implanted by the Ottomans.[13] By the eighteenth century, however, they had developed strong corporate identities and would mobilize independently to defend their corporate interests.[14] The wealth of regimental officers came from their domination of trade. The households and regiments were not discrete groups: they were interconnected loci of power. Some households were headed by regimental officers and others by beys, who had no regimental affiliation but sought to manipulate the regiments by placing their protégés in key positions. Finally, this society was split in two by a division between the Qasimi and Faqari factions. The origins of these factions are shrouded in myth, but in the early eighteenth century most beys identified with one or the other, and each faction was associated with one of the two main regiments: the Faqaris with the Janissaries and the Qasimis with the 'Azaban.[15]

Cairo was the center of Egyptian political life. As well as the Ottoman governor's residence, the regimental barracks were based there, as were the major households. Much of the wealth of Egypt, of course, came from the countryside, produced by the Nile delta's rich alluvial soil. Other important sources of wealth were located not in Egypt's fields but on its coasts: both Egypt's agricultural exports and the long-distance trade between the Indian Ocean and the Mediterranean passed through the customs posts at the ports of Suez, Rosetta, and Alexandria. But those who controlled these sources of wealth, through tax farms, customs farms, and endowments, tended to base themselves in Cairo, appointing agents to manage their affairs on the ground in the villages and ports.[16] The channeling of Egypt's wealth through Cairo made it a prosperous city, with vibrant markets in the city center and the grand mansions of the notables in the southern and western districts.[17] The struggles of Egypt's political-military class affected life in Cairo in numerous ways: through the patron-client networks that saw many Cairenes affiliated with particular households; through the interpenetration of the regiments with the merchant and artisan classes; and through the patronage the wealthy elites were able to dispense.[18] When political struggles became violent, the impact on the safety and property of Cairenes could be grave.

What kinds of violent confrontations did these political elites engage in? Violent acts common to political life ranged from assassinations of individual people to pitched battles between large militias belonging to particular households or between the regiments. It is helpful to distinguish between two basic types of conflict, because each had quite different implications for the city. I emphasize that this distinction is an analytical device I am using to help clarify the type of violence that interests me. Within the narrative of Cairo's eighteenth-century political history, it is not always possible to categorize neatly each violent incident in this way: some confrontations involved elements of both types, and some morphed from one type into the other.

The first type of conflict pitted a relatively unified provincial military elite against the Ottoman governor. Conflicts of this type tended to focus on specific locations of symbolic and/or practical significance. A classic confrontation would involve crowds of soldiers congregating in Rumayla Square, a large open space on the outskirts of the city at the foot of the Muqattam hill, upon which stood the citadel. From this position the soldiers' show of force was clearly visible to the governor and his entourage, and the soldiers were able to cut communications between the citadel and the city. Such a standoff could end with the negotiated resignation of the governor or with a forced deposition.[19] If, however, the protesters failed to garner sufficient support, the governor might prevail, with the soldiers dispersing and the ringleaders executed. However they ended, the violence of such conflicts was contained and at least partly symbolic. While the populace was certainly aware of such conflicts—the soldiers' demonstrations were noisy and ostentatious; the severed heads of unsuccessful rebels were publicly displayed at Bab Zuwayla, the southern gate into the center of Cairo—their impact was not too disruptive of the lives of ordinary Cairenes.

The second type of conflict was the intra-elite factional conflict, fought between households or regiments. In these conflicts, the violence was much more dispersed throughout the city. The most significant example in the early eighteenth century was the war of 1711, fought between the Janissary regiment, backed by the Ottoman governor, and a group of dissident Janissaries allied with the 'Azaban.[20] Smaller intra-elite conflicts were frequent throughout the period. Intra-elite conflicts could involve pitched battles in large open spaces: much of the 1711 war was fought on the Qasr al-'Ayni fields to the west of the city. But such conflicts more often took place within the city's narrow streets. They revolved around the residences of the main combatants, as each side sought to capture and kill their enemies and plunder their property. These conflicts had a far greater impact both on the urban fabric and on the lives of Cairo's civilian population. This chapter focuses on these factional, intra-elite conflicts fought within Cairo's residential and commercial neighborhoods, which impacted public space and private property in numerous ways. Through a discussion of how contemporary chroniclers described these confrontations, I draw out the norms that governed, or at least were expected to govern, political violence.

I first examine the norms surrounding violence and private property. Under what circumstances was it deemed legitimate for disputing parties to attack one another's properties? What constraints or taboos surrounded private property? I then discuss attitudes to violence in public space that involved public property. To what extent was it considered acceptable for those engaged in conflict to appropriate public buildings for violent ends or to engage in behavior that disrupted public space and damaged public infrastructure?

PRIVATE PROPERTY

The most prominent violation of private property during political conflicts was the invasion and plunder of an enemy's house. The household was the primary unit of political organization in Ottoman Cairo, and the house of its leader was the headquarters of this unit and an expression of its power. The houses of the leading beys were large and imposing complexes consisting of a reception hall where political business was conducted, petitioners received, and visitors entertained; quarters for the bey's retainers; and the harem, where his wives, children, and female slaves lived.[21] Such houses were ostentatiously furnished and decorated and were also the location of the bey's personal treasury. For a bey's enemy, the capture of his house could serve several purposes. Sometimes, if a bey involved in a feud had retreated to his house with his retainers and mamluks, the goal was to arrest or assassinate the bey himself, and a fierce battle might be fought to take the house. On other occasions, a bey who had been warned of an impending assassination attempt would have fled Cairo or have gone into hiding, but his house would still be attacked for the symbolic value of seizing his power center and for the plunder it offered.

The chroniclers report the invasion and ransacking of beys' houses without any suggestion that this was in itself considered problematic. Rather, such actions were the routine of politics. Politics was, for its participants and for the chroniclers, largely a competition for control of sources of wealth: tax farms, customs farms, endowments, and protection rackets. It is not surprising, then, that the seizure of wealth itself during a conflict was considered legitimate. It is worth noting that confiscation of wealth was also a tactic used by the sultan and the Ottoman governor. Confiscation as a penalty for disobedience was often formalized: tax farms could be seized on the order of a *firman* (imperial order) and might then be transferred to an offender's rival. But official confiscation could also be less procedural: the soldiers sent to arrest a bey or other notable were often given free rein to plunder his house for their own profit while they were there.

Despite the general consensus on the legitimacy of house invasion and plunder during political conflict, there were norms surrounding how one should treat the house and property of an enemy. The principal norm was the sanctity of the harem. Beys' houses, in common with the houses of all Cairenes of sufficient means, were physically divided into the *selamlık*, the public section of the house where visitors were received, and the harem, where the women of the household lived and which only the bey, his immediate relatives, and his eunuchs could enter. The sanctity of the harem and the seclusion of the women who lived within it were supposed to be respected even by attackers invading a house to plunder it. This norm was not always respected, but it was recognized and could be manipulated by elite figures to preserve their wealth during conflicts.

In narrative rather than prescriptive sources, it is often the report of a violation that reveals the norm, through the critical tone of the chronicler. An example is a story from 1700–1701 related by Damurdashi. The incident occurred during a dispute between 'Abd al-Rahman Bey and the Hawwara Bedouin of Upper Egypt.[22] 'Abd al-Rahman Bey had seized a number of villages belonging to the Hawwara when he was governor of the subprovince of Girge in Upper Egypt. The Hawwara enlisted the Janissaries in Cairo to assist them in securing compensation for the lost revenue. The Janissaries prepared a lawsuit against 'Abd al-Rahman Bey and summoned him to the governor's *diwan*.[23] 'Abd al-Rahman refused to attend, summoned his main ally Ahmad Odabashi al-Baghdadli and all their retainers, and barricaded himself in his house. A force of soldiers from the Janissary and 'Azaban regiments attacked the house, and while defending it, both 'Abd al-Rahman Bey and Ahmad al-Baghdadli were killed.

Once 'Abd al-Rahman Bey was dead, his retainers and mamluks abandoned their positions, allowing the Janissaries to enter the house. 'Abd al-Rahman Bey's mamluks had emptied the treasury and fled through a back door. So the Janissaries plundered the rest of the contents of the house, including the silverware, copperware, furniture, tents, tools, food, and livestock. They then entered the harem and captured the slave women and 'Abd al-Rahman Bey's daughter. Damurdashi expresses shock at this violation of the norms governing violent conflict. He emphasizes the unprecedented nature of the incident, claiming that it was the first conflict in Egypt in which a harem had been plundered and women taken captive. He stresses the scale of the plunder, claiming that everything in 'Abd al-Rahman Bey's house was looted. He also voices condemnation through the words and actions of other characters in the story. The mother of 'Abd al-Rahman Bey's daughter appeals to the soldiers kidnapping her: "You have killed her father and taken her trousseau, and now you'll take her too? Don't you fear God?" (*qataltu abuha wa akhadhtu jihazaha wa ta'khudhuha ma takhafu min Allah*).[24] Recognizing the justice of her plea, an officer of the 'Azaban corps called Mustafa Qaysarli steps in to rescue the daughter and her mother: he secures an orphan's pension for the daughter and arranges both her own and her mother's marriages to two of 'Abd al-Rahman Bey's manumitted slaves. It is perhaps no accident that the one soldier involved in the invasion who showed some propriety, as narrated by Damurdashi, belonged to the author's regiment.

While this incident demonstrates that the norms surrounding violence were sometimes violated with no immediate consequences for the perpetrators, other stories suggest that, for the most part, the norm of harem sanctity was adhered to, even when there was a clear cost to the attacker in doing so. Damurdashi tells the story of a plot hatched by four Qasimi beys and two aghas in 1727–28 and of its fallout.[25] This story shows that chroniclers were not rigidly partisan in their analysis of events. Although the plotters were members of the Qasimi faction, with which Damurdashi sympathized, he is critical of these particular individuals, portraying them as both immoral and incompetent. Nevertheless, one was able to use the norm of harem sanctity to avoid the repercussions of his actions.

The story begins by introducing the plotters: 'Ali Bey Abu 'l-Adab, Mustafa Bey 'Awad, Yusuf Bey al-Kha'in,[26] Yusuf Bey al-Shara'ibi, 'Abdullah Agha, and Sulayman Agha Abu Diffiyya. They are described as inveterate drunkards: they were "in love with drinking liquor and licking wine cups dry" (*mula'in bi sharb al-rah wa mass al-aqdah*).[27] Their intoxication was behind both the hatching of the reckless plot and its failure. During one of their regular drinking sessions at Mustafa Bey 'Awad's house, they decided to assassinate Dhu 'l-Faqar Bey and his allies 'Ali Bey al-Hindi, Muhammad Bey Qatamish, 'Ali Bey Qatamish, and the Ottoman governor Muhammad Pasha al-Nishanji. This was to be a revenge killing: Dhu 'l-Faqar Bey was responsible for the murder of Mustafa Bey 'Awad's brother. In their drunken state, the plotters had forgotten that Mustafa Bey 'Awad's *shurabdar* (drinks waiter) had previously been a slave of 'Ali Bey al-Hindi. The *shurabdar* retained a deep affection for his former master, in whose household he had grown up, so he informed him of the plot. 'Ali Bey al-Hindi informed Dhu 'l-Faqar Bey, who in turn informed the governor Muhammad Pasha. The governor acted quickly and ordered the Janissary agha to arrest all six plotters and raid their houses. Three of the plotters were arrested and executed, while the other three managed to flee. One of the fugitives, Sulayman Agha Abu Diffiyya, also managed to retain much of his property, thanks to a friend in the Janissary barracks called Yusuf Katkhuda. When Yusuf learned of the Janissary Agha's orders, he sent servants to Sulayman Agha's house to move all of his possessions into the harem. When raiding the house, the Janissary agha would not enter the harem, so Sulayman Agha's property was safe.

PUBLIC SPACE AND PUBLIC PROPERTY

The type of public building most frequently caught up in Cairo's violent conflicts was the mosque. Mosques were strategically useful buildings: they were large spaces that could accommodate many soldiers and were easily defensible, making them good bases for holding a particular area of the city. Furthermore, their minarets were the tallest points in the city and provided sight lines and firing lines into the streets and into the courtyards of houses.

The story of the battle between 'Abd al-Rahman Bey and the Janissary and 'Azaban regiments is an example of how mosques were used in urban conflict. 'Abd al-Rahman Bey's house, where he retreated with his ally Ahmad al-Baghdadli, was opposite the mosque of Amir Maridani, just south of Bab Zuwayla. The Janissaries and 'Azaban split into two parties for their assault on his house. One party opened a breach by blasting a hole in the outer wall of the house. The other party climbed the minaret of the Maridani mosque; this gave them a vantage point from which they could fire into 'Abd al-Rahman Bey's courtyard and reception hall, preventing anyone from entering or leaving the house through the main entrance. Both 'Abd al-Rahman Bey and Ahmad al-Baghdadli were shot dead by snipers in the minaret while trying to return fire.[28]

A similar example comes from a conflict that took place in 1725–26 between Çerkes Muhammad Bey al-Kabir and his ally Qasim Bey, and Yusuf Çorbacı and the 'Azaban regiment, who were backed by the Ottoman governor 'Ali Pasha. This conflict came in the wake of tension between Çerkes Muhammad Bey and the previous governor, Muhammad Pasha al-Nishanji. Çerkes Muhammad Bey had coerced the commanders of the seven regiments and other notables into petitioning the sultan to dismiss Muhammad Pasha on the grounds of abuse of power. The imperial government in Istanbul sided with Muhammad Pasha but pretended to accede to Çerkes Muhammad Bey's demand in order to lure him into a trap. Muhammad Pasha's replacement—the governor of Crete, 'Ali Pasha—was to unite with Çerkes Muhammad Bey's rivals in Cairo to kill him or force him into exile, at which point Muhammad Pasha would be restored to the governorate and 'Ali Pasha would return to Crete.[29] During the final stages of the campaign against Çerkes Muhammad Bey, Yusuf Çorbacı's 'Azab soldiers were sheltering in the Mahmudiyya mosque on Rumayla Square while men loyal to Çerkes Muhammad Bey and Qasim Bey were based in Qasim Bey's house nearby. Yusuf Çorbacı's men climbed the Mahmudiyya's minaret, from where they were able to fire into the Qasim Bey's courtyard and shoot Qasim Bey dead.[30]

Often, mosques were themselves the focus of fighting. A mosque made a defensible base where fighters could both shelter and control the surrounding area. Thus, the occupation of a mosque was the means by which a force would hold a particular area of the city, and urban conflict often revolved around the occupation of strategically placed mosques.

The best example of this is from the 1711 war. The earliest stage of this war saw a group of 'Azaban soldiers barricade themselves in the Sultan Hasan mosque, which faced the Janissary barracks across Rumayla Square. The 'Azaban and Janissaries bombarded each other with cannon fire for several days. Each side then sought to gain control of the main roads between Rumayla Square and Bab Zuwayla by seizing the mosques that stood on them. The Janissary commander Ifranj Ahmad sent Ahmad, the agha of the Tüfekçiyan regiment, to occupy the mosque of Sudun Mirzada in the 'Izzi marketplace, which controlled the Suq al-Silah road from Rumayla to Darb al-Ahmar. He also sent 'Umar, the agha of the Çerakise regiment, to seize the mosque of Qijmas al-Ishaqi in Darb al-Ahmar, the road that led to Bab Zuwayla from the east.

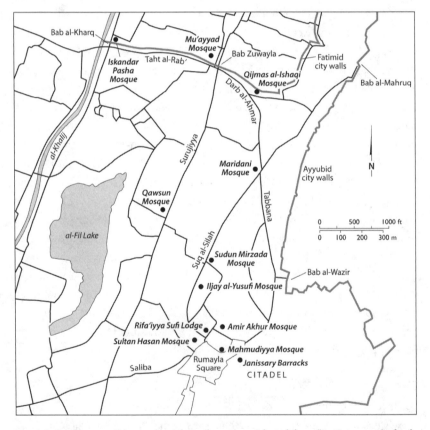

Map 3.1. Southeastern Cairo in the eighteenth century. Adapted from "Le Caire vers la fin du XVIIIe siècle," in André Raymond, *Artisans et commerçants au Caire au XVIIIe siècle* (Cairo: Institut Français d'Archéologie Orientale, 1999).

Meanwhile, the ʿAzaban seized the mosque of Iljay al-Yusufi on Suq al-Silah and the Maridani mosque in Tabbana. These two mosques were, respectively, just south and just north of the Sudun Mirzada mosque; the Maridani also commanded the end of Darb al-Ahmar, which led to the Qijmas al-Ishaqi mosque. The ʿAzaban then forced their opponents out of both mosques. One contingent entered a house several doors away from the Sudun Mirzada and then broke through the wall to enter the next house, and so on until they reached the mosque, at which point Ahmad Agha and his occupying force fled. Another detachment of ʿAzaban under Salih Çorbacı al-Razzaz attacked the Qijmas al-Ishaqi mosque and captured it from ʿUmar Agha, who fled to Bab Zuwayla, where he occupied the Muʾayyad and Iskandar Pasha mosques.[31]

Neither Damurdashi nor Ahmad Shalabi appear to have had many qualms about fighting in and around religious buildings or about potential damage to some of the outstanding examples of Islamic architecture. They narrate the events in a matter-of-fact tone that displays no disapproval of the use of mosques for military purposes. Their spiritual and aesthetic value appears to be irrelevant; it is their location, size and shape, and relationship to the urban topography that are significant. Mosques are described solely in terms of the access they allowed to particular streets, areas, and houses. Indeed, in the story about the conflict involving Çerkes Muhammad Bey, Qasim Bey, and Yusuf Çorbacı, Damurdashi praises the use of the Mahmudiyya minaret by Yusuf Çorbacı's soldiers to assassinate Qasim Bey, because it silenced the gunfire from Qasim Bey's house into the streets, which had been endangering the people of the neighborhood.[32]

Damurdashi also appears to have seen no problem in killing people within a religious building: he did not recognize any concept of sanctuary. He reports an incident during the 1711 civil war when Muhammad Bey of Girge and his Hawwara Bedouin allies were engaged in a long-running battle with ʿAwad Bey and the ʿAzab troops on the Qasr al-ʿAyni fields. One of Muhammad Bey's horsemen was being pursued by a group of ʿAzab soldiers and attempted to escape by entering the *takiyya* there.[33] His pursuers followed him into the *takiyya*, where they stripped him, cut off his head, and took his horse. Damurdashi, who was an ʿAzab soldier, claims to have been present and to have witnessed this event, although he does not say he participated in the killing himself. He relates the incident, carried out by his comrades in front of him, without embarrassment.[34]

Damurdashi and Ahmad Shalabi were both close to Cairene political life: Damurdashi was a soldier in the ʿAzaban regiment, and Ahmad Shalabi was probably a bureaucrat in the provincial administration. Shadhili, however, seems not to have had any close connections with elite political circles. Interestingly, he had a more critical view of the conduct of violence within mosques. He empha- sizes the damage caused to mosque buildings: during the mutual bombardment between the Janissary barracks and the Sultan Hasan mosque at the beginning of the 1711 war, Shadhili writes that cannon fire smashed the windows, broke the walls, and burned the minaret of the Mahmudiyya mosque and also damaged the mosque of Amir Akhur.[35] He also notes the impact fighting had on the reli- gious practices of the population: he complains that when the ʿAzaban seized the Maridani mosque, they prevented people from praying there.[36] These comments form part of a pronounced critical stance toward the 1711 war, which focuses on the suffering of ordinary Cairenes during the fighting. Damurdashi and Ahmad Shalabi also regret the suffering of ordinary Cairenes in ways that I discuss later, but in Shadhili's text the comments on the damage to mosques and the impos- sibility of worship form a distinct line of criticism. It is striking that this differ- ence in perspective coincides with a difference in background, suggesting that those connected with political life were more tolerant than the ordinary popula- tion of Cairo of the appropriation of public space and religious buildings for the violent conduct of politics.

The permissive attitude concerning the conduct of violence within mosques displayed by the politically connected was not applied equally to all sections of Cairene society, however. When civilians were violent within mosques, Ahmad Shalabi heaped opprobrium upon them. A fascinating example is a conflict that broke out in March 1709 over the rectorship of the Aqbughawiyya madrasa, one of the madrasas attached to the Azhar mosque complex.[37] The rectorship of the Aqbughawiyya was left vacant by the death of the shaykh Muhammad al-Nasharti. A scholar called Ahmad al-Nafrawi moved quickly to obtain a *hujja* (certificate) from the qadi and a *buyuruldu* (order) from the governor granting him the posi- tion. However, the followers of the late Nasharti supported another scholar, ʿAbd al-Baqi al-Qallini, who was not present in Cairo at that time. They sent him a message urging him to return to the city to claim the rectorship. The students at the madrasa divided into two parties supporting each of the candidates.

Having obtained the support of the qadi and the governor, Nafrawi attempted to assume the rectorship before Qallini arrived back in Cairo, but he was pre- vented from teaching his classes by the Qallini faction among the students. Dur- ing the night of 23 March 1709, a group of Nafrawi's supporters armed with guns attacked the Azhar mosque and drove out the supporters of Qallini, breaking down the door of the madrasa and physically installing Nafrawi there. The following afternoon, Qallini's party retaliated. They entered the Azhar mosque and locked the doors behind them. A gun battle ensued inside the mosque between supporters of Nafrawi and Qallini. Ten people were killed and many more injured; the vaults of the Azhar were looted, and many lamps were broken in the melee. Eventually, the police chief arrived to disperse the fighting students and remove the dead bodies.

In contrast to his reports of battles around mosques involving the military elite, in this case Ahmad Shalabi is highly critical of the violence. He emphasizes the damage caused to the mosque and its emptiness after the battle, bemoaning that no one at all prayed there that day—the first time ever that the Azhar had been entirely empty of worshippers. The following day Nafrawi went to the governor's *diwan* to appeal for his support, and Ahmad Shalabi reports the dressing-down he received from the *naqib al-ashraf* Hasan Efendi.[38] Even though, from the perspective of the governor's administration, Nafrawi had the right to claim the rectorship, Hasan Efendi called Nafrawi's supporters a *jamaʿa al-mafasid* (party of evil-doers) and accused them of proclaiming disobedience and cursing from the minarets and pulpits, as well as firing weapons inside the mosque. The attention Ahmad Shalabi gives to Hasan Efendi's words suggests that the chronicler agrees with him: he is expressing his own disapproval of the students' behavior through Hasan Efendi's voice. It was perhaps the dissonance between the status of Nafrawi as a member of the 'ulamaʾ and his violent behavior that outraged Ahmad Shalabi.

These stories show a range of responses to violent conduct in mosques. Those written by people within political society—Damurdashi and Ahmad Shalabi—suggest a tolerance of fighting within mosques when it was conducted by members of the military class. The fact that Ahmad Shalabi was outraged by civilian students fighting in a mosque suggests that the norms surrounding violence differed according to the perpetrator. Greater leeway for violent behavior was allowed to the military class than to the population in general. What was seen as legitimate in the context of the political struggles of the great households and the regiments was judged inappropriate in the context of the internal politics of the Azhar mosque-university. This license to the military elite to behave violently in mosques was not recognized by everyone, however. Shadhili, who was not directly connected to elite political circles, took a much more critical attitude to violence in mosques. He linked the damage to mosques and the prevention of prayer with the suffering of ordinary people, as part of a general critique of the effect of political violence on Cairo.

PUBLIC UTILITIES

There was a rough consensus between Damurdashi, Ahmad Shalabi, and Shadhili about violence in public space when it impacted the daily domestic and professional lives of ordinary civilian Cairenes. When Cairenes were prevented from going about their daily business by elite violence, this was a matter of concern for all three. As we have seen, in his account of the battle between Yusuf Çorbacı and Qasim Bey, Damurdashi praises Yusuf Çorbacı for assassinating Qasim Bey from the minaret of the Mahmudiyya mosque because it silenced heavy gunfire from Qasim Bey's house into the streets. The shooting had been so intense that it had prevented anyone from walking in Rumayla Square. Reporting this, Damurdashi exclaims: "We seek refuge in God from such a time."[39]

The theme of the hampering of circulation in the streets appears in other stories too. Shadhili describes the takeover by the Janissaries of the mosques of al-Mu'ayyad and Iskandar Pasha during the 1711 war. This gave them control of the area called Taht al-Rab' between Bab Zuwayla and Bab al-Kharq. He notes that the occupation prevented worshippers from entering the mosques and also that the local people could not move around the area. For Shadhili, this act was an example of oppression and iniquity (al-jawr wa 'l-fujur).[40] When Ayyub Bey sought to broker a cease-fire during the 1711 war, the issue of freedom of movement was foremost in his mind. According to Damurdashi, he wrote to Ibrahim Bey suggesting that they persuade the governor to settle the dispute with the eight dissident Janissaries that was the cause of the war and that, in the meantime, he should open the streets to allow the people to move around (iftahu tariq li 'l-nas tamshi 'ala ba'diha).[41]

In addition to restrictions on the movement of civilians, interruption to the water supply was another consequence of political violence that the chroniclers roundly condemned. A story from the 1711 war concerns the force of Hawwara Bedouin whom Muhammad Bey of Girge had brought to Cairo to support Ifranj Ahmad. Damurdashi reports that the Hawwara were attacking and robbing people on the main roads in the outskirts of Cairo. He claims that their predations made the area so dangerous that the water carriers stopped plying their trade between Cairo and its suburb Bulaq, situated on the Nile about a mile northwest of the city.[42] Damurdashi's dislike for the Hawwara is clear—he refers to them as the "bastards" (awlad al-zina); as an 'Azab soldier Damurdashi was on the other side in the war. This story ends in a rather mysterious fashion, reflecting the nature of Damurdashi's chronicle as a compendium of legends and anecdotes as well as a narrative history. An unnamed Maghribi, on horse-back and armed with two muskets, began escorting the water carriers along the Bulaq road each morning and continued to do so until the end of the war. The Hawwara were afraid to attack him; Damurdashi does not explain why. Re-gardless of the legendary quality of this story, the important point is that the interruption of the water supply, with its obvious consequences for the daily lives of Cairenes, was seen as unacceptable within the norms of violent conflict: Damurdashi uses the story to criticize the Hawwara.

While Damurdashi's story is polemical, his claim that the transport of water along the Bulaq road was disrupted during the 1711 war is corroborated by Ahmad Shalabi and Shadhili. Ahmad Shalabi also blames the Hawwara Bed-ouin and claims that the people of Cairo nearly died of thirst.[43] Shadhili men-tions neither the Hawwara nor the mounted Maghribi, but he confirms that the water supply was interrupted. When the roads were briefly opened to traffic, Shadhili reports that the people rushed to Bulaq to buy fresh water, which they had not been able to obtain. He claims that the price of a jar of water increased to one silver *nisf*.[44]

Interestingly, in the accounts of both Damurdashi and Ahmad Shalabi, the armed hostilities in 1711 begin with an attack on the water supply. The war had its origins in an internal dispute within the Janissary regiment, which esca-lated into a conflict between the Janissaries under Ifranj Ahmad and the Otto-man governor Khalil Pasha on one side and the 'Azaban, dissident Janissaries, and several Qasimi beys on the other. The serious fighting started when Khalil Pasha declined a petition from the senior officers of the 'Azaban asking that the dissident Janissaries, who had been banished from Cairo, be allowed to return to the city. The Qasimi beys and the 'Azaban decided to apply pressure by cut-ting the water supply to the citadel, where Khalil Pasha and Ifranj Ahmad were based. They broke the water wheels and seized the oxen that were used to turn them; meanwhile, a force of 'Azab soldiers occupied the Mahjar gate immedi-ately below the citadel to prevent anyone from leaving.

Here, the victims of the interruption of the water supply were the senior members of the opposing faction rather than the population in general. Neither Damurdashi nor Ahmad Shalabi is particularly critical of this act, both report-ing it in a neutral tone (it may be relevant that both supported the 'Azaban in the 1711 war). But both report that, in obtaining authorization from the 'ulama' to respond with violence, the governor Khalil Pasha and his allies emphasized the cutting of the water supply as the key hostile act that justified a lethal response. According to Damurdashi, Khalil Pasha wrote to the 'ulama' asking, "What is your opinion of people who cut the water supply of the Muslims and seize the roads with arms?" The 'ulama' issued a fatwa stating that such people were brigands (qutta' al-tariq) and that it was incumbent upon the governor to execute them.[45] In Ahmad Shalabi's account, the chief qadi, who was present in the citadel with Khalil Pasha and Ifranj Ahmad, stated that the 'Azaban's cutting of the water supply made it legitimate to wage war against them.[46] The norm within political society against interfering with the water supply appears to have been reflected in formal legal discourse: while the details in their accounts differ, both Damurdashi and Ahmad Shalabi portray legal authorities pointing to the cutting of the water as the key act that made its perpetrator liable to execution. It seems likely that the popular norm was influenced by the legal position.

The particular concern for the impact of political violence on practical utilities such as the streets and the water supply—rather than for its effects on religiously and aesthetically significant buildings—fits with a wider discourse of justice in eighteenth-century chronicles that focused on the daily lives and economic activities of Cairenes. This discourse held that hindering people's access to basic necessities—food, water, and the opportunity to make a living—was the worst possible behavior that officials and elites could engage in. Beyond violence, activities that attracted the scorn of chroniclers included hoarding and speculation that pushed up the prices of basic commodities, coin clipping that led to price inflation, and the semi-official racketeering in which technically illegal "protection" taxes (himayat) were levied on small traders and artisans.[47]

. . .

The violent struggle among urban political elites over the domination of Egypt's resources was not an anarchic free-for-all. Although much of this violence was illegal—often flagrantly so—it was constrained by a set of norms broadly recognized by the participants. These norms were reflected in the way contemporary Egyptians wrote about political violence and in the acts they praised and criticized. The stories discussed here allow us to draw some conclusions about these norms.

It is not adequate to look to Islamic religious doctrine to explain these norms, as studies of violence in the premodern Muslim world often do. Of course, they were connected with and informed by Muslim beliefs and principles in many ways, as we would expect in a society in which Islam was the dominant cultural and religious tradition. But the norms also departed from orthodox Islamic principles in many ways, such as in their lack of respect for private property rights. Both the connection and the distance are illustrated well by the norm of harem sanctity. Clearly, underlying this norm was the principle of the seclusion of women—a value that can be described as Islamic, as it has a scriptural basis, is widely discussed in Islamic legal literature, and was recognized as an ideal, if not always practiced, across most premodern Muslim societies. But the norm of harem sanctity in eighteenth-century Cairo—that when plundering an enemy's house, one must not enter the harem—cannot be described as Islamic, because it implicitly legitimizes the act of plundering the rest of the house. Rather, these norms were specific to eighteenth-century Cairo, and in particular to the city's political classes: those directly engaged in the violent struggles and those affiliated with them through service. This is suggested by the difference in attitude between Damurdashi and Ahmad Shalabi, on the one hand, and Shadhili, on the other. Although certain elements of their conceptions of justice were shared, Shadhili, who does not appear to have been closely connected with political society, tended to see political violence as illegitimate *in general*, rather than only when specific norms were broken.

The norms of eighteenth-century Cairo's political classes were the product of numerous sources: they were connected with notions of personal honor, valor, and manliness, as well as with a conception of justice that centered on the importance of ordinary Cairenes being able to attend to their basic daily needs. I have not seen evidence that these norms were written out as a code, such as the manuals of rules for dueling written in western Europe at the same time. A written code may exist: modern researchers have so far made barely a dent in the extensive manuscript collections of eighteenth-century Egypt. But what is certain is that the norms were expressed and reinforced through stories of heroism and cowardice that were circulated both in the form of written historiographical texts and in the form of oral legends. The chronicle of Damurdashi represents an interface between these two modes of expression.

The stories discussed here also suggest the mechanisms through which these norms constrained violence. It is clear that sometimes they did not constrain it: many of these stories focus on incidents when norms were broken. But there are other examples in which political actors did conform with the norms, even when to do so went against their immediate political or economic interests: for example, when the Janissary agha refused to search the harem of the fugitive Sulayman Agha Abu Diffiya. Given that, on other occasions, people broke the norms without suffering formal sanctions, it seems that those who complied with the norms did so voluntarily. They did so because a reputation for integrity was important in building political capital among their allies and retainers and within the general population. Some actors in these stories intervened to ensure that norms were respected—for example, the 'Azab officer Mustafa Qaysarli, who protected 'Abd al-Rahman Bey's daughter after the plundering of his harem, and Ayyub Bey, who sought to reopen the streets during the 1711 war. These actors were then celebrated in the chronicles for their ethical behavior—as they were, we can presume, in the oral accounts that circulated at the time. The acclaim that their acts received bolstered their reputations and their political capital. In this way, the narration of violent conflict by contemporary Egyptians both established these norms and played a role in enforcing them.

4 URBAN SPACE AND PRESTIGE

When Festivals Turned Violent in Jeddah, 1880s–1960s

Ulrike Freitag

IN 1884 AND EARLY 1885, the Dutch Orientalist Christiaan Snouck Hurgronje resided in Jeddah, the major port town of the Hijaz region, preparing for a visit to Mecca. On 10 January 1885, he noted in his diary that, since the arrival of the pasha (the new Ottoman governor), the city had witnessed daily "big musical entertainments," as well as visits by the authorities and foreign consuls:

> The ovations by the inhabitants are given per *hara* [quarter; in Arabic letters in the original manuscript] and apparently organized by the *shaykh al-hara* [the head of the quarter]. One of these ovations gave rise to a quarrel between the *awlad al-hara* [sons of the quarter] of the Mazlum and those of the Yaman [two of the four quarters of Jeddah], which ended, as usual, in a violent fight. Askaris [soldiers] were whipped up from various corners and at around eleven o'clock the crowd was dispersed, whereas under different circumstances the merry-making lasts till deep into the night. A few days before, there had already been a fight between Mazlum and our quarter (Sham). Some of the ringleaders who had been brought before the *qa'im-maqam* [the Ottoman official in charge of the district], he personally thrashed them in front of his house, and under blows from the sticks they were led to prison by the askaris. The main reason for the fights over the ovations is envy. Each *hara* [in Arabic letters] has its own *mahmal* [litter] which is carried by four men, and creates its own fantasia, for instance a Pasha [Ottoman commander], a *qadi* [judge], etc., who are all presented by people from the neighbourhood. These come to present their *salam* [welcome] at the house where the real Pasha has taken up residence. When the *mahmal* of one district is distinctly more beautiful than that of another, a mere spark sufficed to ignite the fire. The *proxima causa* of the quarrel between Yaman and Mazlum was that a member of one district had joined behind the banner of the other, and then had been chased away in an extremely rude manner.[1]

What seems significant in the wider context of trying to understand urban violence is not only the seldom-reported relative frequency of inner-urban brawls and conflicts at which this quotation hints but also their potential for escalation. This links the questions raised in this chapter to a systematic investigation of the containment or escalation of violence, its scaling from very localized to international levels, and its links with individual and collective manifestations of masculinity.

I first address some conceptual and methodological considerations relating to the relative lack of attempts at analyzing possible links between what is generally known as "popular culture" and urban violence. I also give some background on the urban organization of Jeddah before discussing one particular popular practice, the *mizmar*, which articulated both masculinity and quarter identity.

CROWDS AND VIOLENCE IN HISTORY

In the episode in the quotation, Snouck Hurgronje describes the outbreak of violence in a small Arabian city, of around fifteen thousand to twenty thousand inhabitants, under Ottoman rule during a ceremonial occasion—the greeting of the new Ottoman governor in the late nineteenth century. Violence between different quarters occurred quite frequently in the history of Middle Eastern cities. In Jeddah, as elsewhere, it was often linked to particular ceremonies— notably to occasions that incorporated performances of the famous Hijazi dance, the *mizmar*, or other "popular games" (*al'ab sha'biyya*).[2]

This opens an interesting perspective on possible connections between expressions of masculinity, popular festivals, and urban violence. Can we draw connections between routinized expressions of masculinity, their violent eruptions in locally circumscribed rituals, and violent crowd behavior? Are there links between everyday types of gatherings, male competition, the formation of crowds, urban organization, and violent crowds? It is beyond the scope of this chapter to engage with the wide and multidisciplinary body of theories on masculinity, crowd formation, and behavior, or with the connections between masculinity and aggressive, or even violent, crowd behavior.[3] Rather, it starts from the empirical observation that, in many cities, both premodern and modern, certain rituals performed by men often seemed to result in outbursts of violence and that these could, on occasion, become linked to crowd formation and political confrontations. Following Norbert Elias, the underlying assumption is of course that certain aggressive behavior is part of human nature, although it can find very different expressions and be sublimated in various forms—for example, rituals and sports—in different social formations.[4]

Drawing on examples from Middle Eastern cities, and taking as its starting point the ritual of *mizmar* in nineteenth- and early twentieth-century Jeddah, I analyze this ritual and its social function, then draw on the available literature on this and other case studies in order to discuss possible links to other incidents of the transformation of urban rituals into the crowd violence that has been observed in other times and places.

How does one investigate such issues historically? Certainly, the question of sources, and their reliability, ranks high on the agenda. In particular, and in the case of Jeddah, archival sources are not very helpful, at least in the absence of police records from the period under consideration, when the city was under the rule of the Ottoman Empire (until 1916) and under the Sharifs of Mecca, until it became part of Saudi Arabia in 1925. There are very few travel reports that adopt the anthropological gaze of Christiaan Snouck Hurgronje. A range of local histories tend to mention popular games, usually on the basis of literature on 'adat wa-taqalid (customs and traditions), memoirs and oral information collected by the authors.

Obviously, present-day publications discussing the history of past games that were later often condemned as un-Islamic are often tainted by nostalgia, a sense of local assertion of identity, or a certain sanitization. They sometimes also adapt their descriptions of a historical phenomenon to the religious norms that became prevalent after 1925 in order to avoid religiously founded criticism of a locally important tradition. They thus need to be read with such present concerns in mind. Such a "taming" of the originally enthusiastic tradition is clearly visible in the folklorized and sanitized official versions of the *mizmar* dance, for example. Indeed, clips on YouTube seem to indicate that performances in smaller localities or possibly poorer quarters are still characterized by dancing around a real fire and may also be marked by quick transformations of a friendly competition into actual acts of violence.[5] The skillfully handled sticks can then quickly turn into weapons with which to pursue one's opponent, and the spectators may get involved and try to pursue supporters of the opposing side. I have also made use here of religious opinions (fatwas) and newspapers.

I interviewed a number of elders who still remember the practice of *mizmar*, which local authors clearly link to the construction of masculinity. Although of a younger generation, two of the present 'umdas (formerly elected, nowadays appointed), heads of quarters in the old city of Jeddah, are from families who have held that office for a number of generations and are very knowledgeable about the traditions and changes in their respective quarters. Unsurprisingly, neither local literature nor my interlocutors mention any link between the dance and wider social mobilization, which would have made the dance even more dubious from a current perspective. My considerations of such a link have therefore been inspired by comparative literature on other Middle Eastern, and southern European, cities. This literature not only suggests such links but also draws attention to incidents such as the one described by Snouck Hurgronje, which I otherwise would not even have noticed. The argument presented in this article is therefore somewhat suggestive. Given that crowd formation is one of the key issues in urban violence, and that links between notions of masculinity, quarter identity, and crowds have hardly ever been addressed, it seems essential to probe the available historical evidence on popular culture with a view to these issues.[6]

THE QUARTERS OF JEDDAH

Urban quarters were historically an important organizational unit in the walled city of Jeddah—as in Istanbul, Damascus, Cairo, Sanaa, Dezful, and elsewhere in the Middle East.[7] They provided security and a sense of (spatially connoted) identity and can therefore almost be compared to the role played by tribes outside and inside cities. Nevertheless, there were significant differences between Middle Eastern urban centers.[8] Thus, Serjeant argues that the quarters of Sanaa were much less tightly organized and less prepared to fight over their territories than those in the Hadhramawt region of Yemen. He ascribes this to the presence of strong rulers who were not bound up with local society—an argument to which I return.[9] What is interesting about the Jeddah case is that the urban quarters developed a strong sense of identity even though they were not separated by walls and the urban population was composed of many different ethnicities. As the urban population experienced a rather unusual degree of flux, one could possibly even argue that the integration of newcomers occurred through their rapid incorporation into the life of the quarters.

It is necessary to briefly describe the urban setting and organization of old Jeddah (locally known as al-Balad), which in many ways resembled other small- to medium-sized Middle Eastern cities, in order to understand the socio-geographical specificity of what follows. In the nineteenth century, Jeddah— surrounded only by a few villages and a market catering mainly to pilgrims and travelers outside the gate leading toward Mecca—was composed of four quarters (*hara* or *mahalla* in Arabic and Ottoman Turkish, respectively): al-Yaman to the south, al-Bahr on the sea, Mazlum in the center, and al-Sham to the north. This latter *hara* expanded rapidly in the last quarter of the nineteenth century, when many government offices and rich merchants moved into the area's larger and airier new buildings. Even if these quarters were not separated from each other by walls and gates, their borders (*hudud*) were well known to their inhabitants. Boundaries might have shifted over time—quarters could split or merge—but at any given time, they were well established.[10]

The quarter formed a basic administrative unit within the city, which, in spite of the dramatic change in the social composition of al-Balad, holds true to this day. Thus, quarters not only featured buildings such as mosques, basic infrastructure such as local food sellers, or squares for socializing. They also had an official representative, the *shaykh al-hara* (also known elsewhere as *mukhtar*, and nowadays as *'umda*). Together with his deputy, who headed a group of night guards (*ra'is al-'assa*) and warned the inhabitants of intruders, he was responsible for basic issues of security within the quarter.[11] Furthermore, he was primarily responsible for managing conflict and mediation, both within the quarter and in cases concerning residents and representatives of the subsequent political regimes, whether Ottoman, Sharifian, or Saudi. He also organized neighborhood help in times of crises—for example, to cover the debts of a deceased person. To accomplish these tasks, he maintained a regular *majlis* (council) that was accessible to everyone.[12]

At the informal level, the *hara* was an intermediate space between the relative intimacy of the house and the anonymity of the major thoroughfares, markets, and other urban spaces, where complete strangers interacted with one another. Thus, it had its own rules of access and social relations, analogous to those ascribed by sociologists to modern neighborhoods in other regional contexts, albeit with culturally specific rules—the most prominent of which regulated gender relations.[13] Socially, the city squares (*barha*, pl. *barhat*) were the main regular meeting place for children and one of the locations where groups of men (*shilal*, sing. *shilla*) would have their *mirkaz* (a group of wooden benches). Here, they met to exchange news and views about current events.[14] Sometimes, simple coffeehouses were located on these squares. They, too, were frequented mostly by locals, except during the pilgrimage season, when they catered to the much-increased population of Jeddah, and at times even offered shelter to itinerant pilgrims.

Women visited each other inside their houses, often sitting in alcoves sheltered by carved latticework. From here, they overlooked the alleys and squares so that there was usually somebody supervising the children as well as the comings and goings in the quarter. Women hardly left the quarters unless for specific errands, such as attending school or fetching goods from the main market, using established thoroughfares at regular times.[15] If strangers or individuals identified as intruders were seen and did not follow suggestions to leave, the local strongmen (*futuwwa*) could be called on to intervene.[16]

The quarters of Jeddah thus quite closely resembled not only their Ottoman (and post-Ottoman) counterparts but also those of the south Arabian town of Shihr, described by Sylvaine Camelin—particularly in their constitution of space, which enabled identification on the basis of physical and social proximity and the everyday practices of their use.[17] This obviously entailed a great deal of social, religious, and moral control over the members of the quarters.[18] Festivities within the quarter, such as celebrations of marriage or circumcision, further strengthened internal cohesion.[19] Marriages across quarters, which required the marriage procession to cross the (invisible) urban boundaries, needed to be negotiated ahead of time, often between the 'umdas, in order to prevent trouble. In one famous case, the bridegroom, one of the city's notables, had neglected to obtain such permission and was held up when trying to cross from Sham into Yaman, where his bride resided. The ensuing fight was stopped only by the intervention of other notables.[20] Thus, the quarter was an important social formation that defined people's sense of belonging, although families could live in different parts of the city. Professional organizations including guilds, administrative bodies, and military groups were the other major formations cutting across quarter boundaries.[21]

Many of *the al'ab sha'biyya*—the popular pastimes recorded under the rubric "customs and traditions"—contributed to both the internal and external definition of quarters as sociopolitical units. The three annual highlights for the performance of such traditions in Jeddah were Ramadan; the 'Id (festival) that brought Ramadan to an end, when inhabitants of different quarters visited each other in a defined sequence; and the hajj.[22] The end of the hajj, for example, was marked by an all-female carnival involving elements of competition between the quarters over the originality and lavishness of the costumes.[23]

THE *MIZMAR*, MASCULINITY, AND QUARTER IDENTITY

Among the various dances performed during celebrations in Jeddah, the most famous was possibly the *mizmar*. There are several theories about its origins. According to the specialist on folklore Hind Ba Ghaffar, this dance goes back to the period from the tenth to twelfth centuries when Fatimid delegations brought sugar cane sticks to the Hijaz.[24] These are used elsewhere in the Middle East as pipes or flutes. In the Hijazi context, however, *mizmar* does not refer to these instruments—which were played by themselves or in accompaniment to a dance, as in Yemen—but to the sticks wielded by the dancers. As these are also more solid than sugar cane, the real geographical origin of the dance might be East African rather than Egyptian, and it may have arrived with pilgrims or migrants from that region.[25] The dance developed from an individual into a collective pastime and became increasingly elaborate in terms of its music and the accompanying lyrics.

Regardless of origins and development of the dance, it seems that its basic form was established by the nineteenth century and survives to this day in modified form. Usually two groups meet each other in an open space—often the major *barha* of a quarter—either forming two opposing rows or grouped around a fire.[26] The dancers advance in pairs to the sound of drums and singing, with lyrics often intended to incite the two sides and sometimes including sexual innuendo.[27] Brandishing their sticks and performing various movements, the dancers symbolically challenge each other without touching the body or stick of the opponent with their own. However, if this occurs by accident or intention, a general fight can quickly erupt between supporters of the two groups, and the dance can end in a public brawl—sometimes even causing loss of life.[28] Before the banning of the *mizmar* except under strict supervision, it was therefore important that senior representatives of the quarter—or, on more ceremonial occasions, the *'umda*s themselves—opened the dance and tried to control it.[29]

Writing about the (historically unspecified) recent history of Mecca, local historian Abkar describes the *mizmar* as the "factory of men" (*masna' al-rijal*), noting that it

> was employed in many necessary matters of the quarter, such as security and courage [*shuja'a*] and protection and some important private matters, and it came particularly to the fore on occasions such as the celebration of the 'Id and marriage, or the arrival of the king or amir, and other such matters that occurred on the squares . . . inside the quarters and outside them.[30]

The men involved in these performances were the quarter's *futuwwa*. These *futuwwa* seem to have been mainly young men, though whether they were bachelors, as Noémy Lévy-Aksu observes for their Istanbul equivalent, is difficult to establish. They attained their recognition not least through their ability to dominate the *mizmar*. The masculinity expressed therein was embodied in the mastery of their bodies, the suppleness of movements, and the boldness in challenging opponents with or without actually violating the rules of the game. Upon recognition as *futuwwa*, they became the ones called on when the quarter needed to be defended against intruders. In this way, their behavior was clearly associated with chivalry and recognized as fulfilling an important social function, to the extent that the leader of the *futuwwa* was counted as the third central personality of the quarter, besides the *'umda* and the leading local *wajih* (notable). This shows that demonstrations of physical strength, at times even associated with violence, could attain positive connotations if framed in a socially acceptable way.

This tallies well with what Lévy-Aksu has described for Istanbul. There, most of the quarter strongmen were bachelors, and their frequent and ritualized use of violence, notably in defense of what was perceived as an infringement on their honor but also as small-scale criminals, was their major characteristic as a group.[31] This is particularly interesting because the very same individuals could also be perceived in a completely different way—as loitering bachelors posing a moral danger to the quarter.

In Jeddah, this was at least partly exacerbated by the *futuwwa*'s social origin. Although the *mizmar* could on specific occasions include members of all social groups, it was usually performed by members of the *shaqawiyya*, as only members of this group could become part of the *futuwwa*. *Shaqawiyya* here is a local expression for those performing manual labor and is contrasted, in local oral tradition, with the *effendiyya*, the group of merchants and bureaucrats to whom the *wajih* of the quarter belonged. In the absence of literature on this topic for Jeddah, the exact delineations of these social categories in different periods remain uncertain; while the contrast between *shaqawiyya* and *effendiyya* is quite clear, which professional status or economic conditions qualified individuals for membership in either of them is not exactly specified and might have varied over the decades.[32]

Before participating in the more famous quarter or even citywide celebrations orchestrated and organized by the *'umda*s, young men had to learn the *mizmar* in lesser contests. Local conflicts in the quarter provided such a training ground, as they could be solved through challenging one's adversary to a *mizmar*.[33] It is very likely that here, too, *mizmar* was quite regularly connected with small-scale violence. Such contests, as well as local celebrations, were limited to the "sons of the quarter" (*abna' al-hara*). If people from other quarters attempted to join in, the verses recited by the dancers indicated whether this was welcome or not.[34]

Although it appears that members of different occupational backgrounds participated in these events, the more senior and affluent inhabitants took an active role in the *mizmar* only during important occasions such as the 'Id festivities and the arrival of Ottoman governors, and later of the Saudi king.[35]

QUARTER COMPETITION ON POLITICAL OCCASIONS

As we have seen, *mizmar* dances—as emblematic expressions of the competition between young men for social recognition and hegemony within the quarter and as representations of competing quarters—were among the performances that greeted new political leaders. Performances on political occasions such as religious celebrations and visits to the city by state dignitaries were highly charged, as they placed the honor of the quarter at stake. Besides decorating elaborate litters, sometimes filled with sweets for the children present, quarters tried to excel in their performances as well as in their verbal praise of leaders.[36] Praise was often integrated into the chanting that accompanied the *mizmar*, as illustrated by the following example from Ottoman times, reported by Ba Ghaffar:

'ala l-basha salam
Welcome to the Pasha

billah raddu li 'ala l-basha salam
in the name of God, answer me: Welcome to the Pasha

wa-llah jallijall jana min al-Sham.
and God, great, great, he came to us from Sham.[37]

A fascinating article published in 1924 by the local newspaper *Al-Qibla* describes in detail the ceremonies with which King Husayn b. 'Ali (r. 1916–24) was received when returning to the Hijaz from a journey abroad.[38] Visitors from settlements in the vicinity and from among the Bedouin flooded into the city. They gathered at the pier with members of the ruling family, the government, and the military (including a military band). Schoolchildren, Hadhramis, and the shaykhs of the various quarters had also assembled. When King Husayn disembarked, he was hailed with shouts of welcome and then marched to the municipality, where he was greeted with poems and speeches. Although the article does not give details of the quarters or specific performances, it confirms that the tradition of greeting high dignitaries and rulers with chants, music, and processions continued well into the interwar period.

For the reign of 'Abd al-'Aziz b. Sa'ud (since 1926 king of the Hijaz, from 1932 to 1953 king of Saudi Arabia), local historian Trabulsi relates an episode that might well be imagined in a similar manner:

> It is being told that when King 'Abd al-'Aziz . . . returned from his trip to Egypt, the sons of the quarters [abna' al-hawari] greeted him in the seaport of Jeddah . . . and they were standing in rows at the Bunt-gate. . . . [F]rom the Mazlum quarter, Shaykh Jamil Qumsani . . . stood out, crying: [His Highness the King may live,] and the sons of the quarter answered [he may live; he may live; he may live]. Then the king asked about the shaykh of this quarter and was told [Shaykh Muhammad Hazuqa], and he and those who were with him were taken by the king, who bestowed upon him a *mashlah* [honorary cloak] and two hundred riyal. . . . [T]he present and the attention shown became famous in the quarters.[39]

Such an incident inspired both pride and envy and could have caused violence similar to that described by Snouck Hurgronje in January 1885. However, Trabulsi is conspicuously silent about such consequences. This silence might be linked to the later banning of the *mizmar*, allegedly amid fears for the life of the Saudi kings after the assassination of King Faysal in 1975.[40] Local historians of the Hijaz are not keen on potentially discrediting local traditions, notably in the context of regional rivalries in present-day Saudi Arabia.[41]

However, political issues were not the only reason for banning the *mizmar*, as Wahhabi doctrine explicitly and repeatedly condemned music and dance.[42] These cultural practices had already been declared un-Islamic by Muhammad b. 'Abd al-Wahhab in the eighteenth century. His twentieth-century successors regularly reconfirmed this view, both through the practice of the Committee for the Propagation of Virtue and Prevention of Vice and through the issuing of fatwas.[43] Those successors include Ibn Baz as well as the Permanent Committee of the General Presidency of Scholarly Research and Ifta' (the issuing of legal opinions).[44] One fatwa, probably dating from the early 1990s, explicitly takes up the issue of the *mizmar*, which, as the document seems to suggest, had recently reappeared in Medina. The scholars declared it illegal for five distinct reasons: the kindling and circumambulation of fire, the use of forbidden musical instruments such as drums, dancing, clapping, and "obscene songs that propagate sensuality and forbidden passions."[45]

This, as well as Wahhabi attacks on other local traditions, might explain the extremely defensive tone adopted by Meccan historian Abkar, who concludes his lengthy exposition of the topic of *mizmar* by lamenting a tradition that has lost most of its social content and become relegated to the realm of folklore.[46]

CROWD VIOLENCE AND POLITICAL VIOLENCE: CONCEPTUAL CONSIDERATIONS

The Jeddawi *mizmar* was clearly associated with crowd violence on the levels of intra- as well as inter-quarter conflicts, despite implicit arguments, such as the one by Abkar, that defend a tradition that official doctrine has come to deem un-Islamic. It was also one of the occasions on which representatives of the *effendiyya* and the *shaqawiyya*—the *wajih* and the *futuwwa*—joined forces. In this respect, the *mizmar* resembles the frequent violent clashes on ceremonial (in those cases, decidedly religious) occasions that have been, to cite just two examples, described by Reza Masoudi Nejad for Iranian and Sylvaine Camelin for Hadhrami processions. It might be even more closely related to the Damascene *'arada*, a type of procession accompanied by chanting and a number of physical competitions such as wrestling, sword games, and horse racing, which was performed on a variety of occasions.[47] Given the lack of more specific examples from the local context, the following comparative considerations draw on material from a variety of Arab cities to tease out further the connection between the display of masculinities on festive occasions and social mobilization that led to urban violence.

There are numerous descriptions of how such festivals could turn very violent, and decidedly political. This ties in with George Rudé's interpretation, based on investigations in the western European context, that ceremonial demonstrations tended to spark urban violence particularly in cases when "the 'lower orders' . . . were denied all means of peaceful agitation to secure a redress to grievance."[48] Rudé points out that ceremonies often provided one of the few means of mass assembly and offered the participants an experience in which sudden outbursts against the authorities could be more effective than peaceful attempts to achieve the same aims. This is presumably one of the reasons why the authorities in different locations chose a hard course against such cultural performances and eventually banned many dances and processions at political events.

Hitherto, little research has been conducted on Middle Eastern ceremonies and their link to urban mobilization and violence. Thus, even the question of whether ceremonies based around competing groups identified with quarters turned violent more frequently than those that united urban crowds from dif-

ferent neighborhoods—both of which can be found in the Shiʻi ʻashura' processions, for example—cannot be answered at the moment. The case that has
probably been best researched is that of the Damascene ʻarada. It was, among
other events, associated with the departure and arrival of the pilgrims' caravan, symbolized by the *mahmal* procession. This gave it some of its political
significance—echoing to some extent the association of the *mizmar* in Jeddah
with the arrival and departure of political dignitaries as well as religious occasions.[49] This connection between religion and politics might have been exactly
the nexus that invited the politicization of such manifestations (both in terms
of legitimizing as well as criticizing the authorities) in modern times.[50]

Roberto Mazza has shown how the 1921 Nabi Musa processions in Jerusalem were effectively used for nationalist mobilization.[51] Philip Khoury, discussing Damascene nationalist politics in the 1920s and 1930s, describes how,
through alliances between the Syrian *qabadayat* (the equivalent of the Hijazi
and Egyptian *futuwwa*) and the nationalist notables (the *wujaha'* or *a'yan*), usually originating from the same quarters, the urban population could be mobilized for what effectively were party politics.[52] One may safely assume that in
both cases, the bonds between the *futuwwa* and the *a'yan* were based on cli-
entelist practices but regularly rehearsed on ceremonial occasions such as the
ʻarada or the Nabi Musa procession.

I propose that the mobilization of the urban crowd for political ends by notables in Jeddah functioned along similar lines, both during ceremonial occasions and beyond them. Why else would ceremonial occasions have been so
closely monitored and eventually curbed? Admittedly, the Wahhabi scholars
were not very happy about such performances, but it took a very long time for
this discontent to be translated into a concrete ban, even if the 1970s date is
apocryphal.

In terms of tangible violence, there is little in the sources on politically
motivated disturbances that can be directly linked to the *futuwwa*. Given developments elsewhere, however, I suggest that we need to reexamine crowd
mobilization during cases of urban violence to test the thesis of popular quarter
organizations as their basis. The best-known case of political violence in historical Jeddah is the 1858 massacre of Christians. There, we can be almost certain
of the links between notables (*wujaha'*) and a popular crowd but have so far
lacked clearer understanding of how this crowd was mobilized.[53]

It remains to be investigated whether other incidents of urban violence in
Jeddah can be conceptualized in a similar way, given the dearth of sources.

Yet the fear of crowd violence—though by no means always linked to ceremonial occasions—clearly remained a factor in the transition from the nineteenth to the twentieth centuries. Its association with the *futuwwa*, meanwhile, was mostly lost with the disappearance of the walled city of Jeddah and its social organization. When people moved outside its former boundary in the urban extension made possible by the provision of water to a much wider area and by the destruction of the city wall in 1947, the cohesion of the quarters started to dissolve. Although the old *futuwwa* and their descendants are still in touch with the present *'umda*s, the type of *rujula* (masculinity) embodied by the *mizmar* and associated practices has ceased to exist.

This does not necessarily mean that collective and publicly performed rites of masculinity have disappeared altogether. I argue instead that they have become transformed. In Jeddah, the sport of football became a new locus of masculine competition, this time starting from the elites in the late 1920s but quicky encompassing all sectors of society. It was initially practiced in the very same spaces in which *mizmar* was performed, the squares of the quarters, but quickly began to draw large crowds. Early incidences of hooliganism and violence by overenthusiastic supporters led to a ban of the game in 1934.[54]

At present, such a collective expression of—in this case lower-class—masculinity is the practice of "car drifting" (*tafhit*), described by Pascale Ménoret and Awadh al-Utaybi and observable throughout the kingdom.[55] Ménoret shows convincingly the nature of this practice as a contestation for urban space between marginalized youth, urban developers, and the state. Its social condemnation fits well with the more general tendency of denouncing and criminalizing lower-class expressions of masculinity—a phenomenon described by Wilson Jacob and Hanan Hamad for Egypt in the first half of the twentieth century.[56]

In order to understand urban violence, it might therefore be necessary to take a closer look at the interface between political modernization and social transformation. Only if the state, be it an empire or a modern nation-state, could guarantee a certain degree of security did it have a chance to impose its understanding of security and thus eventually eradicate the older forms of what now might be called a mixture of chivalry and neighborhood watch, as expressed in the *futuwwa* and its rituals like the Jiddawi *mizmar*. The bourgeois norms that came to devalue and criminalize nonbourgeois types of association and masculinity are thus also tied to particular political forms.

In the case of Jeddah, the incremental establishment of security under Saudi rule—both inside the city and, perhaps more important, in the surrounding countryside formerly controlled by Bedouin—was clearly one important step in the shift of power to the state. This was, in many ways, a crucial precondition for the eventual full absorption of *'umda*s and quarters into a top-down bureaucratic system. This contrasts with an earlier system based more on negotiation between local governors and urban units. Obviously, the earlier urban institutions were also part of the state structure but were nevertheless also a mouthpiece for locally chosen spokesmen. This transition was a gradual one, as the continuity of the office of *'umda* in certain families beyond this transition demonstrates; nevertheless, the structural change is not insignificant. This is exemplified in the new, and different, expressions of urban masculinity and contestation such as those linked to football since the late 1920s and car drifting in contemporary Saudi Arabia.

It is perhaps the slow nature of these changes that has allowed older forms of social organization to make an unexpected return, albeit in partly new garb, as demonstrated during the Arab Spring in a number of Arab cities. I am thinking here of the capacity of city dwellers to organize themselves, both for the defense of their quarters in times of urban upheaval (as in Cairo in 2011) and in establishment of even more comprehensive systems of very localized self-government (as in war-torn Syria at the time of writing). An indication of this is provided by Salwa Ismail's investigations of male youth organizations in Cairo's poor new quarters, where she draws explicit comparisons between the old *futuwwa*-style organizations and new forms of male sociability, both religious and more secular. Particularly striking are the association of such "fraternities" with their quarter, the social origins of the youth involved, and their assumption of a certain responsibility for issues of morality and order, including night patrols. Nevertheless, Ismail is careful to emphasize the strong contextual variations between these groups.[57] A systematic investigation of the continuities and discontinuities in male urban organization in relation to space and violence thus remains a fertile area for future research.

5 CITIZENSHIP RIGHTS AND SEMANTICS OF COLONIAL POWER AND RESISTANCE

Haifa, Jaffa, and Nablus, 1931–1933

Lauren Banko

IN SEPTEMBER 1931, the Palestine Mandate government recognized the town of Nablus as "a centre of extreme Arab Nationalism [that had] become a focus for concentrated expression of Arab discontent and hostility to British rule."[1] The language used by the authorities to depict Nablus was relatively new: the British had not referred to a Palestinian town or city in such alarmist terms before 1929. The statement came just weeks after Arab populist leaders of Nablus convened an assembly and firmly resolved to call a general strike throughout Mandate territory as a show of opposition to the government policy allowing Jewish settlements to be armed. Both the Nablus resolution and the British response to it can be placed within the framework of the discursive interplay between peaceful noncooperation tactics and the escalation of violent colonial repression in the port cities and large towns of Palestine. Here an important transition had occurred by the early 1930s as Arab leaders and urban and newly urbanized residents turned largely nonviolent anti-colonial sentiment into a political discourse of resistance that legitimized violence, labeling the British as colonial usurpers of political and civil rights. In response, the administration's colonial vocabulary increasingly construed urban populations as potential enemies who subverted state attempts to impose order and control, a phenomenon that became particularly apparent after the riots that engulfed the port city of Jaffa in 1933.

As an expression of nonviolent resistance against Mandate policy, the 1931 resolution embodied new forms of urban contention that expressed the viewpoints of large segments of Nablus's residents. It voiced civic belonging to the "nation of Palestine" and became an integral part of a repertoire of civil disobedience, including protests, processions, petitions, and strikes that carried the seed of violent action. According to Margaret Somers, general changes toward radical, and therefore potentially violent, nationalism occur when individuals feel that a sense of who they are has been fundamentally violated—especially in relation to their self-identity and perceived natural rights. Individuals and

leaders lay claims to these rights, justified by membership in historically constructed political communities. Citizenship and national identity thus become
"contested truth[s]" that give meaning to "rights" as political practices rather
than abstract notions.[2] In Palestine by the early 1930s, such practices of citizenship and civil rights became prominent not only in Nablus but also in the port
cities of Haifa and Jaffa where socioeconomic changes linked to urbanization influenced a new type of political socialization between the middle-class nationalist movement and the new migrant and often impoverished Arab working class.

Under the Mandate, Palestinians held a local citizenship that was independent of British nationality. When these citizens were outside Palestine, the
Mandate's provisions placed them in the position of British-protected persons.
More important, the Citizenship Order in Council of 1925 did not grant Palestinian citizens the rights they agitated for *as citizens*: leaders asked for sole Arab
control over the government, direct franchise, and rights of control over Palestine's borders, educational affairs, public works, election laws, taxation and
tithe rates, and trade laws.[3] It is no coincidence that by the early 1930s the practice of citizenship and its associated rights, as understood by the Arabs, nurtured an atmosphere ripe for both agitation and violence in urban areas such
as Jaffa, Haifa, and Nablus. In his study of colonial Bombay, Sandip Hazareesingh argues that cities and civic rights are historically linked, as cities provided
the social space to accommodate the modern practices of citizenship.[4] In urban
Palestine the violent nature of agitation for citizenship derived from contestation against the limited and thus expendable rights of colonial citizenship developed by the British Mandatory administration.[5] Violent opposition to such
expendable rights was an outcome of particular trajectories of colonial state
building that unfolded through mechanisms of institutional control that were
particularly prone to producing violence. In this context of state formation, factors such as urbanization and socioeconomic change also contributed to bring
about a violent rhetorical and mobilizational shift in the Palestinians' quest for
citizenship rights.

URBAN NETWORKS AND CONTENTION IN HAIFA, JAFFA, AND NABLUS BEFORE 1933

Rural villages near Jewish settlements were the first to experience violent unrest prior to the establishment of the Palestine Mandate. As suggested by Joel
Beinin, conflict shifted to towns only in the 1920s.[6] To a large extent, before the
late 1920s urban centers were unregulated political spaces where the authorities

did not impose rigorous press censorship and where public gatherings and protests were allowed in times of relative peace. This enabled the creation of civic
links between anti-Mandate Arab activists who endorsed nonviolent tactics of
demonstration and Arab laborers who did not generally adhere to a cohesive
political program. In the early 1930s these links were instrumental in the creation of grassroots organizations that transformed towns such as Haifa, Jaffa,
and Nablus into pivotal arenas of anti-colonial discourse and political action.
As a result, Arab urban residents actively joined civil society organizations in
increasing numbers and participated in public gatherings coordinated by the
nationalist movement. In the ports of Haifa and Jaffa, and in Nablus, which was
located inland, farmers, students, workers, and other residents were brought
together by populist national leaders who organized the population at grassroots level through associations, religious and sporting clubs, and unions and
congresses.[7] The uncensored press served as the main instrument to express
this discourse of opposition to the Mandate and to publicize demonstrations,
protest letters, and meetings.

The population of Haifa, which had a large Christian minority, had become
increasingly Arab and Muslim in the early twentieth century. By the end of the
1930s the city was one of the largest in Palestine. The growth of the port attracted
both Arab and Jewish workers; in the 1930s the two communities were represented in equal numbers, but the Muslim Arab working class was much larger
than its Jewish counterpart. Haifa was second only to Jaffa in its number of unemployed Arab workers.[8] The presence of wage laborers altered the urban social
structure and its physical space, as this new group was largely made up of poor
Arab rural migrants who clustered in bourgeoning slum districts and retained
links to the rural hinterland. Jewish immigrants added significantly to this mix,
as by 1933 nearly 70 percent of all Jews who entered Palestine came through the
port of Haifa.[9] Haifa was thus a tense city for a variety of reasons: economic inequalities that divided Jewish and Arab workers and the presence of large numbers of poor Arab laborers of rural extraction, and importantly, of a virulent
anti-Zionist rhetoric popularized by newspapers and civic societies such as the
Young Men's Muslim Association (YMMA) and the Muslim-Christian Association (MCA).

In contrast to Haifa, in the port city of Jaffa an Arab urban proletariat that
could challenge Jewish organized labor failed to develop by the early 1930s because of the increasing economic and demographic dominance of the Jewish
community both in Jaffa and in neighboring Tel Aviv. Jewish political parties

and labor unions began to implement the Zionist conquest of labor (*kibush ha'avodah*) as early as 1920, which required Jewish employers to hire exclusively Jewish workers.[10] Unrest and violence between the Jewish and Arab communities had occurred in Jaffa in the 1920s, precipitated strictly by intercommunal social tensions. Contestations over political and social space played a significant role in the riots that broke out in 1921, first between Jewish communists and socialists during a May Day demonstration held by moderate Jewish socialist groups. Arab residents reacted violently in turn: crowds started to attack Jewish residents, property, and businesses. In the aftermath, colonial officials blamed violence on religious divisions. The British justified violence by—in the words of Samir Khalaf—"deflecting" genuine social protests "into confessional rivalry."[11] This early incidence of violence, however spontaneous, reflected a small but growing threat of foreign intrusion in Palestine that continued to shape sporadic violence in the decade to follow.

Nablus—a medium-sized settlement in the Mandate period—developed as the stronghold of pan-Arab nationalist ideology. The town had a more homogeneously Arab population than Haifa or Jaffa, and by 1933 it was the center of a populist, radical movement headed by youths and intellectuals who saw themselves as part of a wider Arab nation.[12] Its pan-Arab young activists attended conferences in the port cities and Jerusalem, published periodicals read throughout urban Palestine, and established branches of national political, social, and civic organizations. Nablus remained a more ethnically Arab town in spite of the Jewish settlements that dotted its immediate hinterland. By 1930, there were no significant socioeconomic tensions between residents, and little contestation over physical space and economic resources had taken place as a result of both urbanization and industrialization. British officials and security forces did not have a heavy presence in Nablus if compared with Palestine's port cities and Jerusalem, as the town had a negligible economic and strategic importance for the British.

The political behavior of Nablus's Arab leadership differed from that of the nationalists in Jaffa and Haifa. Indeed, according to a British observer who served in the Palestine police, the traditional Arab families of Nablus had no recent history of stirring crowds to riot in public places.[13] Thus, the British did not impose strict control over the town or its prominent personalities prior to the mid-1930s. At the same time, because Nablus remained out of the geographical space and administrative reach of Palestine's port cities, the resulting lack of intervention on the part of the Mandatory administration favored the development of its more ardent pan-Arab ideology. The self-professed "radical" younger middle-class leadership did not provoke anti-Mandate violence but supported a new strategy: peaceful noncooperation with the administration, including the refusal to attend government functions or pay taxes. These tactics influenced younger national leaders throughout Palestine, who increasingly endorsed them by 1931.

Expressions of colonial power as well as the economic and social changes caused by the intervention of the Mandate administration increasingly left their mark on urban spaces, often subverting them: from the construction of coastal ports to new government buildings, and from the increasing presence of the Palestine police to greater surveillance and public security measures. As an urban phenomenon that organized large crowds of protesters, strikes forced the Mandate's security apparatus into emergency mode to prevent political, social, and economic disruption. As acts that aimed to "reconfigure" urban space, strikes brought those individuals traditionally excluded from public politics into the sphere of potential political violence as witnesses, actors, or victims of colonial repression.[14]

By the early 1930s, changes to the socioeconomic and political makeup of the Arab communities in Haifa and Jaffa laid the groundwork for communal disorder. As ports, both Haifa and Jaffa were of great importance to British and Zionist plans for economic development. They served as transportation centers, the bases for the country's industries, and in the case of Haifa, the terminus of the British-controlled oil pipeline from northern Iraq. Jewish immigrants and Zionist companies and entrepreneurs benefited the most from urban economic and infrastructural growth. Consequently, the majority Arab population of these cities, as well as their rural migrants, had fewer opportunities for employment, even as skilled workers, while the unskilled workforce faced quite precarious employment as day or seasonal laborers.[15] As explained by Carter Wood, urbanization is in itself a cause of disorder because of the tension between different forms of order embedded in new and old urban spaces.[16] In the case of Jaffa and Haifa, and to some extent Nablus and Jerusalem, by the late 1920s urban expansion had resulted not only in the creation of new neighborhoods but also in the enlargement of the popular membership of nationalist and civic associations. These processes changed traditional modes of urban political socialization: they created new social networks and political ties in the impoverished and largely working-class Arab quarters of the port cities of Palestine. Support for violent forms of protest appeared within the framework of the emergence of Palestinian Arab civil society, with newspapers playing a central role in publicizing small and large protest actions.

The tensions embedded in the demographic and socioeconomic makeup of Haifa and Jaffa started to become apparent before 1933. The rate of unemployment caused a considerable amount of discontent, and the Arab press portrayed the British administration's lack of welfare policies as the cause of the economic stagnation of the Arab community. Haifa and Jaffa's economies could support neither the high numbers of Jewish immigrants nor the increasing Arab newcomers from rural areas.[17] The discontent of the poor and of recently urbanized shantytown dwellers (a group that had an increasing influence on the social structure of these cities) fed into the radicalization of other segments of the population. According to May Seikaly, a larger stratum of urban residents had become politicized—not only the peasant workers but also the lower bourgeoisie. The latter participated in various protests, including demonstrations, strikes, and boycotts. They did so by using a written and spoken language of injustice that allowed them to voice demands for greater rights. As Seikaly notes, this antagonism was "not immediately translated to violence," but by 1933 "the ground was being prepared for the revolutionary potential of the Arab urban population."[18]

To add to the mix of tensions, by 1930 a new, populist movement started to emerge. It coalesced around the YMMA, the Youth Congress, and the recently established al-Istiqlal (Independence) Party based in Nablus, whose activities received much attention in the Arabic press.[19] These groups attempted to address the anger of the Arab population at their unequal political, social, and economic treatment; this anger was also channeled toward Jewish Palestinians. As Charles Tilly has suggested, when social and political arrangements are threatened and nonviolent routines fail to pay off, violence is likely to escalate.[20] As Nablus, Jaffa, and Haifa started to be connected by dense civil society networks, youth associations with branches in these three urban centers used their own publications, public lectures, and conferences to inform the population of their shared nationalist aims to end the Mandate and addressed those aims to the government.[21]

The Arabic press and its less moderate editors linked with Nablus or al-Istiqlal Party challenged Mandate institutions and policies, especially unrestricted Jewish immigration and the countrywide lack of protection for Arab tenants who lived on land sold to Jewish buyers. Thus, the newspapers disseminated a new discourse of citizenship rights and governmental duties in a language that was easily understood: articles often focused on specific issues such as voting rights, immigration controls, labor organization, education, and taxation.[22] This semantics of contention had a considerable impact on an already-tense struggle between Arab leaders and the government in Palestinian urban centers and became central to the process of defining political and social institutions of belonging, a process in which violence is historically not an uncommon outcome.[23]

VIOLENCE AND NONVIOLENCE:
THE PALESTINIAN LANGUAGE OF "RIGHTS," 1931–1933

In a revealing study of the semantics of political violence in contemporary Venezuela, Fernando Coronil and Julie Skurski argue that historians and other scholars often assume that the way to explain violence is simply to identify its causes. They contend that much less attention has been devoted to the manifestations of violence and to the "meanings that inform its deployment and interpretation."[24] By relating this argument to urban Palestine prior to the 1936–39 revolt, historians can understand how the Arab population came to deploy violence as a tool to demand particular rights and how a new discursive field on rights was key to structure violent action. [25]

The political consequences of the events of 1921 in Jaffa explain why, for a number of years, the Palestinian Arab national movement did not readily endorse violence. After the Jaffa unrest, the Mandate government abandoned the idea of forming a representative parliament in order to persuade the Arab leadership to deter future violence.[26] In parallel, British officials began to use a particular colonial language that legitimized state power and control over the Arab population by demonizing the participants in the 1921 riots and the 1929 Western Wall disturbances. Their vocabulary emphasized mob violence as the act of an enemy or uncivilized "other," thus providing a justification for the absence of representative government.

As these discursive tactics were progressively adopted by the Arab national movement, by the end of 1932 their portrayal of the British administration as "aggressors" played an important role in the shift from nonviolent noncooperation to violent resistance. In public speeches and in the press nationalist leaders increasingly depicted the injustices inflicted on the Arab population as the direct consequence of Mandate policies. This discursive imagery of injustice, coupled with the absence of political and civil rights and calls to reverse the British pro-Zionist stance, would act as a catalyst for popular anger in the Jaffa riots of 1933. In September 1933, just before the outbreak of unrest, the weekly newspaper *Al-Jam'iyya al-'Arabiyya* (Arab society) stated clearly that protests and demonstrations should be part of a movement of resistance (*muqawama*) against the government's policies that threatened the extinction of Arab nationality in Palestine.[27]

This rhetorical turn implied the legitimacy of violent resistance on the part of the Palestinian Arabs confronted by the prospect of ceasing to exist as a nation. The language was anti-colonial in tone and inspired by events in India. Palestinian activists were in fact quite familiar with the nationalist struggle there and with the argument formulated by Indian nationalists in 1909 that a campaign of terrorism, including the assassination of British officials, was a patriotic duty to be undertaken by a citizenry faced with an invasion of its sovereign territory. As in India, in Palestine claims to citizenship shaped a "legitimacy of [Arab] violence committed for a political cause," becoming part of a larger political theory of violence and self-defense framed by nationalist imaginings.[28] In the months before the 1933 riots, the weekly newspaper *Sawt al-Sha'b* (Voice of the people) explicitly stated that "self-defense [was] a sacred right" of every Arab.[29]

British officials had already noted this language at the end of the previous year. In December 1932, the Criminal Investigation Department (CID) in Jerusalem wrote to the Mandate's chief secretary about extensive and subversive political activities carried out under the banner of Nablus's al-Istiqlal Party. The CID accused the party of promoting a policy of hatred against the British Mandate and trying to "cultivate public opinion for extreme measures," such as noncooperation with the administration and civil disobedience. The administration feared that the party "quietly, but diligently" spread "hatred in the minds of young men, students, teachers, etc. in order to organise public opinion for militant activity."[30] Certainly, the political and social climate of Nablus fostered exclusive Arab nationalist ideologies, although the first armed Arab gangs were reported in the mid-1930s in the villages of central Palestine.

In Nablus, the political atmosphere during the consolidation of al-Istiqlal Party was one of nonviolent resistance. The party itself did "not generally raise the slogan of armed struggle"; instead, its leaders, and particularly the young populists, stressed their support for Gandhi's tactics in India.[31] One of the most active members was Akram Zu'aytir. He represented a new generation of Palestinian nationalists who deployed the rhetoric of "citizenship rights" in urban areas. Zu'aytir worked as a schoolteacher, and in early 1930 he became the editor of the newspaper *Mir'at al-Sharq* (Mirror of the East). In his position as editor, Zu'aytir drew attention to Gandhi's activism against British colonialism in

India. He called for the adoption of Gandhi's ideas, strategies, and aims in Palestine, including demands for complete independence and tactical noncooperation with the British. He also advocated an "army of defense" composed of young Arabs from towns and cities who would walk through rural Palestine to spread a patriotic spirit.[32] Zu'aytir also wrote for Haifa's weekly *Al-Yarmuk* and, with his colleagues from Nablus, connected the city's youth bloc to groups based elsewhere in Palestine.[33] Nablusi activists issued a number of statements in 1931 and 1932 stressing the need for the national movement to continue the peaceful struggle (*al-jihad al-salami*) against the Mandate government.

The authors of front-page press reports frequently framed actions of protest—including strikes and boycotts of Zionist and British goods and services—as national civic duties.[34] The participants in these actions were generally the inhabitants of the cities and towns in which they took place. The Nablus weekly newspaper *Al-Hayat* (Life) stressed that the town was the stronghold of the nationalist movement and that its citizens "[knew] their rights and duties" (*huququhum wa wajabathum*) to strike and demonstrate.[35] Thus, Nablus's leaders, despite being described by the British in 1931 as the most radical in Palestine, did not as yet openly promote a turn to violent activism.[36]

By August 1931, however, the Arab national movement's deployment of more aggressive language against the British authorities became apparent. The context was provided by a strike organized in Palestinian cities on 15 August to protest the arming of Jewish settlements. In Nablus, the crowd of young demonstrators was clubbed by the police with rifle butts until they dispersed. The police injured two youths. In response, Nablus's leaders decided to strike again the following week, also putting pressure on the Arab Executive Committee to call a general strike and a demonstration in Jerusalem.[37] Newspaper headlines during the strike used the simple yet repetitive language of the Mandate having denied "Arab rights" in Palestine.

As the authorities sought to prevent street demonstrations, the populist Arab leaders responded by arguing that demonstrating against the government was a civil right. Arab newspaper reports on the Nablus events referred to the unarmed demonstrators as carrying only "the weapon of rights."[38] *Al-Jam'iyya al-'Arabiyya* described those who had been arrested as "examples of national duty and dignity."[39] While the events in Nablus received extensive coverage in the press, they marked a turning point in the rhetoric of al-Istiqlal. A party member, speaking at a gathering in 1932, stated categorically the right of the Palestinians to use force against the British.[40] In mid-1932, Istiqlalist Subhi al-Khadra wrote an article in *Al-Hayat* that blamed the British alone for the hardships faced by Palestinian Arabs. He called the government's pro-Zionist policy "a blatant attack on the holiest of our rights." Other statements by party members called the British usurpers of the legal and civil rights of the inhabitants of Palestine.[41]

THE RIOTS OF 1933

By 1933, the Palestine administration was aware of the potential for the escalation of violence between Arabs and Jews in Haifa and Jaffa, as throughout the summer of that year the press and civil society groups campaigned against increased Jewish immigration and land sales. Yet, as they had done before, national leaders and groups of activists continued to use the language of citizenship rights to justify demands made to the Mandate government and to encourage the urban population toward noncooperation with the colonial administration. In mid-October 1933, when the Arab Executive Committee called a strike and held a protest demonstration in Jerusalem, a headline in one of Palestine's newspapers explained the event as a result of the Arabs' panic over "reckless immigration."[42] The language used by the urbanite nationalist leadership is suggestive of a threat posed by Mandate policies to the vulnerable position of those who were unemployed or earned low wages in the cities of Palestine. The Jerusalem demonstration, which was organized to address that threat, began with the veteran nationalist leader Musa Kazim Pasha al-Husayni—then in his early eighties—marching at its head. The procession was a thoroughly urban spectacle, with its two thousand participants drawn mainly from the city's neighborhoods. As the mixed British–Arab Palestine police met the procession and tried to disperse the crowd violently, demonstrators started to throw stones. The police wounded about thirty Arabs with their heavy-handed crowd-control methods. The march had been largely contained in the Old City, preventing protesters from reaching government buildings but attracting Arabs who lived in the Muslim and Christian quarters located inside the city walls.

The Executive Committee ultimately made the decision to demonstrate in Jaffa on 27 October. In the days leading up to the demonstration, rumors that the Jews were to take political control over the Mandate in collusion with the British fueled "seething" public opinion, according to officials, against the government's policy of support for the Zionist movement. Mandate officials and the police feared that the upcoming demonstration would have a greater impact than the Jerusalem march. They warned High Commissioner Arthur Wauchope that the composition of the popular movement in Jaffa's Arab quarters and slum district might potentially result in the demonstration being led by the "lawless element," such as Arab boatmen and porters.[43] In anticipation of the demonstration, an article in Jerusalem's Arabic newspaper *Al-Jam'iyya al-'Arabiyya* stressed that the British did not consider the Palestinians as Arab nationals and urged the

Figure 5.1. Jerusalem demonstration turns violent in the Old City, 13 October 1933. Photo: American Colony (Jerusalem). Source: Matson Photograph Collection, Library of Congress.

Arabs to assert their citizenship rights in public against the "usurpation of our sacred rights and our independence."[44] This type of agitation continued in the press during the following week and in public meetings of members of civic and political associations organized in Haifa and Jaffa by al-Istiqlal Party.

Foreseeing trouble, the Palestine government approved the deployment of extra police and armored cars and of one company of Royal Ulster Rifles (with two companies in reserve). Royal Air Force bomber squadrons were also to be sent to Jaffa the day before the planned demonstration. Clearly, the administration was planning for a riot, rehearsing measures routinely used in India. John Faraday, the assistant superintendent of the Palestine police, noted that the police were preparing to counter the use of bombs, clubs, stones, and handmade weapons by demonstrators.[45] Arab delegations arrived in Jaffa on 26 October and, alongside boatmen and urban laborers, filled the streets. Unlike in the Jerusalem march, the police and the government considered the crowd in Jaffa to contain a "different class of Arabs" who were "more daring" and anxious—a reference to the possible participation of Arab migrants and workers from the poor quarters of the city. In addition, propaganda in the local Arab press fueled further tension, circulating news to the effect that the British forces had beaten women and political leaders alike during the Jerusalem march.[46] These rumors themselves fueled an increasing atmosphere of violence in the days before the march.

The public spaces of Jaffa became the focus of contention by both authorities and nationalist leaders. British authorities requested detailed maps of the route of the planned procession, which the Arab Executive Committee handed over to the colonial administration; the route, however, did not meet the approval of the British authorities. Passing through the city's Arab 'Ajami neighborhood and Jewish quarters, the procession was to reach the government buildings located in Clock Tower Square. The use of this route was strategic and symbolic and meant to threaten Jaffa's colonial space and institutions. According to Superintendent Faraday's report of the events, on the morning of 27 October, as three thousand Arabs gathered outside the MCA offices, the crowd became "truculent and unruly." This vocabulary expressed a legitimizing motif that justified the use of lethal force against the crowd. British and Arab eyewitnesses reported the numbers of protesters as high as seven thousand—which also justified the disproportionate response of the police in the minds of the latter. The crowd largely ignored initial orders to disperse. Once the march began, it broke through the police cordons along the planned route. Government reports conveyed the highly charged mood and verbal confrontations that combined to produce an atmosphere of agitation before physical violence occurred. The temper of the crowd was "ugly," and demonstrators were armed with clubs, sticks, stones, and other weapons, including boat hooks and other pieces of iron.[47]

Some demonstrators soon started to damage shops and house shutters. As they shouted slogans, members of the crowd grabbed other weaponlike instruments on the way. According to British reports, stones "were coming over like hail" toward the police cordon. Some groups broke away from the main procession, prompting the police to refer to them as "a blood-thirsty mob of Arabs." A large group of demonstrators met with the police at Jaffa's central Clock Tower Square and charged the policemen after shouting "aleihem!" (Go for them!). By that time, disorder was total, and the police made a number of failed baton charges on foot and horseback. One police officer noted that other efforts to stop the protesters "were frustrated by wild Moslem women hurling stones from the roof-tops."[48]

When a member of the crowd fired a number of rounds at the police at Clock Tower Square, the police opened a controlled volley of fire to attempt to

Figure 5.2. Palestine police baton charge against the Arab crowd turns to chaos in Jaffa's Clock Tower Square, 27 October 1933. Source: *Illustrated London News*, 13 June 1936. © Imperial War Museums (HU 89852).

disperse the crowd. By the early afternoon the situation in Jaffa was under control, but twenty-six individuals, including one police officer, had been killed and sixty others wounded. The organizers of the demonstration—members of the Arab Executive Committee and al-Istiqlal—were all arrested while drafting an order for a protest march in Nablus.

When word of the events in Jaffa reached Nablus later that day, many of the city's inhabitants poured into the streets shouting and singing while making their way to Barclay's bank and the post office—the two symbols of colonial authority. What quickly became a "riotous crowd" stoned both buildings. When the Palestine police arrived, officers attempted a baton charge, but with no success. After a warning, the police fired on the crowd after some rioters began to throw stones in their direction, joined by residents who were also targeting the police from rooftops. One rioter later died from bullet wounds.[49] Rifle fire quickly quelled the disturbance, and Nablus remained quiet. The homogeneous ethnic composition of the town's inhabitants and the absence of large numbers of impoverished laborers might very well have been one of the factors that contributed to contain violence.

Meanwhile on the same day, a crowd of about two thousand Arabs gathered in Haifa's urban center, incensed by rumors—often exaggerated—of bloodshed in Jaffa. A disturbance broke out soon after sunset. A crowd broke windows at the police station barracks with stones picked up from road construction sites. The police shot one Arab dead, and one rioter stabbed a constable.[50] The next morning, the situation worsened: a crowd of about three hundred individuals attacked the police station in the center of the city, and the police again opened fire. Meanwhile, other groups stoned cars and managed to set up thirty-one barricades along the main roads of the city. Another crowd gathered at the train station and stoned the train from Jaffa that was transporting British police officers. As acts of violence intensified, with the torching of a truck, the police again fired on the crowds. Four individuals involved in the riot died from bullet wounds. Ten Jewish residents were injured in the crossfire.[51]

The next day, the administration reenacted the Palestine (Defence) Order in Council of 1931, designed in part by Charles Tegart, who acted as police commissioner in Calcutta and had responsibility for devising colonial security orders.[52] Tegart's order was not the first of its kind to be applied in Palestine. The outbreak of violence in Jaffa in 1921 had led to the first application of martial law by a civilian high commissioner. Until 1933, however, subsequent defense orders were mainly put in place for rural areas in response to agrarian crime such as theft or destruction of property, with the imposition of collective fines on villages. As military reinforcements had not been deployed in urban areas since 1921, Tegart's order brought unprecedented disruption to urban social and political life.

THE AFTERMATH: FROM CITIZENS TO "THE POPULATION"

The large-scale violence deployed by urban crowds of activists and protesters in 1933 transformed the position of the Palestinian population in relation to the Mandate authorities in both discourse and colonial practice. The British authorities used a particular vocabulary to legitimize their use of force to both the Arabs and the government in London, turning civilians into armed rioters, mutineers, or otherwise enemies of law and order.

The measures taken by officials in Palestine and London in the aftermath of the disturbances aimed at preventing the outbreak of further unrest in urban areas, following colonial practice in India. Previous experience in India also informed the discursive characterization of Palestine's unruly population after the riots, as they started to be held collectively responsible for security breaches. British officials in Palestine were well aware of the implications of using harsh tactics to disperse urban crowds and the need to phrase their actions as necessary. The massacre of Amritsar in the Punjab in 1919 had led to an official government debate on the "legitimacy and limits of colonial state-violence." In the case of Amritsar, some colonial officials maintained that the harsh action taken by the army was unavoidable and justified because some Indians in the crowd were guilty of having incited violence.[53] Palestine Police Assistant Superintendent John Faraday used the same line of argument in defense of his own actions in Jaffa when faced with a British commission of inquiry convened in late 1933 to investigate the riots.[54]

The emergency regulations stripped the urban inhabitants of Palestine (now perceived as a potentially violent mob) of their few basic rights and protections—in particular the right to civil trial, the right to assemble, and freedom of the press. It is useful to note the difference between the terms "the citizens" and "the population," as used by the Mandate government, in light of the response to the unrest. In terms of policy "the citizens" and "the population" are often viewed as separate groups in colonial situations. By the end of 1933, senior military officers in London were referring to the Arab citizens as "the population" and authorized the high commissioner to use tear gas and live rifle fire to disperse "mobs."[55] Partha Chatterjee has argued that the concept of the citizen carries with it "the ethical connotation of participation in the sovereignty of the state," while the concept of the population "makes available to government . . . a set of rationally manipulable instruments for reaching large sections of the inhabitants of a country as the targets of their 'policies.'"[56] With the outbreak of collective violence in urban Palestine, the emergency regulations removed basic rights given to the Palestinian Arabs, treating them as colonial subjects rather than citizens of the Mandate.

The Order in Council put into effect during and after the violent events of 1933 defined armed rioters in Palestine as "enemies." The correspondence and various reports produced by the Mandate administration termed the demonstrators "rioters," clearly signposting the subversive nature of their actions. While officials were surely aware that not all protesters engaged in rioting, this language authorized widespread repression. It was also largely directed at urban residents in response to the city-based nature of the violence. The authorities could censor all publications; restrict communications; arrest, detain, or deport "enemies" without trial; and even appropriate the property of suspected

Figure 5.3. Members of the Palestine police with batons and horses, after forcing Arab demonstrators back in Jaffa, 27 October 1933. Protesters and onlookers remain on the roofs of buildings. Photo: American Colony (Jerusalem). Source: Matson Photograph Collection, Library of Congress.

culprits.[57] From 1933, such responses to urban (and rural) violence were indeed Chatterjee's "manipulable instruments." While the Palestine government could easily apply these public security measures against colonial populations, it was more difficult to justify their application to legal citizens.

Citizenship continued to play a role in the aftermath: the discourse of the Arab leadership continued to emphasize concepts of justice and rights, as well as the illegitimacy of the force used by the police against the largely unarmed demonstrators. Within two days of the Jaffa riot, the National League in Syria sent a letter to the British foreign secretary that deplored the use of force among an "unarmed and peaceful population" and appealed for the immediate granting to the Palestinian Arabs "of their just rights . . . as Citizens."[58] The Palestinian Arab press argued that the citizens of Palestine's urban centers largely refused to act violently and reported the beating of the elderly Jerusalem politician Musa Kazim al-Husayni by police during the Jaffa riot. In this fashion, the British were accused of making illegitimate use of violence to protect Mandate interests and policies. The violent deeds of some elements among the urban crowds were explained as the legitimate response of a defenseless population that had the "right" to resist the cruel actions of the police.[59] In Jerusalem the leaders of the Arab Executive Committee used similar language, noting that the citizens of Haifa and Nablus felt that something must be done so that "the people should be granted their rights."[60]

. . .

Until the outbreak of the 1936 revolt the reaction of the Arab nationalist movement as a whole remained one of rhetorical engagement rather than further violent confrontation with the Mandate authorities. Cities and towns in Palestine remained quiet through the final months of 1933. The Arab Executive Committee held demonstrations in several major towns on 16 January 1934, coinciding with the Muslim festival of 'Id al-Fitr. The committee received a permit, and the demonstrations took place without disturbances. Even though these demonstrations were peaceful, radical Arab activists continued to appropriate city spaces through rallies, marches, and strikes organized on public holidays.

In 1933 Jaffa and Haifa became the centers of violent contestation in the name of citizenship rights, while Nablus remained a site of relative nonviolence. The composition of the Arab urban population in Jaffa and Haifa—working class and increasingly made up of migrant rural farmers—contributed to the violent nature of popular contestation during and after the October riots. Here in the coastal cities of Palestine changes precipitated by migration and urbanization mobilized a strong imagery of injustice that was instrumental in the explosion of violent unrest. In a somewhat different fashion, in Nablus the same language of rights connected with the national movement played a significant role in endorsing urban noncooperation and nonviolent tactics of resistance against Mandate policy.

The verbal tensions and semantic contention that came before and after violent unrest were an essential ingredient that allowed "the meaning of citizenship [to be] recast through practice."[61] When in 1933 the colonial state responded to the riots by introducing new legislation criminalizing protest in order to prevent further violence, British soldiers and police officers labeled the urban population a "violent mob," construing them as military enemies who threatened the British administration. The police not only named but also confronted the crowd as a criminal gang, and the CID and other officials treated the crowds' leaders as subversive agents. The violent tactics utilized by the Mandate administration, including the language used in the enactment of the Emergency Regulations, demonstrated the power of the colonial government in Palestine, the readiness of that government to call on British military forces, and the Mandate's disregard for the civil and political rights of its Arab inhabitants. In Palestine "while popular violence was circumscribed . . . state violence was unbounded, as if its aims were to trap popular will."[62]

A study of the colonial reaction alone gives little attention to the specific reasons for the manifestation of violence as linked to the socioeconomic situation in Jaffa and Haifa and the increased radicalization of the homogeneous population of Nablus. In all three cases, disturbances, scuffles, and outright riots had socially constructed significance and were conditioned by the discourses popularized by newspapers and a powerful rhetoric deployed during public meetings and demonstrations. These discourses nurtured a new nationalist mythology surrounding citizenship and civil rights that became firmly anchored in specific urban milieus of resistance as a result of the short-term legacy of colonial and Zionist intrusion into Palestine's towns and cities.

URBAN CONNECTIONS

The City as a Front Line

Part 3

6 CHALLENGING THE OTTOMAN *PAX URBANA*

Intercommunal Clashes in 1857 Tunis

Nora Lafi

BETWEEN 1857 AND 1864, Tunis and the wider Ottoman province of Tunisia were the theater of a series of violent events that challenged the Ottoman governance of diversity and the imperial *pax urbana*. These clashes also redefined the very relationship between the city, the local dynasty, and the empire in the midst of a changing international situation characterized by increasingly forceful attempts by the European powers to assert their interests in local politics.[1] More than twenty-five years after the colonization of neighboring Ottoman Algeria by the French, it became clear that Tunisia had become the object of foreign appetites of colonial nature. At the same time, the implementation of the Ottoman reforms known as the Tanzimat was under way in the provinces of the empire. Though the local Husainid dynasty had ruled Tunis since 1705, the province was still much more integrated into the Ottoman imperial system than historiography might lead us to believe, mainly as a result of a Eurocentric bias. The reforms, and their local interpretation by the local dynasty, were aimed, at least partially, at avoiding mounting foreign influence through the modernization of the institutional framework of the empire.[2]

Such reforms required a redefinition both of the pact between Istanbul and local elites and of local features of the Ottoman system for governing diversity. This system was based on an official recognition of non-Muslim confessional communities as part of specific institutions at the scale of the empire, the *millet*s, and on the delegation of various competences (particularly fiscal and judicial) to such communities at the local scale.[3] It was not equality as theorized in modern political philosophy but an old-regime style of organized coexistence.[4] As the reforms challenged the old regime, the outbreak of violence can be seen as an expression of their limits, as well as an instrument of pressure. The reforms were the object of difficult negotiations that sometimes involved moments of tension, exacerbated by foreign interference. Ussama Makdisi has illustrated in his research on Mount Lebanon the importance of the Tanzimat in challenging old-regime equilibriums and changing the social meaning of communal belonging and religion.[5]

This chapter first presents the characteristics of the local *pax urbana* under the old regime—that is, before the reforms—and the challenges to this system brought about by the imperial reform program of the Tanzimat and by its local interpretation and implementation in beylical Tunis, in a specific international context. An episode of violence that occurred in Tunis in 1857, much less known than the 1864 revolt, is then used as evidence of a change in the paradigm of urban violence and as an indicator of broader transformations in society.[6] My aim is to propose a series of criteria for interpreting the meaning, stakes, and typology of the various manifestations of violence that occurred in these crucial years.[7]

THE NATURE OF THE OTTOMAN *PAX URBANA* IN TUNIS DURING THE OLD REGIME

In the cities of the Ottoman Empire, peace and civil security were the central object of a complex system of governance. Security as a value was attached to the very notion of urbanity, and order was—beyond the mere actions of security forces and justice officials—the result of numerous mediations and a system of "canalization" of violence. This idea of the city as a safe haven had its roots in the medieval philosophy of al-Farabi,[8] which reflected ideas of disparate origin within the Islamic and ancient worlds, and in the construction of features of urban governance that characterized the Ottoman old regime between the sixteenth and eighteenth centuries.[9] This specific Ottoman approach to the *pax urbana*, which mirrored a general imperial demand for order as well as a vision of the governance of diversity, reinforced the power of local notables in the streets and quarters throughout the city and that of guilds and social groups such as confessional communities, to which the maintenance of public order and most aspects of urban governance were delegated. The Ottoman presence in the city was mediated through this assigning of power to notables and the social networks and civic institutions they supported and was not limited to imperial institutions external to the city. Thus, the *pax urbana* resulted, on the one hand, from a fragile equilibrium between urban factions and groups and, on the other, from the intersection between imperial ideology and local practices. It was often maintained by alliances between the imperial central government and a local faction (urban notables and their clientele) at the expense of rival factions.

The potential for the escalation of factional violence was generally contained by procedures of mediation: deliberations by the council of urban notables; the actions of the leaders of the various quarters, streets, communities, and guilds; and petitions to the Ottoman sultan and governor (or, in the case of Tunis, the representative of the local Husainid dynasty that ruled on behalf of the empire).[10] Legal intermediation was also crucial, as suggested by the role of Islamic courts (*mahkama*), judges (qadi), and local religious dignitaries (*'ulama'*) in the resolution of disputes. The latent violence of groups of young men, more or less explicitly affiliated with urban factions, was also the object of specific attention. Civic festivals (*mawssem*) with dances, games like the *fantasia*, and processions served as mechanisms of symbolization.

Local authorities were also in charge of public security and thus functioned as "controllers" of violence, as did the police under Tunis's *shaykh al-madina*, the leader of the city's civic administration.[11] This distinctively Ottoman system of mediation was built around the procedure of the petition.[12] Each group or individual was entitled to write a petition either to the chief of the confessional community, the *shaykh al-madina*, the governor, the local ruler, or the sultan in Istanbul. In fact, the Ottoman administrative system during the old regime was based on what can be called a "petitioning dialogue." Petitions were in no way just the expression of discontent for a perceived abuse of power; they were also the first act of a codified bureaucratic process in various phases, including an inquiry and a demand for explanation sent to the individual allegedly responsible for the abuse. In cities, it is clear that petitions were part of the construction and constant renegotiation of the Pax Ottomana at the local level.

In the case of Tunis, the chronicler Ibn Ben Abi Diyaf (1804–74)—who wrote during the transition between the old and new regimes as part of his duties as *katib* (secretary) of the local government and personal secretary of several beys (the local Husainid rulers)—provides many details about the nature and operation of this petitioning system.[13] Ibn Ben Abi Diyaf, himself the son of a *katib*, not only recorded events but also took part in public affairs, from a very young age, between the mid-1820s and the 1870s. Describing the procedure leading to the writing of a petition to the sultan in Istanbul, he listed all the required preparatory meetings and official steps. The rhetoric used in writing petitions was intended to expose a problematic situation to the sultan on the part of local notables.[14] The petition was validated by the seals of the notables in question (*khatim al-maktum*). Petitions could also be sent to the bey via the religious court.[15] Yet mediation procedures were not always successful, and in many cases their failure could spark episodes of violence. Moreover, in times of rupture between local and/or imperial factions, cities became the theater of violent events that can be interpreted as the expression of a direct challenge to imperial governance.

Such events could also signpost the passage to a new order. This is particularly true of the period of the Tanzimat—the imperial reforms implemented between the 1830s and the 1880s, which also coincided with the extension of European influence in the cities of the empire, particularly those located along the Mediterranean coast. Julia Clancy-Smith has illustrated how in such cities, and particularly in Tunis, new patterns of European migration and new forms of European imperialism partially defined the context of the Ottoman imperial reforms.[16] At stake was not only the role of local notables in urban governance but also the redefinition of collective and personal identities precipitated by changes in the nature of the coexistence between confessional communities. These developments were particularly momentous in Tunis, especially given the influx into the city of growing numbers of European and Maltese immigrants.[17]

In Ottoman cities the organization of coexistence between different religious and/or ethnic groups was part of the Pax Ottomana. Beyond the legal status of the various communities, there were precise instruments of daily regulation of coexistence at the level of the city, quarter, and street. This system was designed to prevent the escalation of violence. In Tunis, streets, markets, and public spaces were patrolled night and day by the police of the medina. In cases of serious threats to public order, the network of civic institutions controlled by the notables of the confessional communities was supposed to provide a framework for mediation and the prevention and resolution of conflict.[18] The chief (*shaykh al-Yahud*) of the Jews (*Yahud al-Balad*), a group of approximately twenty thousand residents in the mid-nineteenth century, was not only in charge of matters of personal, professional, and fiscal status but also acted as the representative of the community in civic institutions such as the council of notables.

EARLY NINETEENTH-CENTURY SIGNS OF DISRUPTION
OF THE OTTOMAN *PAX URBANA*

The violence of 1857 was not a new phenomenon in Tunis; during the old regime, rivalries between factions of notables had been quite common.[19] These episodes of unrest were of course not disconnected from the international and imperial arenas, but they appear to have been quite different from the type of violence experienced by the city after the 1850s. The most obvious difference is the lesser importance of foreign consuls in influencing local urban politics before the reforms.[20]

Both the chronicle of Ibn Ben Abi Diyaf and the imperial archives in Istanbul provide valuable information on several revolts and episodes of unrest that marked the early nineteenth century. Some of these conflicts were triggered by earlier reforms, as was true of the disbandment of the Janissary corps in 1826.[21] In Tunis, as in many cities of the empire, this decision resulted in decades of uncertainty, as Janissary soldiers had come to represent a strong local force both in the army and in the administration. Growing contestation by European powers over the nature of the predatory, but highly codified, Mediterranean economy resulting from the action of corsairs also seems to have played a role in fomenting urban unrest.[22]

For instance, during the reign of Bey Abi Ithna' Muhammad Hamuda Bacha' (r. 1782–1814), a very violent episode took place in 1811, resulting in the destruction of the city markets (suq) by what Ibn Ben Abi Diyaf describes as the Turkish army (*jund al-Turk*). During the revolt (*al-thawra*), some of the soldiers were trapped in the citadel (*al-qasba*), where they opened fire on the inhabitants of the city. The mutineers tried to kill the bey, who was rescued thanks to the intervention of the *shaykh al-madina*, al Hajj Muhammad al-Ghammat, and of a notable, Shaykh Ali Mahawid.[23] The revolt ended with the killing of all the rebels and the bey's decision to promote greater equity between the various corps of the army, notably the "Turks"—a term that included the Janissaries and the local regiments known as *zwawa*. In this case, violence was clearly a consequence of tensions within the various forces of the Ottoman army, including its local Tunisian branch. Its urban character was accentuated by the fact that the various corps stationed in the city were also acting as urban factions, as is also suggested by the involvement of the *shaykh al-madina*, the chief of Tunis's civic administration.

The Ottoman archives in Istanbul report another episode of violence a few years later—a revolt (*isyan*) that broke out in 1815 under Mahmud Pasha (r. 1814–24). This revolt illustrates the consequences in both Tunis and the province of Tunisia of European warnings issued during the Congress of Vienna (1814–15) against North African corsairs,[24] as well as American naval intervention in the Mediterranean.[25] In 1816, the coincidence of the reform of the Janissary system with the initiation of a new power arrangement in the Mediterranean following the Congress of Vienna led to yet another urban revolt, which featured one of the factions of notables (*min a'yan al-thawra*)—probably the faction most affected by the new restrictions on the commerce of slaves and captives.[26] The city gates were closed, and it was only thanks to the mediation of Muhammad al-Ghammat that violence did not degenerate into open conflict.[27] As the chronicler Ibn Ben Abi Diyaf states, because the shaykh knew how to talk to the rebel faction and to the soldiers, he succeeded in bringing them back to reason. But the city was pacified only during the following month, when the bey pardoned all rebels.[28] Following these events, the central government in Istanbul proposed creating the position of anti-riot chief within the local Tunis police.[29]

In 1828, serious unrest broke out again—this time threatening the European population of Tunis, who fled the city and sought refuge in La Goulette, Carthage, and La Marsa.[30] These events confirm that, by the late 1820s, outbreaks of unrest had become intimately entangled with certain developments characterizing the eventful new century: the beginning of Ottoman army reform; changes in Mediterranean trade imposed by Europe, which placed the first severe limitations on the action of corsairs and the slave trade; and, more generally, the greater involvement of Great Britain and France in the affairs of the western provinces of the Ottoman Empire.

ANTI-JEWISH VIOLENCE AND THE BREAKING
OF OTTOMAN COEXISTENCE (1857)

During the 1850s, amid growing French-British rivalry for influence in Tunisia and the difficult implementation of the Tanzimat,[31] violent incidents occurred that were not only a sign of unprecedented crisis in the relationship between the city and the empire, and a result of the growing power of foreign consuls, but also the manifestation of a breakdown in the coexistence of confessional communities.

In 1857, Tunis became the theater of a violent riot against its Jewish residents triggered by the so-called Sfez affair. After a banal street incident, Batou Sfez, a Jewish coachman working for Nessim Shamama (the *qa'id* and *ra'is al-Yahud*, chief of the Jewish community) was accused of blasphemy and executed in June.[32] It was the first time in the nineteenth century that the law punishing blasphemy had been invoked and applied. The sentence was severe because Mohammed Bey (r. 1855–59) was probably looking for a pretext to target the Jewish community. A Muslim had been executed sometime before for the murder of a Jew—a course of action that had sparked resentment in the city through factional conflicts around the nature of the reforms.[33] The type of local mediation that was a feature of the old regime would have probably helped ease tensions. In fact, faced with widespread popular discontent, by ordering the execution of Sfez, the bey was willing to reestablish what could be perceived as a kind of communal balance at the expense of the first Jew against whom a pretext could be found.[34]

Yet it became clear from the beginning of the affair that conservative opponents of the reform agenda of the local government were ready to instrumentalize communal tensions in order to counter foreign influence and arrest the implementation of the Ottoman reforms. The bey chose to execute Sfez in a public display of state violence in order not to lose control of a potentially violent crowd. He expressed this view during an audience with the British consul, Richard Wood, a few weeks after Sfez's execution: "If a rapid introduction of innovations and reforms created an apprehension that our Faith was in danger, the people would rise to a man and my Governement would fall."[35] Batou Sfez, whose status as a native Jew did not place him under consular protection,[36] was sentenced to death by a local tribunal of 'ulama' and swiftly executed so that neither petitions to the Ottoman government in Istanbul nor intervention by foreign governments could save his life. In conversation with Consul Wood, the bey justified his decision to have Sfez immediately tried by the religious court (which he knew was going to pass a severe sentence) as an attempt to avoid anti-Jewish riots:

> I was obliged to abide by the decision of the Sheraa [Islamic Law]. Had I refused to do so the immediate consequences would have been more disastrous. Several hundred Moors inhabiting the quarter of Bab Sueka had armed themselves and were prepared, upon any hesitation on my part to carry out the sentence, to attack the Jews and Christians, two or three hundred of whom [had] taken measures for their protection. Should I have been justified to run such a risk and to expose them and myself to this direful catastrophe? In the case of a Musulman who was condemned for Blasphemy, was not my relative obliged by the ulemas and the people to sanction the sentence and sacrifice the Blasphemer in order to avoid an insurrection and the effusion of the blood of thousands? Nevertheless, for six days and nights I and my Minister revolved the matter in our minds in the hope of finding the means of saving the accused whose life I call God, who will judge me hereafter, to witness, I would have spared if it had been in my power. . . . Governments are not always prepared for a "coup de main" or for suppressing a popular outbreak. Why should they [foreign governments], therefore, suppose

that I am in [a] more favorable position than themselves in preventing a sudden insurrection of my people who are barbarians, and whom you call fanatics?[37]

State violence, here in the form of the capital punishment inflicted on Sfez, is presented as a means to prevent the escalation of popular violence potentially coming from Bab Souika, a neighborhood known for its violent gangs of young men prone to be cynically mobilized by local political factions. In the same conversation, the bey also voiced his general opinion on the Jews:

> The Jews enjoy in this Regency as much civil freedom and liberty of conscience as they do in most countries: but if in England you find reasons for excluding them from your Legislature, why will you not assume that there exist also motives here, though of another nature, which would render dangerous any sudden attempt at their emancipation? Personally I have no objection to it, but I must be allowed to take my time in bringing it about without imperilling their or my own position.[38]

Clearly, the bey was following the debates about the political rights of Jews that were taking place in Great Britain at that time; the first Jew was admitted to the British Parliament only a year later.[39]

The Sfez affair also illustrates the growing ambiguity in the perception of Jews in Tunis: the protégés of European consulates—Ottoman subjects who had been given an official document by a European consular administration admitting them for protection and allowing them to escape Ottoman justice and fiscal administration— tended to be seen increasingly as foreigners, while the natives who were under Ottoman jurisdiction began to suffer from this ambiguity and to be used as scapegoats. Old communal resentments that, under the old regime, had been managed and usually eased by a mix of social mediation and hierarchical authority became entangled with more aggressive sentiments that placed the Jewish community in a more vulnerable position.

Communal tensions in this period took a new form in an entanglement of stakes and scales between the local and the international arenas. Even after Sfez's execution tensions remained high in the city, as a letter sent by a Jewish-British resident to Consul Wood testifies: "The Jew was not only executed, but his corpse was insulted by the fanatical crowd of the Musulman population, who would have dragged it through the town had not the Jews, zealously facing the jury of the mob, succeeded, not however without blows and many wounds, in giving it burial."[40] In fact, the whole summer was marked by tensions on three fronts: intercommunal friction among the urban population, tensions between reformists and conservatives, and pressures on the bey from foreign consuls to support more reforms. At the end of June, a group of Jewish merchants (British protégés of Italian culture) appealed to the British government in fear for their security, emphasizing the various threats they faced:

> We might also cite several acts of Tyranny by which the Bey of Tunis marked the first steps of his administration; but since the event now in question is of such importance as to suffice to show the character of the Bey, of his Tribunals and of his Musulman Population and to point out the danger which we run who live in these parts, without dwelling on them, we think we may hope to see such Reforms established in this Regency as may relieve us of all alarm incompatible with our position of British Subjects.[41]

It seems that the protégés felt that only the British Crown could protect them, as no other petition was sent either to the bey or to Istanbul.[42]

A few weeks later, on 9 August, violent anti-Jewish incidents occurred in Tunis, mostly in the Bab al-Bahr neighborhood. The most striking feature of the 1857 riots was their clear anti-Jewish character, as Jews were specifically targeted by Muslim mobs and chased in the streets. Many of them were beaten. The most detailed narrations of the events are to be found in French and English consular records.[43] The chronicle of Ibn Ben Abi Diyaf remains silent on these events, for a reason not easy to interpret. Was the relevant passage later cut from the text, or did the chronicler choose to avoid exposing these facts? Either way, this omission is very telling about the new situation of fear engendered by the profound divisions that were polarizing urban society.

The French consulate compiled a list of all those who had suffered damages and injuries.[44] It also gathered testimonies. Here, for example, is the statement given to the French consul by a witness to the events, David Ben Kaïche, an Algerian Jewish trader working in Tunis: "I was returning into town by Bab al-Bahr gate when I saw the tumult on the square. I took refuge in the building of the Stock Exchange but part of the crowd converged to this very place in order to loot it. I fled but I was caught by a group of Moors in front of the Castelnuovo pharmacy." Abraham Mahsen, another Algerian Jew employed as a menial worker, recalled: "As I came back into town through the Bab al-Bahr Gate, I found myself in the middle of the crowd and I was assaulted without any reason."[45] These testimonies confirm that Jews were indiscriminate targets of the violence, regardless of their social status or profession. The same file in the archives evokes the fate of Nessim Cafala and David Ben Aïch, who escaped death by seeking refuge in a European house. This list of injured persons compiled by the French consulate is once again very telling about the clear anti-Jewish character of the unrest:

- seven Algerian Jews (Choual Zarkas, Chalom Betron, Jacob Soria, Isac Benchmion, Braham Bensan, Benamia, former officer of the Spahis and his pregnant wife, who lost her child)
- one Roman Jew (Emmanuel Sonnino)
- two British subjects (protégés) of Jewish religion (Andrea Faruggia and Michel-Ange La Rosas)[46]
- two Sardinians (Luigi Costa, carpenter, and Lanfranco)
- thirteen Tunisian Jews (Joseph Rosas, Choual Nattaf, Nessim Ksaif, A. Chouchan, H. Deyana, Ould Gounes, Abraham Portes, Moïse Portes, Moïse Hammena, Haou Pires, Moïse Attal, Mordekai Belaïche, Hais Darmon)[47]

The British consulate also produced several accounts of the riots that confirm their anti-Jewish character. Consul Wood's report to London two days after the events is particularly instructive:

I venture to state with regret that on Sunday the 9th Instant an *émeute* [riot] occurred at Tunis, which threw the European and Israélite populations into great consternation. A Tuscan Jew having inquired of a Moorish shopkeeper the price of a piece of cord, he offered him two thirds less than he demanded, upon which the latter abused him in offensive language which led to an altercation. Another Moor then struck him; and when his brother endeavored to protect him, he was assailed by other Musulmans who dragged both to the square before Her Majesty's Consulate where the Europeans and Natives assemble either to transact business or to loiter at the coffee shops. The attempt of the Foreigners to rescue them increased the tumult; and the Moors assembling from every direction with sticks and stones attacked the Jews indiscriminately. They broke into the Exchange, the furniture of which they smashed and from which they carried away a sum of money. Some time elapsed before the military, which the English and French consulates demanded should assist the local police, could restore order in the Square or in the Jewish quarter where the Musulman populace had commenced to molest the inhabitants. Twenty-two individuals, amongst them a Maltese and some French Subjects were more or less seriously injured.[48]

This narrative provides a number of clues to the dynamics of the events. The local police seem to have been unable to stop the escalation of tension. In such a closely supervised space as the suq, every small incident was normally dealt with immediately. The absence of the police in this case is striking and raises the issue of a possible laissez-faire attitude on the part of local notables (who supervised policing in the neighborhoods) eager to capitalize on communal tensions in order to challenge both the reformist government and the strengthening foreign grip over the city. Although there is no direct evidence to this effect in relation to this episode, the attitude of Tunis's notable class was generally conservative because their interests were threatened by new provisions giving foreigners the right to own property. The granting of equal status to confessional communities such as the Jews was also seen as a challenge to the privileges enjoyed by a largely Muslim notable class and urban population. The presence of Tunisian Jews among the victims indicates that Algerians were not being targeted specifically as subjects of a French colony, once again confirming the indiscriminate anti-Jewish nature of the riots.

Anti-Jewish sentiments and actions were of course not entirely a novelty in Tunis. But such targeted mob violence was unprecedented, marking a turning point away from the previous balance of urban coexistence. Even if, during the old regime, diversity had not been based on equality (a concept unknown in the political philosophy of the pre-Tanzimat Ottoman state), and the Jews were subject to a limitation of their civic rights and a specific dress code, they were allowed to maintain their communal organization. The civic nature of this organization is clearly suggested by their participation in the management of urban administration and their right to petition the public authorities as Ottoman subjects. The violence that erupted in the summer of 1857 sanctioned the birth of a new divide in society. Paradoxically, the violence resulted from the attempted application of imperial reforms in Tunisia promoting, among other things, equality for all Ottoman subjects.

In a time of redefinition of communal and legal identities, violence erupted as popular anger directed against the Jews and foreign powers that were increasingly tightening their political and economic control over the province. Resentment against the Jews nicely served the anti-reform objectives of local conservative notables but also the agenda of European consuls keen to promote more rights for European merchants. The consequence was a growing identification of the Jews in public opinion with the threat of foreign domination. Those who attacked Jews in August 1857 were never brought to justice.[49]

Another expression of the intersection between the local and international contexts was the ways in which the reformist counselors of the bey—such as Khereddine and Khaznadar [50]—and the partisans of the old regime found allies in international diplomacy and in the violent factions of the street, respectively.

The violence against the Jews had far-reaching repercussions. After the 1857 incidents, Tunisian Jewish notables increasingly sought the status of European protégés—a factor that contributed to their further alienation from local society.[51] European powers also used the events of the summer of 1857 to increase their pressure on Tunis; the consuls swiftly forwarded protests of the French and British governments to the bey. On 22 August 1857 a French naval escadrille entered the port of Tunis, forcing the bey to implement the reforms on 9 September 1857 and to sign the fundamental pact (*Ahd al-Aman*) on 25 September 1857.[52] From then on, the reforms were no longer completely Ottoman, and a path was opened toward the French colonial occupation of 1881, making colonization come a step closer.

THE AFTERMATH OF 1857

In 1861 a new series of incidents occurred—of a different nature but linked to the same cause—when many cities in the empire became theaters of political and social tensions. The main bone of contention was negotiation for continuation of the social and political power of the urban notables after the reform of 1858 had created a new form of municipality replacing that of the old regime.[53] Another source of dispute was the reform of the courts of justice. In Tunis a group of residents, led by a few notables, sent a petition to the new municipal council demanding that local notables maintain their influential role in the new institution.[54] As they received no answer, on 25 September 1861 the discontented notables and their clientele gathered at the Great Ezzituna mosque.[55] Al-Tahir al-Mu'addib, Muhammad al-Manna'i al-Bransi, 'Ali Gurji, and Muhammad al-Iskandarani—the leaders who represented important urban factions—decided that on the next day they would close the suqs and march to the Bardo, the palace of the bey, to demand disbandment of the new courts of justice. To intimidate the bey and prepare for violence, al-Mu'addib asked the shaykh of the Bab Souika neighborhood to provide men.[56] This was an allied neighborhood known for its gangs, which had played a prominent role in the 1857 incidents.

In Ottoman cities, the combination of political protest by notables and action on the part of groups of young men was a customary and frequent factor that would ignite violence. On the next day, about one thousand men gathered at the Sidi Muhriz ibn Khalaf mausoleum for a brief propitiatory ceremony;[57] they then marched to the Bardo, where they asked to meet with the bey. Muhammad al-Sadiq Bey (r. 1859–82) received a delegation of ten leaders but arrested some of them afterward. Outside the palace, the protesters broke the symbols of the saint Sidi Muhriz that they had taken with them—a sign that the tension was likely to grow. Ibn Ben Abi Diyaf states that incidents began at this moment in various parts of the medina. Yet French records show that the unrest did not degenerate into a full-scale revolt as a result of the military intervention of the bey's forces.[58] As Consul Léon Roche reported,

> The inhabitants of Tunis are ready to join the demonstration. The lower class, which has everything to gain from disorder, was ready to begin looting. From there we would be only one step away from the scenes of bloody massacre like [those] in Syria. It was only thanks to the firm control of the Dey and of Kheredine that Tunis was spared such desolation. . . . The fanatic party was defeated, and its influence was reduced.[59]

After two days of unrest and repression, the bey announced that he would treat any form of protest as a rebellion against the government.[60] Although those who dared to participate in demonstrations were arrested, the new court of justice showed leniency, forcing the bey to pardon all protesters a few months later. These incidents further illustrate how contestation over the transformation of government and the justice system, but also tensions within the empire and among urban elites, took the form of violent unrest. This unrest followed old patterns of crowd and elite mobilization but was shaped by new dynamics active at all scales, from the street to court intrigues.[61]

Three years later, the whole province revolted. The 1864 revolt, which has been studied more extensively than the 1857 and 1861 incidents, was not specifically urban; on this occasion the entire province rose up in arms against the new regime.[62] Many Christian and Jewish residents abandoned their houses in Tunis and took refuge in Malta, fearing violent attacks. Even the chief of the Jewish community left the city. Ottoman reports show that the question of property—in particular, of rights of foreigners to own it—furnished the central pretext for violence.[63] Yet the unrest must also be interpreted as a consequence of the uncertainty about the fate of the whole province, suspended between Ottoman sovereignty and foreign claims that were increasingly assuming colonial overtones. Thus, the French became increasingly unpopular.

In July 1864, the French consul sent a report to Paris voicing his concern: "People from all our vessels came to the same conclusion: children ask us whether we are British or French. If we answer French, they insult us and even throw stones at us. Children are the mirror of the truth!"[64]

7 A TAMED URBAN REVOLUTION

Saudi Arabia's Oil Conurbation and the 1967 Riots

Claudia Ghrawi

DURING THE JUNE 1967 WAR between Israel and its Arab neighbors, the urban centers of Saudi Arabia's oil-producing Eastern Province were hit by demonstrations and riots during which the protesters demanded a cessation of the supply of Saudi oil to the United States (and, indirectly, to Israel) and closing of ranks of the Arab countries against Zionism and Western imperialism. Similar reactions to the war also came from other Middle Eastern countries.[1] Reports issued by the US consulate and the Arabian American Oil Company (Aramco) in Dhahran in the immediate aftermath of the events interpreted the violent unrest in Saudi Arabia's oil conurbation as a spontaneous outburst of Arab nationalist and anti-American sentiment among Saudi oil workers and the local population. An account of the events popularized in the early 1970s by the revolutionary People's Democratic Party of Al Jazeerah Al Arabiah buttressed this reading of the 1967 riots.[2] The party account concentrates on the beginning of the Six-Day War on 5 June as the event that triggered the demonstration and riots at the US consulate building and military airfield in Dhahran, the heart of American activities in Saudi Arabia.[3]

Later historiography has adopted this version of the events, using them as a baseline from which to develop what are now familiar stereotypes of the violent nature of Middle Eastern petro-autocracies and societies.[4] Yet reading the violence that occurred in June 1967 in Saudi Arabia's oil conurbation solely in the context of regional conflict and petro-politics obscures most of the motives and rationales behind the event. As Nelida Fuccaro has recently argued, it is simplistic to approach societal contexts such as the city, company town, or oil conurbation in petro-states "as a mere accessory of state power, as an appendix to the national and global oil economies."[5] This chapter demonstrates that the riots of 1967 marked the peak of an "urban revolution," in the spirit of Henri Lefebvre's famous formulation of the concept.[6] I argue that Saudi Arabian oil development in the 1960s was accompanied by accelerated urban growth and socioeconomic transformations that were only marginally regulated by the state but largely dictated by the interests of oil extraction.[7] Furthermore, oil development was marked by the appearance of new sociopolitical actors, such as an industrial labor force and a politicized urban youth who displayed a remarkable readiness for political mobilization, which could be also translated into violent action. At the same time, the disciplinary activities of the Saudi authorities led to a tangible increase in the levels of systemic violence routinely deployed against the communities living in the oil conurbation. In the wake of the intensified regional conflict of 1966–67, this ongoing struggle assumed the form of an open rebellion against the Saudi-American petro-regime, with the Arab war effort against Israel serving as a rallying point for the mobilization of various urban groups that were already politicized.

The complex dynamics underlying this rebellion are revealed both by taking a closer look at the forms, timing, and spaces of the protests that took place in the oil conurbation throughout the 1960s, and during the 1967 riots in particular, and by focusing on the modes of suppression and deescalation of violent protest employed by the Saudi security forces and government officials. It appears that the anti-American demonstrations and rioting at the American consulate building and military airfield in 1967 were readily supported, and even partly staged, by the Saudi authorities, which attempted to redirect the demonstrators' genuine anger about corrupt and violent modes of governance toward the symbols of Western imperialism.

OIL AND THE "URBAN REVOLUTION"

At the heart of Henri Lefebvre's "urban revolution" lies the transformation of the city as a product of capitalist forces—a process he saw at work in the Paris of the 1960s. Lefebvre perceived this transformation as "the tremendous concentration (of people, activities, wealth, goods, objects, instruments, means, and thought) of urban reality and the immense explosion, the projection of numerous, disjunct fragments (peripheries, suburbs, vacation homes, satellite towns) into space." For Lefebvre, the process of the dissolution of meaningful sociopolitical urban space, and thus the end of a politically empowered urban society, is denoted by the term "implosion-explosion." It culminates in the emergence of "a shapeless town, a barely urban agglomeration, a conglomerate, a conurbation," in which people lose physical and formal access to political centers and become marginalized in dormitory towns and slums that are removed from the impenetrable islands of power and wealth.[8]

Despite their specific geographical and cultural context and conceptual embellishment, Lefebvre's ideas easily conjure up familiar images of the cities and conurbations that emerged in Middle Eastern oil-exporting countries at roughly the same time—products of a capitalist urbanism that brought to the fore issues of citizenship and civil rights that were not dissimilar from those that had sparked the violent Parisian tumults of 1968 (and Lefebvre's thinking about the urban revolution). Yet there are evident differences between Lefebvre's urban revolution and what unfolded under the aegis of oil. Unlike in late-1960s Paris, oil urbanization in the Middle East often coincided and interfered with the process of state formation. Both oil urbanization and state formation were intrinsically tied to industrial, institutional, and infrastructural developments facilitated—and often largely controlled—by foreign oil companies, more or less in collusion with Western governments. In the case of Saudi Arabia, the capacity of the Saudi state to exercise control over the key resources of oil provided the main source of political patronage and authority at both the national and local levels—a phenomenon particularly pronounced in the oil-producing areas of the Eastern Province.[9] Furthermore, in sustaining the Saudi regime, Aramco and the US administration were instrumental in the marginalization of the Saudi labor force, as discussed in vivid detail by Robert Vitalis.[10] This remarkable amalgamation of state, corporate, and foreign power shaped the contours of the Eastern Province's oil polity by radically transforming space, society, and political dynamics and by enforcing stark socioeconomic inequality and the spatial marginalization of large segments of the local populations.[11]

According to Lefebvre, the sociopolitical disparities created by capitalist urbanization must eventually become an issue of revolutionary struggle: "By 'urban revolution,'" he referred to

> the transformations that affect contemporary society, ranging from the period when questions of growth and industrialization predominate . . . to the period when the urban problematic becomes predominant, when the search for solutions and modalities unique to urban society are foremost. . . . The words "urban revolution" do not in themselves refer to actions that are violent. Nor do they exclude them.[12]

It would fall short of Lefebvre's understanding of urban revolution to reduce it to acts of violence. Yet, for him, radical struggle always also included "justified responses to state repression and corporate injustice, to the 'latent violence' of power."[13] In Saudi Arabia, oil urbanization led to the creation of segregated and tightly controlled spaces and societies. The "latent violence" inherent in the exercise of power periodically turned into the violent repression of oil workers and the local population, triggering acts of counterviolence.[14] By the 1960s, the Saudi government was readjusting its labor policies and began to formalize its paternalistic attitude toward the oil industry workforce. While the 1960s are usually considered the initial years of oil development, they are also rightly seen as marking the beginning of an important historical trajectory toward the violent consolidation of political authoritarianism.[15] The dependence of the Saudi regime on foreign economic and political interests in the oil industry made the latter a target of radical politics. Hence the Eastern Province's oil conurbation was drawn into increasingly violent struggles on various levels—industrial, urban, national, and regional.

SPATIAL AND SOCIAL GEOGRAPHIES OF OIL DEVELOPMENT IN THE CONURBATION

When commercial quantities of oil were found in Saudi Arabia's Eastern governorate of al-Hasa in 1938, a process of radical spatial, political, and socioeconomic transformation was set in motion. By the early 1940s, the American oil consortium had built three company towns at the main oil installations of Dhahran, Ras Tanura, and Abqaiq. Dhahran and Ras Tanura were located immediately on the Persian Gulf, the former five miles from the small fishing village of al-Khobar and the latter ten miles from the old oasis town of al-Qatif—one of the centers of the Eastern Province's Shia population. Abqaiq developed about fifty miles inland, approximately thirty miles from the al-Hasa oasis and the old town of al-Hufuf, another town with large numbers of Shia residents. Dhahran, the seat of Aramco's headquarters, served as a pivot for American political and military activities in the province and in the wider region. In 1944, the United States established a consulate on the road connecting Dhahran to al-Khobar. Two miles farther down this road lay the Dhahran military airfield—the base for Saudi Air Force troops and the US military training mission. Both the US consulate and the military airfield became theaters of the 1967 riots.

Following corporate hierarchy and imperatives for industrial security and social control, the three company towns were planned and built to enforce a strict separation between the professional ranks and nationalities that constituted the Aramco labor force. For reasons of security—real or merely perceived—Aramco discouraged its US employees from living among the native

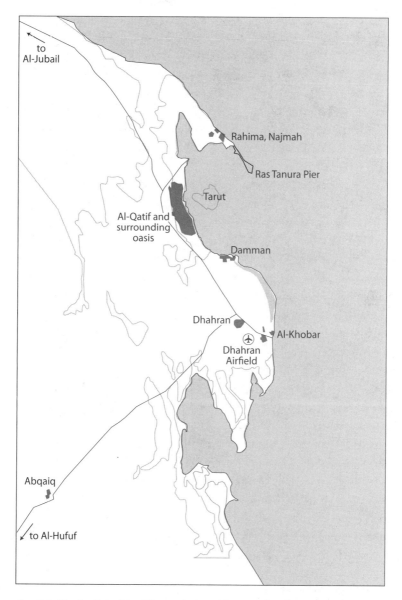

Map 7.1. The Saudi Arabian Oil conurbation. Adaptation based on geographical maps issued by the US government and the Ministry of Petroleum and Minerals, Saudi Arabia, 1958.

Labels on map:

to
Al-Jubail

Rahima, Najmah

Ras Tanura Pier

Tarut

Al-Qatif and
surrounding
oasis

Damman

Dhahran

Al-Khobar

Dhahran
Airfield

Abqaiq

to Al-Hufuf

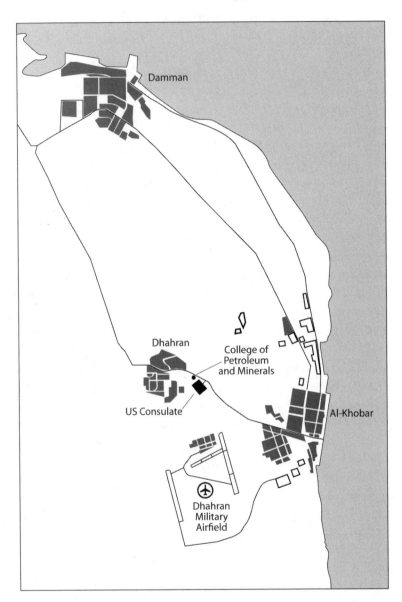

Map 7.2. Detail of Dhahran and surrounding areas. Adaptation based on cartographic material of the Arabian American Oil Company Exploration Department, 1953 and 1975.

communities. Within Aramco's fenced senior staff residential areas US employees enjoyed a living standard similar to that of middle-class suburbs in the United States. Saudi and so-called third-nation workers (Italians, Indians, and Pakistanis, as well as Palestinians, Yemenis, and other Arabs) lived in separate labor camps under lamentable conditions that became a rallying point for labor protests. As a result of Saudi labor strikes in 1945, 1953, and 1956, the Saudi government urged the company to improve the situation of its Saudi employees, though without questioning the segregation of different national groups. The labor movement was forcibly crushed with the help of the Saudi military and use of intelligence gathered by the company about the organization of the movement.[16]

By the 1960s, segregation in the three company towns was again being challenged, as increasing numbers of Saudi employees rose to higher positions in the oil company and could technically no longer be refused accommodation in the senior staff residential areas dominated by US employees. But the overtly racial pattern of accommodation, ranking, and income that had come to define social hierarchies in the oil towns in the previous decades had also created a lasting feeling of discontent among many Saudis, who felt they were regarded as inferior to—and even resented by—Americans. This discontent occasionally spilled into open aggression.[17] A consular report written in 1960, for example, relates several cases of verbal abuse, beatings, attempted stabbings, and sexual harassment involving Saudi police and members of the American airfield police.[18] Although such incidents appear infrequently in US records, they suggest the continuing disparity between the Saudi and American communities that inhabited the oil conurbation, which was deepened by mutual perceptions of cultural "otherness" and incompatibility. This and reasons of industrial security probably prompted the company and the Saudi government to develop the native towns and villages located in the vicinity of the oil installations to accommodate the growing Saudi population.

In the 1960s, the number of Saudis residing in the three company towns had declined considerably, and their character as segregated, affluent, and largely American settlements had become more pronounced. The new Saudi settlements in the oil-production area, on the other hand, had grown into middle-sized towns.[19] Al-Khobar developed into the commercial center of the oil conurbation, while another new town, Dammam, expanded on the coast ten miles north of al-Khobar. In 1953, Dammam was instituted as the capital of the newly established Eastern Province, which encompassed the old governorate of

al-Hasa with its oil installations and the vast and uninhabited Rubʿ al-Khali desert. By the end of the decade, both company-built and Saudi towns had gained
the status of municipalities under the rule of the provincial government. Attempts to decentralize the urban administration further during a short liberal
phase under King Saʿud (1953–64) were abandoned under his successor Faisal
(1964–75).[20] Political authority in the oil conurbation remained largely in the
hands of the provincial governor, the amir of the Eastern Province. He was the
regime's strongman, in charge of enforcing civil order both in the province and
inside the oil conurbation.

Another significant share of power was held by the oil company. During the
labor struggles of the 1940s and 1950s, Aramco had already assumed a leading
role in the surveillance of its workforce, which constituted a considerable por-
tion of the local population. The company's assistance in the implementation of
many of the government's modernization projects fostered the convergence between company and state paternalism, which targeted many among the urban
communities. Saudi employees who had spent many years in the service of
Aramco and had a good track record were eligible for company training, retire-
ment plans, and interest-free loans for building family homes. With the help
of the company's housing scheme, so-called labor quarters (ahyaʾ ʿummaliyya)
were established in Dammam, al-Khobar, Madinat Abqaiq, Rahima (close to
Ras Tanura), the al-Hufuf oasis, and the al-Qatif area, on land developed by
Aramco. These quarters were connected to the electric grid, fresh water, and
the sewage system—services that for many years to come were absent in large
parts of the conurbation.[21]

The uneven impact of oil on urban development accentuated social divisions within urban communities. On the one hand, oil wealth introduced new
commodities and lifestyles in the oil conurbation. Movie theaters, sports clubs,
literary and women's associations, libraries, and newspaper agencies made their
appearance in an area that twenty years earlier had been one of the poorest and
most underdeveloped in the world. Considerable development also took place
in the fields of medical care and education of Saudi children.[22] In 1963, the College of Petroleum and Minerals was founded in Dhahran. On the other hand,
due to strong differences in education and income, material and social development reached only a segment of the Saudi population. While well-trained Aramco employees, affluent commercial entrepreneurs, and some civil servants
were able to afford "modern" lifestyles, many others lagged behind.[23] This was
particularly true for the thousands of day laborers who flocked to the oil con-

urbation seeking work with Aramco or with its numerous contractor firms in order to sustain their families in more distant areas of the kingdom. In 1961, an American consular report estimated the number of Saudis seeking work at 45,000 out of a total population of 361,000. These men often had no technical training and competed in the labor market with more qualified labor migrants both from neighboring Arab countries and from South Asia.[24]

Foreign labor migrants, who were mostly employed in the fast-developing local construction industry, occasionally attracted the resentment of Saudi residents, placing further strain on peaceful cohabitation.[25] More important, in the eyes of the local authorities they posed a significant threat to internal security. Yemenis and Palestinians, in particular, came to be suspected as "troublemakers" in the second half of the 1960s—likely to cause social disorder by inciting the local population against the Saudi government, whose role in the Yemen civil war and close alliance with the United States were resented by many Saudis. The fear of politically motivated acts of sabotage against oil installations contributed to the development of the oil-production area into a high-security military zone, as the result of the deployment of the Saudi army and the National Guard, both of which became permanent features of the human geography of the oil conurbation.[26]

FROM LABOR TO URBAN STRUGGLE

The rise of Lefebvre's "urban problematic" in Saudi Arabia's oil conurbation was preceded and nurtured by the mobilization of Saudi oil workers in the first half of the 1950s and, despite the ban imposed on organized labor protests in 1956, was revived in the mid-1960s.[27] In March 1964, sailors on Aramco tugs went on strike, demanding overtime payments. As the first strike staged by company workers for several years, it instigated a new era of labor mobilization. In May 1964, a six-month boycott of Aramco's industrial cafeterias began, followed by a boycott of the company's dry ration stores. The protesters, who came from the lowest ranks of Aramco employees and were mostly Saudi citizens, demanded higher wages and the right to establish labor unions. The Saudi government identified different groups behind the organization of the 1964 boycott, including leftist activists from al-Qatif and alleged "communists" among high-ranking government officials and labor office employees. The demand for labor unions was first articulated by Saudi oil workers during the famous 1953 strike. However, unions were never established, and the Saudi state instead acted as the only legal representative of Saudi laborers through

the so-called Labor Office, which dealt with the demands of Aramco and contractor workers.[28]

Discontent in the workplace was tightly connected to the hardships of providing for basic needs at home. The high cost of living in what had by then become a booming oil area was a constant trigger of social mobilization. Among
the demands of Aramco's Saudi employees in 1964 was an increase in living
allowances to compensate for the constantly rising prices for food and other
basic commodities in the province's urban centers. The same demands were
articulated in June 1966 during workers' demonstrations in Dhahran and Ras
Tanura.[29] Aramco's workforce used the platform of labor struggle to find solutions to the most pressing problems of their daily existence, such as the all-too-
frequent electricity and water shutdowns in the Saudi towns and the problem
of transportation to and from their workplace.[30] Tactics such as walkouts and
demonstrations were also subsequently adopted as means of popular contention by residents with no connection to the oil company. Anger at the inefficiency and corruption of local administrations was a common rallying point
for urban struggles—even by groups not predisposed to civil disobedience. In
1964, several hundred policemen in Dhahran staged a walkout after the administration had failed for twenty months to grant them a pay raise. Within two
days, the protest spread into the Saudi towns, involving twenty-five hundred
men in what was reported as the first police strike in Saudi history. Growing resentment among residents was further directed against new forms of taxation
introduced by the municipalities in July 1964.[31]

Considerable political mobilization took place among young people. The
generation of secondary school and college students who had grown up under
the influence of populist Arab nationalism (most notably Nasserism) was politicized through the labor movement. The long struggle of Saudi oil workers
against company discrimination and political marginalization had produced
a number of radical political groups, such as the Union of the People of the
Arabian Peninsula (UPAP), which was founded by the former Aramco worker
and labor activist Nasir al-Said, and the Saudi branch of the Ba'th Party, which
had participated in the organization of the Aramco workers' strike in 1956.
The latter became the nucleus for other Ba'thist groups, such as the Revolutionary Students Vanguard, which until the arrest of its members in 1964
was particularly active in Dammam, and the Popular Democratic Front in
the Arabian Peninsula, which consisted largely of leftist activists and intellectuals from the local Shia population.[32] As in neighboring states, the class-

room became a major venue of political activism and a recruiting ground for underground political organizations. In January 1964, "revolutionary" leaflets containing anti-Aramco and antigovernment propaganda with strong Ba'thist overtones were confiscated from secondary schools in Dammam, al-Hufuf, and al-Qatif. Occasionally, the police arrested students who had voiced open criticism of the government.[33]

Local authorities answered ongoing political unrest with an increase in urban control and forceful repression of any signs of opposition. Thousands of unruly workers, students, and members of the Shia minority, as well as government officials deemed too critical, were imprisoned, often without charges or trials.[34] The close links between labor and urban struggles and increasingly palpable social despair enhanced the growing anxiety of the Saudi authorities about civil disorder and smoldering unrest. In 1964 this anxiety was confirmed by rising crime rates and everyday violence. With the intent of "cracking down on crime and lax public morals," the provincial government further intensified its efforts to enforce social order.[35] This expansion of the disciplinary power of the state in the oil conurbation was accompanied by an increase in symbolic violence as a preemptive measure against social unrest. By order of the provincial amir, bodily punishments of criminals were increasingly carried out in public, not within the confines of local prisons.[36] The US administration, which monitored the political and security situation in the area of oil production very closely, showed a keen interest in the growing number of cases of theft and murder and in the drastic punitive measures taken by the Saudi authorities. In August 1965, the American consulate reported the mutilation of two young thieves near the main mosque at Dammam and, one month later, the beheading of two people accused of murder in Dammam and al-Khobar. Similar reports for 1966 mention the mutilation of a thief who was caught stealing an Aramco pipe, several public incidents of sexual harassment against women, and a fatal brawl among armed taxi drivers.[37]

By the mid-1960s, the disciplinary powers of the Saudi government were further tested by its involvement in the Yemen civil war and the Arab-Israeli conflict. The government's engagement in both made the Saudi oil industry the focus of the attention of radical underground groups, with ramifications abroad.[38] In December 1966, a few months before the outbreak of the 1967 riots, the oil installations, the seat of the provincial government, and the headquarters of public security in Dammam were hit by a series of bomb explosions for which UPAP claimed responsibility. Aramco and the provincial government reacted to the threat by tightening security around the oil installations and in the town, stationing one hundred additional security guards in Dhahran alone.[39] A curfew was imposed on both Dammam and al-Khobar, while foreign Arabs were rounded up everywhere in the oil conurbation. The American consul promptly reported that the prison of al-Khobar was "full to overflowing with Yemenis."[40]

THE RIOTS OF 1967

A first crucial observation on the 1967 riots is that, prior to the outbreak of the Arab-Israeli war, the Saudi government had stripped the oil installations and surrounding area of Saudi military forces and the National Guard in order to secure the border with Yemen and the northwestern part of the country.[41] One week before the start of the war, the US consul in Dhahran expressed his concern that hostilities between Israel and its Arab neighbors might produce an "explosive local reaction" among foreign Arabs and Saudi citizens.[42] The only security forces present in the province at that moment were small numbers of National Guard, *khawiya* (armed retainers of the provincial amir who had a supplementary function as civil police), and local police forces, whom a few years earlier the Saudi director of public security in the Eastern Province had described as being in a "low state of morale and training" and "by and large illiterate, inexperienced, unappreciated and underpaid."[43]

While public opinion throughout Saudi Arabia—fed by state propaganda and backed up by high-ranking government officials—was confident that the Arabs would defeat Israel, resentment toward the United States grew in strength, fueled by articles in the Saudi and Arab press and by radio broadcasts.[44] Despite the anxiety of the US administration, the outbreak of hostilities between Israel and Egypt on 5 June did not lead to immediate disorder and unrest. Although reports about the war had reached Dhahran at noon, the day passed relatively quietly. Even the morning of 6 June, when Egyptian and Saudi radio broadcasts reported the planned US naval support for Israel, the response of the local population seemed rather subdued. The first public reaction to the war came from the students at the College of Petroleum and Minerals in Dhahran, who initiated walkouts in small groups, carrying banners and looking for a place to enlist for military service against Israel.[45] A meeting organized in Dhahran by Saudi oil workers and Aramco employees to discuss financial assistance to the Arab cause was short and peaceful. In the late afternoon, about 150 people took part in a march to the local government building in Abqaiq.

Here the head of the local religious committee spoke about the duty to fight foreign aggression against Muslim lands, with the police registering the names of Saudi war volunteers. All in all, the atmosphere in the province remained peaceful, even cheerful, and the local authorities ordered only a minor increase in security at the gates of the three company towns.

It took the whole day before the atmosphere shifted. In the evening, first signs of unrest emerged when a group of about four hundred Aramco employees assembled in the Saudi residential area of Ras Tanura and walked toward the company's main gate, demanding a cessation of oil supplies to the United States and occasionally throwing rocks. The gathering was eventually dispersed by the local police.[46] The next day, on 7 June, tension in the oil districts continued to rise after Saudi and Egyptian radio broadcasts had reported that Israeli troops had reached the Suez Canal. Demonstrations took place in Abqaiq and Ras Tanura, where the local chief of police identified a larger number of Shia from al-Qatif and Safwa among the demonstrators. In Dhahran demonstrators gathered at the north and main gates of the company compound and prevented workers on the way to their day shift from reaching the oil installations. It seems that agitation among Aramco employees was stirred by a small group of activists whose identity remains unclear. Orders to abandon the workplace were spread by telephone and word of mouth. Those who hesitated or refused to obey were threatened.

Meanwhile, the local authorities, who feared that the demonstrators would enter the Aramco compound, ordered the deployment of additional police and *khawiya* to the north and main entrances and the closure of the gates. The demonstrators then reassembled on the road heading toward al-Khobar and were joined there by several newcomers who had arrived at the scene by car and taxi. Before noon, the group of several hundred demonstrators began to march toward the US consulate, while the local authorities struggled to position their limited security forces around the oil installations, American residential areas, consulate, and military airfield. The limited presence of security forces dictated a strategy of deescalation, which was readily adopted by the provincial governor, who issued orders to refrain from using force against the demonstrators.

When the protesters arrived at the American consulate, they started shouting anti-American slogans but, according to several eyewitnesses, were not "in a particularly vicious mood." As Saudi policemen joined the crowd, the protesters began throwing rocks at the windows of the consulate building. At this point, the Saudi commander of the Dhahran military airfield, who had arrived at the consulate earlier in the day with the Dhahran chief of police, rightly assumed that the demonstrators would disperse if the American flag on the consulate roof was lowered and replaced by the Saudi flag. The whole incident passed without casualties, although a few protesters were injured while attempting to climb up to the consulate roof. When the crowd began to disperse shortly afterward, the deputy director of police sent for buses to take the demonstrating workers back to their residential areas.[47] The US consul later commented on the role of the Saudi authorities and of the commander of Dhahran's airfield: "In our opinion the assistance by the police and military in [removing] the US flag [and] hoisting the Saudi flag [was intended] to satisfy the mob by giving them symbols and encouraging them to go away. Whatever one may conclude about the courage of such action, it worked."[48]

Yet, at this point, events took an unexpected turn. Instead of all the protesters being driven back to their homes, several of them were transported, probably on a National Guard truck, to the military airfield, where its Saudi commander instructed the guards to open the main gate and allow the crowd in. Between eight hundred and two thousand protesters were admitted to the compound of the US military training mission, where they started demolishing vehicles, a cinema, a snack bar, and a bowling alley. They then proceeded to the living quarters of the US mission staff, where they broke windows, doors, and furniture. Saudi military personnel also joined in the unrest.[49] After the riot had subsided, a small number of protesters proceeded to the Aramco compound, where they entered the American residential area and started demolishing cars and looting houses. Members of the Saudi security forces stood by, simply watching, until the local governor sent around a dozen policemen into the compound. The rioters were dispersed, and some of the leaders immediately arrested.[50]

The behavior of the Saudi authorities during the riot left US eyewitnesses puzzled. What is obvious in the reports issued by Aramco and by the consulate after the disturbance is that, in the eyes of the Americans, the Saudi authorities were neither expecting such an outbreak of destructive behavior nor in a position to put an end to it. Unequivocally, the reports state that the local authorities had underestimated the rebellious mood of the protesters and that the actions of the airfield commander represented a helpless attempt to control the mob once members of the Saudi security forces had joined the riot.[51] A more persuasive interpretation of the dynamics of the event can probably be drawn from the unrest that occurred in other towns in the area. In Dammam, several thousand protesters assembled in front of the building of the provincial government, demonstrating against the role of the Saudi government in the Arab-Israeli political crisis, shouting anti-regime slogans, and damaging cars. The demonstrators were dispersed by Saudi security forces. One day after the Dhahran riot, Saudi demonstrators stoned the house of the deputy director of security for the Eastern Province in Dammam. Others tried unsuccessfully to call a general strike by attempting to persuade shop owners and entrepreneurs to close their businesses.[52]

Later reports of the mass looting of shops in al-Khobar shed light on an important dimension of the violence as linked to a new type of class animosity.[53] One account quotes a local Saudi informant: "[I]t was an eye-opener to the Saudis to see on that occasion how quickly anger and action against American institutions spread to the town of al-Khobar where scattered groups of youths roamed residential sections throwing stones at large houses which had air-conditioning units in the windows. These were Saudi houses." He concluded that the al-Khobar rioting was "a grass roots phenomenon, i.e. that urban Saudi youths are tuned in on the popular lines of neighboring Arab and European socialist states."[54] Clearly, the uneven effects of oil development had created deep fissures along class lines among the residents of the oil conurbation. Young Saudis, in particular, were angered by their inability to share the wealth offered by the Saudi-US oil bonanza as much as by the political role played by the Saudi government in the region.

Hence, during the riots that occurred in front of the US consulate in Dhahran, the local authorities were quite apprehensive of a possible expansion of the unrest toward the native towns. When the Dhahran rioting was still in full swing, representatives of the local security forces voiced the fear that the protesters might relocate from Dhahran to Dammam and al-Khobar. Rumors of an assembling crowd of five hundred protesters in al-Khobar had also reached the US consulate.[55] These concerns explain the decision of the Saudi authorities to prevent the protesters from reassembling in the native towns and instead to divert them toward the highly secure military airfield. This move can also be interpreted as an attempt to redirect the anger of the protesters toward a readily available and highly symbolic target representing US power.

The mayhem unleashed by the outbreak of popular unrest and the assaults against the local government and security forces eventually prompted the Saudi government to tighten military control over the oil conurbation. On the evening of 8 June, a few hundred National Guardsmen arrived from Riyadh and took up positions around the airfield and US consulate. Others paraded through the streets of al-Khobar and Dammam.[56] In the following weeks the local authorities "moved against anyone implicated or suspected of implication" in the riots.[57] In October the US consulate estimated that one hundred alleged rioters were under arrest, probably half of them non-Saudis.[58] US reports issued in the immediate aftermath of the riots largely attributed the unrest to radical anti-American individuals among Palestinians and Yemenis in the oil conurbation and were predominantly concerned with the events that took place in Dhahran. These accounts were silent on any signs of social conflict behind the unrest, and it remains a matter of speculation as to why two years later new interpretations appear in the reports. It might be that the mass arrests that took place in the Eastern Province immediately after the unrest and again in 1969 and 1970 drew the attention of the Americans to social tensions as motives for political opposition.

Saudi primary sources or oral accounts on the 1967 riots are difficult to obtain. One reason for this relative silence might be that the events marked the beginning of a process of political "cleanup" in the Eastern Province that lasted for years. Whereas the Ba'thist Popular Democratic Front in the Arabian Peninsula was most probably involved in the demonstrations that took place in the three company towns, it is highly doubtful that the unrest in the oil conurbation was the result merely of agitation by a few political radicals or Shia activists. These more recent interpretations convey a rather biased perspective on the events since they downplay the social component of the unrest and its geographical scope, therefore missing their real significance. It seems instead that multiple groups with no uniform political or sectarian affiliation—Saudi and foreign workers, members of the Saudi security forces, and particularly the urban youth—had triggered the rebellious events of 6–8 June.[59]

The former Saudi ambassador in London, Shaykh Hafiz Wahbah, whose son was arrested on the charge of participation in the demonstrations and possession of incriminating literature, was quoted in US consular reports as saying that the demonstrations "were begun by young schoolboys the police were too inept to control." Saudi students from the College of Petroleum and Minerals had indeed played a major role in staging the initial demonstrations in Dhahran that led to the rioting at the US consulate and military airfield and in the Aramco compound. Students who had taken part in the unrest later claimed that they had thought they were expected to do so.[60] Confronted by the Saudi government, the college dean, Saleh Ambah, categorically denied any involvement on the part of his students. But after 1967 the college was regarded as a hotbed of unrest, and in early 1970 Ambah was arrested over doubts about his loyalty to the government.[61]

. . .

By the second half of the 1960s, a culture of rebellion and disobedience had evolved among large segments of the urban communities of the Saudi oil conurbation, striving to bring forward their demands for economic welfare and political participation. Violent forms of popular protest were not only confined to strikes and demonstrations but materialized in incidents like brawls, physical aggression, and even criminal activity such as theft and robbery. While clearly a symptom of social malaise, these actions can also be read as attempts to challenge the socioeconomic imbalances created by rapid urbanization and the subjugation of urban life to the imperatives of oil extraction. The expansion of the state's capacity to control and discipline the urban population resulted in the substantial routinization of everyday violence. This violence was enacted in a variety of ways, and in some cases in collusion with the oil company through the segregation of urban communities, the presence of police and security forces, frequent mass arrests of protesters and foreigners, and the public enactment of punishments.

The riots of 1967 must be read as a popular response to dramatic socioeconomic transformations rooted in the oil boom, the violent routines of state authority, and the multiple forms of discrimination that plagued large segments of the Saudi citizenry and Arab migrant workers. This response was sparked by the traumatic events of the Arab-Israeli war and amplified by the Janus-faced policy adopted by the local authorities during the unrest. The riots were thus far from being a reflexive recourse to violence as a spontaneous expression of Arab nationalist and anti-American sentiment, as is suggested by the historiography. Furthermore, the conclusion that the rationale for the riots was located in anti-American and Arab nationalist sentiment seems far less compelling in light of the dynamics of the 1967 events. The initially peaceful protests, and the signs of agitation and intimidation of the workers by a small, unidentified group of activists, do not corroborate the interpretation of the disturbances as a spontaneous and unified act of violence. Even more intriguing is the way in which the local Saudi authorities and security forces guided the protesters toward specific US targets, thus in some respects coordinating their actions. While this certainly allowed for a controlled release of aggression, the Dhahran rioting gives the impression of a partly staged event that was able to absorb broader social discontent throughout the oil conurbation. By adopting a role of patronage during the riots and playing the card of Arab solidarity and xenophobia, the Saudi authorities succeeded, at least momentarily, in taming the disruptive effects of an ongoing urban revolution.

8 MAKING AND UNMAKING SPACES OF SECURITY

Basra as Battlefront, Basra Insurgent, 1980–1991

Dina Rizk Khoury

The [Iran-Iraq] war transformed the city into the rear lines of the conflict. A great number of people opened restaurants to feed the army. I mean, there was a new aspect of life in the city. Even the geographical space of the city changed. The most important area in Basra became Sa'd Square. All the traffic poured into Sa'd Square because it became the center for the network of transportation to the front. [War] changed the economic nature of the city and province. Important agricultural areas such as Shatt al-'Arab, Tannouma, Zreiji, and Abu al-Khasib lost their most important agricultural products. There were a million palm trees in the east of Basra. I saw with my own eyes these palm trees being destroyed. The tanks would go in a straight line and remove the trees once and for all so that the area could be prepared for fighting. Until today East Basra is not good for cultivation because of all the chemicals, some used by the Iranians and some by the Iraqis.

For me, [however,] the most disastrous war that Basra lived through was the Kuwait war. The eight-year war could not destroy the structure [bunyawiyat] of the city of Basra. Do you know the state's economic investment, the support of the Arab countries of the Iraqi government—all of this allowed the city to keep its foundation, even its infrastructure. At the moment of the defeat of the Iraqi army in Kuwait and its murder within the borders of the city of Basra, a dangerous change occurred. The city of Basra was no longer the same. The dismantling of the structure of Basra began then. The 2003 war, the last war, the war that brought the regime down, did not start for the people of Basra in 2003 but started in 1990–91. It was on that date that the basis of our urban society began to unravel.

Haytham Abbas, Amman, 2007 (author interview)

SPEAKING SEVENTEEN YEARS AFTER the end of the First Gulf War (1990–91), Haytham Abbas, a Basrene intellectual and soldier in the Iran-Iraq War, tells the story of Basra's social and cultural transformation in the last twenty-three years of Ba'thist rule as a tale of war. For him and other Basrenes, the narrative of Iraq's national wars was subsumed under that of their city. It is Basra, dubbed by the Ba'thist regime during the Iran-Iraq War the "city of cities" (*madinat al-mudun*), that suffered these wars most, as it became the rear line for the mobilization of troops and the urban headquarters of the main army corps stationed in the southern sector. Situated less than twelve kilometers from the Iranian border, it experienced steady and heavy bombardment and depopulation. From a major port city with a relatively productive agricultural region, Basra was transformed into the center for the mobilization of troops and goods, while its hinterland was destroyed by Iranian bombardment and the Iraqi government's forced removal of the population living on the eastern side of the Shatt al-'Arab waterway.

Less than eighteen months after the conclusion of the cease-fire agreement with Iran, Basra became a launching point for the invasion of Kuwait and a battleground in a much shorter and more brutal war. At its conclusion in March 1991, under heavy bombardment by US-led forces, retreating and leaderless Iraqi troops instigated an uprising that soon spread to fifteen of Iraq's eighteen provinces. As Haytham Abbas's reflections demonstrate, wartime conditions transformed the political economy and spaces of the city and its hinterland and by 1991 undermined the urban fabric of the city.

There is a rich literature on "reading" episodic violence in urban history, as the chapters in this volume attest. However, less has been written about cities at war—particularly in national wars that involve the mobilization of populations and resources.[1] Most histories of war have been written from a national rather than an urban perspective. But by privileging urban history in narrating the history of war, we are able understand the differential impacts of war on the national landscape. Wars are national, but the Iran-Iraq War was experienced differently in cities like Basra and Khorramshahr than in Baghdad, Najaf, Tehran, or Tabriz. These distinctive experiences have transformed relations between cities and their surrounding areas, redefining urban identity politics and shaping the politics of contestation to state power.[2]

The Iran-Iraq War fostered a hierarchy of citizenship within the various urban centers of Iraq. Cities and their inhabitants made claims to state resources based not only on their strategic position in the national mobilization for the war but also on the price they paid in loss of life and destruction of environment. Thus, while the state's infrastructural investment in hospitals, schools, roads, and cultural institutions provided a privileged sense of citizenship to certain cities at the expense of others, this was mitigated by the dispro-portional destruction that the war wreaked on some cities. Unlike the interior urban centers, borderland cities like Basra and Amara were centers of large mil-itary bases and thus crucial stops for troops moving to and from the front. The cultural and spatial landscape, as well as urban institutions, was more heavily militarized in Basra than anywhere else in Iraq—with the possible exception of Kirkuk, which became the center of counterinsurgency against the Kurdish na-tionalists. The war led to the end of the city's municipal autonomy over civilian matters. In its place, the Ba'th Party, the military (the Ministry of Defense), and the security and civil defense services (the Ministry of Interior) were the bu-reaucracies that came to ensure national and internal security, as they did the security of the population.

Basra suffered various, overlapping forms of violence: the human, physical, and environmental destruction of the two wars; the more systemic violence, often extrajudicial, of the various security agencies and the Ba'th Party; and the intense, episodic antigovernment violence of the uprising and its brutal sup-pression. The deployment and containment—that is, management—of these forms of violence became the primary concern of the state and the Ba'th Party. Central to the managerial vision of the state and the party was the remapping of Basra and its surrounding rural and urban areas into spaces of security. The Ba'th Party, the Ministry of Defense, the Directorate of General Security (Min-istry of Interior), and various municipal and state institutions developed a set of spatial strategies, many in response to specific security challenges. How did the security-informed spatial strategies of the Ba'th Party reconfigure the orga-nization of populations and space in Basra and its hinterland? What role did these strategies play in the organization of violence during the 1991 uprising? In answering these questions, I attempt to show how the specific forms of securi-tization and militarization of space in Basra between 1980 and 1991 shaped the spatial distribution of violence during the short-lived uprising, partly by deter-mining the targets of insurgent populations.

I use the term "security" in two senses. First—following Michel Foucault—it denotes a specific political practice of the state (distinct from sovereignty and discipline) focused on the welfare of populations as a "politics of life," exhibited by the developmental and welfare policies of a state such as pre-1980s Iraq, in the management, among many other things, of the education and health of the population. During wartime, this aspect of security was di-rected toward the preservation of life and the management of death—hence the concern with the movement of populations, the regulation of the families of martyrs, the social fallout of desertion, and the militarization of society.[3] The second meaning, involving the critical issue of the deployment and regulation of violence, concerns matters of national security and insurgency, the disciplining of insurgent or potentially insurgent populations, and the retention of territorial sovereignty—categories understood by Foucault as aspects of state power but from which he distinguished the notion of the "politics of life."[4] I borrow the phrase "spatial strategy" from Satish Deshpande, who used it to explain the national and communal spatial ordering of India. "A spatial strategy," according to Deshpande "not only unfolds in space, it is also about space—its appropriation, deployment and control."[5] It refers to the physical organization of lived spaces but also to the ideologies of spatial ordering. These might include modernizing, insurgent, sectarian strategies that inform the social life of city dwellers. As will become clear, the security practices deployed by the Iraqi state and the Ba'th Party drew on multiple spatial strategies.

FROM SPACES OF DEVELOPMENT TO SPACES OF SECURITY

Basra city is intimately linked to a cluster of rural and smaller town settlements organized, by the 1970s, into seven adjacent administrative districts.[6] Until the development of the Basra oil fields, it was the center of trade networks that linked Iraq to the Indian Ocean trade, as well as the major port of entry into landlocked Iraq. Basra's spatial grid was developed outward from its port area; by World War II this system had been greatly expanded and was linked by rail to Baghdad and the surrounding regions. Modern buildings—enhanced after 1938 by the construction of shops by the British Petroleum Company north of the port area, between the al-Ma'qal and al-'Ashar neighborhoods—formed the nucleus of what would become the center of the new city, ringed by mud huts (*sarifas*) inhabited by rural migrants to service the growing trade sector. Farther west, closer to old Basra, the British built a hospital and a prison in what would become the center of the city's modern and popular Jumhuriyya district. Outside these two areas, many of the older patterns of settlement predating World War II remained—in old Basra and the areas south of the al-'Ashar river district, where the markets were located, and in the older port and residential areas on the western side of the Shatt al-'Arab.[7]

The development of the oil industry and the expansion of the state's development projects after the mid-1950s transformed and intensified the links between Basra and its hinterland. Basra became, after Kirkuk, the main oil

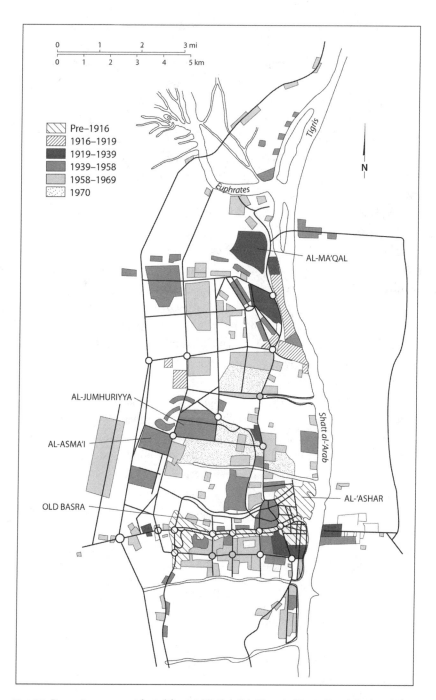

Map 8.1. Basra city, 1919–70. Adapted from Adill Abdullah Khattab, "Basra City: A Study in Urban Geography" (PhD diss., SOAS, University of London, 1972).

city in Iraq. An accelerated process of urbanization, which saw the urban population more than double between 1958 and 1965, was fueled by the migration of the rural population from the southern marshes and other rural parts of Basra. In 1957, 42 percent of the city's population consisted of *sarifa* dwellers, mostly employed in the booming construction industry. They often settled among members of their own clan on government land. The areas of Khamsa Mil, Jumhuriyya, and Hay Hussein had heavy concentrations of *sarifa* dwellers, as did other areas of the city. In addition, a survey conducted in 1970 found that more than 40 percent of Basra's retail merchants were migrants to the city.[8]

Beginning in the 1950s, the Iraqi state mapped Basra and its environs as a space for planned and controlled development. Funded by the Iraq Development Board—created under the monarchy in 1950—foreign consultants and architectural companies presented the government with plans to create modern urban spaces and ordered settlements of rural migrants, build government and commercial spaces, and regulate the flow of goods and population in and out of the city. Like other Iraqi cities, Basra became an object of the emerging field of urban planning, with the first plan presented by the British architect Max Lock in 1955.[9] Although the Lock plan was shelved, plans to develop Basra together with the towns in its hinterland and to create new towns became more ambitious after the overthrow of the monarchy and the establishment of the republic in 1958. The expansion of the state sector of the economy under the Ba'thist government that came to power in 1968 and the nationalization of the oil industry in 1972 allowed the government to embark on a grand project of development in Basra. Two aspects of the Iraqi government's development strategies are relevant to the spatial ordering of Basra and its surrounding areas.

The first was the creation of modern neighborhoods to supplant the haphazard manner of previous patterns of settlement—particularly by *sarifa* dwellers. The government's attention turned to development projects in the western, northern, and port areas of the city and on major road and rail links between Basra and Baghdad and the south. Plans began in the mid-1950s, and by 1958 the Ministry of Housing had developed a residential area for poor government employees on the western fringes of the city, adjacent to the densely populated neighborhoods of Jumhuriyya.[10] By 1966, close to eleven thousand housing units had been built west of the old residential areas of the port. In addition, the sparsely populated al-Haritha neighborhood, in the northern part of the city, was included in the development plans of the municipality. By 1970, its population had more than tripled since 1957, to reach twenty-eight hundred.[11]

The strategic al-Maʻqal and al-ʻAshar areas in the vicinity of the port and close to a highway were designated for higher-income housing. The University of Basra was established on the eastern side of the Shatt al-ʻArab in 1965, turning what had been an area inhabited by *sarifa*-dwellers into a modern neighborhood.[12] By 1970, several new commercial areas developed alongside the older ones. Al-Maʻqal, al-ʻAshar, and al-Jumhuriyya were the modern business and commercial districts. Located in the midst of a thick network of roads, al-ʻAshar displaced old Basra both as the new administrative center of the city and as its central business district. The corniche in the al-ʻAshar area was the center of high-end entertainment, with several casinos along the river and across from the university. By 1980 the two major modern hotels in the city—the Sheraton and the Novotel—were located here.[13] Municipal and private buses, as well as taxis, conveyed passengers to other parts of the city and other areas of Iraq.[14]

The second aspect of the development was the program instituted after the Baʻth Party came to power to develop industry in the city and its hinterland and to expand the relatively small towns in the various districts of the province. The largest paper manufacturer in Iraq was established in the northern suburb of al-Haritha, a cement factory was built in Umm al-Qasr, and plans to create industrial cities to manufacture steel and petrochemicals in Khor al-Zubayr, between Basra and Umm al-Qasr, had been developed by 1974. Zubayr, Umm al-Qasr, and Abu al-Khasib began to compete with Basra, attracting settlers involved in servicing the various industries.[15] An exponential increase in trade to service the development projects in Iraq led the government to expand existing port facilities and build new ones. The port of Umm al-Qasr became the main port for oil exports. In addition, the government built the al-Bakr, al-Khafja, and al-ʻAmiq port facilities. Between 1957 and 1970, industrial production in Basra Province increased by 202 percent.[16]

By the outbreak of the Iran-Iraq War in 1980, the state's development and modernization projects had expanded Basra's municipal boundaries, transformed a number of its satellite towns into modern centers of trade and industry, and led to the extensive urbanization of the province. More important for subsequent developments were two interrelated processes. The first was the transformation of Basra into the premier city of Iraq—second only to Baghdad. This represented a critical aspect of the government's attempt to subsume

Basra's distinctive features as a port town into its national project and narrative of development. With the outbreak of the war with Iran in 1980, the Iraqi government had to jettison the developmental project and its attendant narrative in favor of a narrative presenting Basra as a crucial space for the nation's security—the battlefront that protected the whole of Iraq from the threat of an enemy intent on seeking to undermine and sectarianize the Arab national character of Basra. In the narrative of the war propaganda that emerged, Basra represented the gateway into Iraq, and its population the vanguard of a national struggle to maintain the modernity and Arab character of the country.

The ideology that informed the spatial strategies of the government was no longer one of development, with its attendant notions of security as a "politics of life," but one of spatial ordering—now focused primarily on the disciplining of populations and spaces. As will become clear, the government's rhetoric constructing Basra as the premier city in a national war was undermined by the practices of the Ba'th Party on the ground. Many of the spatial strategies of the party turned Basra's neighborhoods and outlying areas into spaces of security and were informed by the vision of Basra as a space facing the dual threat of Iran and a potentially insurgent and "lawless" population. This rhetoric of insecurity identified Basra as distinct from other urban spaces in Iraq.

The second development resulting from new settlement patterns was the processes of politicization that marked various sections of Basra and its satellite cities. Data that might allow a mapping of political affiliation by neighborhood are sparse, but a rough outline may be drawn from the analysis of the records of the General Directorate of Security—particularly from school registers detailing the political affiliations of matriculating male students in Basra Province for 1987–88. This year was marked by the depopulation of the city of Basra as a result of Iranian bombardment and the growth of its satellite towns of al-Madina, Zubayr, and al-Qurna. The records suggest that there were much higher percentages of students with family members belonging to the outlawed Shia Islamic al-Da'wa and communist opposition parties in these towns than in Basra city. It is not easy to say whether such patterns of political affiliation were a product of the resettlement of politicized Basrenes away from the city to its safer satellites farther north and west; but it is important to keep in mind that links between the city and these satellite towns were reinforced by clan networks of migrants that often defined political affiliation—networks that might explain patterns of participation in the 1991 uprising and the location of the more intense outbreaks of violence deployed by the rebels.[17]

SPACES OF SECURITY AND SPACES OF LAWLESSNESS

On 25 March 1985, the Ministry of Defense sent a letter to the Presidential Office asking that the leadership consider the prospect of forcibly removing the population of the villages and towns east and west of the Shatt al-'Arab to create a line of defense against Iranian forces. The Presidential Office called for the formation of a committee including the minister of the Region of Autonomous Rule (a ministry created in 1974 to administer the Kurdish areas); the leadership of the Southern Bureau of the Ba'th Party; a representative of the Directorate of General Security; and the leadership of the East Tigris Command, which encompassed the three army corps stationed in the southern military sector. Headed by the provincial governor of Basra, the committee planned to displace more than twelve thousand Iraqis inhabiting areas east and west of the Tigris, extending from the town of 'Uzayr, in Maysan Province, to the marshes of the city of al-Qurna at the mouth of the Shatt al-'Arab, in Basra Province.

By August 1985, the displacement (*tarhil*) of the population had been completed, and they were settled in the province of Dhi Qar. The physical landscape of the twenty-one villages and other rural locations that were evacuated was also transformed. The villages and their date groves were destroyed, and their marshes were drained. The destruction was not only physical—the villages also disappeared as administrative units in the census and for the purposes of government bureaucracy. In other words, they were both physically and administratively eradicated. In their place, the government erected a line of defense in a forlorn attempt to save the sixteen million dinars' worth of oil and electricity generators that fed the province of Maysan and the city of al-Qurna.[18] The 1985 operation in the southern sector marked a systematic effort on the part of the government to create a *cordon sanitaire* around the southern border areas similar to the one it had created in the Kurdish north during the 1970s.[19] Over the following three years the process of destruction and displacement extended farther south, to East Basra, as Iranian shelling and urban warfare wreaked havoc on the southern borderlands.

Unlike in the 1985 operation, the Iraqi government rarely planned a systematic process of displacement and resettlement.[20] Rather, the Ba'th Party, and the military and security agencies in charge of the southern sector, followed a reactive and piecemeal policy in responding to the shelling of Basra's eastern hinterland. They carried out military campaigns against the borderland towns and villages that were suspected of harboring deserters and saboteurs without removing or resettling the population. The result was that towns like Tannouma, Abu al-Khasib, and Fao became uninhabitable: their built environment was destroyed, and they were emptied of their populations.[21] By the end of the war, the smaller towns that had dotted the banks of the Tigris and Euphrates Rivers, as well as the towns around the Shatt al-'Arab, which had accounted for some 84 percent of the province's administrative units, had declined to a 45 percent share. Except for the larger settlements, few regained their existence as towns. Their populations returned to their lands in the 1990s but were left without government administrative offices and infrastructural development.[22] Many of their inhabitants migrated to safer towns within the province.

The process of deurbanization in some areas of the province and in Basra itself was offset by the demographic growth of urban areas that swelled with the influx of populations from eastern Basra and Fao. By 1987, Basra's population had declined by 30 percent from its 1977 numbers, while those of towns north and southwest of the city, including Zubayr, Umm al-Qasr, al-Madina, al-Qurna, and al-Dayr, increased between 25 and 150 percent.[23] The mid-Euphrates Bureau of the Ba'th Party reported that it had settled some 36,000 Basrene families—consisting of 226,127 individuals—in the region between 1986 and 1987.[24] Although no studies are available that allow us to map which parts of Basra were depopulated, it is safe to assume that those closest to the port area, around al-Ma'qal and al-'Ashar, suffered most—as did the area around the eastern part of the Shatt al-'Arab, around the University of Basra. With the decline in trade and oil production, the areas of al-Ma'qal and al-'Ashar were transformed into centers of the war economy. The heaviest concentration of hospitals was located in neighborhoods on the southwestern shores of the Shatt al-'Arab. Ma'qal Airport became a locus of the movement of goods servicing the war economy. The city's commercial activity moved west and south, around Sa'd Square and the Jumhuriyya district, and north toward al-Qurna.

Management of the dislocation of populations and reorganization of urban life—and the maintenance of a measure of social peace during the mobilization of hundreds of thousands of troops throughout the province and the city—became major undertakings for the Ba'th Party's Southern Bureau. Particularly after 1984, when Iraq's defenses began to erode along the length of its border with Iran, the Iraqi regime increasingly allocated to the Southern Bureau, headquartered in the city of Basra, the task of managing the social and security repercussions of the war. Thus, not only did the Southern Bureau ensure the social welfare of soldiers and martyrs' families and coordinate civil defense; it was also tasked with the control of desertion from the army and the security implications of the informal economy that developed to service deserters and soldiers. The Southern Bureau had a dual role: it was a social organization tasked with managing the security of the population and a security organization responsible for disciplining a population at war. It became an arm of the state. Its cadres coordinated with different state agencies, sometimes supplanting some of their functions, monopolizing the right to speak and act with the authority of the state in areas affected by the war, and sometimes leading campaigns to pursue deserters, thus supplanting the role of the military police.

The impact of the Southern Bureau's interventions is difficult to overestimate: it coordinated with the various media organizations to ensure the movement of the hundreds of journalists who flocked to the city to cover the war; its leadership cadres helped put in order the work of various popular organizations, from youth, labor, and peasant federations to the General Federation of Iraqi Women; its various committees, many set up to help manage the

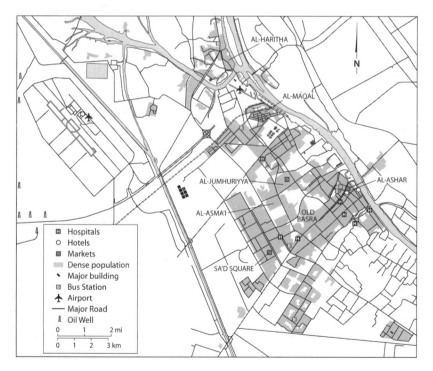

Map 8.2. Basra city. Adapted from US government map, http://www.lib.utexas.edu/maps/middle_east_and_asia/basrah_2003.jpg.

war effort, counted the dead, missing, and prisoners of war; it organized propaganda campaigns and monitored dissent.[25] The head of the Southern Bureau, Mizban Khidr al-Hadi, began the reorganization of the Ba'th Party in the
south. He established more divisions and subdivisions in townships and rural
areas and ensured that the party cadres inserted themselves as mediators between the population and the various institutions of the state. For example,
Ba'th Party cadres spent three months in 1984 visiting rural and urban branches
in the south—partly to monitor the war mobilization of the residents of towns
and villages and partly to ensure that the various administrative branches of the
state were carrying on their services efficiently, particularly when it came to
the management of agricultural production and municipal services in smaller
towns.[26] In 1986–87, when the Abu al-Khasib, Tannouma, and Shatt al-'Arab
areas experienced heavy Iranian shelling, the local party cadres liaised with the
civil defense brigades under the control of the Ministry of the Interior and produced their own reports on losses in life and property.[27]

But it was in its role as a security organization concerned with the disciplining and control of populations—and in the particular spatial strategies it
deployed—that the Ba'th Party had most impact on the targets and patterns
of rebel activity that developed during the 1991 uprising. Two spatial strategies
were particularly significant: mapping the various neighborhoods and schools
of the cities and towns of Iraq into spaces of security; and mapping Basra's
spaces, including its satellite towns and rural hinterlands, as spaces of threat,
insurgency, and lawlessness. In the latter case, the party and the security apparatus developed a set of practices, often extrajudicial and violent, in response to
challenges from within the population to war mobilization.

The outbreak of the Iran-Iraq War provided the leadership of the Ba'th
Party with the support and encouragement of the regime and thus with the opportunity to undertake the systematic Ba'thification of social life and politics.
Although the process had begun in the aftermath of the Ba'thist seizure of power
in 1968, its direction and reach were contested both from within the party and by
other parties, including the Iraqi Communist Party and the Kurdish Democratic
Party. Until 1978, when the politics of the National Front was finally put to rest
and the Iraqi Communist Party and the Da'wa Party were declared illegal—and
belonging to them a crime punishable by death—the popular organizations and
professional syndicates remained a bone of contention between the Ba'th and the
other parties. The process of Ba'thification was from the beginning viewed as a
question of security.

In 1979, when Saddam Hussein came to power, the Ba'th Party and the General Directorate of Security began coordinating the process of "securing" Iraq. For the present purposes, the most significant aspect of this process was the mapping of Iraqi cities, towns, and villages into spatial grids in which individuals were located within a network of family, school, and political affiliations and their threat to security was assessed. One available example of such a mapping is a series of school surveys (collected in registers) of matriculating male students in middle and high schools undertaken by the Ba'th Party and by the Directorate of General Security. The surveys, which produced similar if not identical information, were clearly undertaken after coordination between the security apparatus and the Ba'th Party and were intended to remind students and their families of the dual system of monitoring to which they were subject.

These registers provide a window into the ideology of security underpinning the spatial strategies of the Ba'th Party. The twinning of documentation and control was central to the security of the Ba'th in Basra, as elsewhere in Iraq. The registers were designed as information banks on students as potential recruits for the party and for various Ba'thist state institutions (mostly having to do with security and propaganda). The categories developed in these surveys indicate several strategies of control. Perhaps the most obvious is the space of the school itself, which became a zone of both threat and promise, of both surveillance and mobilization. Included in the categories of these registers was information about the birthplaces of an individual's father and grandfather, the reputation of the family, and any political affiliations, including the family's political leanings. In a section devoted to commentary, the surveys state the number of family members who were martyred in the war, executed for belonging to other political parties, belonged to outlawed political parties, or had deserted or become prisoners of war.[28]

The registers point out the level of coordination between the Ba'th Party and various state institutions—most notably the Ministry of Education but also the Directorate of General Security, which provides information on the family's political affiliations and the criminal records of its members. At the level of the neighborhood, the headman was the linchpin of this information system. Thus, for example, family reputation was tied to the ability of the headmen to provide information on such matters as the virtue or lack thereof of the women in the household. Unlike statistical surveys, these registers mapped the individual and his family: they individuated rather than abstracted. They were meant to locate each student within a particular spatially conceived grid—within a school, a neighborhood, and a home. They were intimate and invasive particularly because these spaces were conceived of as spaces of threat.

The second spatial strategy evident in these registers was the colonization of the space of neighborhoods—a colonization marked by a tension between, on the one hand, the desire of the Ba'th Party and the security services to manage the war in all its aspects, and, on the other, the unplanned and uncontrollable social realities created by the movement of goods and populations in the spaces of Basra and its surrounding area. This colonization took two forms: the ideological inscription of Ba'thist culture onto different spaces and their militarization. Both of these processes developed to contain threats and create support and could be challenged at any moment by the uncontrollable fallout of the war itself. A state of persistent eventfulness permeated the lives of neighborhoods: processions were organized by Ba'th Party divisions, there were perpetual celebrations, and posters of Saddam Hussein were plastered everywhere—a strategy clearly employed by the Southern Bureau as a security measure.[29]

Hazim Najm, a resident of the eastern side of the city, near the University of Basra, tells the story of growing up within the Ba'thist youth movement—of going on trips, dutifully recorded by Ba'th Party cadres in the school, to clear areas of Shatt al-'Arab for the tanks that would roll into Baghdad Street in Basra city. He remembers being taken to the city's Jumhuri Hospital to help with the wounded coming from the front. He also recites the adaptation by women of a chant sung in *husayniyya*s (Shia houses of mourning), as part of the ceremonies in remembrance of the martyrdom of Imam Hussain, to glorify the martyrs and fighters of the Iran-Iraq War:

> First woman: My son is a fighter in the army.
> Second Woman: My son is the lion of the battle.
> First Woman: My son is the thundering deluge.
> Second Woman: Ay by God we saw his power.[30]

Party cadres created meeting places (*madhayif*) to combat, in the words of the head of the Southern Bureau, the unsettled "psychological" situation in Basra and to avoid the chaos and "defeatism" that had ensued after the fall of Muhammarah (Khorramshahr) in 1982.[31] These *madhayif* generated popular support for the war and were viewed by the residents and the organizers as a collective investment in the fight. Hazim Najm remembers in particular the *madhayif* that were set up to feed and welcome families who had traveled to Basra to inquire about their sons on the front and those set up to welcome the inhabitants of Fao who had been forced to evacuate. Posters glorifying the Ba'th, the war, and the leadership competed with black banners with Quranic verses that graced the homes, mosques, and neighborhoods that had lost martyrs to the war. Thus, in addition to sanctioned images of the war, these black banners could act as reminders of its costs and become—as they did during the uprising—a locus of dissent.[32]

As important as the visible transformation of the organization of public rituals was the militarization of Basra's neighborhoods. The offices of the Directorate of General Recruitment and of the Ba'th Party were increasingly transformed into security offices, manned by cadres who took turns to monitor the "peace" of the city. The Ba'th Party recruited, armed, and trained the Popular Army as the party's militia. A critical aspect of its claim that it was part of the military mobilization for the war effort was its ability to recruit "volunteers" from the schools and neighborhoods of the city and its satellite towns. Thus, between 1985 and 1987, the Southern Bureau trained 23,689 men and women in the province of Basra to carry arms.[33] In addition, its security committees policed various neighborhoods in the city—particularly those deemed to pose a potential threat. Najm remembers the fear that the security committee's patrols elicited among members of the Shia community who had relatives associated with the Da'wa or whose relatives had deserted from the army. Sandbags and security checkpoints became a common feature of Basra's streets after 1986.[34]

The expansion in the party's role, its positioning at the intersection of various state institutions and the population at large, and its centrality to the mobilization and security efforts of the state were fueled by an exponential increase in its organizational reach. Between 1985 and 1987, the Southern Bureau added four divisions and thirteen new subdivisions, amounting to a total of ninety-eight subdivisions.[35] This expansion and multiplication of functions created a number of problems for the party. Chief among them were the recruitment and promotion of party cadres into leadership positions and the identification of enough cadres to carry out its disciplinary, surveillance, information-gathering, and mobilization functions. Thus, expansion was circumscribed—and sometimes defined—by the threat of loss of control, of lawlessness. This was particularly true in the city and its hinterland, which were subject to perpetual upheavals, troop and ordnance movement, and the challenges in an area that was virtually a battlefront.

In his report on the activities of the Southern Bureau between 1985 and 1987, Mizban Khidr al-Hadi reassured the General Secretariat of the party that each

of the ninety-eight subdivisions of the Southern Bureau had formed committees to collect and archive information for a number of categories of people
(martyrs, deserters, prisoners of war, the missing) to facilitate control (*ihkam
saytara*) and to integrate (*isti'ab*) the "negative and positive" social repercussions of the war. After the Iranian attack on Fao in February 1986, the bureau
and its various divisions and subdivisions had moved with "exceptional speed
and determination" to deal with the situation, calling for more meetings and
marches. The battles that ensued, particularly in 1986 and 1987, had resulted in
the flooding of Basra and its immediate area with deserters from the army, leading to a spike in robberies. The party organization (the Committee to Pursue
Deserters) was given the authority to apprehend deserters and execute those
who attempted to flee. Party cadres also visited the families of deserters, pressuring them to surrender their relatives. The party was successful in apprehend-
ing 7,832 deserters, while 58,984 others had surrendered to party cadres, and
more than 600 were either killed or executed in pursuit. In total, the party was
successful in inducing some 67,522 deserters to return to the armed forces.[36]

Al-Hadi's report highlights the multiple disciplinary roles that the party
played in maintaining security and the enormous scale of the problems it faced
in controlling the movement of men during the last two years of the war. A complex intelligence network linked the party cadres' military office at the front, the
various army corps, and the local cadres who created information banks on deserters and their families.[37] While not all deserters were from the south, many
remained in Basra and its environs. In its attempts to deal with this lawlessness,
the Ba'th Party itself became an organization in which the suspension of law—
in the form of its arrogation of extrajudicial powers—became the norm.[38]

The priorities of both the party and the state increasingly revolved around
questions of security: the pursuit of deserters, the control of illicit trade, and the
suppression of insurgent populations in border areas, particularly those who
had fled to Iran or fought alongside Shia opposition parties funded by Iran. To
that end, it ran counterinsurgency campaigns in the eastern areas of Basra and
Maysan Provinces and provided intelligence on links between urban residents
and their families in rural areas. In towns settled by the newly displaced, particularly al-Madina and al-Dayr, neither the party nor the other institutions of
state could answer to the social needs of the population. Thus, despite the massive presence of the state in Basra and its hinterland—in the form of the military, the security forces, and the Ba'th Party—a sense persisted that Basra was
living on the edge of lawlessness, and anxieties about social and political break-

down continued to mark the reports of Southern Bureau heads to the General Secretariat of the party.

In a letter from the Ministry of the Interior addressed to the party's general secretary, the Directorate of Criminal Affairs requested that the Southern Bureau's security committees monitor and arrest the deserters and other criminals who gathered in the gardens along the Tigris and frequented bars and casinos. Some of these soldiers were on military furloughs, and their apparent fraternization with deserters created an atmosphere of chaos.[39] Equally troubling— even to those within the Ba'th Party—was the increasing lawlessness of the militias and various ad hoc security personnel among the Ba'th themselves. In that same letter, it is related that the security personnel of the party had shot at a soldier who was on an approved furlough and that his Ba'thist relative had raised the question of whether it was lawful for the party's security man to shoot or whether the matter should have remained within the purview of the security personnel from the Ministry of the Interior.

Lawlessness was engendered by the massive influx of men into the city and the reconfiguration of its spaces. Sa'd Square replaced the port area as the main transport hub for soldiers coming by bus and other means to the southern front from periods of leave. Around the square and the area of the train station in the western part of the city, an informal economy developed based on the sale of goods. Cheap consumer products smuggled from Kuwait through Zubayr, often sold from one soldier to another, created an underground network of smugglers with the tacit support of the military.[40] Certain hotels on Jumhuriyya and Corniche Streets were transformed into hubs of the national and international news outlets, attracting an international group of journalists and their facilitators. Soldiers seeking prostitutes, looking for bars, or hoping to buy fake identity cards that would allow them some extended leave found their way to Bashar Street.[41] Deserters, who often congregated in abandoned spaces, found work in this informal sector and were sheltered in a number of safe houses in the city. Like all frontline cities at war, Basra saw its economy transformed, along with the spatial hierarchy of its neighborhoods. The inability of the state and the Ba'th to manage this transformation as effectively as they had done before the war might explain the state of lawlessness.

The unforeseen effects of war mobilization only partially account for the spike in violence and the militarization of social life in Basra. The disciplinary practices of the Southern Bureau played an equally significant role. The violence of the 1991 uprising, the targets chosen by the rebels, and the chaotic manner in

which events unfolded can be understood as results of the spatial strategies deployed by the Ba'th and the various security agencies of the state to deal with the
threats of lawlessness and insurgency. The rebels were also able to take advantage of the massive and disorderly withdrawal of troops from Kuwait.

BASRA AND ITS HINTERLAND INSURGENT

> *I ran to the armored vehicle with my friend. He said, "Let us go to Basra, and I will
> take you to your grandfather's house so we can get some food and water." When we
> got there, to Sa'd Square, which is right after Khalid Bridge [the point of entry of
> retreating troops from Zubayr], we saw that the streets were empty. Weren't there
> Iraqis in the streets of Basra who in our war with Iran had madhayif [meeting places]
> and tents that cooked for us? . . . The people in Basra province used to salute the Iraqi
> army and the Republican Guard. . . . I said to myself: Is it possible that they don't
> know that we have withdrawn from Kuwait and we are tired and hungry? I asked
> my friend this, and he said the situation in Basra was worrisome. Let us go back to
> our divisions on Khaled Bridge. We were given an order to withdraw to al-Qurna.
> On our way to al-Qurna we were ordered (to attack rebels) by Iyad al-Rawi [General
> Rawi, head of the Republican Guard divisions that put down the uprising], who told
> us that there was an intifada in Basra. . . . My friend was from Basra, a Shia from
> al-Jumhuriyya neighborhood. . . . He went to check on his family. . . . We got the
> order that we must hit Basra—not only Basra but all those [areas] that contained the
> people of the intifada. They were in al-Jumhuriyya, Zubayr, Sa'd Square, al-'Ashar,
> and in many areas in Basra.*
>
> **Sabir Farah, July 2007, Amman (author interview)**

The 1991 uprising is said to have started on 2 March, when a soldier shot at
Saddam Hussein's picture in Sa'd Square. It is perhaps an iconic image and a
telling narrative of the "beginning" of an uprising that had come at the end
of a devastating retreat by the army, in a square that the Iran-Iraq War had
turned into a hub of a militarized city. The choice of the target—a symbol of the
colonization of space by the regime—and the instigator of the act of rebellion
reflect the nature of the uprising. Initiated by soldiers, supported by residents of
the city, and drawing on clan networks beyond its borders, it marked Basra as
the city of the uprising. It was violent, chaotic, and without direction. Unlike a
number of other areas, Basra itself never completely fell to the rebels, although
they had much better success in controlling its suburbs and satellite towns for a
few days. Three days after the start of the uprising, Ali Hasan al-Majid directed
the Second and Third Army Corps in the process of violent pacification. Headquartered in Sa'd Square, the army undertook the suppression of the rebellion
in areas extending from al-Haritha in the northern part of the city to al-Qurna

and the eastern part of the Shatt al-'Arab.[42] Days later, the city and its suburban areas had been brought under the tenuous control of the regime.

Although short-lived, the continued fighting in certain areas of the city—even after the regime had reestablished control over the central areas of Sa'd Square and the Jumhuriyya neighborhood—highlights the links between Basra's position as a battlefront city, the security strategies of the regime and the party, and the intensity of rebel activity. From Sa'd Square, the rebellion quickly spread to the northeastern suburbs of the city, particularly to al-Haritha and al-Dayr—both close to military camps where soldiers and their families went to demand food—and threatened to take over the camps.[43] In the al-Ma'qal neighborhood the rebels—mostly soldiers and residents—attacked the brigade of the Republican Guard after it had bombed a mosque to which citizens had fled to avoid the fighting.[44] So violent was the suppression of the rebellious al-Ma'qal neighborhood that people talk of bodies floating down the river and of mosques being filled with the bodies of the dead.[45]

The city itself seems to have been subdued fairly easily. The suburban areas and the satellite towns, however, were more difficult to bring under control. A complete breakdown of state control, coupled with near-apocalyptic narratives of violence, pervades the recollections of men who lived through the uprising's early days in the Basra area. Bands of men who had confiscated military ordnance dominated the roads out of the city, particularly in the areas of al-Qurna, while barefoot soldiers sold their guns for food. Rebels and their extended kin stormed military bases in the south of the country asking for information about their loved ones who had not returned from Kuwait. All communication lines were severed. No telephone, television, or radio communications existed to inform people of the military and political situation.[46] The disintegration of the social fabric that held Basra and its satellite communities together is reflected in Sabir Farah's recollection of the beginning of the uprising as a time of violence and of the threat of violence—and of an almost incomprehensible suspension of relations between soldiers and the city that had supported them during the Iran-Iraq War.

But some patterns emerge despite the chaotic nature of the uprising. These have to do with the targets of the rebellion and the levels of participation in it. Not surprising, perhaps, was the targeting of visual representations of the Ba'thist regime and its leader and of exaltations of the war. As parts of the city and satellite towns returned to the control of the regime, the military and Ba'thist cadres—now severely eroded by mass defections from their lower ranks—restored visual

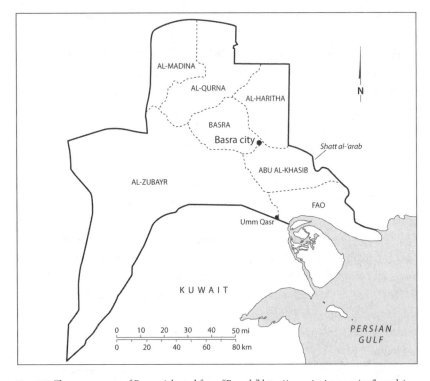

Map 8.3. The governorate of Basra. Adapted from "Basrah," http://www.jauiraq.org/gp/basrah/.

representations of the regime, particularly images of Saddam Hussein. The institutions of the Ba'th Party, and of the military and security agencies, were systematically emptied of their contents. So devastating was the result of such attacks
that, within weeks of the restoration of order, the Ba'thist security services and
the Directorate of General Security felt compelled to undertake the collection
of new data—particularly on the participants in the uprising and those Ba'thist
cadres who had failed to defend the regime.

It is instructive to consult the reports of Ba'th Party cadres on the 1991 uprising, as well as surveys conducted by the Directorate of Security and the Ba'th
Party of the male matriculating secondary school student population, which
also entailed an assessment of the level of participation of their families months
after the suppression of the revolt. The surveys indicate the link between state/
Ba'th practices during the Iran-Iraq War, the distribution of rebel activities during the uprising, and the state's policies of punishing families of those it deemed
a national security threat. In the province and city of Basra, these policies af-

fected the families of both Communist and Daʻwa Party members, the families of prisoners of war suspected of working for the Iranians or recruited into the Iran-financed Badr Brigade, and the families of deserters. In the few chaotic days of the uprising, rebels from the Basra suburbs and the surrounding region descended on the city and with other Basrenes attacked the offices of the local recruitment organization of the Baʻth Party and of the security apparatus. Clearly, they were targeting spaces that represented the power of the state and the party.[47]

The reports and surveys highlight the correlation between the spatial distribution of violence and the security practices of the party and the state during the Iran-Iraq War. In areas of the city and its hinterland that had suffered most dislocation during the war there was a link between the targets of violence and patterns of participation. Thus, the town of al-Madina, to the north of the city, which had more than doubled its population during the war as a result of the influx of displaced populations and had suffered the heaviest losses of life during the war, had the largest number of rebels recorded by the Directorate of General Security.[48] The sources tell us little about the targets of the rebels, nor is it clear which family or neighborhood networks they mobilized. But it is clear that some of the participants must have been from the displaced families that had lost their livelihood and been subject to counterinsurgency measures instituted in the eastern areas of Basra.

. . .

To write the history of cities at war is to move from a national narrative to one focused on urban communities. This shift allows us to understand the disparities in the ways that various Iraqi communities experienced the Iran-Iraq War and the First Gulf War. The military, the security apparatus, and the Baʻth Party created some of the conditions that transformed social life as they attempted to manage the unforeseen consequences of these wars. But the wars—the shelling, the mobilization of troops, and the larger and often less controllable movement of people and goods across the south—created conditions that could not be easily managed. Certainly, the militarization and securitization of southern border cities like Amara, Basra, and to a lesser extent al-Nasiriyya, had a significant impact on the sense of grievance of their citizens about both the wars and the regime. Just as important, the wars brought tens of thousands of internally displaced people into the cities, helping to feed the 1991 rebellion against the government. The Iran-Iraq and the First Gulf Wars were national wars but also wars of regions and their cities. The differential impacts of war and of state practices led to a drastic reworking by the military and the Ba'th of the organization of social life, of the urban landscapes of Basra, and of a number of urban areas in southern Iraq.

It is in the context of the sustained and massive dislocation of the violence of war, and of state and party practices designed to secure and manage this dislocation, that the episodic and chaotic nature of the 1991 uprising needs to be read. The spatial strategies devised by the state and the party to securitize and control the lawlessness generated by the transformation of Basra into a militarized space since 1980 contributed in no small measure to defining the targets of the rebels. The chaotic and intense violence of the uprising and the fact that it remained leaderless and was easily suppressed are results of the erosion of the organization of civilian social life and municipal underpinnings of the city and its environs as they were transformed into battlefronts.

EVENTFUL RUPTURES

Order and Disorder

Part 4

9 A PATRIOTIC UPRISING

Baghdadi Jews and the Wathba

Orit Bashkin

A COMMITTED COMMUNIST, Iraqi Jewish bard David Semah dedicated one of his Arabic poems to the people of Baghdad. Semah was living in Israel at the time, yet he felt it necessary to comment on the revolutionary zeal of the people of his old hometown. He therefore wrote a poem in memory of the Iraqi Wathba (Leap), a name given to massive waves of urban rioting in Baghdad during the winter of 1948. The poem, "The First Wathba" (*Al-Wathba al-ula*), celebrated Baghdad as a city of rebels and a city belonging to a nation (*umma*) suffering from perpetual oppression. The city's rebels, however, did not fear death, thus providing the Eastern homeland (*watani bihadha al-sharq*) with a radical model.[1] The poem can be seen as an attempt to commemorate the urban heroism of Baghdad in the Israel of the late 1950s and to remind Semah's Jewish and Palestinian readership of its significance.

Thinking about the momentous importance of the Wathba to Iraqi Jews, I try in this chapter to describe Jewish participation in the Wathba and its importance for Iraqi Jews, for the Iraqi left, and for our understanding of the connections between urban violence and sectarian and minority identities. I argue that the urban violence that took over the city during the Wathba had cemented the loyalty of Iraqi Jews to their city and its people. During these days, Jews positioned themselves, albeit very carefully, against the state and with the Iraqi people. Moreover, the Wathba helped establish the influence of the Iraqi left among radical young Jews—most notably students. It also enabled the Jewish community in its entirety, during a time when Judaism was increasingly equated with Zionism, to distance itself from Zionism and stress its commitment to domestic Iraqi concerns.

The Wathba was an outcome of the noticeable changes in the urban landscape of Baghdad during the 1940s. Iraq at the time was a constitutional monarchy whose pro-British elites relied on support from landed and tribal elites. Opposition to the ruling household, the Hashemite monarchy, and to its networks of supporters came from two directions: the left, which included the Social Democrats and the illegal Iraqi Communist Party (ICP), and the ultranationalist camp, which included proto-Ba'thists, members of al-Istiqlal (Independence) Party, and other pan-Arab radicals.

After World War II ended, Baghdad expanded. The migration of poor tribesmen from the south, which had begun in the interwar period, increased. These migrants populated Baghdad's new slums and were therefore the object of public debates concerning their employability and the violence and criminality they might be responsible for.[2] On the other hand, the middle and upper classes became richer during the war years; middle- and upper-middle-class neighborhoods expanded, while ambitious modernist projects changed the city's architecture in well-to-do neighborhoods and main streets. Consequently, the gap between rich and poor in Baghdad in particular, and in Iraq more generally, became more pronounced. It is no wonder, then, that Iraq experienced a series of strikes and demonstrations during the years 1945–48.

In the 1940s, Baghdad also experienced a cultural and literary renaissance, and its artists, poets, and novelists were a source of interest to students frequenting the city's cafés and attending its university halls. The Baghdadi public sphere thrived, with its literary salons, political clubs, women's organizations, and youth societies. The Baghdadi colleges, like the College of Arts and Sciences and the Teachers Training College, as well as the city's high schools and vocational schools, attracted more students, including many from provincial towns and the countryside. These schools quickly became centers of radical activity, as the influence of left-leaning and nationalist organizations, both legal and illegal, colored their extracurricular activities. The radicalization of Baghdad's students meant that the state found itself at an impasse. As part of its modernizing agenda, it wished to increase the number of educated Iraqis. At the same time, however, the expansion of education exposed men and women to the ideas of the opposition. In addition, the Baghdadi print market (although operating under severe censorship) was mostly identified with the opposition. For most leading intellectuals, social and economic issues represented the most important domains in which the Hashemite state failed to provide for its citizens and needed to be corrected. These demands found their expression in the Wathba.[3]

The Wathba began as a series of protests against a newly proposed agreement with Britain known as the Portsmouth Treaty. The riots broke out when Prime Minister Salih Jabr was out of the country negotiating the treaty, which was to replace one ratified in 1930. The Wathba started with students' demonstrations at the Law College on 4 January 1948. The college was closed down and arrests were made among the students. On 6 January the college reopened, but other colleges joined in the strike. The publication of the text of the treaty itself on 16 January caused a major outbreak of strikes over a three-day period in the colleges and stirred the activity of student organizations. Students and workers continued protesting, and demonstrations spread in Baghdad between 20 and 26 January. Dissent paralyzed many places in the capital when professors and doctors resigned in protest over police brutality. Protests entered another phase when Jabr returned from England, when demonstrations affected all parts of the city, while police brutality increased in response. The unrest arguably reached its peak on 26 and 27 January, as Baghdad and its suburbs were flooded by protesters. Casualties resulted when people tried to cross the city's bridges in the face of police fire. Bodies were left in the streets, some hanging from bridges. Although the opposition leaders did not initiate the Wathba, they were careful—like the city's poets, writers, and journalists—to join it. By the time the demonstrations were over, between one hundred and four hundred demonstrators lay dead.[4]

British accounts from the time reflect tensions between the perception of the Wathba as the outcome of an organized political plot, on the one hand, and the uncontrolled movement of bloodthirsty mobs in the city's streets, on the other. The British ambassador, Sir Henry Mack, tried to minimize the importance of the events by arguing that the protest against the treaty was used as a pretext "to enlist the unthinking xenophobia of Iraqi youth in the task of driving Saleh Jabr from office." He dismissed the attempts of "nationalist extremists" and liberal reformers to glorify "the so called 'national uprising'" as the opening of a new millennium in which the Iraqi government and the people would march forward together, divided no longer by the intrigues of "the British and their Iraqi jackals." He also suggested that even the principal architects of the national uprising were, in fact, badly frightened by "the devil of the mob violence they had unchained."[5]

The uprising was also depicted as a "storm" ignited not only by the students' actions but also by the opposition press—in particular the rightwing *Al-Nahda* (Revival) and *Al-Yaqza* (Awakening) and the leftist *Sawt al-Aharar* (Voice of the Free), as well as by opposition parties that "were very active during this period, preparing public opinion to suspect the good intentions of the negotiations." They thus saw the riots as the outcome of efforts by the communists, who wanted to produce chaos, and the ultranationalist al-Istiqlal Party, whose members wished to oust the British and the Hashemites. In this atmosphere, extremism ruled, since "moderate opinion" could not withstand the students' demands for full national sovereignty and young people's disgust with the inefficiency and corruption of the Iraqi government. Along with depictions of such organized violence, however, were also depictions of mob behavior, portraying the actions of the youth as "looking for trouble," carrying bricks in their pockets and sticks under their clothes. At the height of the events, the police were depicted as being engaged in urban battles.[6] But Mack believed that "the agitators in Baghdad" had learned from the Wathba that demonstrations could be very effective.[7]

The Wathba was a Baghdadi event, although its implications went far beyond the urban sphere, primarily because it was carried out by the city's youth, students, workers, protesters, and politicians. The state responded by suppressing the revolt brutally and violently. The violence of the state was underwritten by its portrayal of the actions of the demonstrators as acts of "agitation" and "disorder," and through its depoliticization of the demonstrators by referring to them as "dissidents" and "saboteurs" who were damaging public property and endangering the city's safety. The demonstrators' responses were both physical (marching, shouting, and chanting) and political (producing leaflets, engaging in counterpropaganda efforts, and composing poems and speeches against the state and in commemoration of the martyrs). Although political leaders affiliated with the ruling elites later tried to represent themselves as patriots who had supported the Wathba, the anxiety of the state at the potential outcomes of these events was demonstrated not only by acts of police brutality—as the police clashed with demonstrators, beat civilians, and confronted the youth in the city's streets—but also in the actions of the state after the Wathba. The fear of chaos overtaking the city led to the enactment of severe disciplinary measures, including the arrest and jailing of nationalists, Social Democrats, and communists; severe censorship; and the execution of the leaders of the ICP. These tactics of intimidation were effective only to a degree, as a new wave of violence and urban disorder erupted in 1952. During this series of riots, known as the Intifada, the streets were again occupied, and the attempts of the state to pacify the crowds ended in failure.[8]

While much has been written about the wave of urban violence against Baghdadi Jews, the Farhud, during which over 170 Jews were killed in the aftermath of the Rashid 'Ali al-Kaylani coup (1–2 June 1941), the involvement of Jews in the Wathba has not been explored at great length. Both Arab and Zionist national historiographies have silenced important aspects of the Wathba. Iraqi pan-Arab historiography—which was extremely hostile to the ICP and excluded Jews from many of its official accounts under the Baʻth—produced decidedly partial accounts of these major events. Zionist historiography has highlighted the Farhud as a crucial event that has forever changed the history of the Jewish community and led to the Zionization of the entire community. But the very same historiography mostly ignored the participation of the Jews in the Wathba because it did not want to acknowledge the fact that Iraqi Jews participated in a patriotic Iraqi urban revolt at a time when, according to Zionist narratives, they were supposed to be supporting the Zionist cause and yearning for migration to the Land of Israel. Despite these silences, however, the Wathba is of immense importance to our understanding of Jewish urban history, sectarianism, and violence.

PERFORMING PATRIOTISM

Jews played a significant part in modern Baghdadi life. Numbering around ninety thousand men and women, Baghdad's Jewish population grew considerably in the first half of the twentieth century, partly because of waves of Jewish migration to the city from the north and the center of Iraq and partly because of the activities of the Jewish middle and upper classes. By 1948, many Jews had left their Jewish neighborhoods and moved into mixed areas, although the urban Jewish poor tended to live in exclusively Jewish neighborhoods. During the years 1921–48, young Jewish men who were graduates of high schools, middle schools, and universities came to have much in common with other members of the urban middle classes by virtue of their education, leisure practices (such as visiting cafés, literary salons, cinemas, and cultural associations), and interest in Arab and global politics. Jewish intellectuals wrote in Arabic and stressed that they saw Iraq as their homeland and Arabic as their mother tongue.

Baghdadi Jews—especially the community's parliament and senate members, but also its chief rabbi, journalists, and writers—also disassociated themselves from the goals of political Zionism and stressed their patriotism and loyalty to Iraq's national and domestic concerns.[9] After 1945, however, the very same Jewish elites had to come to terms with the activities of right-wing and ultranationalist organizations, whose members were voicing their concerns that Iraqi Jews might be clandestinely supporting their Jewish brethren in Palestine and should therefore be considered disloyal citizens. During 1948, the Iraqi state itself engaged in activities against its Jewish community in its attempt to uproot Zionism in Iraq; arrests of alleged Zionists and Jewish communists led to the imprisonment of dozens of innocent Jews during the spring of 1948, while 796 Jews employed at government ministries were dismissed from their positions.[10]

The Wathba, however, provided an opportunity for Baghdadi Jews to express their patriotism and loyalty to the Iraqi people. The protests attracted Jewish students, Jewish workers, and Jewish Iraqi nationalists, because Jews were part of all the urban institutions and locations from which the Wathba sprang—schools, colleges, newspapers, cafés, literary salons, stores, factories, and shops. Abraham Twaina, a historian and community leader, notes that Jews closed down their stores, Jewish students went on strike, and Jewish communists attempted to gain control over events.[11] Some Zionist emissaries did report that the demonstrators turned against the city's Jews, blaming them for not assisting the protests.[12] Jewish Iraqi intellectual Ishaq Bar-Moshe likewise describes how the demonstrations quickly became anti-Zionist—and occasionally anti-Jewish—events.[13] But other Zionist emissaries state that the attempts to turn public opinion against the Jews failed.[14] In fact, community leader Abraham Twaina recalls that the Iraqi secret police wanted to divert the attention of the demonstrators by inciting them to loot Jewish stores, but the protesters were under instructions not to respond to such provocations.[15]

Important insights regarding the demonstrations can be drawn from an account by a Jewish soldier in the Iraqi army, who wrote to his relatives in Mandatory Palestine about the events. The soldier noted that all the schools in the city were demonstrating, and many Jews attended the funerals of the martyrs. The soldier was shocked by the violence of the police. He and his fellow soldiers were ordered not to demonstrate or go out onto the streets. Yet he recalled his impressions from what he was able to see in the city (in defiance of his orders): the city, he felt, had undergone "a massacre." He described policemen positioning themselves at the top of the minarets so they could open fire at the demonstrators; even when demonstrators snatched machine guns from the police, they did not know how to operate them and were thus exposed to further peril. He also paid attention to the violence of the protesters, noting that two policemen had been killed and their bodies thrown into the river, while another policeman's body was defiled, and two police cars were burned to the ground. In this situation, the solider explained, most policemen wanted to resign from their posts.

But the letter mostly conveyed the soldier's horror at the state's violence, as he described the floors of the bridges colored by the blood of the fallen.[16]

Nonetheless, the soldier was very impressed that the city was passionately sympathetic with the demonstrators and the dead. Most businesses had been shut down. For example, cinemas were closed down as a sign of mourning for the souls of the dead (an important fact, as most cinema owners in the city were Jews), as were stores that sold alcoholic beverages (again, a type of business usually operated by either Jews or Christians). Similarly, the lights in al-Rashid Street, Baghdad's main thoroughfare, were turned off for seven nights as a gesture of grief and bereavement.[17]

The letter reflects the feelings that overtook Baghdad, as a city in rebellion and in mourning. Most important, it conveyed the sympathy expressed by a young Jewish soldier whose heart went out to the people in the streets protesting against the state's actions, even though he was serving that state. Other Jewish demonstrators reported that the protesters made the city their own. They changed the name of al-Ma'mun Bridge, on which many demonstrators had been killed, to the "Bridge of Martyrs," and the street leading to the bridge was renamed "Martyrs' Street."[18] The bridges, it seems, were the major urban symbol of the Wathba. On 26 January, students and workmen came from the districts of al-Rusafa (in the east of Baghdad) and A'zamiyya (north Baghdad) to al-Ma'mun Bridge. They wanted to cross to al-Karkh (in west Baghdad) but were butchered under police fire. Salim Fattal, a Jewish high school student—and a communist—commemorated a porter who had died during these protests; "the porter's bag, soaked with his blood, was hanged on al-Ma'mun Bridge, close to where he had died, and was *the memorial* of the uprising."[19] Noticeably, the new memorial in the city, the porter's bag, was not constructed by the state but by demonstrators, in order to commemorate their suffering and the regime's violence.

Slogans of Arab-Jewish solidarity and Arab-Jewish-Kurdish brotherhood were chanted during the Wathba, and the participation of rabbis, qadis, and other religious authorities in the demonstrations contributed to their nonsectarian nature. The leadership of the Jewish community—Chief Rabbi Sasson Khaduri, several members of parliament, and one senator, as well as its leading intellectuals—were extremely careful not to attack the government or the monarchy directly. In fact, their speeches, public notices, and proclamations during the Wathba were gathered into a small booklet published in memory of the martyrs of freedom (*shuhada' al-hurriya*), which was dedicated to none other than King Faysal II, Regent 'Abd al-Ilah, and the prime minister. All were represented as individuals who stood with the Iraqi people during these difficult times.[20] However, as many legal political parties—which often participated in Iraqi governments, like the social democratic al-Hizb al-Watani al-Dimuqrati, as well as the ultra-nationalist al-Istiqlal—took part in the demonstrations and set up committees in the city, the Jewish leadership felt that it, too, could express its sympathy with the martyrs and the goals of the Wathba. Moreover, the leadership used Jewish participation in the events to express their loyalty to Iraq.

One demonstration in the city was orchestrated by Jews. An eyewitness estimated the number of participants at two thousand, but as more and more protesters joined, their number grew considerably. The Jewish demonstrators carried with them black flags, possibly as signs of mourning, and the Iraqi national flags, as well as posters. Some played the drums, while others lit candles, as they walked from Bab al-Mu'azzam to al-Rashid Street. Gunshots were heard, and Muslims were impressed by the audacity of Jewish protesters who had brought guns to the demonstration. These Jewish men and women, reported the eyewitness, were crying for the Muslims who had died that week, and they also mourned the Jews who had been martyred during the Farhud. All the dead, Jewish and Muslim alike, seemed to have been perceived as victims of the state. The Muslims who participated in the rally

> appreciated the demonstration, and many voices were heard among them, saying: there is no anti-Semitism in our hearts toward you. We did not know that the Jews loved us so much. The Jews passed by Bab al-Sheikh, and their cries went to the Heavens. No one could hold back his tears, and Baghdad became a city in tears. This demonstration lasted to the very late hours of the night.[21]

The demonstration—with its sounds (drums, cries), its signs (flags), and the marching of an entire Jewish group in the city—was crafted in such a way as to underscore Jewish loyalty to Baghdad. This performance, it seems, was extremely effective.

The community's leader, Rabbi Sasson Khaduri, took part in these ceremonies of collective mourning. He declared that the Iraqi people had lost its sons for the sake of patriotism (*wataniyya*) and blessed the Wathba. The rabbi prayed in his chambers for the souls of the dead, which "made a great impression on the Muslims. Wondrously, hundreds of Arabs visited him." The most important commemorative events were indeed the funerals of victims from all religions, mostly Muslims, which were attended by the leaders of the community. A community leader reported that "thousands went after every coffin," as days of mourning were set to commemorate the dead.[22] Abraham Twaina noted that countless Jews visited the houses of the families of the dead: "the Jewish visitors entered alleys they have never imagined they would ever set foot in before."[23] Rabbi Khaduri, who attended several of the funerals, depicted the martyrs as the innocent sons of the Iraqi people who had sacrificed themselves on the altar of patriotism. The Wathba, to Rabbi Khaduri, was an expression of unity: all Iraqi people, regardless of ethnicity, religion, or dogma ('ala ikhtilaf 'anasirihi, adyanihi, wa madhabihi) wanted to serve the dear motherland (watan) "where we live, and where our sons would continue living, in peace and security, God Willing [in sha' Allah]." The people in Iraq, he announced, were aware of their honor, sovereignty, and independence, and this awareness motivated their actions. He ended his eulogy by expressing a hope for a united Iraq under the protection of the king and the regent.[24]

Shalom Darwish—journalist, short story writer, and member of parliament for the Social Democrats—gave a passionate speech, delivering flowers on behalf of the community to the graves of the "innocent martyrs" (shuhada') who had been killed in the demonstrations. He opened his speech with the following words:

Honorable Sirs,
In the name of Iraqi Jews, who are represented by the Honorable Hakham Sasson Khaduri, the head of the Jewish community in Baghdad, we put these flowers on the grave of the deceased Qays bin Ibrahim al-Alusi, who sacrificed his dear life . . . together with his brothers, the eternal martyrs. May God bless them all.[25]

The martyrs sacrificed themselves for justice and freedom (haqq wa huriyya), said Darwish; yet their deaths were not in vain. Marching under fire, these fallen heroes were part of a blessed and bloody campaign for freedom and unity.

Or, as the poet said,

They have died and brought life to their people [sha'bihim] with their death;
How wondrous is a death that revives a life![26]

A proclamation by the community that read "No More Sectarianism [ta'ifiyya] after today!" applauded the people of the nation who demanded liberty and constitutionalism as they shouted against sectarianism. Another proclamation noted that the Jewish community expressed its "brotherly feelings toward this great, honorable nation, as it attended the funerals, the demonstrations, and chanted popular slogans and songs with the other demonstrators." The pains of suffering and oppression brought the nation together. The nonsectarian nature of the events appeared in another statement of the community professing that the Muslim, Christian, and Jewish youth formed a bond and were not deterred by death.[27]

This sense of patriotism was shared by Muslims—both Sunni and Shia—who welcomed Jews into mosques and shared the Jewish desire to understand the Wathba as an antisectarian event. One of the victims of the Wathba was Ja'far al-Jawahiri, a Shia engineering student and the younger brother of the famous bard Muhammad Mahdi al-Jawahiri. The eulogy of Ja'far al-Jawahiri was delivered at the Sunni Haydarkhana mosque, where Muhammad Mahdi al-Jawahiri read a poem commemorating his brother. Sasson Somekh, a Jewish high school student at the time, attended the packed memorial with fellow Jewish students, who were warmly welcomed by the Muslim organizers of the rally.[28] The fact that Somekh attended the gathering should also be seen as a change in his own practices. His parents, Somekh writes in his autobiography, did not want him to go to certain places in Baghdad because they considered the locations perilous. For example, he had never visited the poor Jewish neighborhood of Tatran in Baghdad. When he visited the Sadda region, populated by poor Bedouin immigrants, he was overwhelmed by "pity and nausea"; to him, these Baghdadis seemed "like creatures from another planet."[29] Somekh was a young patriotic intellectual who took part in the urban culture of cafés and clubs, where artists and poets gathered and sent poems and articles to journals and newspapers. Yet class differentiations were still a very important factor shaping his life. The juxtaposition of Somekh's depictions of his class-based urban isolation with his impressions of the Muslim-Jewish solidarity of the Wathba reveals the importance of crossing sectarian lines physically, in urban space, since the violence that took over Baghdad erased such differences, albeit for a short while.

Abraham Twaina reflected on the atmosphere in Iraq following the Wathba: "It seemed as if Iraq turned into a paradise, and its people into angels. The friendships between Jews and Muslims were strengthened, but new enemies surfaced as well. At the end of March, however, the honeymoon was over. In the Land of Israel, 'Abd al-Qadir al-Husayni was killed."[30]

Twaina's remarks, I think, capture the spirit of the Wathba—how the uprising gave the Jews of Baghdad a chance to illustrate their loyalty to the people of Iraq. Both Avner Ben-Amos (writing on republican France) and Peter Wien (writing on Mandatory Syria and Iraq) examine public funerals as a part of a larger project to build a secular but sanctified community based on a civic religion and its heroes and modern-day saints. This form of commemoration became, in the Middle Eastern context, a vital symbol of the efforts to fend off colonialism.[31] The careful staging of the funerals and demonstrations, and the mass participation in these ecumenical religious services, served to emphasize national solidarity and nonsectarian patriotism in the urban topography of Baghdad. The commemorations created an anti-statist yet national culture, establishing the practices of naming streets and bridges and mourning for the city's martyrs and heroes. Historians today have become very suspicious of the slogans chanted during the Wathba. They identify the speeches about the eternal spirits of the martyrs, sacrifice for the sake of the nation, the unity of the homeland, and the desire for oneness with the kitsch, violence, and murderousness of fascist and dictatorial regimes in Iraq and elsewhere in the Middle East.[32] In the Jewish context, however, these attestations about the unity of the nation were a response to state discrimination against them and to their fear of being marked as traitors. Such slogans represented the sentiments of Jewish intellectuals and public figures who wanted to reassure the Baghdadis who attended the demonstrations and funerals that they were part of the Iraqi people—that they belonged to the *sha' b*, shared its pains, and hoped for a better future. They used specific sites in Baghdad—especially mosques—to articulate these sentiments.

MERGING INTO THE CROWD

The Wathba was intimately connected with the history of the left in Iraq. The failure of the pan-Arab camp to liberate Iraq from British domination, as it became manifest in the failure of Rashid 'Ali al-Kaylani's coup in 1941 (a pro-German military takeover that included many pan-Arabists and nationalists) created a political vacuum. At the same time, during World War II the British eased censorship with respect to Russian publications. The small ICP (established in the mid-1930s) was consequently able to emerge as an important power. The Iraqi communist leadership, which had not initiated the Wathba, made sure to take an active part in it. Dhu Nun Ayyub, a communist novelist, depicted Baghdad in his 1949 novel, *The Hand, the Land and the Water* (*Al-Yad wa'l Ard wa'l Ma'*), as a city whose streets were blocked by workers, students, and protesters shouting, "May colonialism and Zionism fall!"[33] According to Ayyub, the demonstrators, many of whom were among the urban poor, denounced "the thieves" who had "stolen their property and starved the people."[34]

For the communists, the hunger, frustration, and lack of bread finally matured into a full-fledged revolutionary zeal, generating a power that was able to topple the regime. During the Wathba, they set up a students' committee (Ittihad al-tullab al-'amm) to deal with the various aspects of the events and orchestrated many demonstrations and protests.[35] Their efforts were successful, even though the ICP's leadership was jailed at the time, because of the communists' intimate knowledge of the city. An illegal party, the ICP used many venues to gather support, spread its networks of activists, and increase its popularity. The ICP enlisted members in the city's colleges, especially the Teachers' Training College and Baghdad's Law College, as well as in high schools and middle schools. The urban nature of the ICP was instrumental in determining the party's large Jewish membership, as the community was mostly centered in Baghdad. Young Jews joined the ICP for "purely Jewish" reasons, such as the ICP's antifascist stance and its condemnation of Iraqi ultranationalists who equated Judaism with Zionism. But they also joined for reasons common to all Iraqi communists—the desire to attain social justice in Iraq and to minimize British hegemony over Iraqi foreign policy.[36]

Jews played a vital role in the Baghdadi activities of the ICP. Two Jews, Sasson Dallal and Judah Siddiq, belonged to the top ranks of the ICP, and Jewish members organized communist groups in the city, such as women's organizations and local committees, and operated cells in Baghdadi factories and schools. They often found themselves either working or living in neighborhoods that were very different from either the middle- and upper-class Jewish neighborhoods, like Batawin, or the older exclusively Jewish quarters, such as Tatran and Tawrat. Jews worked in poor Shia neighborhoods like Karkh and Kazimayn, in mixed neighborhoods like Karada, and everywhere the ICP sent them. The houses of Jewish members of the party were used as safe houses and locations for communist meetings, while Muslims and Christians in Baghdadi neighborhoods also offered shelter to Jewish communists they did not know.

Party members acted as couriers distributing newspapers—*Al-Sharara* (The spark) and *Al-Qa'ida* (The principle)—leaflets, and books printed in the ICP's publishing house, *Dar al-Hikma*, in the city's streets.[37] Jewish activists collected money from the party's supporters in the shops and markets. Jewish women traveled the streets of Baghdad carrying letters, visiting prisoners, and educating other women. Cell members used to meet in open spaces in the city, such as cafés and gardens, and in business premises affiliated with the party. Some cell meetings were conducted while simply walking in the streets. As the ICP had organized demonstrations before the Wathba, especially in 1946, it had a reservoir of specific locations (crossroads, major squares), as well as public symbols (like the statue of General Maude),[38] that would attract protesters. Although these demonstrations included people from all walks of life, the party knew how to operate in the city and effectively engage its networks of members, supporters, and sympathizers in the city's public space. Jews played a crucial role in all these efforts.

During the Wathba, communist Jews interacted with the city at a few major sites where demonstrations took place. The street itself became a symbol of national unity. Salim Fattal, a communist teenager, professed that his desire to be part of the Iraqi people was materialized spatially, as he became a part of a marching crowd that had no racial, ethnic, or religious features and was simply a great mass moving in the city's streets. Shim'on Ballas, who joined the ICP in 1946, recalls:

> These were the days . . . when I marched arm in arm with demonstrators whom I had not known before, and when I loudly called for the toppling of the government of national betrayal, the release of political prisoners, and for free elections. . . .
>
> The communists courageously fought publications that incited anti-Jewish feeling in the right-wing press. . . . In demonstrations along al-Rashid Street the demonstrators chanted: "We are the brothers of the Jews; we are the enemies of imperialism and Zionism!" I remember this rare sight, how as the demonstration approached the commercial and banking area, and, as this slogan was chanted by the demonstrators, merchants, and bankers, all Jews, came out to the balconies and clapped their hands enthusiastically.[39]

Ballas's experience marching in the anonymous crowd bolstered his conviction that his concerns were also the concerns of the Iraqi people. The communist pro-Jewish position made him proud of his political affiliations and, moreover, elicited the enthusiastic response to the ICP of Jewish merchants and bankers, who did not normally support a communist agenda. In fact, Jewish communists Ibrahim Sha'ul, Mir Yaqub Cohen, and Sahyun al-Bazzaz collected money from Jewish merchants during the Wathba. These funds helped, at least according to one account, to sponsor trucks bringing women, students, and workers from the countryside to the city to participate in the protests. On certain occasions the communists also invited famous individuals to take part in the protests—for example, the poet Muhammad Mahdi al-Jawahiri honored the demonstrations by his presence.⁴⁰ Iraqi Jewish communist Sami Michael believed that it was the efforts of "boys with no experience" that led rabbis, qadis, and priests to join the Wathba.⁴¹

The residents of neighborhoods needed to come to terms with a paralyzed city. At times, the communist activists were made central figures in their own neighborhoods and were seen as individuals with knowledge of events. Shoshana Levy (who at the time was ten years old and lived in a mixed middle-class neighborhood) wrote that she heard from her parents about the demonstrations and about the politicians whose names were chanted at protests. The protests affected the social order in her neighborhood; a neighbor, the Jewish communist Eliyahu Ezer, explained to her about the battle between the people and the reactionary government: "I noted that the communist neighbor began visiting our home often and became a main source of information about what happened in the city. In general, I felt that there was a harmony and intimate solidarity between the houses and the families populating our neighborhood."⁴² In Shoshana's view, then, the Wathba created a feeling of intercommunal solidarity; her account reflects the sentiments of a young Jewish girl who grew to appreciate her communist neighbor, whom she saw as the link between the Jewish neighbors and the protesters.

Besides the streets and neighborhoods, other urban sites very much connected to the communist involvement in the Wathba were the schools (middle, high, and college level), from which students embarked on demonstrations. For the communists, schools served in the same way as mosques for the nationalists and the more established members of the Iraqi community—as sites where people were normally gathered, which could therefore be transformed into places where students were incited to rebel and protest. Kamil Kahila, a Jewish high school student, depicted the effects of the Wathba in his school as follows:

> The Jewish communist youth was the most militant and rabble rousing. The communists . . . demanded from all pupils participation in the demonstrations. They even confronted the schoolmaster, who preferred seeing his students focusing on their studies rather than partaking in dangerous activities. I remember them talking to the schoolmaster: "We must go and demonstrate. All of us." The schoolmaster finally capitulated, and the students went to the protests. The same happened in all the schools of Baghdad, Jewish and non-Jewish. I was among the hundreds of students who marched toward the center of the demonstrations in Baghdad. We carried posters and chanted against the treaty and

British imperialism. The communists led the rally, whereas the Zionists left on the first occasion. These demonstrations were the most meaningful memory in my political and public consciousness.[43]

Notably, whereas the state's representative, the school's principal, is portrayed as powerless in the face of his politically motivated students, the school itself serves as a convenient location for encouraging students to act against the state. The Wathba, more broadly, pushed many young Jews to go out onto the streets. Iraqi police files indicate that dozens of young Jews who were arrested in 1948 and 1949 on charges related to communism had taken part in these events.

SHORT-TERM EFFECTS AND STATE VIOLENCE

After the Wathba, the state unleashed a fierce campaign against Iraq's civil society in general, and the communists in particular. Hundreds of activists were arrested and jailed, and the centers of communist activity shifted, in many cases, from the city's streets and cafés to its jails. A British account from 1949 noted that the National Democrats and al-Istiqlal Party were very weak. Furthermore, the government manipulated the martial law that had been declared throughout the country following Iraq's entry into the 1948 war in Palestine in order to crush the communist opposition.[44] Communist committees were broken up, and leftist activities came to a halt as "police action against the communists was pursued with renewed vigor" throughout the year. The British saw the implementation of martial law as crucial to the maintenance of public order and noted that the Iraqi police feared that lifting of martial law at the end of 1949 would endanger their efforts to root out communism.[45] Communist Jews who were arrested as part of this campaign, however, were often not accused of being communists but were rather tried as Zionists (or as Zionists *and* communists). Naturally, the state's association of communism with Zionism helped discredit the former.[46]

Given this context, many communists expressed anxiety concerning whether the memory of the Wathba could serve as a revolutionary model or had been erased by state violence. The communists realized that the Wathba had not followed a classical Marxist model; although the factory proletarians took part in the movement, the demonstrators were much more diverse and included students, members of the middle class, and nationalists. In this sense, it was not a moment of class unity but one of unity against the state's unjust social policies and pro-British stance. The Wathba also did not start in the poor neighborhoods of Baghdad but in its main streets and spread from the colleges and commercial centers to the rest of the city. Therefore, much theorizing was required to fit the Wathba into a broadly Marxist framework.[47] However, the Wathba came to symbolize the possibility of a revolution and was therefore commemorated in communist cells and gatherings and in prisons. In an autobiographical essay, Jewish communist Yaʻqub Mir Masri argued that the communists had in fact prepared the setting for the rebellion during the 1940s.

The ICP newspaper, Al-Qaʻida (established in 1943), reminded its readers of the importance of ousting all foreign armies from Iraq, organizing the peasants, and defending Kurdish rights. The Wathba was later constructed as the manifestation of all of these ideas in the streets of Baghdad.[48] In January 1949 the Jewish secretary of the party, Sasson Dallal, wrote "a message to the public" in which he devoted much attention to the fact that the Wathba should be remembered as the embodiment of a true revolution. He suggested that flowers should be laid on the graves of the martyrs in the cemeteries (thus appropriating the sites of the martyrs' graves from the nationalists) and that these acts should be accompanied by public speeches. Working with students, peasants, and soldiers, the ICP should organize a general strike. He hoped, then, that the revolution would come back to life through its mere commemoration. Dallal also suggested the use of violent means against those who refused to remember the Wathba. Those who "betray the blood of the martyrs . . . deserve the rage of the masses and their contempt."[49]

Dallal's efforts were unsuccessful. Shortly after he wrote this message to the public, he was jailed and ultimately executed by the state; this very same letter was used as evidence for his subversive activities. A British account from 1949 reported that the government had made full use of martial law against the commemoration of the Wathba and communist activities more generally; some demonstrators were arrested, tried, and sentenced on the same day: "Troops stood by, police were reinforced and no serious disturbances took place."[50] Communist Jews, however, remembered the Wathba. For them, it was the last moment before everything collapsed—before the mass arrests of Jewish citizens by the state (on the false charge that they were affiliated with Zionism); before Jewish communists were exiled and denationalized; and, most important, before the Jewish community was displaced in its entirety, in 1950–51, and the distinction between Judaism and Zionism became insignificant in Iraq. It was thus not only a successful moment for the ICP; it was a testament to the fact that, for one moment in Iraqi history, social justice, class issues, and the anti-colonial struggle seem to have eclipsed sectarian divisions.

•   •   •

Jewish participation in the Wathba illustrates that friendship, nonsectarian solidarity, and Iraqi patriotism were celebrated by Iraqi Jews during, and because of, this urban revolt. The Jews who demonstrated at the protests, and who were victimized by state violence, saw themselves as loyal Iraqi citizens. They used these violent events in the city to claim a part in the Iraqi national narrative and to underscore the fact that they thought of Iraq as their homeland. Leftist Jews felt that their hopes for equality and a class-based battle against the regime were materializing in the Wathba. Nevertheless, many Jews were victims of the state's campaign against the left in the aftermath of the events, which was often disguised as battle against Zionism. Considered in a broader Middle Eastern context, these demonstrations are not so different from the demonstrations that were seen at the beginning of the Arab Spring in Cairo. The same signs of Coptic-Muslim solidarity seen in Tahrir Square were also present in the Baghdadi Jewish context. In both cases, groups of students, as well as many individuals belonging to the middle classes and the urban poor, protested against their governments' social policies and commitments to foreign interests, demanding sovereignty, justice, and honor. The category of "the people" (*al-sh'ab*) and their demand—the fall of the regime (*isqat al-nizam*)—were articulated clearly in both cases. In Baghdad, these demands were soon brutally and effectively silenced.

10 DISSECTING MOMENTS OF UNREST

Twentieth-Century Kirkuk

Nelida Fuccaro

VIOLENCE HAS CAST A LONG SHADOW over Kirkuk's modern history. For almost a century, its troubled public life has been molded by the geopolitics of oil and nation building and, since the 1990s, by the gradual fragmentation of the Iraqi state, which in 2014 has led to the occupation by the Kurdish regional government. As one of Iraq's most multicultural cities, Kirkuk has been a powerful symbol of the communal, ethnic, and nationalist conflicts that have unfolded in Iraq since World War I. The fierce political and rhetorical battle that still inflames the city has centered on its "ethnic" identity and features multilayered struggles that have involved its Turkmen, Kurdish, and Arab residents. It is no surprise that ethnic antagonisms and nationalist claims have framed our understanding of the violent manifestations of the explosive mix of animosities that have fragmented Kirkuk's public life.[1] Yet—as recent literature on Indian communalism has suggested—broad analytical categories such as ethnicity and nationalism do not fully account for intricate urban realities and experiences of collective violence. These categories tend to simplify and homogenize the richness, complexity, and diversity of Kirkuk as an urban society, replicating monolithic and ahistorical conceptions of its residents—particularly Kurds and Turkmens—as communities of violence, both as victims and perpetrators.[2]

This chapter dissects two momentous episodes of bloodshed that took place in 1924 and 1959 in order to bring to light some constitutive elements of Kirkuk's civic strife: the city's civilian population and its military forces; contingent historical factors such as British colonial intervention and the development of the oil industry; and Kirkuk's urban space as a place of bloody conflict, state intervention, and communal memory. Literature of urban riots in India has convincingly shown how taking a close look at civic conflict as an event provides an ethnographic, experiential, and urban reading of violence, bringing into the discussion agency, time, and space as constitutive elements of public action.[3] These elements have been often ignored in the study of Iraq's popular uprisings, communal clashes, and repressive state action. Although clearly staged *in* cities, they often have not been treated as an urban phenomenon but analyzed through the lens of imperial, national, and regional politics.[4] This chapter also moves beyond the immediate temporality of Kirkuk's violent events to consider the long-term symbiotic relationship between the imposition of state discipline, the outbreak of urban conflict, and the restoration of order. It also draws attention to various discursive modalities of violence by discussing the role played by different languages *of* violence and *on* violence in producing and sustaining Kirkuk's moments of bloodshed and in mediating their interpretations.

MUTINY AND REPRISAL IN THE COLONIAL TOWN: MAY 1924

The main protagonists of the bloody events of May 1924 were Assyrian Christian soldiers of the Iraqi Levies, Britain's colonial army in Iraq. Deployed in Kirkuk in late 1923, the Levies served as a frontier force under the command of the Royal Air Force (RAF). They were used to quell disturbances in the town's Kurdish hinterland and to protect the disputed border between Iraq and Turkey. Kirkuk's Levies included both Assyrian Christians (originally from southeastern Turkey) and Kurds—the two martial races that made up a considerable proportion of this colonial force.[5] The disturbances of May 1924 were sparked by a trivial incident in Kirkuk's central markets—a quarrel between a shopkeeper and some Assyrian soldiers belonging to the Tiyari tribe who were notorious for their belligerent and unruly behavior.[6] As attempts to restore calm by the local police and by Levy officers failed, large numbers of Assyrians carrying rifles and wearing bandoliers started to attack the town, creating panic among residents. Some opened fire from the roofs of their living quarters on the west bank of the river Khasa, targeting the markets and the citadel (Qal'a), the ancient core of the Ottoman city, located on the east side of the river. Many marched toward the citadel from various directions, discharging fire at regular intervals. A British Levy officer saw "groups of men [Assyrian soldiers], in a crazy state of excitement, moving about on the road, and parties in extended order, making what looked like a regular attack on the town [the citadel]. . . . They were all quite crazy, eyes glazed, and faces dead white; they were like men out to fight and nothing would stop them."[7]

Once they had crossed the bridge, they occupied some houses in the citadel and from the rooftops started firing at the police headquarters and markets, which were set ablaze. As residents responded to Assyrian fire, RAF patrols arrived at the scene and started flying in circles over the citadel in an attempt to force the Assyrian mutineers to surrender, while civilians started to shoot at the planes. Eight hours after the news of the disturbance had reached Baghdad, five armored cars and two platoons of the Royal Inniskilling Fusiliers arrived in Kirkuk, the latter airlifted from the capital. By then the Assyrian rebels had been disarmed and marched outside the town under escort of military convoys. The following day, several of Kirkuk's local Christian residents were murdered, while infuriated crowds pillaged the empty quarters of the Assyrians and the property of local Christian residents, and bands of looters, including residents and Kurdish Levy soldiers, ransacked the markets.[8] According to British reports, the death toll was approximately forty-eight civilians, including eight Christians killed on the second day of the unrest, five Levy soldiers, and three policemen.[9]

This blatant breach of public order can be partly explained in terms of the militarization of the old Ottoman-Iranian frontier in northern Iraq after the British occupation of the region in 1919. As towns like Kirkuk and Mosul became the logistical bases of Levy forces during the British Mandate (1920–32), acrimony between these forces and the civilian population often led to bloodshed. It is no accident that a casual encounter in Kirkuk's markets was the trigger of unrest, as the markets were the only public space in which Assyrian soldiers came into regular contact with the local population. Confined to the barracks and to civil-

Figure 10.1. Kirkuk's citadel and the Khasa riverbed. On the left, the stone bridge built by the Ottomans, ca. 1925. Source: Edwin Newman collection. Courtesy of the San Diego Air & Space Museum.

ian residences requisitioned by the army in west Kirkuk, the Assyrians lived in social isolation and were often engaged in training and military operations outside town. Their tribal ethos and martial virtues were undoubtedly key elements in organizing their mobilization as combat forces during the assault against the citadel and the markets. Some formed lines waiting to cross the bridge, while others, following the basic principles of infantry training, advanced in short rushes along the west bank of the river Khasa.[10]

Yet the seemingly wild behavior of the Assyrians was not the result of their primordial instincts, as the description by the British Levy officer might suggest. Their seemingly manic killing spree was a response to the vulnerable situation they faced inside Kirkuk—particularly those soldiers who had brought their families with them and lived in the so-called married lines, civilian houses requisitioned by the army. In fact, the fracas in the markets seems to have been exacerbated by a perceived infringement of family honor rather than the bullish bargaining over the price of merchandise by the Assyrian privates, for which they were notorious. According to Assyrian sources, the soldiers became incensed as a result of the inappropriate remarks and behavior of the shopkeeper and customers toward their wives and daughters. Although it is unlikely that women were present at the scene, British accounts confirm that the atmosphere among Assyrian soldiers was tense, as they feared for their families' safety, since

Figure 10.2. Levy soldiers with a Royal Air Force airman in the outskirts of Kirkuk, ca. 1925. Source: Edwin Newman collection. Courtesy of the San Diego Air & Space Museum.

they were about to leave town on military duties. Their attitude was also shaped by dramatic events in the markets of Mosul in August 1923, when some Assyrian children were killed by local residents.[11]

The waves of looting and the murder of local Christians that followed the removal of the Assyrians from Kirkuk cannot be interpreted merely as a sign of Muslim-Christian animosity. This would imply that the violation of Christian property and the destruction of lives were premeditated, that clear-cut divisions existed between Kirkuk's Muslim and Christian residents, and that the Assyrians were identified, by virtue of their religious status, with local Christians. In fact, the Assyrians' recent arrival, and their tribal background, language, and confessional affiliation, set them apart from Kirkuk's Christian residents—a long-established urban community of Turkish and Arabic speakers that included a large number of members of the Chaldean (Catholic) Church.[12] Assyrian fire did not specifically target Muslims: eyewitness accounts confirm that the soldiers shot at the population at random. Moreover, the violence against Christian residents on the second day of the disturbances seems to have been a matter of individual retribution rather than outright collective religious animosity.

From the testimonies collected by the commission of inquiry convened to investigate these events, it appears that, although several local Christians were murdered because they were said to have sheltered Assyrian soldiers, it was in fact the Assyrians who broke into private residences, often threatening their occupants.[13] The actions of the "mob" that ransacked the markets and private property did not conform to a racially and religiously motivated collective ethos, and the violence was not random but clearly encouraged by material gain. Particular houses became a target of the looters not because they were Christian but because they were empty—their residents, fearing for their lives, had sought sanctuary in the Kirkuk police headquarters. Shops were ransacked by Kurdish Levy soldiers—who, unlike the Assyrians, remained in town—together with effendis (notables) and street urchins. In the words of a RAF intelligence officer based in Kirkuk who had witnessed the sacking of the markets, "the entire town joined in the proceedings."[14]

The most salient aspect of the 1924 violence—both for its time and for the future—was that those who perished under Assyrian fire were mostly Turkmens, members of a racial group that constituted the overwhelming majority of Kirkuk's population.[15] As a Turkmen town, early 1920s Kirkuk was the archetypal post-Ottoman frontier society of British-controlled Iraq, its cultural

Figure 10.3. A section of Kirkuk's markets with a Christian house in the background, ca. 1925. Source: Edwin Newman collection. Courtesy of the San Diego Air & Space Museum.

outlook shaped by centuries of Ottoman rule. The town was mostly Turkish speaking, and the political orientation of its socially conservative elites—which included both Turkmen and Kurdish families, mostly Sunni Muslim—was toward Anatolia and the old Ottoman order rather than Baghdad. Many Turkmens in Kirkuk read the actions of the Assyrians as an attempt on the part of the colonial regime to destabilize the community, an interpretation that still permeates Turkmen communal history.[16]

RIOTING CROWDS IN THE POST-REVOLUTIONARY CITY: JULY 1959

> *The city of Kirkuk, for its part, has become addicted to death like other cities. . . .*
> *Death followed death, and insanity succeeded insanity. . . . The city lost its innocence*
> *and became filled with scoundrels and killers.*
>
> **Fadhil al-Azzawi, *The Last of the Angels*** [17]

This almost apocalyptic image of Kirkuk after the 1958 revolution, sketched by the Kirkuk-born novelist Fadhil al-Azzawi, tallies with accounts of the bloody events of July 1959. The scene of the violence was one of flamboyance: the celebrations organized for the first anniversary of the military revolution that had swept away the British-backed Hashemite monarchy in 1958.[18]

Rioting started on anniversary day—14 July—along the route of the procession coordinated by a number of popular organizations whose numbers had mushroomed after the revolution, including the People's Resistance Forces (al-Muqawama al-Sha'biyya), a militia linked to the government but controlled by the Iraqi Communist Party (ICP). As the parade was crossing the new bridge that separated west Kirkuk from the old citadel, shots were fired in the vicinity of a Turkmen coffeehouse, either by demonstrators or by individuals lining the procession route. The account of Kirkuk's chief of police relates that, before this incident, the cortege was disrupted by the sudden appearance of Turkmen demonstrators eager to join the procession and by a large group of soldiers of the Iraqi army stationed in Kirkuk.[19] We can assume that many of Kirkuk's Turkmens were effectively excluded from the official parade on the grounds of their conservative political inclinations. By 1959, the bulk of the popular base of the professional and youth associations that formed the backbone of the anniversary parade included recently urbanized Kurds employed in the oil industry. These associations were linked to modern political organizations—the ICP and the Kurdish Democratic Party. Turkmen accounts of the episode suggest that the community had organized its own celebrations to show its support for the government. They also blame Kurdish communist sympathizers and activists, mostly from outside Kirkuk, for having started the violence after they infiltrated the procession.[20]

After the first shots were heard near the Turkmen coffeehouse, demonstrators and spectators became excited, tension escalated, and a violent commotion disrupted the procession. Meanwhile, in the coffeehouse, twenty Turkmens, including the owner, were killed and their bodies dragged out into the streets. According to the chief of police, shots were fired by soldiers, members of the People's Resistance Forces, and unspecified civilians. In the meantime a mixed crowd (allegedly including members of the People's Resistance Forces, unspecified Kurds, and bands of residents) started to loot Turkmen properties in central Kirkuk, after having seized arms and ammunition from a nearby police station.[21] On the following day, as the looting and killing continued—as well as the macabre ritual of hanging corpses for public display and dragging them around the city—the Second Division of the Iraqi Army stepped in to restore order and protect the Turkmen residents. Various reports suggest that Kurdish soldiers and junior officers of the Fourth Brigade refused to follow the orders of their superiors and joined the aggressive crowd roaming around the city. It was only on 17 July that military reinforcements sent from Baghdad managed to disarm the rebellious Fourth Brigade and the rioters, and the town was sealed off. The bodies of approximately thirty-one people were recovered, mostly Turkmens—though many other bodies were said to have been buried. Some 130 people were injured, and hundreds of Turkmen properties were ransacked, gutted, or burned. Scores of terrified residents fled the city.[22]

This episode of Kirkuk's civic violence was radically different from that of May 1924. In spite of the heavy loss of life suffered by the Turkmen community on both occasions, new civilian and military actors had now entered the urban arena. Kirkuk was no longer the remote garrison town of the mid-1920s but a thriving city that had grown closer to the central government after the discovery of oil in 1927, Iraq's achievement of independence from British control in 1932, and the deployment of the Second Division of Iraq's national army. Both oil and the presence of the army had transformed Kirkuk's demography and urban landscape, as well as its economy and class structure. One of the most noticeable features of the public culture of Kirkuk in the 1950s was its modern and highly regimented military life—a far cry from the alien presence of the Levies in the mid-1920s. As early as 1933, the British consul in Kirkuk had reported that the Iraqi troops were "well clad, well drilled and well fed."[23] By the late 1950s, the urban landscape was dotted with barracks, public buildings, and entertainment venues that teemed with officers and soldiers. Army parades were important military routines used by central government to instill civic discipline by example and to inculcate national pride among residents. Cavalry and infantry units often marched through the city displaying weapons and artillery—particularly in the summer, when soldiers headed to the mountains.[24]

In contrast to the civic and national ethos promoted in Kirkuk's public spaces by the army, the urban experience of oil development and national politics was quite divisive; the oil industry redesigned Kirkuk's demographic and class structure in fundamental ways. As the urban economy boomed, particularly after World War II, the city attracted large numbers of immigrants, mostly from the immediate Kurdish hinterland of the city, driving the development of distinctively Kurdish neighborhoods, such as Imam Qasim and Shurjah, in eastern Kirkuk. While forming the majority of menial laborers employed in the oil industry, Kurds also constituted the backbone of the city's trade unions, which had developed under the aegis of the ICP during the monarchy as an underground organization.[25]

Modern politics in Kirkuk reflected the "urban turn" experienced by Iraq's popular activism in the Hashemite era, as well as the increasing politicization of the army that had led to the military takeover of government in 1958. In this respect, the violence of 1959 linked Kirkuk as a modern civic space to the post-revolutionary politics of Baghdad, characterized by a split among officers between followers of Arab nationalism and of communism. The progressive Kurdification of the city acquired increasingly political overtones after 1958, when the new military regime openly supported the communist movement and allowed Mulla Mustafa Barzani, the Kurdish nationalist leader, to return to Iraq from exile in the Soviet Union. The encouragement apparently given to communism by the republican government and its conciliatory stance toward the Kurdish national movement explain the increasing vulnerability of Kirkuk's Turkmen community and the strong communist inclination of some of the Kurdish officers in the Iraqi army.[26]

Given this general political context, the 1959 disturbances are generally considered a manifestation of ethnic animosity closely intertwined with political competitiveness. Contemporary accounts of these events characterize the rioting crowds and their victims as "Kurdish," "communist," or "Turkmen"; academic analyses have tended to follow suit. For instance, the riots are interpreted by Hanna Batatu as the result of the actions of "fanatic Kurds of different tendencies."[27] Without denying the ethnic and political component of the violence, the sources suggest that other forces and motivations were at play. The disturbances were not planned, certainly on the first day. Although groups such as the insubordinate officers of the Iraqi army and the People's Resistance Forces acted on occasion as what Paul Brass has called "conversion specialists" and Stanley Tambiah has termed "riot captains," violence was not systematically provoked for political ends.[28] Not all crowds necessarily conformed to a united collective ethos, as is clearly indicated by the vague and contradictory position of some sources on the question of their composition.

Attaching political and ethnic labels such as "communist," "Kurd," or "Turkmen" to acts of murder, vandalism, and the destruction of property obscures the socioeconomic and other factors that prompted individuals to participate in intergroup violence. A mix of economic opportunism and class hostility played a part in the prolonged attacks to Turkmen property and business, as the community still formed an important segment of Kirkuk's commercial and entrepreneurial class. Class was undoubtedly a new element of crowd behavior since the sacking of Kirkuk in 1924. In addition, the public visibility and highly symbolic nature of violent acts—the exposure of bodies in the streets and the alleged burial alive of victims—mimicked the brutality of the 1958 revolution in Baghdad. It is suggestive of the use of violence as an extreme form of personal empowerment that is at the same time a display of the powerlessness of those of low socioeconomic status.

Again, labeling the disturbances as ethnic or political does not account for the simultaneous or sequential activation of a variety of motives (political, economic, communal, and ethnic) at both individual and group levels. The highly charged political feelings of loyalty to the young republican regime unleashed by the celebrations set the tone of the "mood for violence" that engulfed the procession. For some of the participants—once they caught sight of competing parades, public establishments, and private residences identified as Turkmen

Figure 10.4. Kurdish family in Kirkuk, ca. 1958. In spite of the new political divisions many of Kirkuk's residents were still living the multicultural tradition of the post-Ottoman city. In the middle the father is wearing traditional Arab garb. Photo: Courtesy of the owner, who wishes to remain anonymous.

or militias and military groups recognized as communist or Kurdish—this political feeling swiftly metamorphosed into localized communal animosity. As
communist sympathizers, the insubordinate Kurdish soldiers of the Fourth Brigade and members of the People's Resistance Forces were animated by political
incentives, as suggested by the spectacular shelling of the citadel and Turkmen
businesses with mortar fire during the second day of the disturbances.[29] Yet the
participation of soldiers in some of the looting suggests that they entered into
the vicious circle of personal violence as Kurds—an ethnic affiliation that had
assumed an increasingly class connotation in Kirkuk.

Some of the dynamics of the disturbances show how the space of the modern city became an integral aspect of individual and collective violence. Spatial
tactics guided the actions of militants. Members of the People's Resistance
Forces followed detailed itineraries in pursuit of their political rivals, marking
out the locations of houses and neighborhoods on maps. During the second
day of the disturbances, when the Turkmen population barricaded itself in the
citadel, young militants conducted house-to-house searches, forcibly removing
residents in an act that cleansed spaces of the presence of Turkmens.[30] As in the
case of the takeover of the citadel by the Assyrian Levies in 1924, acts of violence
coincided with the transgression and infringement of personal and communal
space. The intrusion of Turkmen demonstrators and spectators in the ceremonial space of the procession was a key catalyst of the violence. Competition for
control of this space by both demonstrators and public officials defined some of
the dynamics of the unrest. Public officials conceived the procession as a dia-
gram of order; the police oversaw its timing and organization and patrolled the
route that crossed the river Khasa connecting the citadel to western Kirkuk.

Contestation over the commemorative arches erected by residents throughout Kirkuk to celebrate the revolution represented another form of violent
competition over the ceremonial space of the city. Though they had been built
before 1958 to celebrate military victories, after the revolution these arches became celebrations of the new republican regime—a popular tribute to Iraq's
military rulers that narrated a new chapter in the history of the nation.[31] A
series of editorials published in the government-controlled *Al-Ahali* newspaper after anniversary day, in late July 1959, featured detailed descriptions of
the arches erected by municipalities and local communities throughout Iraq.
These descriptions—often dwelling on their elaborate decorative motifs, which
included Iraqi flags and photographs of the president—illustrate how government propaganda used arches to imbue urban and rural landscapes with the

new revolutionary spirit.[32] In contrast to their official image as the bearers of a united civic culture that effaced sectarian, ethnic, and religious divisions, the arches built by the people of Kirkuk for anniversary day—some reports suggest that more than one hundred were sponsored by the Turkmens—became closely identified with communal values and claims. Contestation over an arch sponsored by the Turkmen community and decorated with Turkish writing seems to have triggered the killings in the Turkmen coffeehouse. As well as buildings, arches became a target of reprisals during the fighting, and many were vandalized and destroyed.[33]

THE VIOLENCE IN BETWEEN: STATE DISCIPLINE, 1924–1959

I destroy anarchy . . . anarchy does not last long.

'Abd al-Karim Qasim, president of Iraq[34]

This statement during a press conference highlights how the logic of "order versus disorder" guided the actions of the republican regime in the aftermath of the 1959 disturbances. The government mobilized a variety of legal and military instruments to pacify Kirkuk: the imposition of martial law, the proscription of public assemblies, and the resort to military courts to restore public confidence in the regime. By the beginning of August, the military governor-general of Iraq had issued several proclamations granting extraordinary powers to the army, police, and security forces, including the power to arrest anyone carrying firearms and offensive weapons.[35] The harsh measures taken by Qasim's regime speak volumes about its power to use violent means to organize, coerce, and persuade its citizens. Yet, as in 1924, the events of 1959 show that in Kirkuk government authority and lawlessness, and peace and civic strife, coexisted in a precarious balance but, not surprisingly, worked in close association with one another. As Stathis Kalyvas puts it, "[T]he question of how order emerges and how it is sustained is but the flip side of understanding dynamics of conflict."[36]

The role played by the soldiers stationed in the city during both events offers an illuminating example of how particular moments of violence were produced as a result of the fine lines separating state discipline from insubordination, and legitimate from illegitimate use of force. Stationed in Kirkuk to enforce the authority of the British administration, the Assyrian Levies turned their guns against the civilian population in 1924, setting in motion a vicious cycle of retribution. In 1959, the soldiers of the Iraqi army who joined the disturbances at the side of the riotous crowds became implicated in the murder of civilians. Both military groups derived their subversive power from their privileged status as the upholders of a Baghdad-sponsored order.

The long-term dynamics and effects of the order-conflict-violence nexus in Kirkuk became apparent in the long interlude between 1924 and 1959. At first glance, this appears a relatively peaceful and violence-free period in the history of Kirkuk, at least in terms of large-scale public disturbances. Yet an examination of the basis for peace—rather than of the causes of conflict—reveals that violence was one of Kirkuk's chronic conditions.[37] The apparent state of normalcy concealed a condition of routine coercion and intimidation exercised by the colonial and monarchical regimes. State discipline in Kirkuk took many forms. It did not always produce physical violence, yet the threat of it was always present. In the early years of the Mandate, British inspectors and administrative officials acted vigorously to purge the municipality of Kirkuk and the local police of "undesirable characters." Former Ottoman civil servants and police officers were often dismissed, and in some cases arrested, on charges of corruption, abuse of authority, and, crucially, "pro-Turkish inclinations."[38] After 1924, as Air Command in Baghdad construed the activities of Kirkuk's population as a growing security threat, RAF pilots on reconnaissance patrols were able to "visualize" the city fully in order to map landscapes of subversion. As elsewhere in Iraq, the feeling of "being watched" from the air increased the sense of vulnerability on the part of the local population.

This feeling was compounded by the presence of RAF intelligence officers on the ground. Following an intelligence review in early 1925, operatives in the northern provinces of Iraq were instructed "to see considerably further in advance than other officials and officers on other duties" and "to mark down the exact whereabouts of any prominent pro-Turks, particularly military officers."[39] The reports sent to Air Command by the intelligence officer based in Kirkuk town show how the compilation of lists of "bad hats" (subversive elements) shaped the political geography of Kirkuk in the minds of colonial administrators. As a corollary of intelligence gathering for the purpose of policing the population, cartography was also used to make the space of the city intelligible. This was a state practice that continued throughout the monarchical period. The few maps of Kirkuk still available from that time show urban boundaries, residential areas, public institutions, and military and oil establishments. In identifying these elements of the urban landscape, the maps show concerns with public security, urban development, land tenure, transportation infrastructure, and lines of communication both with the oil fields and Kirkuk's hinterland.

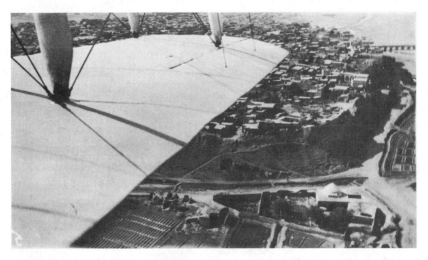

Figure 10.5. Kirkuk from the air: Royal Air Force plane policing the town, ca. 1925. Source: Edwin Newman collection. Courtesy of the San Diego Air & Space Museum.

After independence, in 1932, the observational powers of intelligence officers were also mobilized by the Iraq Petroleum Company and the Iraqi Ministry of Interior. The deployment of plainclothes officers to defuse troubles was a fact of life in pre-revolutionary Kirkuk. Informers reporting to the police, the oil company, and the British vice-consulate were also planted in the secret cells of the ICP, the most active organization in the labor movement since the 1940s. On the one hand, by making the regime of tight surveillance explicit, the often palpable presence of spies forced people into self-discipline. On the other, the bloody repression of the peaceful strikes staged by oil workers in 1946 set an ominous example in methods of crowd control by the military police, effectively forcing the labor movement underground.

After the 1946 strike, and during the imposition of martial law between 1948 and 1950 following the nationwide insurrection known as the Wathba (Leap), the municipal and military police liaised increasingly with the security personnel of the oil company and the Iraqi army in order to combat labor militancy. Individuals suspected of being affiliated with the ICP, in particular, were subject to house searches, arrests, interrogation, and arbitrary detention. The British vice-consul reported with some satisfaction in 1948 that Kirkuk's communists were "shy of open disorder." As well as oil workers, secondary school students were closely monitored, and often threatened, by the deployment of military police in front of their school buildings.[40] The thriving cultural life of Kirkuk in the 1950s also suffered from the close scrutiny of the secret police. In 1954, an attempt to form a theater company ended with the arrest of several intellectuals who were accused of forming an illegal organization.[41]

The cumulative effects of this "stabilizing" violence of the everyday, coupled with the shock waves of the revolution, explain the horrific explosion of civic conflict in 1959. The physical and psychological abuse perpetrated by the monarchy and its agents and the public nature of the reprisals unleashed by the 1958 revolution are the subject of some of the most gruesome images in al-Azzawi's fiction in *The Last of the Angels*. In a macabre carnival in which torturers and victims change places, released communist prisoners make a public display of their torture-scarred bodies, reenacting the physical violence they have suffered in prison before large crowds.[42]

LANGUAGES OF VIOLENCE

Various languages of violence were subtly but unequivocally interwoven with the actions that preceded, produced, and followed the events of 1924 and 1959. Enunciated by the government, community leaders, political activists, and ordinary people before, during, and after the disturbances, these languages used different registers to tell stories of violence. Some stories entered the arena of popular communication as rumors, verbal intimidation, folk tales, and memory. Others were narrated as public discourse. The rhetorical struggle that followed both disturbances does not explain them but shows how interpreting violent events has served competing communal and nationalistic claims to Kirkuk to this day.[43]

Subaltern forms of communication constituted an important ingredient of what Jonathon Glassman has called "the making of violent subjectivities" within crowds. Bloodstained messages were used by the terrified residents of the colonial town in 1924 as a visual signal to the tribes in the hinterland of Kirkuk of the ongoing carnage and as a way to solicit their assistance against the Assyrians.[44] Rumors were also triggers of aggressive behavior, creating an atmosphere of suspicion and vulnerability. In 1924 the British administrative inspector reported to the commission of inquiry that he was convinced that alleged threats against the wives and daughters of Assyrian soldiers were "sufficient to cause fierce resentment in the Assyrian breasts." Under interrogation, the father of the Assyrian patriarch confirmed that, before the market fracas, a rumor had been spreading in town to the effect that local residents were going to molest Assyrian families after the battalions left Kirkuk.[45] Rumors could also travel far. A camp hosting Assyrian refugees in Baghdad was attacked by local residents as unconfirmed and exaggerated reports of the killings in Kirkuk reached the capital. Before 14 July, Turkmen residents believed that Kurdish political activists were evacuating Kirkuk of its women and children, adding to their apprehension of danger during the anniversary celebrations. On a visit to Kirkuk a few months after the violence, British embassy intelligence official Peter Hayman noted that "surface calm, deep underlying anxiety and *plentiful rumour*" continued to linger over the city.[46]

Verbal provocation also encouraged violent action. Foul and improper language set the tone of the market incident of May 1924, which coincided with the celebration of Ramadan and Easter. Local residents accused the Assyrian soldiers of having insulted the shopkeeper. In turn, the Assyrian soldiers complained to their British officers that their religion had been cursed repeatedly during the altercation. The use of fiery language extended to the Assyrian officers. Showing his contempt and anger at the market incident, one of them harangued his men, threw his hat on the ground, and discharged his revolver in the air to encourage his soldiers to attack the population.[47] In 1959 the parade was one of the main discursive sites of ethnic and political provocation. Caught in the frenzy of the celebrations, left-wing demonstrators chanted slogans that praised the government and Iraqi-Russian friendship. Before the fatal incident in the coffeehouse, some reports suggest that loudspeakers mounted on army trucks were blasting out offensive language against Turkmens. Vandalism against the Turkmen arches was accompanied by threatening insults to the community, in response to singing and poetry recitations in Turkish.[48]

Popular stories of bloodshed forged powerful communal bonds, rekindling a shared sense of outrage. The memory of the Assyrian carnage of 1924 was very much alive in 1933, while the young Iraqi army was undertaking military operations against the Assyrian Levies in northern Iraq. On one occasion, bands of Arab villagers entered Kirkuk in a belligerent mood and posted anti-Assyrian notices in the markets demanding revenge for the bloodbath of 1924. In an unrelated incident, angry residents converged on the Assyrian barracks threatening to attack the Levies, enraged by the murder of a local girl whose body had been found in the citadel after she went missing.[49]

In Kirkuk's conservative Muslim religious culture, the violation of female purity and of family honor featured prominently in memories of violence—memories that were also nurtured by a very lively folklore tradition. This folklore is captured in the magic realism of al-Azzawi's fiction, particularly in some of the gruesome stories told by mothers to their sons. These stories feature the severed heads of Assyrian fighters brought to Kirkuk in 1933 by the triumphant soldiers of the Iraqi army: "[T]he eyes in these heads were impudent and kept staring at [the women], casting impertinent glances their way, so that many women had been forced to pull their headscarves around their faces as they cursed Satan and the Assyrians."[50]

A key narrative theme in Turkmen communal history has been the violation of the Turkmen neighborhoods of Kirkuk as the heartland of their ancient nation. Al-Azzawi portrays the largely Turkmen historical quarter al-Chaqur—the setting of *The Last of the Angels*—as a fatherland, the focus of strong community solidarity and collective honor.[51] Since World War I, Kirkuk has become central to the nativist rhetoric of the Iraqi Turkmens. The citadel in particular—which in the 1950s included the three quarters of Maydan, Aghaliq, and Hammam—constitutes an important *lieu de mémoire*, a space that was repeatedly violated by the "illegitimate" intrusion of Arabs and Kurds. Accordingly, the "massacres" (*katliamlar*) of 1924 and 1959 are placed within a linear historical development characterized by the irreversible process of the Arabization and Kurdification of the Turkmen nation. While the 1924 disturbances are remembered as the first attempt by the Iraqi government to eradicate the Turkmens from Kirkuk, the events of 1959 form the basis upon which the community still refuses to accept Kurdish claims to the city. The victims of 1959 have been bequeathed to posterity as martyrs—the victims of attempts by Kurdish communists to annex Kirkuk to Kurdistan and to seize Iraqi oil.[52] In contrast, some of the victims remember the violence as a moment of rupture in Kirkuk's peaceful coexistence. This rupture is poignantly narrated as a rite of passage—a traumatic coming-of-age—in the harrowing account of Resmiye Hanim, a resident of the citadel who was thirteen at the time of the disturbances.[53]

Government officials, political activists, and the press set the terms of the public, national, and communal debate on Kirkuk's moments of violence, conspiring to popularize its communal, ethnic, and political dimensions. The British colonial administration ultimately construed the events of 1924 as an expression of the deep-seated ill feeling between Christians and Muslims, also emphasizing the intrinsic "racial" antagonism between the Assyrian and Kurdish Levies stationed in Kirkuk. Not surprisingly, British accounts of the events of 1959—collated from official and unofficial sources by the embassy in Baghdad—characterized the Kirkuk "mob" as Kurdish communist sympathizers, a poignant reminder of the threat that left-wing politics had posed to the pro-British Hashemite regime during the last two decades of the monarchy.

Yet, as in relation to 1924, these accounts also stress the factional nature of the violence, suggesting that the communists had taken advantage of ethnic clashes between Kurds and Turkmens.[54] The republican regime read the violence through the prism of its rhetoric of progressive revolutionary politics. In the words of President ʿAbd al-Karim Qasim, the Kirkuk incidents represented "a black spot in our history and a stain on the history of the revolution."[55] The apparent resurgence of ethnic and communal divisions, and the horrific nature of some of the killings, caused considerable embarrassment in official circles. In order to minimize the involvement of the Communist Party, the Iraqi president publicly condemned the Kirkuk disturbances as the barbaric acts of criminal agitators and anarchists, questioning the democratic credentials of the progressive organizations involved.[56]

The outcome of official inquiries and trials mediated the version of the disturbances that the government circulated for public consumption. In contrast to the lenient attitude of the court toward the Assyrian Levy officers identified as the ringleaders, the mixed court convened by the republican regime passed twenty-eight death sentences. By sending ordinary activists to the gallows as individuals and not as members of political organizations, the government criminalized the 1959 disturbances. This served its urgent need to underplay the political and ethnic roots of Kirkuk's violence, and in particular the role of the army. Although the regime tried to minimize media coverage, the trials attracted considerable press attention.[57] For instance, the daily nationalist newspaper Al-Hiyad published a full account of the first round of the proceedings and captioned the gruesome photographs of the atrocities "Democracy and Peace in Pictures."[58]

How the court proceedings and the nationalist press scripted the 1959 events contrasted with the apologetic stance and conciliatory tone adopted by the Central Committee of the ICP. In an article published in the communist Ittihad al-Shaʿb in late August, the committee condemned the excesses of the violence and stressed the party's inability to impose discipline on the masses of Kirkuk or to tame their revolutionary energy. Yet, at the same time, the communiqué hinted at violence as an organizing principle of popular politics—a constructive force of modern progress.[59] A dissenting voice came from Dhu al-Nun Ayyub, a leftist intellectual close to the republican regime, who criticized the violent actions of ICP sympathizers in Kirkuk as *al-tatarruf al-yasari*—leftist extremism with sectarian overtones.[60]

. . .

By 1959, violence had certainly become an important means of conducting ethno-nationalist politics in Kirkuk. Yet the deeds, words, and atmospheres that combined to produce, tame, and recall the acts of violence committed in both 1924 and 1959 highlight the complex array of actors and forces that conspired to make communal and ethnic conflict such a salient feature of the city's twentieth-century history. The limitations imposed by the sources make it difficult to gain a tangible grasp of the interests and circumstances of the subaltern perpetrators and their victims. What is clear, however, is that Kirkuk's moments of violence cannot be understood exclusively as ethnic, communal, or politically motivated without taking into consideration the cumulative effects of the stories of violence that circulated during and after the events. These stories reinforced a collective sense of complicity and grievance but also created authoritative interpretations that are still polarizing communities to this day, pitting Turkmens against Kurds.

Alongside idioms of violence, state discipline and the role played by urban space in the conflict indicate the close links between the material and discursive conditions that underlined Kirkuk's disturbances. The interplay of these conditions combined both to produce and to remember violence. The short- and long-term reverberation of state action and propaganda in Kirkuk can hardly be overstated and goes a long way in explaining the delicate balance between order and disorder in the city. The imposition of state discipline—whether through soldiers, airplanes, or police—was deeply implicated in Kirkuk's moments of violence, producing the incremental effects of the overlapping security regimes at work in the period between 1924 and 1959 and in the following decades. Kirkuk's urban space—which represented a microcosm of Iraq's unstable ethnic, religious, and national frontier—represented both the stage of and a stake in the violence and inevitably came to be invested with highly charged political and communal meaning. To this day Kirkuk stands as the symbol of two nations. It is both the "Jerusalem" of the Kurds—a place of return—and the core of the ancient Turkmen nation of Iraq.

11 WAR OF CLUBS
Struggle for Space in Abadan and the 1946 Oil Strike

Rasmus Christian Elling

[W]e cannot be over-nice about legality and fair play where it is a question of vital oil interests.

British ambassador in Tehran to consul in Ahwaz, May 1946[1]

IN ITS MID-TWENTIETH-CENTURY HEYDAY, Abadan in southwestern Iran, one of the Middle East's most modern cities, boasted the world's biggest oil refinery. The 1980–88 war with Iraq turned the city into a mere shadow of its former self, and many locals and former residents today yearn nostalgically for the Abadan of the past, with its harmonious, cosmopolitan society. Yet this romantic popular recollection sometimes glosses over the fact that Abadan's trajectory from a mostly Arab village to a complex multicultural city was interrupted by moments of interethnic violence. Conversely, the nationalist Iranian historiography—which hails the city's fight to oust British imperialism, nationalize oil, overthrow the shah, and resist the Iraqi invasion—also tends to reduce interethnic conflict to the mere result of foreign enemy conspiracies.[2]

In this chapter, I counterbalance neglect, omissions, and distortions by bringing to light a particular event in Abadan's history of violence and placing it within its spatial context. On 14 July 1946, during a strike by oil workers, clashes broke out in Abadan between socialist labor activists and members of a so-called Arab Tribal Union. Using oil company archives, accounts by labor activists, and local memoirs, I investigate this underexamined event that stands at the contentious intersection of local, national and global politics, imperialism, ethnicity, and industrial urbanism.[3] In this investigation, one unit stands out in Abadan's geography: the social club. As a key site of change and strife in Abadan's urban life, the club encapsulates certain important dynamics in the trajectory of the modern Iranian nation-state, its history of anti-imperialist struggle, and the place of its marginalized minorities.

SECURING OUTPUT: ABADAN UNDER COMPANY RULE

Abadan's modern history is inextricably tied to that of the Anglo-Persian—later Anglo-Iranian—Oil Company (henceforth "the Company"). When oil was struck in Iran in 1908, Abadan was a village on an island between two rivers leading to the Persian Gulf—an outpost on Iran's border with Ottoman Iraq. It was inhabited mainly by Arab tribes living in adobe huts, cultivating date palms, fishing, and trading with the neighboring cities of Mohammerah and Basra. Whereas the northern and eastern parts of what is today the Khuzestan Province were inhabited by Lors, Bakhtiyaris, and various Persian-speaking communities, the south had been dominated by Arab tribes since at least the seventh century. By the sixteenth century, it was known as Arabistan,[4] and from 1897, it was under the control of Shaykh Khaz'al of Mohammerah. Like the Bakhtiyari khans in central Khuzestan, where oil was discovered, the shaykh acknowledged the sovereignty of the Iranian Qajar shahs in Tehran but ruled more or less autonomously.

Since the eighteenth century, Britain had treated the Persian Gulf littoral around Bushehr, south of Abadan, as its de facto possession. Moreover, the Constitutional Revolution (1905–11) and subsequent civil war, the 1907 division of Iran into Russian and British spheres of interest, and the increased military presence of the Government of India in southern Iran up to and during World War I all factored into the Iranian central government's dysfunction in Khuzestan. Consequently, when British diplomats and Company officials were tasked with facilitating the establishment of an oil industry in Khuzestan, they circumvented the Iranian government and instead dealt directly with the region's tribal leaders.

Wary of the arrival of a foreign entity in his domains yet keen on generating profit, Shaykh Khaz'al signed a lease in 1909 for the parts of Abadan Island where the Company had decided to build its refinery. Despite challenges and obstacles, European engineers erected a refinery that was able from 1913 to process high-grade petroleum for export. When Winston Churchill, the Company's key lobbyist, decided that the British navy should switch from the use of coal to oil on the eve of World War I, his government acquired a controlling interest in the Company. Securing and expanding Abadan's oil output became a top priority, and Abadan's palm groves soon gave way to a sprawling modern city. The Company insisted that locals did not have the industrial discipline required for the operation, so it imported its skilled labor from India, Burma, Iraq, Palestine, Europe, and even China. Abadan's population increased from around twenty thousand in 1910 to forty to sixty thousand in the early 1920s, and two hundred thousand in the 1940s.[5] To accommodate this influx of workers, the Company reluctantly engaged in urban development and colonial-inspired social engineering.[6]

BRAIM HOUSING ESTATE AND ABADAN REFINERY

Figure 11.1. Aerial photo of the Western enclave in Abadan. Source: British Petroleum Archive. © BP plc.

The British staff was housed in modern bungalows in the district of Braim at one end of the island, where the breeze made the extremely hot climate somewhat tolerable. Here, they were sheltered by the massive metallic barrier of the refinery, which stood in the middle of the island, and could nurture an exclusive, elite lifestyle. On the other side lay the "native town," which consisted mainly of Arab villages, the workers' neighborhood Ahmadabad, and the bazaar—and, from the 1920s, also of sprawling shantytowns. This segregated urban geography was a material manifestation of the ethnically demarcated labor hierarchy with which the Company ran its operation in Abadan: white "senior staff" at the top; skilled and semiskilled Indians, Christian (Armenian and Assyrian) and Jewish migrant labor from the Middle East in the middle; and masses of Iranian ("Persian" and "Arab"[7]) wage earners and unskilled and casual labor at the bottom.

Plagued by labor unrest from its early days, the oil industry was hit by a major strike in 1929, when workers protested against low wages and their appalling working and living conditions.[8] This historic strike inspired nationalist forces across Iran, and with the more resolute Reza Shah in power in Tehran from 1925 the Company was forced to make concessions. Pressured by growing social disorder, overcrowding, crime, and disease in the shantytowns, the

Company began in 1926 to engage in urban planning, building a new bazaar while providing sanitation and infrastructure, electricity, and paved roads. Eventually, the Company would build hospitals, schools, cinemas, and a university and, in the 1930s and 1940s, new, modern neighborhoods for Iranian labor, such as Bahmanshir and Bawarda. Through these developments, the Company sought to present an image of the city as a modern, egalitarian space of welfare and progress.[9]

Yet this image stood in contrast to the lived reality of most Iranians in Abadan. The Company's public relations strategy, combined with some improvements in quality of life and increased social mobility, was in the end not enough to gloss over the unequal distribution of power and resources in Abadan or to deflect criticism of the British exploitation of Iranian resources.

The Company was nonetheless able to manage discontent in Abadan during the boom years of the 1930s. With the ousting of Reza Shah and the British invasion of southern Iran in 1941, the Company further strengthened its foothold in Khuzestan. During World War II, Iran was plagued by food shortages, famine, disease, and insecurity. Citing a potential threat of sabotage against oil installations as well as Khuzestan's strategic position on the supply route through Iran to the Soviet Union, the Company pushed through a demand for martial law, eventually turning the entire province into a "special military zone"

CLUB, RESTAURANT AND PART OF BRAIM HOUSING ESTATE, ABADAN

Figure 11.2. Aerial photo of Abadan. Source: British Petroleum Archive. © BP plc.

under a pro-British military governor-general. The militarization of daily life, increased social control, food rationing, drastic fluctuations in labor demand, widespread hunger, epidemics, overcrowding, and a spike in crime fueled anti-British sentiment and socialist-inspired labor activism against the Company, and in May 1946, the oil worker movement reasserted itself in Abadan. By that time, Western diplomats and Company officials were convinced that the activism was orchestrated by Moscow as part of a bloodless war between Britain and the Soviet Union.

The July 1946 oil strike heralded the demand for oil nationalization that, in 1951, would bring an end to quasi-colonial British rule in Khuzestan. In order to properly grasp the violence that occurred during the 1946 strikes, however, it is necessary to take a closer look at the histories of two of the actors involved—the Arabs and the labor activists.

TRIBES, WORKERS, AND UNREST IN THE OIL CITY

By the 1910s, a modus vivendi had been established between the Company and Shaykh Khaz'al. The former lent the latter recognition, external protection, and loans in return for access to and security on Abadan Island. The Company often used Khaz'al's tribal forces to quell social disorder and labor. Under Khaz'al, Arab notables profited from the presence of the Company, and a handful of shaykhs enriched themselves as contractors or bazaar merchants. Others were able to benefit from Abadan's development, working as guards, servants, or day laborers, while farmers and fishermen sold their produce to the Company. Yet the Company rarely employed Arabs as wage earners and thus prevented their integration into the oil labor force.

The Company's—and indeed Britain's—policy toward the shaykh was ambivalent: they depended on his cooperation to secure their oil output, but they had by the 1920s become wary of his autonomist aspirations. The shaykh revolted against Tehran in 1916 and 1921, even proposing to separate his domains from Iran. Having toyed with the idea, Britain ultimately rejected Arab secession, and in 1925 Reza Khan took Shaykh Khaz'al prisoner and abolished the shaykhdom. A tribal insurgency erupted across Khuzestan, but now the British and the Company supported the state's clampdown against their erstwhile Arab allies. The unrest in Abadan and Mohammerah was crushed, but rural Arabs continued for decades to resist and protest harassment, new taxes, forced conscription, and the expropriation of land, animals, and foodstuffs by state authorities.

Figure 11.3. Caravan transporting oil products from Iran to Iraq, 1910s. Source: Ministry of Petroleum, Iran.

The Iranian central government rapidly consolidated its rule by uprooting traditional authority. While tribal communities throughout Khuzestan (and throughout Iran) were violently subdued, disarmed, and forcibly sedentarized, the Arabs were largely marginalized on the new political and social landscape that appeared after 1925. The free movement of families across the previously fluid national borders was curtailed, the use of the Arabic language in public was outlawed, and cities were given new Persian-sounding names—Mohammerah became Khorramshahr, for example. While the Iranian state was now present in Abadan through municipal, juridical, military, and police authorities, the Company, backed up by powerful British diplomats, retained much real power. In the event of a crisis, the Company either lobbied for British military intervention or used its own security forces, which operated in a legal gray area.

While pockets of urbanization and modern education appeared across the region, most Arabs continued to live in poverty and illiteracy, barred from influence and witnesses to a great influx of outsiders. Displacement of Arabs from Abadan had begun with Khaz'al's land leases in Braim and continued with the Company-led evictions in the bazaar and Bawarda in the 1920s and

1930s.[10] While some Iranian white-collar workers were able to move gradually into the new middle-class districts in the 1940s, Arabs were mostly confined to the squalid, crime-ridden neighborhoods of Kofeysheh, Koshtargah, and Ahmadabad, located outside the Company's housing zones, or lived in simple villages on rural Abadan Island. Some resorted to highway robbery, smuggling, and piracy, and memoirs testify to the fact that Arab tribes would still engage in raids against Abadan's citizens as late as the 1940s.[11]

Against this backdrop of inequality, agitation with ethnic overtones spread among the Arabs in Khuzestan in the 1940s. Contrary to popular historical narratives still prevalent in Iran, which present this agitation as completely stage-managed by the British, recent research has demonstrated the development of a genuine Arab movement across the province.[12] The key grievances of this movement included the lack of land rights and the expropriation of Arab property, yet there were also demands for cultural rights, political recognition, and regional autonomy.

British diplomats regularly reported on Persian-Arab tensions during World War II, on Arab distrust of the Iranian authorities, and on the violent treatment of Arab civilians by the Iranian gendarmerie and military.[13] In May 1944, local authorities reported their worries that Shaykh Jaseb—son of Shaykh Khaz'al— was scheming to return from his exile in Basra to establish an independent Arab state in Khuzestan.[14] In February 1945, the Iranian army attempted unsuccessfully to disarm Arab tribes on Abadan Island.[15] In January 1946, another of Khaz'al's sons, Shaykh Abdollah, launched a futile rebellion. Britain did not— as Iranian nationalists at the time feared and have since maintained—back the idea of an independent Arabistan, and it is clear from diplomatic correspondence that the Arab leaders felt betrayed. The Company was not interested either: as a business enterprise, it nurtured no dreams of state making.

Faced with rising social disorder, political discontent, and troop withdrawal from Iran in early 1946, British diplomats were particularly anxious about the threat posed by the oil labor movement. The dramatic history of this movement began when Indian migrant workers staged protests and strikes in the refinery in the 1910s and 1920s, to which the Company responded with mass deportations and the use of Arab tribal forces to quell disturbances. By the late 1920s, Iranian workers began to extract concessions from the Company by threatening to paralyze the refinery. In a fascinating account, a Soviet-trained labor activist sheds light on the mobilization leading to the 1929 strike.[16] Alarmed by Bolshevik infiltration, the Company pressured the Iranian authorities for

Figure 11.4. British-Indian riflemen guarding the refinery in Abadan, 1941. © Imperial War Museums (E 5327).

tighter security while expanding its own system of surveillance. During World War II, thousands of Iranians were suddenly dismissed from the refinery, and while intercommunal clashes broke out, discontent even spread to British personnel.[17] Underground socialist activism escalated among the oil workers, and by 1946 the Soviet-backed communist Tudeh Party and its affiliated trade unions were ready to take effective control of Abadan.

At that point, the Arabs were practically the only community in Abadan not to have joined the socialist labor movement. There can be several reasons for this. The Company had from the beginning of its operations viewed Arabs as unreliable labor; they preferred Iranians from outside the region or imported labor from abroad. The Arab labor that was employed consisted mainly of day laborers or contractor teams headed by shaykhs. It may be that some Arabs chose to rely on alternative sources of livelihood rather than endure the grueling work conditions in the oil industry or—as Arab activists maintained—that the Company in its recruitment discriminated against the Arabs. Either way, Arabs were underrepresented among the Company's workers and thus simply did not have the same stake in the labor movement as the mostly "Persian" wage earners.[18]

There are also possible sociocultural explanations. While others often severed tribal and traditional ties to their birthplaces when they moved to Abadan, Arabs still lived in their customary setting. Tribal power had even been revived in the political vacuum following the forced abdication of Reza Shah in 1941, and the conservative shaykhs were apprehensive of the Tudeh challenge to feudalism and tribalism. It is also likely that some Arabs felt threatened by socialist rhetoric, which was antithetical to local mores, and perhaps alienated by the liberal spirit of new Abadan. Although Tudeh stressed ethnic equality in its propaganda and translated some of its communiqués into Arabic, the party had largely failed to attract the Arabs. In the summer of 1946, intercommunal differences gave way to political violence.

TALKING SEDITION: SPACES OF CONTENTION IN ABADAN

Despite the Company's vigorous attempts to curb dissent, the success of the labor movement was nonetheless directly tied to the very spaces created by the oil industry. Khuzestan's refineries, oil wells, and workshops afforded activists close proximity to their peers and to sites for communication, debate, and the organization of dissent. In the overcrowded urban sprawl, the control of movement was nearly impossible. Memoirs testify that resentment toward the Company was fueled by the combination of slowly improving living conditions for Iranian workers and the rapidly rising but unfulfilled expectations of modernity that urbanization had generated.[19] One urban space—the club—played a key role in the socialization and politicization of Abadan's citizens. Its history throws light on Company social engineering, as well as on the spatial context of the 1946 clashes.

In the 1910s, the Company opened the so-called Gymkhana Club in the exclusive Braim district, which catered to the British senior staff. The Gymkhana boasted billiard tables, a bar with a dance floor, a restaurant, and a hall for meetings and lectures. As the Western expatriate community grew, the city saw a proliferation of clubs for boating, cricket, football, gardening, and so on—all with annual fairs, shows, matches, and balls. There were various freemasonry lodges, amateur theater groups, scout organizations, and social clubs that would later be graced by jazz legends such as Dave Brubeck, Dizzy Gillespie, and Duke Ellington. The dancing saloons, swimming pools, tennis courts, cafeterias, and bars presented a welcome alternative to the seedy speakeasies, opium dens, and brothels of the "native town." The Company believed that clubs and social activities would not only cultivate Western urbanity but also reduce alienation, restlessness, and disgruntlement among its senior employees.[20] The clubs remained exclusive to Europeans, while a few less well-equipped facilities were provided separately for Indians. Although a handful of Iranians managed to enroll in the latter, and while Iranian Armenians were able to open a club of their own, ordinary Iranian labor was generally barred from these social amenities.

The first organized demand for a club for Iranians was tied directly to the emergence of a nascent socialist movement. When Soviet-trained activists arrived in Abadan in 1927, their strategy to mobilize laborers was twofold: they organized a clandestine network to function as a secret trade union, and they established the first athletic club for Iranians in Abadan. Prepared for Company opposition to such a club, the activists enlisted a number of noncommunist Iranian white-collar workers to persuade a government official to issue

Figure 11.5. Jazz band playing at the Bashgah Abadan club, 1961. Photo: Courtesy of Shahriar Tashnizi.

a permit and then swiftly announced the opening of Kaveh Sports Club to the public. Masses of people attended the inauguration, where they listened to representatives from various guilds giving "stirring speeches unheard of before in Khuzestan"[21]—a dress rehearsal for the 1929 strike. Although Kaveh Club was frequented by many who were unaffiliated with the secret trade union, the Company could not tolerate its existence. With the help of Abadan police, the Company had Kaveh Club shut down after two months of workers' resistance. Indeed, mere membership in the club was later used as a justification for arrest during the clampdown following the 1929 strike.[22] Yet the Company eventually had to allow new professional and recreational spaces. From 1931 onward, the Company built clubs for clerks, seamen, artisans, and eventually the mid-ranking Iranian workers. To entertain the lower classes, the Company also established popular swimming pools and open-air cinemas. As sites of sociability and socialization, even athletic clubs were rightly feared to also function as sites of political activity, and Company managers allocated resources to have Abadan's burgeoning club milieu monitored.

By the mid-1940s the budding labor movement had turned many Company clubs into centers of resistance, even creating a parallel set of clubs for the various trade unions of taxi drivers, welders, and so forth, all considered illegal by the Company. Whereas the communist activists of the 1920s had to congregate secretly in private homes or in the palm groves outside Abadan, the Tudeh activists of the 1940s would use clubs as venues for party meetings, dissident activity, and speeches against British imperialism. The Company was aware that, in order to suppress discontent, the clubs had to be curbed, even if their sheer number made it nearly impossible. In October 1945, the British consulate general in Ahwaz wrote to the ambassador in Tehran that the military governorship and martial law instituted in Khuzestan during the war should remain in effect because

(1) it is easier in that way to prohibit meetings and generally to interfere with the activities of parties and clubs liable to *talk sedition*—though as you say even a Military Governor can't really suppress that sort of thing forever, and (2) malefactors are speedily punished (sometimes, I hear, even before they have done their foul deed) and that creates an excellent impression on other intending malefactors.[23]

As hotbeds of "sedition talk"—the subversive practice of ungrateful subalterns ("malefactors") who had to be punished for their insubordination ("foul deed")—the clubs had thus developed from Company-controlled spaces to nodal points in an urban network of anti-British activism. Within days after the British troop withdrawal from Abadan in March 1946, sedition talk gave way to a series of wildcat strikes and then a huge show of the labor movement's strength for the 1946 May Day demonstrations. The Iranian police first instructed Tudeh to celebrate the day inside the clubs, but, realizing the sheer numbers of participants, local authorities allowed for "overflow orderly meetings outside in the vicinity" of the clubs.[24] In the end, tens of thousands of workers marched throughout Abadan, disregarding all instructions. In a very literal sense, labor activism had spilled over into the streets, transgressing the coercive logics of social control in the oil city. Abrahamian describes the power grab:

> By mid-June [1946], the Tudeh organization in Khuzestan paralleled, rivaled, and, in many towns, overshadowed the provincial administration. . . . Its branches determined food prices, enjoyed the support of the local fire brigades, and controlled communications, especially truck communications, between the main urban centers. Its unions represented workers' grievances before management, collected funds for future emergencies, organized an elaborate shop-steward system, and opened forty-five club houses in Abadan alone. Moreover, its militias patrolled the streets, guarded the oil installations, and impressed foreign observers by quickly transporting 2,500 volunteers from Abadan to Khorramshahr to build an emergency flood wall.[25]

The Company's general manager in Abadan warned that, since clubs had more than twenty-five thousand members, local power was now effectively in the hands of "armed clubs" who were patrolling the streets wearing Tudeh armbands.[26] In the administrative language, *club*—and in the local vernacular, *kolub*—now signified a political actor rather than a material space. Despite a ban on public gatherings, Tudeh organized huge open-air meetings and took over Company buses, ending racially segregated public transport. In one incident, Indians, seen as lackeys of the British, were forced out of a football club by angry Iranians; and in another, labor activists climbed the walls of a club during a theater performance, inviting an outside crowd of between four thousand and five thousand to "take possession" of the premises and demanding an end to discrimination between Iranian and Western staff.[27] Tudeh vigilantes also forced Arab merchants, accused of hoarding, to sell goods to trade union members at reduced prices. The labor movement, in short, had broken the lines of urban demarcation, appropriating formerly exclusive spaces and threatening the Western enclave and its Indian and Arab servants. "Violence," a group of British MPs warned, "can occur *at any moment*."[28] The consul in Khorramshahr asked the Foreign Office in London to draw up a clandestine plan for a possible military intervention.[29] Such a move, however, would have been highly problematic, as Britain and the Soviet Union had just withdrawn from Iranian soil amid great controversy over Moscow-backed rebellions in Iranian Azerbaijan and Kurdistan. Indeed, the Tehran press was already claiming that the British army was in fact secretly using Company facilities as military bases.

The Company and the British diplomats were particularly alarmed by reports of increased Soviet activity and overtures to Arab tribal leaders. In what appeared a blatant publicity campaign inside the British sphere of interest, the Soviet consul at Ahwaz was seen openly socializing and playing dice with commoners in the coffeehouses of Khorramshahr.[30] After a tour of Khuzestan in June 1946, the British ambassador concluded that the Company would soon be forced to defend itself against Tudeh.[31] Looking for alternatives to an actual reinvasion of southern Iran, diplomats were contemplating a resort to an old Company strategy: using armed Arab tribes against labor activists. But there were more complex underlying dynamics in the July 1946 clashes.

ARAB MOBILIZATION AND THE POLITICS OF FEAR

Throughout 1946, Arab shaykhs repeatedly complained to the Company about Tudeh's aggressive campaigning. In Abadan's rural hinterland, Arabs violently confronted itinerant Tudeh propagandists, and during the 1946 May Day parades, the protesting crowds allegedly shouted slogans against the shaykhs, whom Tudeh considered henchmen of British imperialism. Following the parades, a shaykh reported that, due to threats and propaganda, some of the Arab contractors were likely to join Tudeh. This represented a frightening scenario for the Company: whereas the Arab contractors had until then been considered immune to socialist infiltration, there was now reason to fear that some might join the anti-British wave. The shaykh warned that the tensions might end in violence.[32]

From the diplomatic correspondence, it is impossible to ascertain a clear British strategy. On the one hand, the official line was one of caution and, as previously, official Arab requests for support were snubbed. The consul in Khorramshahr, for example, told a shaykh who wanted to bring back the exiled Shaykh Abdollah from Kuwait to Khuzestan that "the Arabs should do nothing which could be calculated to embarrass H. M. Govt. or their own Govt." and that they should not "bring trouble on themselves."[33] On the other hand, some Company officers certainly did assist in mobilizing the Arabs.[34] In May 1946, Abadan's new governor promised these officers that action would be taken against Tudeh, including the deployment of Arab forces.[35] In July, a military attaché to the Company, Colonel H. J. Underwood, noted that violent attacks on Tudeh members by Lor tribesmen east of Abadan had had a "wholesome effect," which could be emulated in Abadan by a "discreet cultivation of good neighbourhood policy amongst the Arabs."[36] Underwood had already met with shaykhs in June, reporting that Arabs were "definitely against the Tudeh" and "ready to help the Company by force." In the same report, he also suggested that it was "perhaps all to the good that the Arabs should form themselves into a patriotic Union."[37]

On the night of 12 June, Arab shaykhs gathered in Khorramshahr and Ahwaz to establish such an organization—the so-called Union of Tribes of Khuzestan (Ettehadiye-ye 'Ashayer-e Khuzestan), or Arab Tribal Union (ATU). Yet this action may also be understood as more than simply a Company ploy. On several occasions in the 1920s, and again in the 1940s, Arabs in Khuzestan had attempted to organize politically. While some initiatives were local in orientation and tribal in structure, others had more elaborate pan-Arabist agendas, yet only few openly championed Arab independence. The ATU established in June 1946 instead appeared primarily motivated by anger with the fact that Tudeh was pressuring the Company to hire Persian rather than Arab contractors.[38] Fearful of Tudeh "threats," the Arabs even sent a telegraph to the prime minister in Tehran protesting "the Tudeh closing of the Bazaar" in Khorramshahr.[39] In turn, Tudeh members warned Tehran that if they did not receive protection, they would have to "arrange their own." Indeed, the British feared that the Soviets were feeding Tudeh weapons through Basra, while the Tudeh claimed that the British were arming the Arabs.[40]

On 23 June, Arab shaykhs gathered for a traditional dance ceremony (*yazleh*) in Ahwaz, and the following day Arabs from across rural Khuzestan descended upon Khorramshahr to inaugurate the first modern Arab club under the auspices of the ATU.[41] A crowd of about ten thousand to twelve thousand people attended the ceremony, allegedly including Shaykh Jaseb, son of Shaykh Khaz'al.[42] The organizers triumphantly read out a charter containing ethnic demands, including parliamentary representation and the right to teach Arabic in public schools, as well as an end to Tudeh interference in provincial affairs and assistance from the Iranian state in developing the local infrastructure and economy. Importantly, the charter also criticized the Company for neglecting Arabs by building its facilities on Arab land but hiring outside labor, which had resulted in "much poverty and distress." In particular, it bemoaned the loss of historic Arab date palm areas and demanded that the Company "examine the legal rights of the Arab labourers and engage Arabs in a much larger proportion to other Persians."[43]

Such wording may put into question Tudeh's accusation that the ATU was a mere Company pawn. The fact that the Union had its own agenda was underscored by its resistance to a demand from Tehran, reiterated by British diplomats, to change its name to the non-ethnic "Khuzestan Farmers' Union." In fact, the anti-Tudeh emphasis indicates that the shaykhs shared mutual interests with the conservative faction of the divided ruling elite in Tehran. This impression is bolstered by correspondence between the ATU and Prime Minister Ahmad Qavvam and by the fact that the ATU also intermittently identified as a "Democratic Union" in order to indicate support for Qavvam's Democratic Party. In short, while Tehran certainly feared Arab separatism, there were probably also forces eager to exploit the union as a tactical counterbalance to the Tudeh. It is important to note that the charter clearly stressed the ATU's adherence to the constitution and territorial integrity of Iran.

After Khorramshahr, the ATU quickly moved to set up clubs in towns such as Bandar Mahshahr (Ma'shur), Hendijan, and Shadegan (Fallahiyah); it then announced it would open a club in Abadan on 5 July. Fearing interethnic conflict, local authorities refused to issue a permit. Tudeh, in turn, distributed pamphlets in Arabic warning people not to let the British and their allied shaykhs "plant seeds of enmity between Arabs and Persians,"[44] and they announced that the ATU was funded and instigated by the British. The trade unions then called for a general strike across the province on 14 July. Among their demands, they included the dismissal of Khuzestan's pro-British governor-general; an end to Company political interference and intrigues with the ATU; and improvements in health services, housing, and transport, as well as the institution of weekend (Friday) pay. According to an article in the Tudeh-affiliated *Rahbar* daily, two thousand workers took control of transport in and out of Abadan on 14 July "so as to prevent the British from inciting the local tribesmen"—a euphemism for Arabs. Other workers, *Rahbar* reported, maintained "perfect order" throughout the city.[45] The trade unions' gradual takeover of the city was recorded meticulously by Company intelligence: from truck garages to hospitals, port installations, and swimming pools, Tudeh moved to capture all facilities. Yet even then, the British consul rejected the governor-general's proposal to arm Arab tribes.[46] As armed Arabs were gathering in Abadan, it was too late, however, to prevent a violent encounter.

MONSTERS OF MAYHEM

Unsurprisingly, Tudeh and Company accounts of what happened on 14 and 15 July differ. Certainly, there was a clash sometime after 6:00 p.m., but the otherwise detailed Company accounts are murky on the exact sequence of events. According to one report, "excited irresponsible leaders" had mobilized "an inflamed roaring mob" of several thousand Tudeh supporters to "attack the Arabs" in order to preempt an Arab attack on a Tudeh club. After this initial attack, a larger crowd poured into downtown Abadan, where the Arab club was burned down. During the clashes, several prominent shaykhs and Arab (as well as non-Arab) merchants were lynched or killed in fights with crowds, labor activists, and possibly police, including Hajj Haddad, Mahdi Hossein Gazi, Shaykh Naser, and Yusef Kowaiti. These killings, Company officers feared, would "definitely mean an immediate and serious Arab versus Tudeh war."[47] The houses and warehouses of shaykhs were looted, while files in the Arab club were confiscated. Police opened fire on looters, and by 2:00 a.m. on 15 July, the Company had received reports of "about 150 casualties in the hospital, and the mortuary already full," with between fifteen and twenty deaths. Injuries, the hospital reported, included "mostly clubbing, some knife and gunshot wounds; several broken limbs." Most wounded and dead, according to this report (and to Tudeh accounts[48]) were Persians; according to other reports, most casualties were Arabs.[49] Tudeh spoke of more than fifty dead but claimed that actual numbers could never be ascertained since corpses were dumped in mass graves outside Abadan.[50] Around seventy arrests were made, and there was similar unrest in other cities of Khuzestan. The following day, the atmosphere was tense and full of rumors of impending Arab retribution. Abadan's governor had initially suggested "that Arabs might be 'allowed' to burn down Tudeh H.Q." to settle the score,[51] but the Company apparently pressured the police to prevent this.

In a lengthy report, counselor of the British embassy in Tehran, Sir Clairmont Skrine, claimed that Tudeh pamphlets called on locals "to make mincemeat" of agents of "the colonising foreign powers" and that when violence broke out, the crowd acted on this invitation by targeting the Arabs.[52] Indeed, British intelligence claimed that it had recorded speeches by Tudeh leaders on

14 July calling on workers to kill named Arabs collaborating with the Company.[53] According to Skrine, Tudeh had planned that Arabs be "murdered brutally *pour encourager les autres* [in order to encourage others]; the Arabs were to be cowed, and the power of their Union was to be finally broken by terroristic methods." He provided a vivid depiction of the violence:

> At the monster meeting at 6.30 p.m. inflammatory speeches must have been made, for at about 7.30 the roar of a mob out for blood terrified all within earshot. Within an hour the Arab Union Headquarters had been attacked, cars and houses set on fire, and at least three prominent Arab Union supporters brutally murdered in their houses. Bodies were mutilated and thrown into the river, women hacked with knives, houses set on fire. As might have been expected, the Arab population hit back in force and being in greater numbers than the Persians they cudgelled and chopped at a considerable number of Tudeh supporters, perhaps 150. Only the resolute action of Major Fatih [the Abadan head of police] and his men who used rifle fire to quell the mob saved Abadan from much greater catastrophe. Left to themselves, the Arabs might easily have beaten or hacked to death every Persian in the place.[54]

The killing of Hossein Gazi was described by another Company officer: "The crowd found this unfortunate man at home and brutally beat him to death with clubs. In the end his head was torn off and carried away. The crowd blooded themselves and their clubs with the blood of their victims."[55]

The language is dramatic and the depiction of the crowd racist: the mindless, monsterlike mobs of bloodthirsty Orientals out to terrorize, mutilate, and behead each other—and in the process, to raze the modern urban order. The description of violence is marked by feral viciousness: bodies—even the bodies of women—were "hacked," "cudgelled," and "chopped" with primitive weapons, while the attackers ritualistically smeared themselves with blood. The only force that quelled the mob and saved Abadan was the rational thinking, modern rifles, and "resolute action" of Major Fatih—the only official Company ally in this situation. Thus, the British diplomats and Company officers maintained that Tudeh had started the violence but that both sides constituted irrational crowds. Unsurprisingly, in their testimonies before a military tribunal convened by the Iranian authorities after the unrest, Tudeh activists presented a quite different account. Their testimonies were recorded by Farajollah Mizani (a.k.a. Javanshir), a prominent Tudeh activist who published them in exile in 1980 in the form of a booklet.[56]

During the trial, Tudeh leader Hossein Jowdat outlined a conspiracy. Aided by British forces and Iraqi Arab nationalists, the Company had incited the Arabs to crush the labor movement. According to him, the first step was to bring Shaykh Abdollah, along with weapons and ammunition, from across the Shatt al-'Arab (Arvand Rud, in Persian) into Abadan's vicinity. By arming the Arabs, the Company would create chaos during the general strike, thus spoiling an otherwise orderly and legitimate industrial action. The end goal, Jowdat maintained, was to destroy Tudeh and stir the Arabs toward a separatist rebellion that could secure Britain's oil interests. To prove the British hand in this conspiracy, Jowdat claimed that those scheduling the opening of the Arab club had made calculation errors between the Islamic and Iranian calendar and that an ATU proclamation calling for violence against Tudeh bore signs of a clumsy translation from English to Persian.[57]

Furthermore, Jowdat claimed that the Company had distributed employment notices in the region on the first day of the strike to attract hordes of unemployed riff-raff to Abadan. When these people converged in the city and were informed that the jobs had already been taken, they would drift around aimlessly in the streets, creating an atmosphere of disorder, and eventually loot the residences of prominent shaykhs and merchants. Jowdat explained that clashes started when Arabs attacked a car carrying two Tudeh members who were about to inspect their own club. A melee resulted in the shooting of a Tudeh member, which in turn attracted others to the scene, including the aforementioned loitering riff-raff. Violence escalated from here, just as the Company had planned.[58] The next day, the military ejected the drifters from Abadan, rendering a proper investigation impossible. With this account, Jowdat exonerated Tudeh from the violence, placing the blame squarely on the Arabs, "the British," and the unemployed mobs.

Although this explanation differs from the official British line, some of the wording is quite similar. For example, Jowdat explained that the Company had unleashed a "monster of turmoil and disorder and mayhem" (*hayula-ye eghteshash va na-amni va harj-o-marj*). The violence of the real culprits—certain Arabs (referred to euphemistically as "contractors") and the "loiterers" or "riff-raff"—was either mindless or rooted in suspicious motives. The Arab tribes and the riff-raff had "terrorized" ordinary people and ruined the state of peace and order instituted by Tudeh. Underlying this language, I argue, is a tangible urban/rural discrimination, which intersects with perceived ethnic and ideological differences between the Arabs and Persians. While Tudeh leaders are careful not to indict the Arabs wholesale, and instead distinguish between loyal Arab compatriots and suspicious Arab "outsiders," they nonetheless paint a picture of regressive tribes and treacherous separatists hiding across the river in Iraq. The Arab enemy, in this account, has descended from the backwaters, armed by the British, and then was placed in the heart of Abadan's modern urban space, thus reawakening a backward monster and unleashing it on the progressive order championed by socialism.[59]

Apart from Company records and Tudeh testimonies, there is an eyewitness account by the esteemed writer and translator Najaf Daryabandari that contains interesting details. According to Daryabandari, Shaykh Haddad, who was killed during the violence, was a famous character in Abadan's urban life: he was a well-paid contractor and would tour the city every day in a fancy open jeep; his office was stormed by Tudeh activists because it functioned as headquarters of Arabs working for the Company. Daryabandari acknowledged that, during the clashes, "a sort of Persian-Arab fight took shape" but argued that the real reason for the clashes was to be found in Company-Tudeh relations. He added that no ethnic violence had occurred after 1946. The day after the clashes, Daryabandari witnessed that "the ground and walls of [Haddad's office building] were smeared in blood," while "martial law was declared, the trade unions were besieged and labor activism in Abadan curtailed." However, Daryabandari recalls, activism "stayed in our hearts and minds and attracted us to the Tudeh Party and to resistance against the Company."[60]

Whether they had instigated the Arabs or not, the British reacted to the violence with trepidation. First, a sloop was anchored in the Shatt al-'Arab, threateningly facing Abadan. A British-Indian brigade was then deployed to Basra, ready to move into Khuzestan.[61] British diplomats feared that the strike had only been the first step of a larger Soviet-backed scheme to disrupt oil production and ultimately oust the British from Iran. The Foreign Office, however, remained opposed to the idea of arming the Arabs in the event of further labor disturbances. Yet maybe such action was already redundant: the consul in Khorramshahr triumphantly declared in August that the combined effect of a British military presence in Basra and Iraqi agitation over the repression of Iran's Arabs had had "the very desirable effect of stimulating the [Iranian] Central Govt. into taking more vigorous measures against the Tudeh."[62]

Although the Company eventually agreed to Friday pay, thus ending the strike, the violence was utilized by Company-loyal local authorities as an excuse for draconian measures against the labor movement. There were mass arrests of

Tudeh members, and all gatherings of more than three people were outlawed. Jowdat describes this situation as resembling a military occupation. The Company's "Iranian-lookalike" forces placed sentinels with machine guns on the roofs of private homes, holding the laborers hostage in their own city: "Soldiers and armed policemen had occupied the streets, public centers and thoroughfares of the city, and everywhere you could see the flash of bayonets."[63] Tudeh was forced to retreat and reorganize underground, as the laborers had lost their control of Abadan. Yet the Company's foothold was unsustainable. Across Iran, newspapers gave extensive coverage to the violence as yet another example of British meddling in Iranian affairs and of the peril of Arab separatism. The experiences of July 1946 radicalized the leftist and anti-imperialist current, and in the aftermath of the strike, Prime Minister Qavvam conceded a number of cabinet posts to pro-Tudeh politicians. Five years later, with the nationalization of Iran's oil industry, British hegemony in Khuzestan came to an end. The very last remaining Company employees in Abadan, "toting tennis rackets and golf clubs" along with all their belongings, gathered in the Gymkhana Club— the first club in Abadan and a symbol of segregation—from where they were evacuated from Iran on a British gunboat to the sound of a military band playing "Colonel Bogey."[64]

Meanwhile, the disheartened Arab shaykhs were concerned that their peers would end up joining Tudeh out of fear of retribution. British diplomats reported that the military tribunals set up by the Iranian authorities were severely biased toward Tudeh and that the Arabs themselves had not cooperated in a proper manner by documenting their side of the events.[65] Leading shaykhs went into hiding, while others headed to Baghdad and Cairo, where they presented the Khuzestani Arab case before the Arab League.[66] The Iraqi and Egyptian press expressed solidarity with their Arab brethren and outrage at the Iranian government and Tudeh. In the end, however, the Arabs did not receive international support sufficient for relaunching an autonomist movement, nor did they win any justice from the Iranian state. The Arab clubs were shut down, and to this day it remains virtually impossible for Arabs—still considered with suspicion by the authorities—to organize politically inside Khuzestan.

·   ·   ·

The city of Abadan was simultaneously the stage for and the object of the July 1946 clashes. The fight over a particular socio-spatial unit—the club—in the urban landscape of a city such as Abadan was an expression of multilayered conflicts over resources and power in a modern nation-state. The club developed from being the symbol of a British/European/white enclave in a segregated city to become a symbol of resistance against imperialism in a multicultural city marked by leftist mobilization and, for some Arabs, a symbol of a minority's fight for representation in a nation-state dominated by a Persian-speaking majority. Thus, there were multiple interests at work in the violence that interacted in more complex ways than the simplified binaries of Arab/Persian, contractor/wage earner, or tribal/leftist suggest.

Ethnicity certainly played a role: there is ample evidence that the mobilization, contention, and violence were perceived by all sides at least partially to reflect ethnically framed emotions, demands, and interests. But it is important not to reduce the clashes to a straightforwardly ethnic conflict: the presence of some Arabs among the labor activists and the fact that not all Tudeh targets were Arabs underscore that the lines were blurred. Although the Arab community remained partially marginalized from the rest of the city, Abadan was also a place of intermingling, cosmopolitanism, and peaceful coexistence. As Daryabandari mentions, there have been practically no overt interethnic tensions in Abadan since 1946, with the partial exception of the heated days of the Islamic Revolution of 1978–79. In other words, it would be wrong to perceive the 1946 violence as an expression of inherent primordial animosity between "Arabs" and "Persians."

Similarly, the conflict should not be boiled down to a mere British conspiracy against Iran. Although some Company officers—perhaps on their own initiative and perhaps in conflict with official British policy—were directly involved, there is also ample evidence that the British government was reluctant to back the shaykhs. Furthermore, the Arab mobilization was not only aimed at the labor movement and Tudeh but also expressed grievances against the Company. Sober historical research into the relationship of the anti-Tudeh faction in Tehran with the Arab shaykhs in Khuzestan could furthermore shed light on the underexamined topic of center-periphery politics in Iran. But this does not mean that the British government and the Company, with its coercive policies in Khuzestan, can be exonerated. The oil industry was established according to a colonialist, segregationist logic that was expressed in both its urban development and its labor policy, which favored some groups and marginalized others, thus exacerbating ethnic divides in Khuzestan.

This inequality spawned a struggle for physical spaces of political representation such as the club—a key urban space for articulating claims, expressing identity, and demanding representation and inclusion. The club must therefore be located within the context of the various scales of activity at the time: the new global economic imperialism of a Western-owned oil company, Iranian nationalism, leftist labor activism, and the ethnically framed mobilization of a marginalized minority. The stake invested in the club during the urban violence of 1946, then, had as much to do with control over public space in Abadan as with a contestation of national space in Iran.

12 URBAN RUPTURE

A Fire, Two Hotels, and the Transformation of Cairo

Yasser Elsheshtawy

IN JANUARY 1952 an anti-colonial crowd set fire to numerous buildings in downtown Cairo. One of those was the famed Shepheard's Hotel—the ultimate symbol of British colonialism. These events eventually led to those of 23 July, when the monarchy was overthrown and a group of military officers assumed power. They engaged in a far-reaching attempt to modernize Cairo. The barracks located along the Nile, at the edge of the city's downtown area, were a particularly poignant target given their affiliation with the British army. They were replaced in 1959 by the—at the time—ultramodern Nile Hilton.

This violent incident reveals a specific moment in Cairo's history in which the past was cast aside, removed, destroyed, and replaced by a new vision that aimed at engaging Cairo, and in turn Egypt, with the wider world and illustrating that the city had finally escaped the shackles of colonialism. Shepheard's became a symbol of the British occupation, *Life* magazine describing it in a lengthy pictorial in 1942 as a "British base in Cairo."[1] Yet it was not Shepheard's by itself, of course, but rather the entire downtown area that was, in the eyes of many, an enclave for the privileged, promoting social practices that set it aside as an elite space. In a very different way, after 1959 the Nile Hilton represented a new face of Cairo by encouraging progressive social practices that sought to cast away the backwardness of antiquated traditions. This came to an abrupt end with the death of President Nasser in 1970 and the subsequent adoption of socially and economically conservative policies.

Cairo's twentieth-century urban development can be read through this violent upheaval that occurred in 1952. The fire that burned down Shepheard's Hotel set in motion a process that led to the city's current urban form. To trace the trajectory that began with this incident up to the construction and subsequent use of the Nile Hilton is to reveal the kind of rupture, both spatial and social, that characterized the urban development of the Egyptian capital.[2]

This chapter looks first at the idea of urban rupture, and at the founding myth of this rupture, as a point of entry into the downtown Cairo of the period between the nineteenth century and the 1952 Cairo fire. It also examines the notion of "urban reverberation"—that is, the spatial impact of this violent event. In both sections the story of the two hotels is used as a baseline to relate specific events, providing both visual and spatial reference points. The chapter concludes by discussing how we can read this rupture and reverberation in the context of pre-2011 Cairo and the impact, if any, that it may have on future developments.

URBAN RUPTURE: THE DESTRUCTION OF COLONIAL CAIRO AND THE FOUNDING MYTH

> *The Nadhir [gazer] stood in the square. Here was the opera, a complete piece of Europe designed by Facioti and Rossi in the style of La Scala in Milan. The opera is in the middle of the square, and to its left the treasury department, which is still standing. He looked across the street; there was Shepheard's hotel, a small piece of England, as if it were the British consulate.*
>
> **Radwa Ashur, *Qit'a min Uruba* (A piece of Europe)**[3]

Urban violence may refer to willful acts of destruction—for instance, through the agency of crowds seeking to overturn a political order. Government officials and planners razing neighborhoods and districts under the pretext of enforcing order and health measures could be construed in a similar manner. Violence can also be seen as a process of homogenization and reconfiguration of urban space taking place over an extended period of time—a kind of urban rupture that seeks to achieve a radical break with the past. Indeed, David Harvey argues that this is one of the defining features of modernity, a process of "creative destruction" in which the city dances "to the capitalist imperative to dismantle the old and give birth to the new." Furthermore, "modernity is, therefore, always about 'creative destruction,' be it of the gentle or the democratic or revolutionary, traumatic, and authoritarian kind." Harvey also introduces the idea of the "founding myth"—a desire to show that what happened before is irrelevant, in order to justify the inevitability of a radical break with the past.[4]

Conceptualizing urban violence along these lines—that is, viewing it in terms of both process and agency, a creative destruction accompanying modernization and contributing to a founding myth for new regimes—is crucial in understanding the events leading up to the Cairo fire of 1952. Furthermore, in this chapter I am applying the construct "creative destruction" to urban interventions such as the reconfiguration of the Cairene downtown space, physically and socially, the displacement of the city's center, and the promotion of a new planning paradigm.

The Context: Modernizing Cairo

Christine Rosen argues that the "aftermath of great fires" provides historians with a unique opportunity, since the durability of structures and in turn the continuity of urban development are brought into question.[5] Events such as fires thus reveal underlying societal structures and power relations. But in order to understand this more clearly in the context of Cairo in 1952, it is necessary to recognize the city's urban morphology and sociopolitical geography at the end of the nineteenth century.

A map dating from 1846 shows the medieval city of Cairo still intact, characterized by a dense maze of narrow alleyways. Significantly, it is removed from the Nile River, with large agricultural fields separating it from the waterfront. The only outlet to the water is Bulaq, a largely industrial district and port area at the time.[6] Substantive changes occurred with the planning of Isma'iliyya, the city's new downtown area initiated by Isma'il, Egypt's ruler who in 1863 succeeded his uncle, Sa'id Pasha. Four years after assuming power, he began his transformation of Cairo into a European city modeled after Paris, with wide boulevards and spacious squares. This "modernist" project proceeded, and in 1869, during the opening of the Suez Canal, Egypt presented its modern face to the civilized world.[7] Cairo thus became what was arguably a dual city, composed of a European quarter, Isma'iliyya (or downtown, as it is known today), and the medieval city. A map from 1874 clearly show the contrast between these two realms.[8]

Much has been said about these transformations and the extent to which they ushered in a new phase in Cairo's urban history. Some scholars, such as Timothy Mitchell, have rightly noted that bringing in modernity was primarily a spatial project whose main defining feature was a "juxtaposition" between the old order, represented by the older quarters of Cairo, and the new, embodied by the staging of a "miniature Paris in Wust al-Balad" (downtown).[9] And it is precisely this duality that led urban historian Mara Naaman to note that elements of violence were embedded in the urban planning process.[10]

An obviously distinct feature setting the downtown space apart from the medieval city were broad avenues built along straight lines, which define the area's urban form to this day. But it was not just roads that defined the city's new

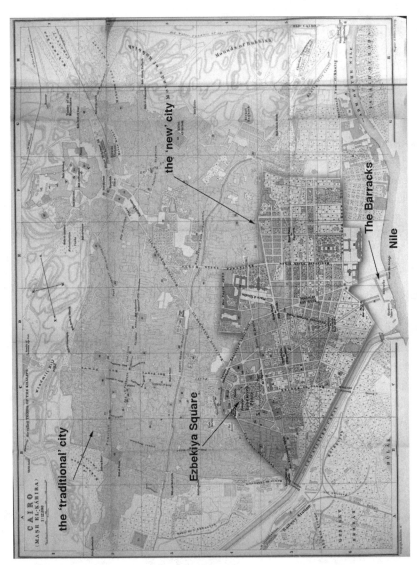

Map 12.1. Map of Cairo indicating clear separation in street layout between the old and new city, 1885. Source: Travelers in the Middle East Archive (TIMEA), Rice University, https://scholarship.rice.edu/handle/1911/9305.

shape—there were also massive improvements related to landscaping and the construction of new buildings, some of which introduced new social practices related to consumption and entertainment. For instance, among Isma'il's major projects was the improvement of Ezbekiya Square—the city's heart, standing at the threshold between the European quarter and the medieval city. This also included Ezbekiya Gardens, which were "laid out afresh with formal gardens, grottoes, fountains and modern cafes."[11] This was a distinctly European space. As Naaman notes, Ezbekiya Gardens, built after the draining of an existing pond, was a "European-style garden modeled by Pierre Grand and Barillet-Deschamps after the Parc Monceau in Paris."[12] Moreover, a brand-new Opera House was constructed, overlooking a square with the same name. Shepheard's Hotel was of course nearby, and the entire area acquired a reputation as an entertainment district.

The social scene was distinctly elitist. Trevor Mostyn, who in his chronicle of Cairo describes that era as the city's Belle Époque, evokes scenes reminiscent of a European city rather than an oriental setting: Albanian doormen, Parisian-style cafés such as Groppi's, fashionable window displays, and imposing gentlemen's clubs.[13] Anne-Claire Kerboeuf has also characterized this new area as being elitist, noting that it became an enclave of sorts. Thus, in order to enter one of its many stores, it was necessary to have an "*effendi* look (shoes, suit, and a *tarbush*) and speak a foreign language. Financial means were consequently required."[14] She argues that Isma'iliyya was a European micro-society closed to many Egyptians.

The presence of a range of European shops and other establishments further cemented the reputation of downtown Cairo as an alien space in the eyes of ordinary Egyptians, while introducing new habits and social customs to the rich and wealthy of Cairene society. Radwa Ashur, in her semi-fictional depiction of Cairo's transformation, writes extensively about one such import—the famous Groppi establishment. She notes that it was founded by Giacomo Groppi, a Swiss entrepreneur who arrived in Egypt in the 1880s, and that in its heyday it not only served food but also became a trendsetting cultural establishment.[15]

More branches were opened in the downtown area, highlighting Groppi's success. He also introduced a new type of restaurant: an American-style diner serving coffee, sandwiches, and pastry on counters while patrons stood—named, appropriately, "L'Americaine." The use of the French word demonstrated the extent to which French (that is, European) culture permeated everyday life as a way of signaling sophistication. Such practices seemingly confirmed that

Figure 12.1. Ezbekiya Gardens, 1938. Source: Library of Congress.

downtown was an exclusively European space in which "European modernity" was "compartmentalized in one district."[16] Downtown was also a site of decadence—a place where weary soldiers returning from the battlefield could find some relief in the form of alcohol and brothels.[17]

But some scholars have disputed the claim that downtown Cairo was an exclusively European setting. Nancy Reynolds, for example, has argued that this area was a hybrid space whose streets and public spaces accommodated both European and local practices of leisure and consumption.[18] This may have been true in some parts of it, but on the whole a clear line of demarcation did exist, laying the ground for the subsequent violent events. Moreover, as Egyptian architects Galila El Kadi and Dalila Elkerdani have argued, downtown was not simply a preserve of Westerners but was also associated with the new Egyptian elite.[19]

The mere fact that the city would be conceived in terms of two spaces—an old, rundown, traditional space versus a clean, modern, and efficient one—lay at the heart of Isma'il's modernization efforts. The mere fact of the state's neglect of these older districts contributed to a series of protests. These include the 'Urabi rebellion of 1881–82, the revolution of 1919, the workers' protest of 1946, and the fires and subsequent revolution in July 1952. The juxtaposition of traditional with modern was clearly in evidence at the site of the Opera House and the Ezbekiya Gardens, which were immediately adjacent to the heart of Fatimid Cairo. And it was in this interstitial space that the events leading to the Cairo fire began. Farther north, toward the Nile, were the British barracks—another space that became the site of violent encounters during the colonial and post-colonial periods. In addition, the downtown cafés became the preferred site for Egypt's intellectuals to debate politics and organize mobilization.[20] The seeds of urban upheaval and violence were thus planted within this Western, elitist space.

Shepheard's: Symbol of Colonial Egypt

Standing in the center of downtown Cairo was Shepheard's—a hotel dating from the 1850s that underwent a series of renovations and extensions until it reached its most historically recognizable form in 1927. The hotel stood for the glamour of Cairo and was a center of its elite social life, visited by notable guests, including President Theodore Roosevelt in 1910,[21] as well as the king of Egypt, whose cars were a frequent sight opposite its main entrance. As a 1958 Associated Press report noted, Shepheard's "was more than a hotel, a centre of life in Cairo, a romantic setting for stories, true and fictional, about the crossroads of the world. It symbolized an era, the age of empire, the high point of colonialism."[22] Anthony Trollope, the famous English novelist, visited Shepheard's in 1858 and wrote: "I know of no place as delightfully mysterious as Cairo. But the English tongue in Egypt finds its centre in Shepheard's Hotel."[23] The hotel was located off Ezbekiya Gardens on the corner of Alfi Bey and Ibrahim Basha Streets and was, according to Mostyn, "a club in itself and proudly advertised itself as 'Patronized by Imperial and Royal Families.'"[24]

One of the most well-known features of Shepheard's was its famed terrace, which overlooked a vibrant and boisterous street. The terrace was raised by eight steps from street level, and this elevated plane symbolized for some the colonial detachment from Cairene street life. Indeed, frequent depictions by travelers highlight the cosmopolitan and refined nature of the terrace's patrons,

Figure 12.2. View from the terrace of Shepheard's Hotel in the early twentieth century. Photo: T. H. McAllister. Source: Brooklyn Museum, Goodyear.

contrasted with the street hawkers and "dragomans" (tour guides), who seemed to pose some sort of threat. This sense of remoteness was emphasized in artistic portrayals, such as the satirical watercolor paintings by Lance Thackeray in *The Light Side of Egypt*, published in 1908. One such painting, titled *Romeo and Juliet*, shows a white Englishman gazing at a pretty English girl sitting demurely at one of the tables on the terrace. Behind the railings, we see the heads of the Egyptian natives surveying the scene with curiosity.

The hotel was known not just for its terrace but also for its numerous popular haunts such as the legendary Long Bar, presided over in the early 1950s by "Joe the bartender," who became a legend in his own right.[25] Additionally, Shepheard's was the center of a lively nightlife, hosting many balls attended by the well heeled. Curiously, it also seems to have been a center of gay life and encounters; various accounts place it alongside other well-known "cruising spots" at the time, such as public toilets in London and the Pink Elephant Club in Manila. Interestingly, the Nile Hilton's Jackee's nightclub and Tavern bar would acquire a similar reputation in the 1970s and 1980s.[26]

Further emphasizing the disconnectedness between the hotel and Cairo life was the fact that behind Shepheard's, and bordering its spacious gardens, stood windowless houses where people lived in appalling squalor. According to Nina Nelson, writer and resident of Cairo at the time, they were hidden from view "by a great lattice screen, some sixty feet high, interlaced with thick greenery, and visitors walking along the trim pathways . . . or among the towering royal palm-trees, sycamores and flowering shrubs were unaware of the different world which lay a few yards away."[27]

Along the same street, overlooking Opera Square, was another important and luxurious hotel, the Continental-Savoy. It was not as famous as Shepheard's, but it too catered to many important guests, including T. E. Lawrence, the legendary British soldier and explorer. Its terrace was not on street level but located on the second floor, providing a sweeping view of Opera Square. Surrounding these two establishments was Cairo's entertainment district, comprising brothels, nightclubs, and cabarets. Its somewhat permissive atmosphere, in addition to its colonial associations, made it a ripe target during the uprising of 1952.

The Continental-Savoy and Shepheard's were not the only institutions exclusively connected to Western modernity and colonialism. Gamal al-Sharqawy, discussing the events that preceded the Cairo fire of 1952, lists a series of establishments that, as the symbol of British occupation, became the targets of boycotts and protests. For instance, Egyptians were asked by various anti-colonial political factions not to enter into Cinema Rivoli because it banned the screening of Egyptian movies, and to withdraw deposits from Barclays Bank so as not to support the colonial economy. In addition, a group of female members from the Bint al-Nil (Daughter of the Nile) party, a feminist association created in 1948, held a sit-in in front of Barclays Bank objecting to Egyptians' conducting business there. Not surprisingly, these venues, like Shepheard's, were targeted during the great fire.[28]

Black Saturday: The Cairo Fire of 1952

Much has been written about the great fire that destroyed downtown Cairo in 1952, portraying it as a singular event. Yet there had been previous incidents that should have acted as forewarnings. For instance, on 2 November 1945 demonstrators denouncing British policy in Palestine emerged from al-Azhar mosque after prayers and headed to Abdin Square, where they destroyed the stores of Europeans and Jews in the Moski area. On 3 and 4 December 1947, large demonstrations occurred in a number of Egyptian cities against the United Nations' decision to divide Palestine. The protesters destroyed Jewish and European stores and institutions.[29]

These and other events showed clearly that there were intense popular anger and resentment against colonial forces, government corruption, and an inept monarchy. The Cairo fire is significant because it became a spatial expression of this anger. Moreover, in her detailed depiction of the fire that consumed most of downtown Cairo, Reynolds has argued that it represented both a rupture and a continuity: "a culmination of the hybridized society that grew in the first half of the century and a break with that world and its attendant versions of Egyptian nationalism."[30] It became an act of rebellion against inequality and colonialism and a way of reclaiming a lost urban space. It was the first sign of a break with national institutions and paved the way for the military coup that took place six months later.

The event itself—prompted by the killing of Egyptian police conscripts in the city of Isma'iliyya in the Suez Canal Zone—took place on 26 January 1952 and was preceded by ongoing fights in and around the vicinity of Shepheard's.[31] There are many conflicting accounts pertaining to the instigators, motives, and so on. As of today no official indictment has been made nor have the culprits been identified. The following is an account culled from numerous sources with an emphasis on the spatial impact and the subsequent reverberations of the Great Fire.

The fire began with an attack on Casino Opera—a popular nightclub made famous by Allied troops during World War II—and was followed by an attack on several famous downtown cinemas, all of which were taken to represent the corrupt influence of the West. The fire consumed ninety-two bars, seventy-three restaurants and dance halls, sixteen clubs, and forty cinemas. Perhaps the most iconic building to be completely destroyed was Shepheard's itself. At least twenty-six people had been killed in the demonstrations, and five hundred more were wounded. Over seven hundred establishments had burned, four hundred buildings lay in total ruin, and the entire downtown business district was pillaged and charred.[32] 'Abd al-Rahman al-Sharqawi, a well-known Egyptian writer, recalled twenty years after the incident that "the fire consumed the heart of Cairo" (*akalat al-nar qalb al-Qahira*).[33]

While there is consensus about the damage inflicted on buildings and people, what remains in dispute, as noted previously, is the way in which the events unfolded and the extent of planning involved. Gamal el-Sharqawy interviewed a number of eyewitnesses, many of whom argued that the mobilization occurred in three stages. The first was prompted by "popular anger" due to what happened in Isma'iliyya on the preceding day, intensified by dissatisfaction with the ruling regime. This anger started early in the morning, reaching a climax with the burning of Casino Opera. Then, between approximately 1:00 p.m. and 3:00 p.m., protesters burned entertainment venues and cinemas associated with the British. At this second stage, the attacks acquired a nationalistic and religious overtone. Then came the third phase, in which a variety of buildings were burned. One eyewitness then notes: "In my opinion the fires that happened in the first and second stage were spontaneous, carried out by an angry populace. As for the third stage, a mix of every variety was involved: conspirators, thieves, everybody tried to fish in the murky waters."[34] This seems to be confirmed by other eyewitnesses, who observed that people came by the "thousands" armed with "sticks and iron bars," first attacking Casino Opera before moving on to other establishments.

However, al-Sharqawy—adopting a conspiracy theory—notes the speed with which these events unfolded. In remarkable detail, he writes that the fire at Casino Opera started at 12:27 p.m.; that the second fire, at Cinema Rivoli, began at 12:56 p.m.; and that between 1:15 p.m. and 1:30 p.m. more than ten major fires destroyed Cinema Metro, the Excelsior Hotel, the Ford Agency, the Turf Club, Cinema Miami, and many others. An uncontrolled mob, in al-Sharqawy's view, would not have had the necessary discipline and organization to destroy all of these building in such a short time. Others have noted the sheer determination with which some of these crowds moved. Radwa Ashur writes, with reference to the burning of the Groppi Café, that "the movement of the men was strange as they moved from table to table, from one chair to another and from glass to glass. It was not random, in spite of its loose nature, but strong, continuous and fast . . . as if it knows its course."[35] The conspiracy theory is further confirmed by an eyewitness account attributing the burning of Shepheard's to an organized act by three individuals who arrived at the scene in a "fancy car" and proceeded to set the building on fire deliberately.[36]

The fire was fierce and completely destroyed the hotel, whose charred remains appeared as if they had "gone through an earthquake or . . . been subjected to a direct hit from heavy artillery or an airplane."[37] Jacques Berque, Islamic scholar and sociologist, citing an eyewitness account, notes that the violence was well organized, with tankers dispensing fuel that people were able to collect in drums.[38] The most harrowing description is perhaps that provided by Harold Hindle James—a retired Royal Air Force officer then residing in Cairo. He describes in agonizing detail the unfolding of events—the attack on his apartment and how he survived. The report, written for the British embassy

Figure 12.3. The destroyed Shepheard's Hotel. Source: AP Archive. Reprinted with permission.

in Cairo, illustrates that foreigners were targeted—specifically those at the Turf Club—and the crowds were led by effendis (the educated class of Egyptians):

> In watching the mobs in the streets it became quite clear that the main destruction was part of an organized plan. The mobs were not one disorderly mass but appeared to be in separate groups each under the leadership of one or two effendi types. The effendis directed the attacks, [lit] the fires (I could not see how, but they appeared to be carrying various materials), and then the mobs were left to carry out the looting. In the early stages I saw two cars stopped, and I saw screaming people, apparently Europeans, being dragged out. One could not see what happened to them, but they disappeared. I do not know either what happened to the cars, but they eventually also disappeared, presumably driven off by members of the mob.[39]

Irrespective of the specific motives behind the fire and the existence of a conspiracy to burn downtown Cairo to the ground, the anger was real and caused massive, unprecedented damage. The widespread disaffection that triggered the crowd violence has been variously interpreted. One common view is that these events were orchestrated by the communists to topple the government. Supporting this view is the appearance during the burning, in the city center and in some of its entry points, of billboards that showed red flames emanating from the city of Cairo and leaving it in ruins, accompanied by the caption: "The communists did this."[40] The area did indeed symbolize the excessive wealth of the ruling class, highlighting societal divisions. In support of this class-based motive, one British official noted that the gangs "attacked most places in the centre of the City where alcoholic drinks and luxury goods were sold, where 'high living' amenities were provided, and where 'Western' entertainment was available, irrespective in all these instances of the nationalities of the owners."[41]

Beyond such socioeconomic and political readings, these events can also be interpreted as part of a struggle over what it meant to be modern. According to Naaman, the destruction of so many Western establishments was a way of responding to the question of *whose* modernity they represented—a question that opened up the way for the post-colonial regime of Gamal Abdel Nasser to define a new project of modernity.[42] According to al-Sharqawy, Nasser referred to the fires as the first signs of the social revolution against corrupt institutions. Thus, irrespective of who was behind these events, the inescapable fact is that they heralded the emergence of a new age in Cairo, building on perceived inequality and on the realization that the modernity project was attached exclusively to a foreign elite and a corrupt indigenous class—a circumstance of which the downtown area was the preeminent spatial symbol. After the fire, a shift in the planning paradigm saw the center of the modern city move west, toward the Nile.

URBAN REVERBERATIONS

The Nadhir thought about his idea and where his words were leading. He said: The Free Officers "Egyptianized" the heart of the city and gave it to the middle class.

Radwa Ashur, *Qit'a min Uruba*[43]

The rupture that took place in Cairo during the fire resulted in the dismantling of the colonial city in an act of rebellion that paved the way for the military revolution of 1952. This move can be associated with a certain radical modernity aimed at overcoming decades of traditionalism and European rule, and what was seen as a backward link to an Islamic past. Moreover, this specific moment and its aftermath represented a reverberation and a response to this rupture, leading to a shift of the city's center toward the Nile—away from both the Islamic and colonial quarters of the city. Similar to the configuration of downtown space that took place decades earlier, a form of violence embedded in the planning process, these new developments sought to overturn the prevailing planning paradigm and establish a new orientation by creating a novel center for the city's downtown. And just as Shepheard's had been a symbol of the old order, after 1952 the new regime and the new modernity associated with it came also to be represented by a hotel—the Nile Hilton. Its construction was the result of a new, radical direction in planning that sought to dismantle the existing order and forge a new society.

A New Cairo

Following the fire, Cairo residents awoke to martial law, a suspended constitution, widespread arrests and interrogations, and a devastated downtown area. In response to the Great Fire, the monarchy pursued a series of government reforms, resulting in several cabinet changes.

While the fire destroyed many buildings, rebuilding did not require a reconfiguration of the urban morphology of the downtown area. In fact, the state emphasized that reconstruction would restore the area to the way it had been before the fire.[44] More subtle measures were used to assert control over the city's public spaces, which included renaming in September 1954 fifteen of Cairo's squares and streets. For instance, Ibrahim Basha Street, where the fire had started (overlooked by the Opera and Shepheard's and leading to the Abdin Palace, the residence of the king) was renamed Gumhuriya (Republic) Street, a gesture acknowledging the new political order established by Nasser. Two years later, the public works minister, 'Abd el-Latif al-Baghdadi, initiated the transformation of public squares, including Tahrir (Liberation) Square (formerly Isma'iliyya) and the construction of a public walkway that became known as the Corniche.[45]

What made this process violent was that it entailed an active engagement by state actors in reconfiguring the space and meaning of both downtown Cairo and the larger city. Janet Abu-Lughod has described this process as indigenization; others have referred to it as Egyptianization.[46] Ashur argues that the officers who took power in July 1952, given their military background, dealt with the city as a military barracks. They issued orders and "did not concern themselves much with meanings and implications."[47] Impressed by Europe's post–World War II reconstruction efforts, they built "repetitive matchboxes" throughout the city, such as those in the form of boxlike public housing projects.

Underlying all these efforts was a desire to open up the space of the downtown area and other parts of Cairo to the masses, to whom they had previously been denied access. Reynolds casts these developments as a way of freeing the Egyptian public from the "captivity of local commerce" by emphasizing a "new equation of luxury and accessibility."[48] Accordingly, foreigners were removed from the downtown area, and their real estate was bought by the military officers who had now taken power. This signaled in clear and unmistakable terms that the symbols of colonial rule were being erased, in a process that was essentially a continuation of the violent upheaval of the Cairo fire and "a bringing down of the curtain, so to speak, on the theater of the modern that was downtown."[49] The state invested heavily in the downtown area, engaging in a nationalization program that turned once luxurious establishments—including Cicurel, a major Jewish-owned department store—into state-controlled retail centers, dispensing locally manufactured items. These once-exclusive retail outlets thus became accessible to a much larger segment of Egyptian society. In rebuilding the downtown area, there was great emphasis on a nationalization program emphasizing themes of public ownership, popular accessibility, and continuity. Accordingly, downtown Cairo became more accessible to ordinary Cairenes in the 1950s and 1960s.[50]

In addition to the rebuilding of the downtown area, there was also a clear shift toward the Nile and the new Tahrir Square—a site fraught with symbolism.

Isma'iliyya Square, as it had been known, was the site of Qasr al-Nil, the nine-teenth-century palace of Khedive Isma'il, ruler of Egypt between 1863 and 1879. Qasr al-Nil had housed various government institutions, including the state treasury and the army. Following the British takeover in 1882, it had become known as the "Barracks." Not surprisingly, after 1952 the military officers decided to remove this symbol of oppression and replace it with a series of modern buildings that included the headquarters of the Arab League, the Nile Hilton Hotel, and the headquarters of Nasser's Socialist Union. The use of the riverfront was a deliberate evocation of the 1940s.[51]

Nearby areas were also developed, taking advantage of the newly built Corniche Road. This included the new Shepheard Hotel (this time without the "s"), which was located near the old Semiramis Hotel. With respect to the new hotel's architectural style, Nina Nelson mentions that the old style of Shepheard's was united with a more modern sensibility.[52] According to a *New York Times* report from 1957, the hotel "has combined classic Arabic lines with the utilitarian space-saving concept of modern design. At one side a brilliant blue tile arabesque arch, almost Gothic in simplicity, is like a slender monolith rising from the ground to the roof in the center of the all-white building."[53] Significantly, as a sign of a newfound social equality, the new Shepheard lacked the outdoor terrace of its predecessor. Architecture aside, it was presented as the face of a "new Egypt" and was inaugurated by Nasser in 1957 to coincide with the opening of Egypt's new parliament.[54] The revolutionary government promptly issued a commemorative stamp depicting the hotel facing the Nile.[55] Emphasizing the importance of this area, news footage from 1958 shows a military parade attended by Nasser and other heads of state taking place along the pristine cornice facing the Nile, immediately next to the Hilton, which was still under construction at the time. Like private companies, hotels owned by foreign companies were increasingly nationalized—the Belgian-controlled new Shepheard and Semiramis were taken into public ownership in 1960. Thus, a new assertion of Egyptian sovereignty was achieved both in the national economy and within urban space.[56]

The Nile Hilton: A Break with the Past

Modernism entailed the belief that architecture and planning could enact social change. The construction of new environments characterized by simplicity and efficiency would solve social problems and usher in a new era of prosperity. This was the conviction of many urban planners following World War II, which guided their large-scale, tabula rasa–like developments. Similar thinking was applied in Cairo after 1952. Modernism proved the perfect vessel for the socialist regime's cultivation of a new kind of modernity for the masses. But the building of a new Shepheard Hotel, whose architecture was rooted in conservatism, marked only the timid beginning of the sweeping changes that were envisaged. It was the construction of a new hotel in the international architectural style that represented such a radical departure. What was known as the Nile Hilton Hotel—it is currently being converted into a Ritz-Carlton—is part of a complex of buildings that incorporates the various layers of modern Cairo.[57]

The hotel is located on a site that, until 1952, represented for Egyptians the essence of colonialism and occupation—the English barracks, housing the regiments of the British army stationed in Cairo. A 1904 photograph taken from an air balloon show these barracks next to both the Qasr al-Nil bridge and the museum. The specific location of the barracks in relation to the city and the Nile is significant. A map from 1933 shows them facing the Nile, and behind them is the new downtown area built by Isma'il. Farther back is the old city with its dense alleyways—the backward city that modernizers felt they needed to move away from.[58] A map from 1958, before the Hilton was built, illustrates the extent of the changes that have taken place, the site of the English barracks having been cleared for the construction of the Arab League and the Hilton.

Designed by an American architectural firm—Welton Beckett and Associates—the hotel was opened in 1959. Photographs published in the *New York Times* show distinguished visitors such as Presidents Nasser and Tito—as well as Conrad Hilton, the chain's owner, wearing a cowboy hat.[59] According to Hilton, Nasser's embrace of the hotel represented support for capitalism and America. Similarly, local and international media portrayed the Nile Hilton as a new face for Cairo and thus for Egypt. For instance, in a 1962 issue of *Life* magazine it appeared in all its splendor alongside other Hilton hotels, including Istanbul's. The hotel was also meant to signify a link with the country's pharaonic past through the use of a number of decorative features, such as the back of the hotel covered in large decorative hieroglyphs. At the time of its opening, the twelve-story structure was the tallest building in Cairo. According to Annabelle Wharton, it offered a "spectacle of glamorous modernity" accommodating modern social practices.[60] The building represented an attempt by Nasser to publicize the new face of Egypt, guided and inspired by an ideology of secularization through which the Egyptian state was aiming to regain an international role.

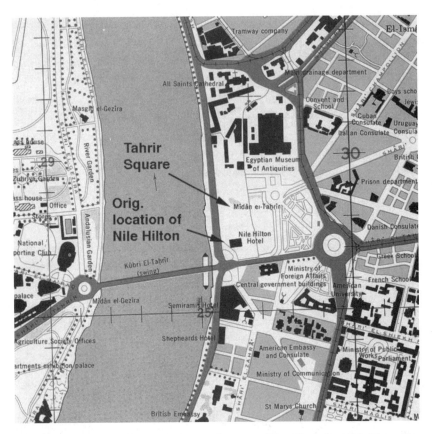

Map 12.2. Cairo, US Map Service, 1958. Source: University of Texas, Perry Castañeda Library Map Collection, http://www.lib.utexas.edu/maps/egypt.html.

Wharton has pointed out that balconies enabled people to be visible, whereas the vernacular architecture of old Cairo, with its intricate *mashrabiyya*s (wood-carved window screens), hid women from the view of passersby.[61] Such an interpretation may be far-fetched, but it is supported by promotional brochures showing modern Egyptian couples enjoying the amenities of the hotel room. That the hotel stimulated new lifestyles was also evident in its daily operations: its cafeteria employed women as waitresses for the first time; the Tavern bar became a center of intrigue; the hotel's main staircase, strategically placed in the lobby, allowed for maximum visibility. This proved particularly significant for weddings, as the traditional walk of the bride and groom took place on the staircase—a tradition that continued up until the hotel's closure for renovation in 2010. In addition, many middle-class Egyptians from Cairo and its surrounding provinces used the hotel as a fashionable and glamorous meeting place.

Aside from its function as a meeting point for ordinary Egyptians, the hotel became a favorite haunt of Egypt's elite. It also hosted a series of historic official events, such as the inauguration of the Arab League in 1969.[62] It was also a customary retreat for many Arab leaders. King Hussein of Jordan enjoyed sitting at the poolside bar, and the hotel hosted the meeting between the king and PLO leader Yasser Arafat following the 1970 massacre of Palestinians known as "Black September." Openly sporting guns, they were brought together by Nasser, who can be seen with them in one of the last photographs of the Egyptian leader, who died shortly afterward.[63]

LOOKING FORWARD

The buildings aged and eroded over time. Rats occupied its light shafts. Their streets were occupied by those who had the money required for shopping. No, they were not necessarily rich, but they were comfortable enough to have purchasing power. No longer were the rich the patrons of Groppi and L'Americaine. The truly wealthy do not buy from Qasr al-Nil Street but go to Europe and the United States to shop. They go directly to the source. Or they go to the malls—large commercial complexes standing by themselves or connected to a five-star hotel.

Ashur, Qit'a min Uruba[64]

In his monumental survey of Egypt's great hotels, Andrew Humphreys correctly argues that the European occupation of Cairo began when Napoleon Bonaparte rode into Cairo in July 1798 and took up residence in the Palace of Alfi Bey, the predecessor of the historic Shepheard's.[65] It ended when the relocated hotel went up in flames in January 1952. Black Saturday was the trigger for revolution and the withdrawal from Egypt of the British rulers, followed by a mass migration of foreign nationals. A new Egypt emerged, resulting in the reconfiguration of its downtown area; the introduction of a new, modernist, and forward-looking architecture; and, more significantly, the institution of new social practices that, for a short while, promoted egalitarian ideals.

Symbols of the past were either removed or built over. The original Shepheard's was never reconstructed but was replaced first by a parking lot and then by an unassuming office building. The local area is unrecognizable today. These developments since the 1970s have reversed the modernizing trends triggered by the reverberations of the urban rupture that occurred in 1952. Indeed, conservative ideologies—inspired by Gulf returnees—have led to a revival of historical architectural forms. Neoliberal discourses, manifested in the disengagement of the state from urban development, have also begun to dominate the region—most notably in the form of an architecture of spectacle inspired by Dubai and replicated in cities such as Rabat and Amman.[66]

Cairo's contemporary urban form emerged from two acts of violence: the popular violence of an angry crowd and the state intervention that followed. Both enabled a process that led to an urban rupture and its subsequent reverberations. Historians like Naaman have referred to this as a "spatial turn" away from the downtown area—a turn that continued for the next half century.[67] Under Sadat, in the 1970s, urban development took place in the center of the city, around Tahrir Square, and along the Nile shore. But it also moved farther inland, to Madinat Nasr, Maadi, Heliopolis, and New Cairo, with its gated communities—all sites of the new urban elite. Thus, in one furious act of devastation, Egyptians ushered in a new era that initially showed some promise but soon lost its way. It remains to be seen whether the country can indeed move forward and whether architecture and urbanism can be deployed in such a way as to remake Cairo, and Egypt in turn. The Great Fire of Cairo may seemingly have been extinguished on that fateful day, but it is still burning.

AFTERWORD

Nelida Fuccaro

THE CONTRIBUTORS TO THIS VOLUME have started to disentangle the "riddle" of violence in the history of the urban Middle East. Seeking to "see like a city," they have explored the links between destructive behavior targeting human lives and built environments; norms, institutions, and spaces governing urban coexistence; and a variety of agents implicated in the production, presentation, and representation of violent deeds and events. Was violence a state of normalcy or exception? Was it part of a toolkit of social and political experience that shaped individuals and collectivities? Or was it a disquieting intrusion in the social, political, and discursive texture of Middle Eastern cities? These are some of the overarching questions underlying this volume, which hopefully will be explored further in the future.

Certainly, violence had multi-sided causes, effects, and manifestations. It was vociferous—able to shape vocabularies of political dissent, local resistance, and state repression—but also discreet as it reached the hidden corners of social life and the interstices between the private and public spaces of the city. The stories of violence included in this book are closely intertwined with the development of cities and societies throughout the Middle East and with the history of the empires, states, and international forces that controlled them in the early modern and modern eras. The main analytical categories employed by the authors (place/space, agency, and discourse), the thematic (as opposed to chronological) organization of the chapters, and the limited number of case studies available to date do not yet allow us to draw a composite picture of violence in urban life across the region in relation to broader historical change.

A few considerations, however, are in order. In the case studies dealing with Ottoman provincial capitals the politics of urban factions—the staple of the historiography on urban notables and the network analysis discussed in Chapter 1—materializes in ways that are very familiar to Ottoman specialists: conflicts antagonizing Cairo's Mamluk leaders in the early eighteenth century, intercommunal strife in Tunis during the Tanzimat era, and quarter rivalries in late Ottoman Jeddah triggered by quarter gangs. From these examples public violence in the age of empire appears firmly anchored in recognizable arenas of factional politics that made up the political and social texture of prenational urban centers. These arenas were dominated by military and civilian elites and their urban clientele and were kept together by a delicate balance between local and imperial forces.

Yet in the process of realignment of political and social blocs, violent behavior took on different meanings, function, and expressions. In Cairo, the exercise of force was instrumental in maintaining the politics of consensus that organized elite groups while shaping norms of urban civility and social morality. In Tunis, the deadly attacks staged by crowds against the Jewish community signposted in a dramatic fashion the collapse of the Ottoman system regulating diversity, quite ironically at a time when central government was investing considerably more resources in the city and in the province of Tunisia. The case of Jeddah highlights the ritual aspects of violence and its latent nature as it was embedded in the patron-client structure of the town's quarters, while elucidating the nexus between ceremonial performance, masculinity, and popular mobilization.

The chapters dealing with the period after World War I depict the ascendancy of riotous urban crowds as the claimants of new types of popular sovereignty. In parallel, they reveal the inexorable advance of national states—and of their protégés and supporters (local elites, interest groups, and police forces)—as masters and controllers of urban destinies. In showing the proliferation and diversification of techniques and actors of violent mobilization, some of the chapters offer sharply defined images of the workings of powerful security regimes, of new bureaucracies of discipline, and of professional and casual practitioners of violence. This plurality echoes the idea of the dual city and captures quite well the violent contours of twentieth-century Middle Eastern urbanism beyond the classic paradigm of colonial Cairo, examined in this volume by Yasser Elsheshtawy. In fact, cities grew increasingly diverse—multiple rather than dual—as state building, nationalism, industrialization, and technological development molded hybrid but highly dynamic colonial, post-colonial, corporate, and authoritarian urban settings.

The chapters examining Mandatory Palestine, monarchical and Ba'thist Iraq, and oil-producing Iran and Saudi Arabia show that some of their largest and strategically and economically important urban settlements came to accommodate increasingly open social and political milieus but also became the sites of rising inequality, segregation, and fear. Rapidly expanding Cairo and Baghdad in the 1940s and 1950s, interwar Haifa and Jaffa, and the oil conurbations of Dhahran, Kirkuk, and Abadan after World War II displayed sophisticated and confrontational political cultures but also the disruptive presence of zones of legal, political, socioeconomic, and spatial exclusion.

In this respect many of the essays included in this volume provide evidence of the coexistence of openness and segregation and how this coexistence could become a conduit for violence. The simultaneity of this condition characterized the leisure and entertainment milieus of multicultural downtown Cairo before 1952 as a hybrid and permissive European micro-society that promoted trends of cultural integration and ethnic and class divisions. It also defined the elite and grassroots political circles of monarchical Baghdad and Kirkuk and of Abadan, which were caught in-between watchful and repressive regimes and latent ethnic and religious conflict but nonetheless were galvanized by a powerful rhetoric of class, national, and communal emancipation. Citizenship legislation in Haifa and Jaffa under the British Mandate is another case in point. While discriminating against Palestinian Arabs, it opened up new vistas on their entitlement to civil rights. Similarly, the socioeconomic gap between the Aramco-sponsored labor quarters of Dhammam, al-Khobar, and Abqaiq and the American camps around them grew wider in the 1950s and 1960s. Yet the residents of the labor quarters became exposed to (and in some cases fatally attracted by) the modern amenities and Western consumer culture popularized by the oil company, which were showcased in the American camps.

This multiple urban condition often guided the mobilization and discourse of violent crowds, nationalist activists, religious and ethnic groups, oil workers, and traditional community leaders. Arson in Cairo and Dhahran, rioting in Jaffa, anti-British slogans in Baghdad, and (seemingly) ethnically motivated killings in Kirkuk and Abadan addressed this condition and used new resources and tactics to transgress or erase lines of separation, often creating new ones in the process. The violence deployed in the conduct of progressive politics, for instance, was not only instrumental to achieve the tactical aims of Abadan's labor movement in 1946 or those of the Iraqi Communist Party in Baghdad and Kirkuk in 1948 and 1959, respectively. It also served to manipulate the social and political meaning of killing and bloodshed among urban groups by imposing particular interpretations of crowd violence: as the result of ethnic and religious confrontation in Abadan and Kirkuk—between Arabs and Iranians, and

Turkmen and Kurds—or as the expression of a newly found national solidarity between Muslims and Jews in Baghdad.

Yet we must not forget that many of the new forms of violent politics produced by cities in the twentieth century cannot be dissociated from the discriminatory, preventive, and punitive action of those in power. This state of reciprocity was ubiquitous and ostensibly more pronounced than in the age of empire. In urban Palestine the exclusion of the Arab population from colonial citizenship ignited nationalist rage and led to the imposition of martial law after the 1933 Jaffa riots, in a dress rehearsal of the 1936–39 revolt. The military intervention of the government in the oil conurbation of the Eastern Province of Saudi Arabia in 1967 closed the vicious circle of decades of discriminatory and highly divisive oil urbanization that culminated with strikes, the sabotage of oil installations, and the destruction of public buildings and urban property. Similarly, the 1991 Intifada in Basra was clearly rooted in the mixed regime of anarchy and security instigated by the Ba'thist reorganization of the city and its hinterland in the 1980s as the frontline of the Iran-Iraq War.

In this volume, the urban matrix and reverberations of violence become particularly apparent in the case studies that explore physical spaces of collective action, the competition for their control, and their use as sites of resistance, repression, and memory. Seen through the violent tactics deployed in episodes of spatial politics, urban sites appear protean and malleable. In 1952, affluent and leisurely downtown Cairo suddenly turned into a burning hell at the hands of furious crowds. In a similar twist in 2011, Tahrir Square switched from being a place of liberation—an orderly venue for the negotiation and exchange of democratic and political positions—to a site of hooliganism and state repression. In 1946 the clubs of Abadan—conceived and lived as recreational spaces—were transformed in political battlegrounds after being appropriated by Iran's labor movement and by the Arab tribal population gravitating around the oil conurbation.

The symbolic transmutation of urban sites also helps us understand the transformative powers and instrumental role of violent events, particularly war and protracted civic conflict. The devastating military operations of the Iran-Iraq War allowed the Ba'thist regime to present Basra as the "city of cities," effectively converting it into an exclusive space for the mobilization of fighters, the commemoration of martyrs, and the punishment of deserters. Kirkuk's massacres of 1924 and 1959 were key moments in the transformation of the citadel into a *lieu de mémoire* for its Turkmen and Kurdish communities. As the

twentieth century progressed, built environments increasingly functioned—
often interchangeably—as urban, communal, and national spaces. By 1946
Abadan's clubs encapsulated the relentless advance of virulent anti-British sentiment across Iran; so did the streets, bridges, and mosques of Baghdad memo-
rialized by the insurgents during the Wathba.

The evidence presented in this volume confirms the assumption that violence is multisided and relational—mirroring the multiple urban condition—
and that it has had both disruptive and ordering effects on Middle Eastern
cities. It also raises the issue of the different intensities and temporalities of
violence: as a routine or exceptional occurrence and as an event or a process.
Authors have used particular episodes as the focus of their analysis, reading
them as indicators of urban sociability and as points of entry in order to explore broader sociopolitical and historical contexts. Explosions of large-scale
episodic violence or protracted conflict such as the Cairo fire of 1952, Abadan's
and Kirkuk's disturbances in 1946 and 1959, and the total war that engulfed
Basra in the 1980s reveal more dramatic scenarios of urban rupture, subversion, and pacification.

Exceptional events of this kind also bring into sharp focus the cumulative
effects of long-term sociopolitical and economic factors in urban transformation: in Cairo, British rule and the penetration of foreign capital; in Kirkuk
and Abadan, the development of the oil industry and the ethnic conflagra-
tion engendered by nationalist and leftist politics; in Basra, the militarization
of authoritarian rule operated by the Ba'th Party. The intensity of the violence
involved often measures our ability to disclose the powers of governments
and their means to coerce, persuade, and manipulate urban spaces and societies. The Iran-Iraq War and the 1952 Cairo fire precipitated momentous acts of
"creative destruction" by the Ba'thist and Nasserist regimes, interventions in the
urban texture of Cairo and Basra that redesigned them in their own image. In
both cases state hegemony was literally advanced "by design," as argued by Eyal
Weizman for Israel after 1967.

It is, however, important to recognize the different economies of scale of violence. Moments of sustained killings and bloodshed do not tell the whole story.
Less flamboyant low-intensity violence—the routine abuse and micro conflicts
marking everyday urban experience—reveals the endemic nature of violence
and its latent condition and how both can conspire to escalate conflict or bring
stability. The martial tradition that nurtured the dance performances of Jeddah's
youth in the late Ottoman and early Saudi eras had potential to trigger both so-

cial reconciliation and quarter antagonism. The seemingly peaceful interlude in Kirkuk's public life after 1924 served as an incubator for the dramatic explosion of interethnic animosity in 1959. Acted out or hidden, visible and invisible, embedded in more or less formal institutional arrangements and processes of urbanization, low-intensity violence also shaped the hierarchical world dominating the routine politics of premodern and modern elites, particularly those operating in highly militarized political societies: Cairo's Mamluk factions, whose bloody quarrels caused almost daily intrusions in the lives of residents, and the Ba'thist cadres that controlled and manipulated the security of life of Basra's residents under war conditions. Systemic and routine violence is more successful when practiced as an imposed sociopolitical norm, a fact that might explain the continuing presence of local entrepreneurs of violence as enforcers of order in the imperial and post-imperial urban centers of the Middle East.

At the time of writing the actions of an entirely new class of such entrepreneurs is sending shockwaves throughout the world as ISIS militias are brutalizing the city of Mosul in ways that are beyond human comprehension. A mix of local, regional, and transnational jihadis are annihilating the city's population, civic tradition, and ancient culture in the name of the revival of a long-lost Islamic caliphate. Since the occupation of the city in June 2014, ISIS has committed unspeakable crimes: killed residents, cleansed neighborhoods, enslaved and raped women, maimed bodies, burned down libraries, desecrated museums, and destroyed ancient monuments. As child fighters roam around the city bearing arms for the caliphate and ISIS ominous black flags hang on courtrooms, checkpoints, and public buildings, one ponders the futility of any intellectual endeavor to tackle such barbarity. Will it be possible one day to treat this as "historical evidence" in the same way that authors in this volume have done with past atrocities? Emotionally, it does not seem so now, but perhaps we should remember that retelling horrific stories might in the future help us come to terms with the rule of violence.

NOTES

PREFACE

1. The role of violence in the contentious politics of modern Middle Eastern cities is discussed in Ulrike Freitag, Nelida Fuccaro, Claudia Ghrawi, and Nora Lafi, eds., "Introduction," in *Urban Violence in the Middle East: Changing Cityscapes in the Transition from Empire to Nation State* (Oxford: Berghahn, 2015), 11–21.

CHAPTER 1: URBAN LIFE AND QUESTIONS OF VIOLENCE

This chapter has benefited from the comments and bibliographical suggestions of Oliver Dinius, Rasmus Christian Elling, Ulrike Freitag, Claudia Ghrawi, Dina Khoury, Franck Mermier, and Shabnum Tejani.

1. Warren Magnusson, *Politics of Urbanism: Seeing like a City* (London: Routledge, 2011), 34–35.

2. For a historical reflection on the Arab Spring as urban violence, see Claudia Ghrawi, Fatemeh Masjedi, Nelida Fuccaro, and Ulrike Freitag, "Introduction," in Ulrike Freitag, Nelida Fuccaro, Claudia Ghrawi and Nora Lafi, eds., *Urban Violence in the Middle East: Changing Cityscapes in the Transition from Empire to Nation State* (Oxford: Berghahn, 2015), 3–7; Marco Allegra, Irene Bono, Jonathan Rokem, Anna Casaglia, Roberta Marzorati, and Haim Yacobi, "Rethinking Cities in Contentious Times: The Mobilisation of Urban Dissent in the 'Arab Spring,'" *Urban Studies* 50, no. 9 (2013): 1675–88; Salwa Ismail, "Urban Subalterns in the Arab Revolutions: Cairo and Damascus in Comparative Perspective," *Comparative Studies in Society and History* 55, no. 4 (2013): 865–94.

3. The state still absorbs theoretical discussions on the violent condition of the Middle East. See, for instance, contributions by Laleh Khalili, Daniel Neep, and James McDougall in the roundtable "Theorizing Violence," *International Journal of Middle East Studies* 45 (2013): 791–97, 810–12.

4. For debates on the slippery nature of violence from different disciplinary and methodological standpoints, see ibid., 791–812; Julie Skurski and Fernando Coronil, "Introduction: States of Violence and the Violence of States," in Fernando Coronil and Julie Skurski, eds., *States of Violence and the Violence of States* (Ann Arbor: University of

Michigan Press, 2006), 1–9; Rasmus Christian Elling, unpublished report on the workshop "The Category of Violence," held at the University of Aberdeen, 23–24 June 2011.

5. There is in fact no inherent contradiction between physical and structural violence, as suggested by Paul Farmer's work on the destruction of the human body caused by Haiti's health-care crisis. Paul Farmer, "An Anthropology of Structural Violence," *Current Anthropology* 45, no. 3(2004): 305–25.

6. Jon Abbink, "Preface: Violation and Violence as Cultural Phenomena," and Göran Aijmer, "Introduction: The Idiom of Violence in Imagery and Discourse," in Göran Aijmer and Jon Abbink, eds., *Meanings of Violence: A Cross-cultural Perspective* (New York: Berg, 2000), xi–xvii, 1–21.

7. An earlier, very instructive discussion of this tension is presented in Sidney Tarrow, "The People's Two Rhythms: Charles Tilly and the Study of Contentious Politics," *Comparative Studies in Society and History* 38, no. 3 (1996): 596–99.

8. For a discussion of the possibilities of studying violence as a military state practice in the context of the Middle East, see Daniel Neep, "War, State Formation and Culture," in roundtable "Theorizing Violence," 795–97. On violent actions as "revisioning moments" that serve to normalize urban experiences of violence, see Tali Hatuka, *Violent Acts and Urban Space in Contemporary Tel Aviv* (Austin: University of Texas Press, 2010), esp. 3–4.

9. Seminal studies on communalism include Gyanedra Pandey, *The Construction of Communalism in Colonial North India* (Delhi: Oxford University Press, 1990); Paul R. Brass, *The Production of Hindu-Muslim Violence in Contemporary India* (Seattle: University of Washington Press, 2003); Veena Das, ed., *Mirrors of Violence: Communities, Riots and Survivors in South Asia* (Delhi: Oxford University Press, 1990); Stanley J. Tambiah, *Leveling Crowds: Ethnonationalist Conflicts and Collective Violence in South Asia* (Berkeley: University of California Press, 1996).

10. For a very constructive debate on the achievements and limits of theories and definitions of violence, see Bruce B. Lawrence and Aisha Karim, "Introduction: Theorising Violence in the Twenty-First Century," in Lawrence and Karim, eds., *On Violence: A Reader* (Durham, NC: Duke University Press, 2007), 1–15.

11. Coronil and Skurski, *States of Violence*, 10, 26. This is in contrast to traditional Western theories, which viewed the exercise of force by a sovereign authority as a historical necessity and precondition for the stable development of both states and cities. See Catherine Besteman, ed., *Violence: A Reader* (New York: New York University Press, 2002), 3–4; and extracts from Max Weber and Charles Tilly in the same volume (13–18, 35–60).

12. Hannah Arendt, *On Violence* (New York: Harcourt, 1970); Frantz Fanon, *The Wretched of the Earth*, trans. Constance Farrington (London: MacGibbon & Kee, 1965); Ted Gurr, *Why Men Rebel* (Princeton, NJ: Princeton University Press, 1970); James C. Scott, *Domination and the Arts of Resistance: Hidden Transcripts* (New Haven, CT: Yale University Press, 1990).

13. Samir Khalaf, *Heart of Beirut: Reclaiming the Bourj* (London: Saqi, 2006); Amy

Mills, *Streets of Memory: Landscape, Tolerance, and National Identity in Istanbul* (Athens: University of Georgia Press, 2010); Lucia Volk, *Memorials and Martyrs in Modern Lebanon* (Bloomington: Indiana University Press, 2010); Sune Haugbolle and Anders Hastrup, eds., *The Politics of Violence, Truth and Reconciliation in the Arab Middle East* (London: Routledge, 2009); Sune Haugbolle, *War and Memory in Lebanon* (Cambridge: Cambridge University Press, 2010), esp. 161–93.

14. See Orit Bashkin's chapter in this volume on the memorialization of Baghdad during the Wathba insurrection. See also "Introduction," in Ussama Makdisi and Paul A. Silverstein, eds., *Memory and Violence in the Middle East and North Africa* (Bloomington: Indiana University Press, 2006), esp. 2–18.

15. Joshua Cole, "Massacres and Their Historians: Recent Histories of State Violence in France and Algeria in the Twentieth Century," *French Politics, Culture and Society* 28, no. 1 (2010): 106–26. Quote from James McDougall, "Martyrdom and Destiny: The Inscription and Imagination of Algerian History," in Makdisi and Silverstein, *Memory and Violence*, 66.

16. Samir al-Khalil, *Republic of Fear: The Inside Story of Saddam's Iraq* (London: Hutchinson Radius, 1989), xxvi.

17. Coronil and Skurski, *States of Violence*, 1–3; Anton Blok, "The Enigma of Senseless Violence," in Aijmer and Abbink, *Meanings of Violence*, 23. The undesirability of interpreting violence as the demonization of the "other" has also been underscored in the context of South Asian studies on communalism. Faisal Devji, "Communities of Violence," in roundtable "Theorizing Violence," 801–2.

18. Mark Mazower, "Violence and the State in the Twentieth Century," *American Historical Review* 107, no. 4 (2002): 1158–78; Jonathon Glassman, *War of Words, War of Stones: Racial Thought and Violence in Colonial Zanzibar* (Bloomington: Indiana University Press, 2011), 230–33; Hamit Bozarslan, *Violence in the Middle East: From Political Struggle to Self-Sacrifice* (Princeton, NJ: Wiener, 2004), 4.

19. David Nirenberg, *Communities of Violence: Persecution of Minorities in the Middle Ages* (Princeton, NJ: Princeton University Press, 1996). For a discussion of the relational nature of violence, see also Benjamin Brower, *A Desert Named Peace: The Violence of France's Empire in the Algerian Sahara, 1844–1902* (New York: Columbia University Press, 2009), 4–9.

20. Gerard Martin, "The Tradition of Violence in Colombia: Material and Symbolic Aspects," in Aijmer and Abbink, *Meanings of Violence*, 164–69; Ussama S. Makdisi, *The Culture of Sectarianism: Community, History and Violence in Nineteenth-Century Ottoman Lebanon* (Berkeley: University of California Press, 2000).

21. Henri Lefebvre, *The Urban Revolution*, trans. Robert Bononno (Minneapolis: University of Minnesota Press, 2003).

22. John Friedmann, "City of Fear or Open City?," *Journal of the American Planning Association* 68, no. 3 (2002): 237–43.

23. For a recent thematic survey of the social history of Middle Eastern cities, see Peter Sluglett, ed., *The Urban Social History of the Middle East, 1750–1950* (Syracuse, NY: Syracuse University Press, 2008).

24. The literature on urban unrest is vast. As representative examples, see Jane Hathaway, ed., *Mutiny and Rebellion in the Ottoman Empire* (Madison: University of Wisconsin Press, 2002); Ervand Abrahamian, "The Crowd in the Persian Revolution," *Iranian Studies* 2, no. 4 (1969): 128–50; Janet Afary, *The Iranian Constitutional Revolution, 1906–1911: Grassroots Democracy, Social Democracy, and the Origins of Feminism* (New York: Columbia University Press, 1996); Zeinab Abul-Magd, *Imagined Empires: A History of Revolt in Egypt* (Berkeley: University of California Press, 2013); Stephanie Cronin, ed., *Subalterns and Social Protest: History from Below in the Middle East and North Africa* (London: Routledge, 2008): Joel Beinin and Frédéric Vairel, eds., *Social Movements, Mobilization, and Contestation in the Middle East and North Africa* (Stanford, CA: Stanford University Press, 2011); Guilain Denoeux, *Urban Unrest in the Middle East: A Comparative Study of Informal Networks in Egypt, Iran, and Lebanon* (Albany: State University of New York Press, 1993).

25. See James Baldwin's chapter in this volume on Cairo's military elites. The violent worlds of urban notables have featured in social science literature dealing with more recent periods. See Michael Gilsenan, *Lords of the Lebanese Marches: Violence and Narrative in an Arab Society* (London: I. B. Tauris, 1995); Michael Johnson, *All Honourable Men: The Social Origins of War in Lebanon* (London: Centre for Lebanese Studies, 2001), and "Political Bosses and Their Gangs: Zu'ama and Qabadayat in the Sunni Muslim Quarters of Beirut," in Ernst Gellner and John Waterbury, eds., *Patrons and Clients in Mediterranean Societies* (London: Center for Mediterranean Studies of the American Universities Field Staff, 1977), 207–24.

26. Ira Lapidus, *Muslim Cities in the Later Middle Ages* (Cambridge, MA: Harvard University Press, 1967).

27. See in particular Freitag et al., *Urban Violence in the Middle East*. This is the first edited volume arising from the project that has inspired this book. It takes the evolution from empire to nation-state as a point of departure, building on sociological and urban studies literature by Charles Tilly, William Sewell, and Henri Lefebvre. See also James Grehan, "Street Violence and Social Imagination in Late-Mamluk and Ottoman Damascus (ca. 1500–1800)," *International Journal of Middle East Studies* 35, no. 2 (2003): 215–36; Dina R. Khoury, "Violence and Spatial Politics between the Local and the Imperial: Baghdad, 1778–1810," in Gyan Prakash and Kevin M. Kruse, eds., *The Spaces of the Modern City: Imaginaries, Politics and Everyday Life* (Princeton, NJ: Princeton University Press, 2008), 181–213; Nelida Fuccaro, *Histories of City and State in the Persian Gulf: Manama since 1800* (Cambridge: Cambridge University Press, 2009), 151–90; Daniel Neep, *Occupying Syria under the French Mandate: Insurgency, Space and State Formation* (Cambridge: Cambridge University Press, 2012).

28. For a recent discussion of Syria, see Neep, *Occupying Syria*, esp. 131–64. On the effects of British urban planning on conflict and the confessionalization of communal identities in Mandatory Jerusalem, see Roberto Mazza, "Transforming the Holy City: From Communal Clashes to Urban Violence, the Nebi Musa Riots in 1920," in Freitag et al., *Urban Violence in the Middle East*, 179–94.

29. Al-Khalil, *Republic of Fear*; Joseph Sassoon, *Saddam Hussein's Ba'th Party: Inside an Authoritarian Regime* (Cambridge: Cambridge University Press, 2011).

30. For example, the erection of walls and the transfer of residents in order to enforce sectarian segregation in Baghdad. See Mona Damluji, "'Securing Democracy in Iraq': Sectarian Politics and Segregation in Baghdad, 2003–2007," *Traditional Dwellings and Settlements Review* 21, no. 2 (2010): 71–87. On the various architectures of security in contemporary Beirut, see Hiba Bou Akar, "Contesting Beirut's Frontiers," and Mona Fawaz, Mona Harb, and Ahmad Gharbieh, "Living Beirut's Security Zones: An Investigation of the Modalities and Practice of Urban Security," *City and Society* 24, no. 2 (2012): 150–72, 173–95, respectively.

31. Eyal Weizman, *Hollow Land: Israel's Architecture of Occupation* (London: Verso, 2007).

32. Richard Sennet, quoted in Magnusson, *Seeing like a City*, 85. For case studies of the role played by imperial and post-imperial states in the definition of public disorder and social deviancy, see Freitag et al., *Urban Violence in the Middle East*, part 1.

33. Asef Bayat, "Middle Eastern Megacities: Social Exclusion, Popular Movements and the Quiet Encroachment of the Urban Poor," in Kees Koonings and Dirk Kruijt, eds., *Megacities: The Politics of Urban Exclusion and Violence in the Global South* (London: Zed, 2009), 97–100; Salwa Ismail, *Political Life in Cairo's New Quarters: Encountering the Everyday State* (Minneapolis: University of Minnesota Press, 2006), 129–60.

34. Ismail, *Political Life in Cairo's New Quarters*, esp. xxxi–xxxv.

35. Lapidus, *Muslim Cities*, 143–84; Edmund Burke, "Towards a History of Urban Collective Action in the Middle East: Continuities and Change 1750–1980," in Kenneth Brown, Bernard Hourcade, Michèle Jolé, Claude Liauzu, Peter Sluglett, and Sami Zubalda, eds., *État, ville et mouvements sociaux au Maghreb et au Moyen-Orient / Urban Crises and Social Movements in the Middle East* (Paris: L'Harmattan, 1989), 45–48. For the role played by mosques, passion plays (*ta'ziyya*), and buildings in the mobilization of women in Qajar cities, see Vanessa Martin, "Women and Popular Protest: Women's Demonstrations in Nineteenth-Century Iran," in Cronin, *Subalterns and Social Protest*, 55, 58–61. For links between the protesting crowd and the courthouse in early modern Damascus and Baghdad, see Grehan, "Street Violence"; and Khoury, "Violence and Spatial Politics."

36. Doreen Massey, *For Space* (London: Sage, 2007), 64–68. On the relationship between space and place from the perspective of social geography, see James A. Tyner, *Space, Place and Violence: Violence and the Embodied Geographies of Race, Sex and*

Gender (New York: Routledge, 2012), 14–18. For an experiential reading of place, see Yi-Fu Tuan, *Space and Place: The Perspective of Experience* (London: Edward Arnold, 1977). On place studies on the Middle East, see Amy Mills, "Critical Place Studies and Middle East Histories: Power, Politics and Social Change," *History Compass* 10, no. 10 (2012): 778–88.

37. This is brilliantly demonstrated by Stephen Legg in his study of colonial Delhi in *Spaces of Colonialism: Delhi's Urban Governmentalities* (Malden, MA: Blackwell, 2007). See also Nelida Fuccaro's chapter in this volume on British aerial control in colonial Kirkuk.

38. See Lauren Banko's chapter in this volume on urban violence and the language of citizenship rights in Mandatory Palestine.

39. Sallie A. Marston, "The Social Construction of Scale," *Progress in Human Geography* 24, no. 2 (2000): 219–42; David Delaney and Helga Leitner, "The Political Construction of Scale," *Political Geography* 16, no. 2 (1997): 93–97.

40. Sarah D. Shields, "Interdependent Spaces: Relations between the City and the Countryside in the Nineteenth Century," in Sluglett, *Urban Social History of the Middle East*, 43–66; Saksia Sassen, "The Global City: Introducing a Concept," *Brown Journal of World Affairs* 11, no. 2 (2005): 27–43.

41. Quote from Christopher A. Bayly, *The Birth of the Modern World, 1780–1914* (Oxford: Blackwell, 2004), 194.

42. Georg Simmel, "The Metropolis and Mental Life," in Kurt H. Wolff, ed. and trans., *The Sociology of Georg Simmel* (New York: Free Press, 1964), 409–24. On the production of space and everyday modern urban life, see Henri Lefebvre, *The Production of Space*, trans. Donald Nicholson-Smith (Oxford: Blackwell, 1991) 31–39, 385–86.

43. For a discussion of the *cordon sanitaire* in the context of colonial urbanism in Syria, inspired by French experience in North Africa, see Neep, *Occupying Syria*, 153–54. On dual cities, see Bernard Hourcade, "The Demography of Cities," in Sluglett, *Urban Social History of the Middle East*, 175–79. On Cairo, see the classic by Janet Abu-Lughod, "Tale of Two Cities: The Origins of Modern Cairo," *Comparative Studies in Society and History* 7, no. 4 (1965): 429–57. On Algiers, see Zeynep Celik, *Urban Forms and Colonial Confrontations: Algiers under French Rule* (Berkeley: University of California Press, 1997), esp. 1–57. For a reinterpretation of Cairo as a dual city, see Yasser Elsheshtawy's chapter in this volume.

44. William J. Berridge, "Object Lessons in Violence: The Rationalities and Irrationalities of Urban Struggle during the Egyptian Revolution of 1919," *Journal of Colonialism and Colonial History* 12, no. 3 (2011), doi:10.1353/cch.2011.0025.

45. On oil urbanism, see Nelida Fuccaro, "Introduction," in "Histories of Oil and Urban Modernity in the Middle East," special issue of *Comparative Studies of South Asia, Africa and the Middle East* 33, no. 1 (2013): 1–6. See Rasmus Christian Elling, "On Lines and Fences: Labour, Community and Violence in an Oil City," Nelida Fuccaro, "Reading

Oil as Urban Violence: Kirkuk and its Oil Conurbation, 1927–58," and Claudia Ghrawi, "Structural and Physical Violence in Saudi Arabia Oil Towns, 1953–56," in Freitag et al., *Urban Violence in the Middle East*, 197–264; and Rasmus Christian Elling and Claudia Ghrawi's chapters in this volume on labor and spatial upheaval in Abadan and Dhahran, respectively.

46. Joel Beinin, "Mixing, Separation, and Violence in Urban Spaces and the Rural Frontier in Palestine," *Arab Studies Journal* 21, no. 1 (2013): 22–26.

47. Florian Riedler, "The City as a Stage for a Violent Spectacle: The Massacres of Armenians in Istanbul in 1895–96," in Freitag et al., *Urban Violence in the Middle East*, 164–78; Juan R. I. Cole, "Of Crowds and Empires: Afro-Asian Riots and European Expansion, 1857–1882," *Comparative Studies in Society and History* 31, no. 1 (1989): 134–61. See also Nora Lafi's chapter in this volume on anti-Jewish riots in Tunis.

48. Jens Hanssen, *Fin de Siècle Beirut: The Making of an Ottoman Provincial Capital* (Oxford: Clarendon, 2005), 84–112.

49. For a concise discussion of police reforms and policing before World War I, see Laleh Khalili and Jillian Schwedler, eds., *Policing and Prisons in the Middle East: Formations of Coercion* (London: Hurst, 2010), 10–13. On colonial policing, see Martin Thomas, *Violence and Colonial Order: Police, Workers and Protest in the European Colonial Empires, 1918–1940* (Cambridge: Cambridge University Press, 2012). And on Istanbul, see Noémi Lévy-Aksu, "A Capital Challenge: Managing Violence and Disorders in Late Ottoman Istanbul," in Freitag et al., *Urban Violence in the Middle East*, 52–69.

50. Elizabeth Thompson, *Colonial Citizens: Republican Rights, Paternal Privilege, and Gender in French Syria and Lebanon* (New York: Columbia University Press, 2000), 175–96. On urban violence and youth culture in Africa, see Gary Kynoch, "Urban Violence in Colonial Africa: A Case for South African Exceptionalism," *Journal of Southern African Studies* 34, no. 3 (2008): 629–45; and Terence Ranger, "The Meaning of Urban Violence in Africa: Bulawayo, Southern Rhodesia, 1890–1960," *Cultural and Social History* 3, no. 2 (2006): 193–228.

51. Haggai Erlich, "Youth and Arab Politics: The Generation of 1935–36," in Roel Meijer, ed., *Alienation or Integration of Arab Youth: Between Family, State and Street* (Richmond, UK: Curzon, 2000), 47–70; Keith D. Watenpaugh, *Being Modern in the Middle East: Revolution, Nationalism, Colonialism, and the Arab Middle Class* (Princeton, NJ: Princeton University Press, 2006), 255–78; Olmo Göltz, "Henchmen or Honourable Men? Violent Non-state Actors in the 1953 Coup in Iran," paper presented at conference "Urban Violence in the Middle East: Histories of Place and Event," London, SOAS, February 2013.

52. Berridge, "Object Lessons in Violence"; see also Yasser Elsheshtawy's chapter in this volume.

53. Fuccaro, *Histories of City and State in the Persian Gulf*, 182–86; see also Claudia Ghrawi's chapter in this volume.

54. Farhad Kazemi and Lisa Reynolds Wolfe, "Urbanisation, Migration, and the Politics of Protest in Iran," in Michael E. Bonine, ed., *Population, Poverty and Politics in Middle Eastern Cities* (Gainesville: University Press of Florida, 1997), 260–62.

CHAPTER 2: THE SEMANTICS OF VIOLENCE AND SPACE

1. Slavoj Žižek, *First as Tragedy, Then as Farce* (London: Verso Books, 2009), 109.

2. Surnames in parentheses throughout this chapter refer to the authors of case studies included in the volume. The research project "Urban Violence in the Middle East: Between Empire and Nation State," which has inspired this volume, featured very enlightening seminars. For this, I would like to thank Nelida Fuccaro, Ulrike Freitag, Nora Lafi, Claudia Ghrawi, and Fatemeh Masjedi. I also thank those who contributed to the 2013 conference at SOAS, University of London. I am grateful in particular for the feedback on my queries from Benjamin Brower, Are Knudsen, and Saghar Sadeghian and for Stephen Legg's inspiring comments.

3. David E. Apter, *The Legitimization of Violence* (Basingstoke, UK: Palgrave, 1996), 13–14.

4. Fernando Coronil and Julie Skurski, "Introduction: States of Violence and the Violence of States," in Fernando Coronil and Julie Skurski, eds., *States of Violence* (Ann Arbor: University of Michigan Press, 2006), 289.

5. See Göran Aijmer and Jon Abbink, *Meanings of Violence: A Cross-cultural Perspective* (London: Bloomsbury, 2000).

6. Deborah G. Martin and Byron Miller, "Space and Contentious Politics," *Mobilization: An International Journal* 8, no. 2 (2003): 143–56.

7. Mark Wigley, "Editorial," *Assemblage (Violence Space)* 20 (1993): 7.

8. Randall Collins, *Violence: A Micro-sociological Theory* (Princeton, NJ: Princeton University Press, 2009).

9. James McDougall, "Savage Wars? Codes of Violence in Algeria, 1830s–1990s," *Third World Quarterly* 26, no. 1 (2005): 117–31.

10. See, for example, Karen Barkey, *Bandits and Bureaucrats: The Ottoman Route to State Centralization* (Ithaca, NY: Cornell University Press, 1996); Dina Khoury, "Violence and Spatial Politics between the Local and Imperial: Baghdad, 1778–1810," in Gyan Prakash and Kevin M. Kruse, eds., *The Spaces of the Modern City: Imaginaries, Politics and Everyday Life* (Princeton, NJ: Princeton University Press, 2008), 181–213; P. Sant Cassia, "Better Occasional Murders Than Frequent Adulteries: Discourses on Banditry, Violence, and Sacrifice in the Mediterranean," in Coronil and Skurski, *States of Violence*, 219–68.

11. Charles Tripp, *The Power and the People: Paths of Resistance in the Middle East* (Cambridge: Cambridge University Press, 2013), 311.

12. Philip Herbst, *Talking Terrorism: A Dictionary of the Loaded Language of Political Violence* (Westport, CT: Greenwood Press, 2003), xi.

13. See Laleh Khalili and Jillian Schwedler, eds., *Policing and Prisons in the Middle East: Formations of Coercion* (London: Hurst, 2010), 1–40.

14. A special thanks to Benjamin Brower for delivering an interesting paper at the conference "Urban Violence in the Middle East: Histories of Place and Event" (SOAS, 2013), for facilitating discussion, and for the e-mail correspondence that forms the basis of this section. See also Benjamin Claude Brower, *A Desert Named Peace: The Violence of France's Empire in the Algerian Sahara* (New York: Columbia University Press, 2009), esp. 261n35.

15. Benjamin Brower, private correspondence.

16. On terrorism, see Partha Chatterjee, "Terrorism," in Carol Gluck and Anna Lowenhaupt Tsing, eds., *Words in Motion: Towards a Global Lexicon* (Durham, NC: Duke University Press, 2009), 240–62.

17. On conspiracy, see Vicente L. Rafael, "*Conjuración* / Conspiracy in the Philippine Revolution of 1896," in Gluck and Tsing, *Words in Motion*, 219–39.

18. Itty Abraham, "*Segurança* / Security in Brazil and the United States," in Gluck and Tsing, *Words in Motion*, 36.

19. See Nasser Hussain, *The Jurisprudence of Emergency: Colonialism and the Rule of Law* (Ann Arbor: University of Michigan Press, 2003); and Stephen Legg, *Spaces of Colonialism: Delhi's Urban Governmentalities* (London: Wiley-Blackwell, 2007), 98.

20. E. P. Thompson, "The Moral Economy of the English Crowd in the Eighteenth Century," *Past & Present* 50 (1971), 76–136; George Rudé, *The Crowd in History: A Study of Popular Disturbances in France and England, 1730–1848*, 2nd rev. ed. (London: Serif, 2005).

21. Ervand Abrahamian, "The Crowd in Iranian Politics," *Past & Present* 41 (1968), 184–210; Joel Beinin and Zachary Lockman, *Workers on the Nile* (Princeton, NJ: Princeton University Press, 1987); W. J. Berridge, "Object Lessons in Violence: The Rationalities and Irrationalities of Urban Struggle during the Egyptian Revolution of 1919," *Journal of Colonialism and Colonial History* 12, no 3 (2011), doi:10.1353/cch.2011.0025; Juan R. I. Cole, "Of Crowds and Empires," in Coronil and Skurski, *States of Violence*, 269–306; James Grehan, "Street Violence and Social Imagination in Late-Mamluk and Ottoman Damascus (ca. 1500–1800)," *International Journal of Middle East Studies* 35, no. 2 (2003): 215–36; Charles Tripp, "Egypt, 1945–1952: The Uses of Disorder," in Michael J. Cohen and Martin Kolinsky, eds., *Demise of the British Empire in the Middle East: Britain's Responses to Nationalist Movements, 1943–55* (London: Frank Cass, 1998), 112–41.

22. On injury, see Lydia H. Liu, "Injury: Incriminating Words and Imperial Power," in Gluck and Tsing, *Words in Motion*, 199–218.

23. See, for example, Marco Allegra, Irene Bono, Jonathan Rokem, Anna Casaglia, Roberta Marzorati, and Haim Yacobi, "Rethinking Cities in Contentious Times: The Mobilisation of Urban Dissent in the 'Arab Spring,'" *Urban Studies* 50 (2013): 1675–88; Adam Ramadan, "From Tahrir to the World: The Camp as a Political Public Space," *European Urban and Regional Studies* 20, no 1 (2012): 145–49.

CHAPTER 3: ELITE CONFLICT AND THE URBAN ENVIRONMENT

I would like to thank the Leverhulme Trust for supporting the research and writing of this chapter.

1. For example, Peter M. Holt, *Egypt and the Fertile Crescent, 1516–1922: A Political History* (London: Longmans, 1966); André Raymond, "Une revolution au Caire sous les Mamelouks: La crise de 1123/1711," *Annales Islamologiques* 6 (1966): 95–120; Jane Hathaway, *The Politics of Households in Ottoman Egypt: The Rise of the Qazdağlıs* (Cambridge: Cambridge University Press, 1997), and *A Tale of Two Factions: Myth, Memory and Identity in Ottoman Egypt and Yemen* (Albany: State University of New York Press, 2002).

2. There are a few exceptions. Jane Hathaway examined the symbolic aspects of violence in *A Tale of Two Factions*, and in "Bilateral Factionalism and Violence in Ottoman Egypt," in Eleni Gara, M. Erdem Kabadayı, and Christoph K. Neumann, eds., *Popular Protest and Political Participation in the Ottoman Empire: Studies in Honor of Suraiya Faroqhi* (Istanbul: Bilgi University Press, 2011), 145–57. André Raymond used the chronicle by Shadhili to explore the attitudes of ordinary Cairenes to political violence in "The Opuscule of Shaykh 'Ali al-Shadhili: A Source for the History of the 1711 Crisis in Cairo," in Daniel Crecelius, ed., *Eighteenth-Century Egypt: The Arabic Manuscript Sources* (Claremont, CA: Regina, 1990), 25–38. Thomas Philipp studied the importance of ties of personal loyalty in the conduct of violence in "Personal Loyalty and the Political Power of the Mamluks in the Eighteenth Century," in Thomas Philipp and Ulrich Haarmann, eds., *The Mamluks in Egyptian Politics and Society* (Cambridge: Cambridge University Press, 1998), 118–27.

3. On the genres of historical writing in Ottoman Egypt, see Nelly Hanna, "The Chronicles of Ottoman Egypt: History or Entertainment?," in Hugh Kennedy, ed., *The Historiography of Islamic Egypt (c. 950–1800)* (Leiden, Netherlands: Brill, 2001), 237–50. For overviews of the manuscript chronicles in Arabic and Turkish, respectively, see P. M. Holt, "Ottoman Egypt (1517–1798): An Account of Arabic Historical Sources," and Stanford J. Shaw, "Turkish Source-Materials for Egyptian History," both in P. M. Holt, ed., *Political and Social Change in Modern Egypt: Historical Studies from the Ottoman Conquest to the United Arab Republic* (London: Oxford University Press, 1968), 3–12, and 28–48. For detailed studies of various eighteenth-century chronicles, see Crecelius, *Eighteenth-Century Egypt.*

4. Ahmad al-Damurdashi, *Kitab al-Durra al-musana fi akhbar al-Kinana,* ed. 'Abd al-Rahim 'Abd al-Rahman 'Abd al-Rahim (Cairo: Institut français d'archéologie orientale, 1989)—referred to hereafter as Damurdashi A; Ahmad al-Damurdashi, *Al-Damurdashi's Chronicle of Egypt, 1688–1755: Al-Durra al-musana fi akhbar al-Kinana,* ed. and trans. Daniel Crecelius and 'Abd al-Wahhab Bakr (Leiden, Netherlands: Brill 1991)—referred to hereafter as Damurdashi C.

5. Although he uses the title Katkhuda (lieutenant) as part of his name, there is no

internal evidence in the chronicle that he in fact held this rank. Rather, whenever he features in the chronicle as an eyewitness to the events described, he appears to be an ordinary soldier rather than an officer. See Daniel Crecelius and 'Abd al-Wahhab Bakr, "Introduction," in Damurdashi C, 11–12.

6. On the relationships between the different manuscripts of the Damurdashi group, see 'Abd al-Wahhab Bakr, "Interrelationships among the Damurdashi Group of Manuscripts," in Crecelius, *Eighteenth-Century Egypt*, 79–88.

7. Ahmad Shalabi ibn 'Abd al-Ghani, *Awdah al-isharat fi man tawalla Misr al-Qahira min al-wuzara' wa 'l-bashat*, ed. 'Abd al-Rahim 'Abd al-Rahman 'Abd al-Rahim (Cairo: Maktabat al-Khanji, 1978).

8. On Ahmad Shalabi, see 'Abd al-Rahim 'Abd al-Rahman 'Abd al-Rahim, "Yusuf al-Mallawani's *Tuhfat al-ahbab* and Ahmad Shalabi ibn 'Abd al-Ghani's *Awdah al-isharat*," in Crecelius, *Eighteenth-Century Egypt*, 39–50; and Jane Hathaway, "Sultans, Pashas, *Taqwims* and *Mühimmes*: A Reconsideration of Chronicle-Writing in Eighteenth-Century Ottoman Egypt," in Crecelius, *Eighteenth-Century Egypt*, 51–78.

9. 'Ali ibn Muhammad al-Shadhili al-Farra, "Dhikr ma waqa'a bayna 'askar al-mahrusa al-Qahira (sana 1123 H = 1711 M)," ed. 'Abd al-Qadir Ahmad Tulaymat, *Al-Majalla al-tarikhiyya al-Misriyya* 14 (1968): 321–403.

10. Raymond, "The Opuscule of Shaykh 'Ali al-Shadhili," 27–30.

11. The prominence of mamluks within these households has led many scholars to view this elite society as a continuation of the elite of the Mamluk Sultanate that ruled Egypt before the Ottoman conquest. Jane Hathaway has shown that this assumption is incorrect and that elite household culture drew far more on Ottoman models than on the Mamluk Sultanate. See Hathaway, *Politics of Households*, and Jane Hathaway, "Mamluk Households and Mamluk Factions in Ottoman Egypt: A Reconsideration," in Philipp and Haarmann, *The Mamluks in Egyptian Politics and Society*, 107–17.

12. As was common throughout the empire, the collection of much of Egypt's revenue, including agricultural taxes and customs dues, was farmed out to investors who paid a large sum upfront in return for a cut of the revenues they would collect for a fixed period.

13. The two largest regiments in Egypt were the Janissaries (usually called Mustahfizan, the "guards," in Arabic) and the 'Azaban, which were often engaged in fierce rivalry. The other five regiments were the Gönüllüyan, Müteferrika, Çerakise, Tüfekçiyan, and Çavuşan.

14. This transformation of military regiments occurred throughout the Ottoman Empire. Charles Wilkins examines the political and economic role of the Janissary regiment in Aleppo, describing it primarily as an "entitlement group" rather than a military unit. See *Forging Urban Solidarities: Ottoman Aleppo, 1640–1700* (Leiden, Netherlands: Brill, 2010). Baki Tezcan describes this transformation as the broadening of the political base of the Ottoman Empire, accompanied by the emergence of a concept of lim-

ited monarchy, that was prompted by the assertion of the increasingly wealthy Muslim merchant class of its right to participate in politics. See *The Second Ottoman Empire: Political and Social Transformation in the Early Modern World* (New York: Cambridge University Press, 2010).

15. On the bilateral factionalism of Egyptian politics, see Hathaway, *A Tale of Two Factions*.

16. On the system of tax farming (*iltizam*) in the Nile delta, see Kenneth M. Cuno, *The Pasha's Peasants: Land, Society and Economy in Lower Egypt, 1740–1858* (Cambridge: Cambridge University Press, 1992). On the management of endowments (*awqaf*) in the countryside, see Muhammad 'Afifi, *Al-Awqaf wa 'l-haya al-iqtisadiyya fi Misr fi 'l-'asr al-'uthmani* [Endowments and economic life in Egypt during the Ottoman period] (Cairo: al-Hay'a al-Misriyya al-'ama li 'l-kitab, 1991).

17. On the residences of the elite, see André Raymond, "Essai de geographie des quartiers de residence aristocratique au Caire au XVIIIème siècle," *Journal of the Economic and Social History of the Orient* 6 (1963): 58–103.

18. On household formation, see Hathaway, *Politics of Households*. On the interpenetration of the military regiments and the merchant/artisan classes, see André Raymond, "Soldiers in Trade: The Case of Ottoman Cairo," *British Journal of Middle Eastern Studies* 18 (1991): 16–37. For a comprehensive account of commercial life in the city, see André Raymond, *Artisans et commerçants au Caire au XVIIIe siècle*, 2nd ed. (Cairo: Institut français d'archéologie orientale, 1999).

19. A good example of such a demonstration, which concluded with the deposition of the governor, was the revolt against Defterdar Ahmed Pasha in 1676. For a detailed study of this incident, see James E. Baldwin, "The Deposition of Defterdar Ahmed Pasha and the Rule of Law in Seventeenth-Century Egypt," *Osmanlı Araştırmaları Journal of Ottoman Studies* 46 (2015): 131–61.

20. For a detailed account of the 1711 war, see Raymond, "Une revolution au Caire."

21. Notwithstanding the Orientalist fantasies found in some popular literature, the word *harem* does not imply sexual excess but simply refers to the private area of the house, which included the living quarters of the women of the household and to which visiting men were not admitted.

22. Damurdashi A, 59–62; Damurdashi C, 106–11. On the role of the Hawwara Bedouin in Ottoman-Egyptian politics, see Zeinab Abul-Magd, *Imagined Empires: A History of Revolt in Egypt* (Berkeley: University of California Press, 2013), 17–42; Michael Winter, *Egyptian Society under Ottoman Rule, 1517–1798* (London: Routledge, 1992), 78–108.

23. The *diwan* was the governor's council, which both handled administrative business and functioned as a tribunal. For the judicial functions of the *diwan*, see James E. Baldwin, "Islamic Law in an Ottoman Context: Resolving Disputes in Late 17th / Early 18th-Century Cairo" (PhD diss., New York University, 2010), 31–74.

24. Damurdashi A, 62; Damurdashi C, 111.

25. Damurdashi A, 171–73; Damurdashi C, 268–70.

26. Yusuf Bey's sobriquet "the traitor" (al-Kha'in) resulted from his behavior during an earlier violent conflict. Ridwan Bey al-Khazindar had sought refuge in Yusuf's house while fleeing, but Yusuf had informed the Janissary agha, who had promptly arrested him. This suggests a norm centered on the obligations of hospitality. This incident is related by Damurdashi: see Damurdashi A, 168; Damurdashi C, 264.

27. Damurdashi A, 171; Damurdashi C, 268.

28. Damurdashi A, 60–61; Damurdashi C, 109–10.

29. On Çerkes Muhammad Bey al-Kabir and his volatile relationship with the imperial government, see Jane Hathaway, "Çerkes Mehmed Bey: Rebel, Traitor, Hero?," *Turkish Studies Association Bulletin* 22 (1998): 108–15.

30. Damurdashi A, 167; Damurdashi C, 263.

31. There are some differences in the details of these events between the three chronicles. My narrative follows Ahmad Shalabi and Shadhili, which are quite similar and clearer and more coherent than Damurdashi's account. Ahmad Shalabi, *Awdah al-isharat*, 233–36; Shadhili, "Dhikr ma waqaʿa," 359–67; Damurdashi A, 85–94; Damurdashi C, 150–63.

32. Damurdashi A, 167; Damurdashi C, 263.

33. A *takiyya* is a Sufi lodge—a space for prayer and ritual, where some members of the order also reside.

34. Damurdashi A, 93; Damurdashi C, 161.

35. Shadhili, "Dhikr ma waqaʿa," 363.

36. Ibid., 365.

37. Ahmad Shalabi, *Awdah al-isharat*, 220–22.

38. The *naqib al-ashraf* was the head of the descendants of the prophet Muhammad. A *naqib al-ashraf* was appointed for all large cities in the Ottoman Empire.

39. Damurdashi A, 166; Damurdashi C, 262.

40. Shadhili, "Dhikr ma waqaʿa," 367.

41. Damurdashi A, 86; Damurdashi C, 153.

42. Damurdashi A, 90; Damurdashi C, 156.

43. Ahmad Shalabi, *Awdah al-isharat*, 237.

44. Shadhili, "Dhikr ma waqaʿa," 367.

45. Damurdashi A, 85; Damurdashi C, 150.

46. Ahmad Shalabi, *Awdah al-isharat*, 230.

47. Elite political figures who cracked down on such abuses became celebrated heroes in the chronicle literature. A prominent example is Küçük Muhammad, a senior Janissary officer at the end of the seventeenth century. See Peter M. Holt, "The Career of Küçük Muhammad (1676–94)," *Bulletin of the School of Oriental and African Studies* 26 (1963): 269–87.

CHAPTER 4: URBAN SPACE AND PRESTIGE

The research for this chapter was conducted in the framework of and financed by the DFG-AHRB Project on Urban Violence (2010–13). I would like to thank Jihan Akrawi, Nushin Atmaca, Nelida Fuccaro, and Nora Lafi for their comments and for help in gathering the literature and researching side issues, and Nora Derbal for contacting ʿumda Malak Mahmud Ba ʿIsa with a number of questions.

1. Christiaan Snouck Hurgronje, "Jeddah Diary," manuscript (Leiden University Library Cod. Or. 7112), 45–46. I am quoting from the translation by Jan-Just Witkam, which is to be published shortly. I follow his transliteration and translation, including the choice of italics or otherwise. I have indicated those words spelled in Arabic in the original manuscript.

2. ʿUmda ʿAbd al-Samad and local author Abu Zinada contrasted this with another popular entertainment, the *zayr*, in which only drummers competed for excellence. Author interview, Jeddah, 17 November 2011. On the *zayr*, see Hind Ba Ghaffar, *Al-Aghani a-shaʿbiyya fī-l-mamlaka al-ʿarabiyya al-saʿudiyya* (Jeddah: Dar al–Qadisiyya lil-Nashr wa-l-Tawziʿ, 1994), 159–60.

3. A solid survey of recent literature is contained in Rose Challenger, Chris W. Clegg, and Mark A. Robinson, *Understanding Crowd Behaviours: A Guide for Readers* (York: Cabinet Office/University of Leeds, 2009), part 3, https://www.gov.uk/government/uploads/system/uploads/attachment_data/file/192606/understanding_crowd_behaviour-supporting-evidence.pdf (accessed 1 July 2013).

4. Norbert Elias, *Über den Prozeß der Zivilisation* (Frankfurt: Suhrkamp, 1976), 1:263–83.

5. For a spontaneous and folklorized version of the *mizmar*, see http://www.youtube.com/watch?v=ojgILNRkRH0, uploaded 19 January 2010 (accessed 3 July 2013); and Fahad Alajlan, "NKU 20th International Potluck (Mjas and Mizmar Dance from Saudi Arabia)," http://www.youtube.com/watch?v=bw94SyZUjxc, uploaded 10 April 2011 (accessed 3 July 2013).

6. Crowds and crowd violence in the Middle East have been discussed, for example, in James Grehan, "Street Violence and Social Imagination in Late-Mamluk and Ottoman Damascus (ca. 1500–1800)," *International Journal of Middle East Studies* 35, no. 2 (2003): 215–36; and Ervand Abrahamian, "The Crowd in Iranian Politics 1905," *Past & Present* 41 (1968): 184–210. Both texts take their cue from George Rudé, *The Crowd in History: A Study of Popular Disturbances in France and England, 1730–1848* (New York: Wiley, 1964), which also discusses the link with popular festivities, but not explicitly with notions of masculinity.

7. On the notion of quarters in the discussion of Middle Eastern urbanity and their legal and social construction, and Istanbul in particular, see Noémy Lévy-Aksu, *Ordre et désordres dans l'Istanbul ottomane (1879–1909)* (Paris: Karthala, 2013), 215–75. For Damascus, see Jean Lecerf and René Tresse, "Les ʿarada de Damas," *Annales Islamologiques*

15 (1979): 237–64. For Cairo, see Nawal Al-Messiri-Nadim, "The Concept of the Hāra: A Historical and Sociological Study of al-Sukkariyya," *Annales Islamologiques* 15 (1979): 323–48. For Sanaa, see Robert B. Serjeant and Husayn al-'Amri, "Administrative Organisation," in Robert B. Serjeant and Ronald Lewcock, eds., *San'a': An Arabian Islamic City* (London: World of Islam Festival Trust, 1983), 142–60, esp. 146–48. For Dezful, see Reza Masoudi Nejad, "Urban Violence, the Muharram Processions, and the Transformation of Iranian Urban Society: The Case of Dezful," in Ulrike Freitag, Nelida Fuccaro, Claudia Ghrawi, and Nora Lafi, eds., *Urban Violence in the Middle East: Changing Cityscapes in the Transition from Empire to Nation State* (Oxford: Berghahn, 2015), 91–110.

8. Very often, tribesmen had to disarm when entering cities, and their identity remained linked to their extra-urban contexts. See Sylvaine Camelin, "Le territoire du politique: Quartiers et linages dans la ville de Shihr (sud du Yémen)," *Journal des Africanistes* 74, no. 1–2 (2004): 413–33, http://africanistes.revues.org/478 (accessed 10 December 2012).

9. Serjeant and al-'Amri, "Administrative Organisation," 146–47.

10. In this, I disagree with Lévy-Aksu when she writes about quarters that "their limits are not fixed precisely" (my translation). Lévy-Aksu, *Ordre et désordres*, 215.

11. On night guards and quarter strongmen in Istanbul as part of the urban security system, see ibid., 235–52. The night guard (more specifically of the market areas) appears even in the title of Franck Mermier's study, *Le cheickh de la nuit—Sana'a: Organisation des souks et société citadine* (Paris: Sindbad-Actes Sud, 1997). It is noteworthy that, while the system of night guards was restructured in Istanbul during the Young Turk era, this has not affected them in an outlying Ottoman city such as Jeddah, where the *'asas* persisted long beyond Ottoman times (Lévy-Aksu, *Ordre et désordres*, 246).

12. Author interviews in Jeddah with 'Adnan al-Yafi, 22 March 2006; Sami Nawar, 9 March 2011; and Talal Bakur and Muhammad Raqqam, 16 March 2011. See Muhammad Trabulsi, *Jidda . . . hikayat madina*, 2nd ed. (Jeddah: Al-Madina al-Munawwara li-l-Tiba'a wa-l-Nashr, 2008), 180–90. A detailed description referring mostly to the 1950s is provided by 'Abdallah Mana', *Tarikh ma lam yu'arrikh. Jidda al-insan wa-l-makan* (Jeddah: Dar al-Marsa li-l-Nashr wa-l-Tawzi', 2011). Lévy-Aksu argues that, during the Tanzimat and notably in Hamidian times, the *mukhtar* (that is, the *'umda*) was given many of the legal and social functions previously fulfilled by the imams, which might explain their conspicuous absence in the accounts of the important personalities of the quarters in the literature and interviews on Jeddah dating from the twentieth century. Lévy-Aksu, *Ordre et désordres*, 222–23.

13. On these notions, see Fran Tonkiss, *Space, the City, and Social Theory* (Cambridge, UK: Polity, 2005), 69–76. On the Middle Eastern village, see Michael Gilsenan, *Recognizing Islam* (London: I. B. Tauris [1982] 1992), 164–80. See Camelin, "Le territoire du politique," para. 4, which describes this for the town of al-Shihr in Yemen, drawing theoretically on literature on the sociology of modern quarters in Western cities. See, for

example, Pierre Mayol, "Living," in Michel de Certeau, Luce Giard, and Pierre Mayol, eds., *The Practice of Everyday Life*, rev. ed. (Minneapolis: University of Minnesota Press, 1998), 7–34. In this literature, modern quarters are perceived mainly as a social space, though many observations on the sense of space and appropriate behavior are pertinent to Middle Eastern cities.

14. On the *barhat* of Jeddah, see Trabulsi, *Jidda . . . hikayat madina*, 190; and Mana', *Tarikh ma lam yu'arrikh*, 34–35. For the *'umda* and for the regular meetings of various *shilal* of men, see also Trabulsi, *Jidda . . . hikayat madina*, 184 and 202–6.

15. Author interviews with Talal Bakur and Muhammad Raqqam, Jeddah, 16 March 2011.

16. On this institution, elsewhere also known as *qabada'i* in this period, see Lévy-Aksu, *Ordre et désordres*, 253–75. For its historical origins, see Franz Taeschner, *Zünfte und Bruderschaften im Islam. Texte zur Geschichte der Futuwwa* (Zürich: Artemis, 1979); and Claude Cahen, "Mouvements populaires et autonomisme urbain dans L'Asie musulmane du moyen age," *Arabica* 5, no. 3 (1958): 225–50, *Arabica* 6, no. 1 (1959): 25–56, and *Arabica* 6, no. 2 (1959): 233–60.

17. Camelin, "Le territoire du politique," paras. 2, 9.

18. Lévy-Aksu, *Ordre et désordres*, 228–34.

19. Camelin argues the same for Shihr ("Le territoire du politique," para. 27).

20. See Muhammad 'Ali Maghrabi, *A'lam al-Hijaz*, 2nd ed. (Jeddah: Matabi' Dar al-Bilad, 1985), 1:47–48; Mana', *Ta'rikh ma lam tu'arrikh*, 201.

21. In describing these overlapping social ties in Arabian cities, Walter Dostal has employed the term "alliance groups." Walter Dostal, *Der Markt von San'a'* (Vienna: Verlag der Österr. Akademie der Wissenschaften, 1979).

22. Author interview with 'Abd al-Wahhab Abu Zinada and 'umda 'Abd al-Samad, Jeddah, 17 November 2011. For the visits, see Muhammad b. Nasir al-Asmarri, "Tarikh al-hayyat al-ijtima'iyya Jidda: 1300–1343 h./1882–1925 m." (master's thesis, King 'Abd al-Aziz University, Jeddah, 2008), 97.

23. For more details, see my "Playing with Gender: The Festival of al-Qays in Jeddah," in Nazan Maksudyan, ed., *Women and the City, Women in the City: A Gendered Perspective to Ottoman Urban History* (New York: Berghahn, 2014), 71–85.

24. Ba Ghaffar, *Al-Aghani al-sha'biyya*, 173. The following description of the dance is based on her description, unless indicated otherwise (ibid., 173–82). Locally, the African roots of the dance are often emphasized, presumably with reference to black African rather than Egyptian roots. This was confirmed orally by 'umda Malak Mahmud Ba 'Isa to Nora Derbal, Jeddah, December 2012. Further descriptions can be found in Trabulsi, *Jidda*, 339–42; and 'Abbas b. Muhammad Sa'id al-Fadli, *Al-Nuzla al-yamaniyya. Hayy fi dhakirat 'Jidda'* (Jeddah: Maktabat Dar Zahran, 2009–10), 117–19.

25. This theory was advanced by a number of my interlocutors.

26. See Mana', *Ta'rikh*, 193, on the use of a major *barha* of a quarter.

27. Conversation with Professor Abu Bakr Bagader, Berlin, 5 June 2013.

28. Ba Ghaffar, *Al-Aghani al-sha'biyya*, 175. See also http://www.youtube.com/watch ?v=0jgILNRkRH0, uploaded 10 June 2010 (accessed 13 November 2013).

29. Trabulsi, *Jidda*, 341–42.

30. 'Abdallah Muhammad Abkar, *Harat Makka* (Jeddah: N.p., 2007), 206. This and subsequent translations are mine.

31. Lévy-Aksu, *Ordre et désordres*, 261–63. Like that of the night guards, the role of *qabada'i* in Istanbul changed in the late Ottoman Empire but seems to have persisted in Jeddah and probably in other provincial cities. For their role in Mandatory Syria, see Philipp Khoury, "Syrian Urban Politics in Transition: The Quarters of Damascus during the French Mandate," *International Journal of Middle East Studies* 16 (1984): 507–40, esp. 520–23. The transition of *futuwwa* from noble youth groups to thugs in Cairo is of particular interest. Wilson Chacko Jacob, "Eventful Transformations: Al-*Futuwwa* between History and the Everyday," *Comparative Studies in History and Society* 49, no. 3 (2007): 689–713. On armed male youth groups in Najaf in the nineteenth and early twentieth centuries, see Peter Heine, "'Zghurt und Shmurt,' Zur gesellschaftlichen Struktur der Schiiten im Iraq bis 1958," *Al-Rafidayn. Jahrbuch zu Geschichte und Kultur des modernen Iraq* 3 (1995): 7–18.

32. Author interviews in Jeddah with *'umda* 'Abd al-Samad, 21 March 2011, and 'Abd al-Wahhab Abu Zinada, 17 November 2011. On Syria, see also Khoury, "Syrian Urban Politics," 521. This social distinction is also discussed in Jacob, "Eventful Transformations."

33. Mana', *Ta'rikh*, 64; conversations with *'umda* Malak Mahmud Ba 'Isa.

34. Trabulsi, *Jidda*, 341–42; and 'Abd al-'Aziz 'Umar Abu Zayd, *Hikayat al-'attarin fi Jidda al-qadima*, 2nd ed. (Jeddah: al-'Amal al-Thaqafiyya, 2011–12), 112.

35. Author interviews in Jeddah with *'umda* 'Abd al-Samad, 21 March 2011, Abu Zinada and 'Abd al-Samad, 17 November 2011. Ba Ghaffar cites a verse saluting the pasha arriving from Sham, presumably going back to Ottoman times (Ba Ghaffar, *al-Aghani al-sha'biyya*, 181).

36. Author interview with Sami Nawar, Jeddah, 9 March 2011.

37. Ba Ghaffar, *al-Aghani al-sha'biyya*, 181.

38. *Al-Qibla* 776 (Mecca), 11 April 1924, 2. I would like to thank Philippe Pétriat for pointing me to this source and providing me with a copy of the document.

39. Trabulsi, *Jidda*, 190.

40. Verbal communication by a colleague, Jeddah, 6 March 2011.

41. Mark Thompson, "Assessing the Impact of Saudi Arabia's National Dialogue: The Controversial Case of the Cultural Discourse," *Journal of Arabian Studies: Arabia, the Gulf and the Red Sea* 1, no. 2 (2011):163–81.

42. Muhammad Al-Atawneh, *Wahhabi Islam Facing the Challenges of Modernity: Dar al-Ifta in the Modern Saudi State* (Leiden, Netherlands: E. J. Brill, 2010), 108–12.

43. A good survey of Saudi religious policy in the Hijaz is provided by Guido

Steinberg, *Religion und Staat in Saudi-Arabien. Die wahhabitischen Gelehrten 1902–1953* (Würzburg: Ergon, 2002), 511–78. Music and festivities are discussed in ibid., 546–48.

44. Muhammad b. Ibrahim b. ʿAbd al-Latif Al al-Shaykh, *Fatawa wa-rasaʾil*, vol. 8, http://www.alifta.net/Fatawa/DisplayFeqhMoesarTOC.aspx?languagename=en (accessed 3 July 2013).

45. The issue is discussed in Al-Atawneh, *Wahhābī Islam*, 112. The fatwa concerned is no. 14644, pt. 1, vol. 26, 257. It is undated, but one of its signatories, ʿAbd al-Razzaq b. ʿAfify, died on 1 September 1994, and a fatwa with an earlier number mentions the date 1991, so 1991–94 is the likely period during which the fatwa was issued. See http://www.alifta.net/Fatawa/FatawaDetails.aspx?languagename=en&View=Page&PageID=10309&PageNo=1&BookID=7#P257 (accessed 3 July 2013).

46. Abkar, *Harat Makka*, 208.

47. Again, a comparison of the *mizmar* with the Damascene *ʿarada* is interesting here because the *ʿarada* was another celebration that was not exclusively linked to religion and that also sometimes turned violent. Lecerf and Tresse, "Les ʿarada de Damas," 240; see Khoury, "Syrian Urban Politics," 523. Obviously, there were also other types of crowd-related violence, such as bread riots. See Grehan, "Street Violence and Social Imagination," 215–36.

48. Rudé, *The Crowd in History*, 238–39.

49. Here, the *mahmal* is a ceremonial litter sent with the pilgrims to Mecca.

50. Lecerf and Tresse, "Les ʿarada de Damas," 249; Khoury, "Syrian Urban Politics," 523.

51. Roberto Mazza, "Transforming the Holy City: From Communal Clashes to Urban Violence, the Nebi Musa Riots in 1920," in Freitag et al., *Urban Violence in the Middle East*, 179–96.

52. Khoury, "Syrian Urban Politics," 523–27.

53. This event has been discussed in detail by Philippe Pétriat, "Notables et rebelles: Les grands marchands hadramis de Djedda au milieu du XIXième siècle," *Arabian Humanities International Journal* [En ligne], 1, 2013. https://cy.revues.org/1923; Ulrike Freitag, "Symbolic Violence and Urban Politics in Late Ottoman Jeddah," in Freitag et al., *Urban Violence in the Middle East*; and William Ochsenwald, "The Jidda Massacre," *Middle Eastern Studies* 13, no. 3 (1973): 314–26.

54. The playing of football in the squares and alleys is discussed in ʿAbdallah Manaʿ, *Baʿd al-ayyam, baʿd al-layali* (Jeddah: Dar al-Marsa li-l-Nashr wa-l-Tawziʿ, 2009), 36–44; for the ban, see IOR [India Office], L/PS/12/2073, Jedda Reports July 1934, March 1935.

55. Pascale Ménoret and Awadh al-Utaybi, "Urban Unrest and Non-religious Radicalization in Saudi Arabia," in Madawi al-Rasheed and Marat Shterin, eds., *Dying for Faith: Religiously Motivated Violence in the Contemporary World* (London: I. B. Tauris, 2009), 123–37.

56. Pascale Ménoret, *Joyriding in Riyadh: Oil, Urbanism and Road Revolt* (Cambridge: Cambridge University Press, 2014); Jacob, "Eventful Transformations"; Hanan Hammad, "Industrial Violence: *Futuwwa, Effendiyya* and the Making of Urban Masculinity in Interwar Egypt," in Freitag et al., *Urban Violence in the Middle East*, 70–90.

57. Salwa Ismail, *Political Life in Cairo's New Quarters* (Minneapolis: University of Minnesota Press, 2006), 96–128.

CHAPTER 5: CITIZENSHIP RIGHTS AND SEMANTICS
OF COLONIAL POWER AND RESISTANCE

1. Weldon C. Matthews, "Pan-Islam or Arab Nationalism? The Meaning of the 1931 Jerusalem Islamic Congress Reconsidered," *International Journal of Middle Eastern Studies* 35, no. 1 (2003): 11.

2. Margaret R. Somers, "Rights, Relationality, and Membership: Rethinking the Making and Meaning of Citizenship," *Law and Social Inquiry* 19 (Winter 1994): 65, 78–79.

3. National Archives of the United Kingdom (hereafter NAUK) CO 733/71/230–286: "Local Government Interim Report," 11 July 1924. See also Lauren E. Banko, "The 'Invention' of Palestinian Citizenship: Discourses and Practices, 1918–1937" (PhD diss., School of Oriental and African Studies, University of London, 2013).

4. Sandip Hazareesingh, "The Quest for Urban Citizenship: Civic Rights, Public Opinion and Colonial Resistance in Early Twentieth Century Bombay," *Modern Asian Studies* 34, no. 4 (2000): 797.

5. For more on the development of administrative and legislative policies under the Mandate, see Assaf Likhovski, *Law and Identity in Mandate Palestine* (Chapel Hill: University of North Carolina Press, 2006); and Roza El-Eini, *Mandated Landscape: British Imperial Rule in Palestine, 1929–1948* (London: Routledge, 2006).

6. Joel Beinin, "Mixing, Separation, and Violence in Urban Spaces and the Rural Frontier in Palestine," *Arab Studies Journal* 21, no. 1 (2013): 15–16.

7. For more analysis on this style of organization by workers, see Zachary Lockman, *Comrades and Enemies: Arab and Jewish Workers in Palestine, 1906–1948* (Berkeley: University of California Press, 1996).

8. May Seikaly, *Haifa: The Transformation of a Palestinian Arab Society 1918–1939* (London: I. B. Tauris, 1995), 2–6, 138–42. In 1931 the population of Haifa was 50,403; Jaffa, 51,866; and Nablus, 17,189. See E. Mills, *Census of Palestine, 1931* (Jerusalem: The Greek Convent and Goldberg Presses, 1932).

9. Seikaly, *Haifa*, 73.

10. See Mark LeVine, *Overthrowing Geography: Jaffa, Tel Aviv, and the Struggle for Palestine 1880–1948* (Berkeley: University of California Press, 2005), 93–94.

11. Samir Khalaf, *Civil and Uncivil Violence in Lebanon: A History of the Internationalization of Communal Conflict* (New York: Columbia University Press, 2002), 13.

12. See Weldon C. Matthews, *Confronting an Empire, Constructing a Nation: Arab Nationalists and Popular Politics in Palestine* (London: I. B. Tauris, 2006).

13. Edward Horne, *A Job Well Done: Being a History of the Palestine Police Force, 1920–1948* (Essex, UK: Anchor Press, 1982), 32.

14. Alex Tickell, *Terrorism, Insurgency and Indian English Literature, 1830–1947* (New York: Routledge, 2012), 205–7.

15. For example, see Mahmoud Yazbak, "From Poverty to Revolt: Economic Factors in the Outbreak of the 1936 Rebellion in Palestine," *Middle Eastern Studies* 36, no. 3 (2000): 93–113; and Zachary Lockman, *Comrades and Enemies: Arab and Jewish Workers in Palestine, 1906–1948* (Berkeley: University of California Press, 1996), 186–90.

16. Carter J. Wood, "Locating Violence: The Spatial Production and Construction of Physical Aggression," in Katherine D. Watson, ed., *Assaulting the Past: Violence and Civilization in Historical Context* (Newcastle, UK: Cambridge Scholars Publishing, 2007), 22.

17. David De Vries, "Proletarianization and National Segregation: Haifa in the 1920s," *Middle Eastern Studies* 30, no. 4 (1994): 863.

18. Seikaly, *Haifa*, 155–56,171–74.

19. Al-Istiqlal Party, based in Nablus, officially announced its charter in 1931, and its small nucleus of middle-class members declared that the party was aligned with the ideology of pan-Arab unity. The party had been largely dissolved by the end of 1934.

20. Charles Tilly, *The Politics of Collective Violence* (Cambridge: Cambridge University Press, 2003), 76.

21. "Details of the First Palestinian Arab Youth Conference in Jaffa," *Al-Jam'iyya al-'Arabiyya*, 6 January 1932.

22. The importance of the press in Palestine is stressed in Ami Ayalon, *Reading Palestine: Printing and Literacy, 1900–1948* (Austin: University of Texas Press, 2004).

23. See the comparison between Quebec and Ireland during the decades preceding the period under study in Jeffrey Cormier and Phillipe Couton, "Civil Society, Mobilization, and Communal Violence: Quebec and Ireland, 1890–1920," *Sociological Quarterly* 45 (Summer 2004): 489–90.

24. Fernando Coronil and Julie Skurski, "Dismembering and Remembering the Nation: The Semantics of Political Violence in Venezuela," *Comparative Studies in Society and History* 33 (April 1991): 289–91.

25. See Nelida Fuccaro's chapter in this volume for an instructive parallel on the different languages of violence deployed in Kirkuk in the colonial and post-colonial eras.

26. Yehoshua Porath, *The Emergence of the Palestinian-Arab National Movement, 1918–1929* (London: Frank Cass, 1974), 132–33.

27. "Judaizing Palestine," *Al-Jam'iyya al-'Arabiyya*, 18 September 1933.

28. Tickell, *Terrorism, Insurgency*, 137.

29. "The Right of Self-Defense Is the Right to Life," *Sawt al-Sha'b*, 23 September 1933.

30. NAUK FO 371/16926: CID to Chief Secretary, 16 December 1932.

31. Samih Shabib, *Hizb al-Istiqlal al-'Arabi fi Filastin, 1932–1933* [The Arab Istiqlal Party in Palestine, 1932–1933] (Beirut: PLO Research Center, 1981), 63.

32. Matthews, "Pan-Islam or Arab Nationalism?," 7.

33. Ibid., 8.

34. "Palestine Day in Nablus," *Al-Jam'iyya al-'Arabiyya*, 18 May 1931.

35. "We Want a Representative Parliament," *Mir'at al-Sharq*, 29 August 1931.

36. "The Spirit of the Strike and Its Significance," *Sawt al-Sha'b*, 12 November 1932.

37. "In Nablus," *Al-Jam'iyya al-'Arabiyya*, 18 August 1931.

38. Matthews, "Pan-Islam or Arab Nationalism?," 11; "Women's Demonstration in Nablus," *Mir'at al-Sharq*, 24 August 1931.

39. "Free Us from the Prison," *Al-Jam'iyya al-'Arabiyya*, 30 August 1931.

40. Shabib, *Hizb al-Istiqlal*, 76–78.

41. Ibid., 43.

42. "Palestinian Arab Concern Increases over Immigration," *Al-Iqdam*, 13 October 1933.

43. NAUK FO 371/16926: CID report, 23 October 1933.

44. "Our Critical Movement in Its New Direction," *Al- Jam'iyya al-'Arabiyya*, 17 October 1933.

45. Middle East Centre Archives, University of Oxford (hereafter MEC) Jaffa riots, 1933, Box 1, File 3, JAM Faraday papers, GB165-0101.

46. See NAUK AIR 5/1246: Air Headquarters report, 23 November 1933; NAUK FO 371/16926: CID report, 15 November 1933.

47. MEC Jaffa riots.

48. Ibid.

49. NAUK FO 141/699/6: Wauchope to HC Egypt, 28 October 1933.

50. NAUK FO 371/16926: CID report, 15 November 1933; NAUK CO 733/239/6: Disturbances Commission of Enquiry, 4 January 1934.

51. NAUK CO 733/239/6: Disturbances Commission of Enquiry, 4 January 1934.

52. MEC Tegart Papers, Box 3, File 1, GB165-0281.

53. Tickell, *Terrorism, Insurgency*, 185–89. Nearly fifteen years prior to the events in Palestine in 1933, the British government had faced the aftermath of a contentious case of state violence. In 1919, the British Indian army faced a large, unarmed crowd of protesters in Amritsar, one of Punjab's urban centers. The massacre started when a British army commander ordered his troops to fire into a crowd of protesters without warning, resulting in the deaths of about 380 people. Tickell's description of the debates over the legitimacy and limits of colonial violence refers to the discussion in the British Parliament between politicians such as Winston Churchill and Secretary of State for India Edwin Samuel Montagu.

54. MEC Jaffa riots.

55. NAUK FO 371/16932: Situation in Palestine: Cabinet conclusions extract, November–December 1933.

56. Partha Chatterjee, *The Politics of the Governed: Reflections on Popular Politics in Most of the World* (New York: Columbia University Press, 2004), 34.

57. NAUK CO 322/1164/15: Palestine (Defence) Order in Council of 1931.

58. NAUK FO 371/16927: Letter from the National League to Sir John Simon, 30 October 1933.

59. *Al-Muqattam*, 2 November 1933, cited in NAUK CO 733/239/5.

60. NAUK CO 733/239/5: Wauchope to Cunliffe-Lister, 6 November 1933.

61. For a comparison, see Coronil and Skurski, "Dismembering and Remembering the Nation," 330.

62. Ibid., 124.

CHAPTER 6: CHALLENGING THE OTTOMAN *PAX URBANA*

The research for this chapter is part of the joint ZMO-SOAS collaborative project "Urban Violence in the Middle East: Between Empire and Nation State," financed by the DFG and the AHRC. The author wishes to thank Nelida Fuccaro and Ulrike Freitag, as well as all of her colleagues from the Zentrum Moderner Orient and the Unité de Recherche Dirasat in Tunis, for their constructive comments on earlier versions of this essay. All the direct quotations from French are translated by the author.

1. On the history of Ottoman Tunisia in the previous decades, see Asma Moalla, *The Regency of Tunis and the Ottoman Porte (1777–1814)* (London: Routledge, 2003). On the origins and developments of foreign influence, see Jean Ganiage, "France, England and the Tunisian Affair," in Prosser Gifford and William Roger Louis, eds., *France and Britain in Africa: Imperial Rivalry and Colonial Rule* (New Haven, CT: Yale University Press, 1971), 35–72.

2. On the imperial reforms, see Carter Vaughn Findley, *Bureaucratic Reform in the Ottoman Empire: The Sublime Porte 1789–1922* (Princeton, NJ: Princeton University Press, 2012). See also Kemal Karpat, "The Transformation of the Ottoman State, 1789–1908," *International Journal of Middle East Studies* 3, no. 3 (1972): 243–81.

3. See Nora Lafi, "Diversity and the Nature of the Ottoman Empire," in Steven Vertovec, ed., *Routledge International Handbook of Diversity Studies* (London: Routledge, 2014), 125–31.

4. On the Ottoman system of coexistence during the old regime, see Nora Lafi, "Etre juif dans l'Algérie ottomane," in Hélène Hoog, ed., *Juifs d'Algérie* (Paris: Skira Flammarion-Musée d'Art et d'Histoire du Judaïsme, 2012), 69–81.

5. Ussama Makdisi, *The Culture of Sectarianism: Community, History and Violence in Nineteenth Century Ottoman Lebanon* (Berkeley: University of California Press, 2000).

6. The 1864 riots have been used, for example, by Edmund Burke III to construct a typology of Arab protest movements: "Understanding Arab Protest Movements," *Arab Studies Quarterly* 8, no. 4 (1986): 333–45. On 1864, see Taoufik Bachrouch, *Rabi' al-'Urban, Adwa' 'an Asbab Thawra 'Ali Ben Ghadhaham, sana 1864: Watha'iq min al-Arshif al-Watani al-Tunisi* [Reflections on the main characters of the Ali Ben Ghad-

haham 1864 revolt on the basis of documents from the National archives of Tunis] (Carthage: al-Mu'assasa al-Waṭaniyya lil-Tarjamah wa 'l-Taḥqiq wa 'l-Dirasat, Bayt al-Ḥikmah, 1991).

7. This chapter is based on files from the Tunisian National Archives (among them the register of petitions), on the chronicle of Ibn Ben Abi Diyaf, on a reading of the un-edited urban chronicle of the chief of the city (*yawmiyat shaykh al-madina*) also found in the National Archives in Tunis, as well as on the correspondence between various actors in the events found in the central archives of the Ottoman Empire in Istanbul (BOA) and in the archives of the French Foreign Office in Nantes and of the British Foreign Office in London.

8. On al-Farabi's interpretation of Plato's concept of the ideal city, see Christopher Colmo, "Theory and Practice: Alfarabi's Plato Revisited," *American Political Science Review* 86, no. 4 (1992): 966–76.

9. On the construction of the Ottoman bureaucratic apparatus, see Karen Barkey, *Empire of Difference: The Ottomans in Comparative Perspective* (Cambridge: Cambridge University Press, 2008).

10. For a reflection on the beylical system, see Dalenda Larguèche and Julia Clancy-Smith, "The Mahalla: The Origins of Beylical Sovereignty in Ottoman Tunisia during the Early Modern Period," *Journal of North-African Studies* 6, no. 1 (2001): 105–16.

11. Archives Nationales de Tunis (hereafter ANT), SH, 50 602 55. See also Abdelhamid Larguèche, *Les ombres de la ville. Pauvres, marginaux et minoritaires à Tunis (XVIIIe–XIXe s.)* (Tunis: Centre de Publication Universitaire, 2002), 262–83; and Rida Ben Rajab, *Al-Shurta wa Aman al-Hadira, 1861–1864* [Police and security in the capital] (PhD diss., University of Tunis, 1992).

12. On this aspect of Ottoman governance, see Nora Lafi, "Petitions and Accommodating Urban Change in the Ottoman Empire," in Elisabeth Özdalga, Sait Özervarlı and Feryal Tansuğ, eds., *Istanbul as Seen from a Distance: Centre and Provinces in the Ottoman Empire* (Istanbul: Swedish Research Institute, 2011), 73–82.

13. Ahmad Ibn Ben Abi Diyaf, *Ithaf ahl al-Zaman bi Akhbar Muluk Tunis wa 'Ahd al-Aman* [Presenting contemporaries the history of the rulers of Tunis and the funda-mental pact], 2nd ed., 9 vols. (Tunis: Dar al-'Arabiyya lil-Kitab, 2004), 3–4:117–21. On this figure, see Ahmed Abdessalem, *Les historiens tunisiens des 17e, 18e et 19e siècles: Essai d'histoire culturelle* (Paris: Klincksieck, 1973); and Carl Brown, *Consult Them in the Matter: A Nineteenth-Century Islamic Argument for Constitutional Government* (Fayetteville: University of Arkansas Press, 2005).

14. In the original text, *wa narfa' fi dhalika amruna bi 'arduhal li-mawlina al-sultan* (and we send for this affair a petition to our ruler the sultan). Ibn Ben Abi Diyaf, *Ithaf*, 3–4:117.

15. Such documents can be found in ANT, SH 263 1, Qa'ima shikayat al-mahkama al-ma'rada 'la al-bay'.

16. Julia Clancy-Smith, *Mediterraneans: North Africa and Europe in an Age of Migration, c. 1800–1900* (Berkeley: University of California Press, 2010). See also Abdelhamid Hénia, "Le rôle des étrangers dans la dynamique socio-politique de la Tunisie (XVIIe–XVIIIe s.)," *Cahiers de la Méditerranée* 84 (2012): 213–33 ; and Adbelhamid Larguèche, ed., *Les communautés méditerranéennes de Tunisie* (Tunis: Centre de Publication Universitaire, 2006).

17. See Jean Ganiage, *La population européenne de Tunis au milieu du 19e siècle: Étude démographique* (Paris: Presses Universitaires de France, 1960).

18. See Ulrike Freitag's chapter in this volume for a discussion on how masculinity defied traditional systems of mediation in late Ottoman Jeddah. On notables, see Mohamed El Aziz Ben Achour, *Catégories de la société tunisoise dans la deuxième moitié du XIXe siècle* (Tunis: Institut National d'Archéologie et d'Art, 1989). See also Abdelhamid Hénia, ed., *Etre notable au Maghreb* (Paris: Maisonneuve et Larose, 2006).

19. See Paul Sebag, *Une histoire des révolutions du Royaume de Tunis au XVIIe siècle: Une oeuvre de Guillerargues?* (Paris: L'Harmattan, 2003). The relationship between local notables and the Ottoman imperial structure during the eighteenth century has been discussed in Mohamed El Aziz Ben Achour, "Pouvoir central et gestion urbaine: L'exemple de Tunis au XVIIIe siècle," in Luigi Serra, ed., *La città mediterranea* (Naples: Istituto Universitario Orientale, 1993), 287–98.

20. On the influence of foreign consuls, see Anne-Marie Planel, *De la nation à la colonie: La communauté française de Tunisie au XIXe siècle* (Paris: Thèse de doctorat EHESS, 2000).

21. The Janissaries were a corps of elite troops and administrators that included young boys of Caucasian origin trained to serve the sultan.

22. Salvatore Bono, *Corsari del Mediterraneo* (Milan: Mondadori, 1993).

23. Ibn Ben Abi Diyaf, *Ithaf*, 3–4:115–16. See also Tawfik Bachrouch, *La médina de Tunis avant le protectorat* (Tunis: CERES, 2008), 751–52.

24. See Khalifa Chater, *Dépendance et mutations précoloniales: La régence de Tunis de 1815 à 1857* (Tunis: Presses universitaires, 1984).

25. Başbakanlık Osmanlı Arşivi (hereafter BOA) HAT 456 22496 29 Z 1230, 2 December 1815.

26. Ibn Ben Abi Diyaf, *Ithaf*, 3–4: 116 (1 May 1816). On the context, see Ismael Montana, *The Abolition of Slavery in Ottoman Tunisia* (Gainesville: University Press of Florida, 2013).

27. Ibn Ben Abi Diyaf, *Ithaf*, 3–4: 116–17 (1 May 1816).

28. BOA C. AS. 763 32223 23/Ş /1231, 19 July 1816.

29. BOA HAT 458 22558/A 29/Z /1231, 20 November 1816. For the later reform of the urban police, see also ANT, Dossier 653, carton 59, *Amin*, doc. 26. Ottoman intelligence officers also suggested the assassination of some of the leaders of the unrest but faced difficulties as several of them had taken refuge in various port cities of the Mediterranean (BOA HAT 1539 48 29/Z /1232, 9 November 1817).

30. Mahmoud Bouali, *Le temps de la non-révolte (1827–1832)* (Carthage-Tunis: Société Tunisienne de Diffusion, 1978), 48–49.

31. On the rivalry for influence, see André Raymond, "Les tentatives anglaises de pénétration économique en Tunisie (1856–1877)," *Revue Historique* 214, no. 1 (1955): 48–67. For implementation of the Tanzimat, see Ibn Ben Abi Diyaf, *Ithaf*, 3–4:237–39.

32. Ibid., 233. On this figure, see Fatma Ben Slimane, "Définir ce qu'être Tunisien: Litiges autour de la nationalité de Nessim Scemama (1873–1881)," *REMMM* 137 (2015): 31–48. On blasphemy in Islamic jurisprudence, see Abdelmagid Turki, "Situation du 'tributaire' qui insulte l'Islam au regard de la doctrine et de la jurisprudence musulmanes," *Studia Islamica* 30 (1969): 39–72. On Jews in Tunisia, see Claude Hagège, "Communautés juives de Tunisie à la veille du protectorat français," *Le Mouvement Social* 110 (1980): 35–50. For a reflection on the Sfez affair, see also Clancy-Smith, *Mediterraneans*.

33. On the judicial system and the question of Jewish defendants, see Robert Brunschvig, "Justice religieuse et justice laïque dans la Tunisie des deys et des beys jusqu'au milieu du XIXe s.," *Studia Islamica* 23 (1965): 27–70. For a reflection on the death penalty in 1857 Tunis, see Mohamed Kerrou and Moncef M'Halla, "La prostitution dans la médina de Tunis aux XIXe et XXe siècles," *Annuaire de l'Afrique du Nord* (1991): 201–21.

34. Ibn Ben Abi Diyaf, *Ithaf*, 3–4:233.

35. National Archives of the United Kingdom (hereafter NAUK) FO 102/53 n. 24: "Report by Consul Wood of a Conversation with the Bey. Private Audience," 25 July 1857.

36. That is, he was not a protégé, who could not have been taken to court easily. Ibid., 6 July 1857.

37. Ibid.

38. Ibid. A few weeks later the bey answered in the same terms to an official protest by the British government. NAUK FO 102/53 n. 33: 18 August 1857.

39. Michael Clark, "Jewish Identity in British Politics: The Case of the First Jewish MPs: 1858–1887," *Jewish Social Studies* 13, no. 2 (2007): 93–126.

40. NAUK FO 102/53 n. 24: Letter to Consul Wood from the Jewish-British residents of Tunis, 6 July 1857.

41. Ibid., n. 22: Petition, 30 June 1857. The petition was signed by Saverio Zahra, Michele Balzan, Antonio Farrugia, Paolo Azzopardi, D. V. Camilleri Mifsud, Giuseppe Schembri, Zio Maria Pisani, B. Farrugia, I. J. Williamson, E. They, Giuseppe Catajar, Emanuele Caruana, Moses Levy, G. Azzopardi, Giuseppe Bussutil, Moses Agnelos, Moise Levi Sonsino, Salvatore Calleja, Fratellli Crassapopoulo, Thomas A. Hanson, Michelangiolo Larosa, Giuseppe Zerafa, G. Samut, and Gaspare Coschieri.

42. No evidence has been found in the archives of the police. Petitions may have been deliberately destroyed or sent to another administrative department during another phase of the tensions. If the latter is the case, they might emerge one day.

43. Centre des Archives Diplomatiques de Nantes, Ministère des Affaires Étrangères,

Consulat de Tunis (hereafter CADN), 71 PO/1 332 1582-1887 n. 332, "Emeutes populaires"; NAUK FO 102/53 n. 31: report by R. Wood, 11 August 1857.

44. CADN 71 PO 1 332 1582-1887 n. 332. The chancellor of the French consulate, Augustin Ferdinand, and his witness, Gabriel Valensi, also produced an account of the damage reported by Domenico Mangano, the owner of the stock exchange.

45. Ibid.

46. Michel-Ange La Rosas was among the people who sent a letter to Consul Wood on 30 June 1857 stating that they felt insecure.

47. CADN 71 PO 1 332 1582-1887 n. 332. Several of those individuals were so badly injured that they died in the following days and weeks.

48. NAUK FO 102/31.

49. Armand Maarek, "Le pacte fondamental et les réformes à travers les archives diplomatiques françaises," in Denis Cohen-Tannoudji, ed., *Entre Orient et Occident. Juifs et Musulmans en Tunisie* (Paris: Éditions de l'Éclat, 2007), 133–54. See also Habib Jamoussi, *Juifs et Chrétiens en Tunisie au XIXe siècle* (Carthage: Amal, 2010).

50. For information on Khereddine, see Atilla Çetin, *Tunuslu Hayreddin Paşa* (Ankara: Kültür Bakanligi Osmanli Eserleri, 1999). See also Gerard Van Krieken, *Khayr al-Dîn et la Tunisie (1850–1881)* (Leiden, Netherlands: E. J. Brill, 1976); and Mongi Smida, *Khereddine, ministre réformateur (1873–1877)* (Tunis: Maison Tunisienne d'Édition, 1970).

51. On this question, see Claude Hagège and Bernard Zarcal, "Les Juifs et la France en Tunisie: Les bénéfices d'une relation triangulaire," *Le Mouvement Social* 197, no. 4 (2001): 9–28.

52. Ibn Ben Abi Diyaf, *Ithaf*, 3–4:235–45 (22 August 1857).

53. ANT, Dossier 60, carton 55, "Décret du 20 moharrem 1275: *qanun al-majlis al-baladiyya*"; William L. Cleveland, "The Municipal Council of Tunis, 1858–1870: A Study in Urban Institutional Change," *International Journal of Middle East Studies* 9, no. 1(1978): 33–61. See also Nora Lafi, "Les pouvoirs urbains à Tunis à la fin de l'époque ottomane: La persistance de l'ancien régime," in Nora Lafi, ed., *Municipalités méditerranéennes* (Berlin: K. Schwarz, 2005), 223–44.

54. On these events, see Ibn Ben Abi Diyaf, *Ithaf*, 5–6:89ff. On the context, see CADN 712 PO/1 n. 103.

55. CADN 712 PO/1 n. 101. See also Bachrouch, *La médina*, 761.

56. Ibn Ben Abi Diyaf, *Ithaf*, 5–6:89ff.

57. On the power of saints in the Islamic Maghreb, see Nelly Amri, *Les saints en Islam: Les messagers de l'espérance* (Paris: Cerf, 2008). See also Mohamed Kerrou, ed., *L'autorité des Saints en Méditerranée* (Paris: Recherche sur les Civilisations, 1998).

58. Ibn Ben Abi Diyaf, *Ithaf*, 5–6:89ff ; CADN 712 PO/1 n. 101.

59. CADN 712 PO/1 331, Correspondance avec le Ministère, Direction Politique, Gestion de Léon Roche, 1861.

60. Ibid., n. 101.

61. This is also illustrated by Jean Ganiage in his seminal work on the roots of French colonial domination in Tunisia: *Les origines du Protectorat français en Tunisie (1861–1881)* (Paris: Presses Universitaires de France, 1959).

62. Béchir Ben Salama, *L'insurrection de 1864 en Tunisie* (Tunis: Maison Tunisienne de l'Édition, 1967). See BOA HR. SFR. 3 . . . doss. 88 doc. 32 31 5 1864. See also Ibn Ben Abi Diyaf, *Ithaf*, 5–6:112–57.

63. BOA HR. SYS. 58 41, 15 June 1864, and HR. SFR. 3 ... doss. 89 doc. 28, 15 June 1864.

64. ANT, "Correspondance des puissances étrangères au sujet de la révolte des tribus, mission de Haydar Effendi, envoyé du Sultan," 1 July 1864.

CHAPTER 7: A TAMED URBAN REVOLUTION

This chapter is a product of the joint ZMO-SOAS program "Urban Violence in the Middle East: Between Empire and Nation State," financed by the DFG and the AHRC. I would like to thank Nelida Fuccaro, Rasmus Elling, Ulrike Freitag, Nora Lafi, Fatemeh Masjedi, Nushin Atmaca, and Amer Ghrawi for their valuable thoughts and comments and Melody Mosavat and Jim Mandaville for helping me with compiling the cartographic materials. I am especially grateful to the many people who agreed to share with me their firsthand knowledge of the events described in this chapter during a field research trip to the Eastern Province in 2013. Many of them asked to remain anonymous.

1. United States National Archives and Records Administration (hereafter NARA) RG 59 Central Foreign Policy Files 1967–1969 POL27 ARAB-ISR 6/6/67 to POL27 ARAB-ISR 6/9/67.

2. *Struggle, Oppression and Counter-revolution in Saudi Arabia* (Berkeley: Arab Support Committee, ca. 1972), 6–7 (translated from the original Arabic articles appearing in the 1972 issues of *Al Jazeerah Al Jadeedah*, the political organ of the People's Democratic Party of Al Jazeerah).

3. The military airfield in Dhahran was established in 1945 as a base for US Air Force troops on the Arabian Peninsula. In 1951, the lease between Saudi Arabia and the United States expired, and the airfield passed under Saudi command. In 1953, the United States Military Training Mission (USMTM) was established to provide military training to the Saudi army. The USMTM staff compound was located on the airfield.

4. This event is described in Helen Lackner, *A House Built on Sand: Political Economy of Saudi Arabia* (London: Ithaca Press, 1978), 105; Mordechai Abir, *Saudi Arabia in the Oil Era: Regime and Elites; Conflict and Collaboration* (Boulder, CO: Westview, 1988), 111–12; and Mordechai Abir, *Saudi Arabia: Government, Society and the Gulf Crisis* (London: Routledge, 1993), 53–54.

5. Nelida Fuccaro, "Introduction: Histories of Oil and Urban Modernity in the Middle East," *Comparative Studies of South Asia, Africa and the Middle East* 33, no. 1 (2013): 2.

6. Henri Lefebvre, *The Urban Revolution*, trans. Robert Bononno (Minneapolis: University of Minnesota Press, 2003).

7. Toby Jones has made a similar argument but with an emphasis on the deleterious effects of oil production on the local environment and the traditional local economy. Toby C. Jones, *Desert Kingdom: How Oil and Water Forged Modern Saudi Arabia* (Cambridge, MA: Harvard University Press, 2010), 146.

8. Lefebvre, *Urban Revolution*, 14.

9. See Jones, *Desert Kingdom*, 138–78.

10. Robert Vitalis, *America's Kingdom: Mythmaking on the Saudi Oil Frontier* (Stanford, CA: Stanford University Press, 2007).

11. Fuccaro, "Introduction: Histories of Oil," 5.

12. Lefebvre, *Urban Revolution*, 5.

13. Andy Merrifield, *Henri Lefebvre: A Critical Introduction* (New York: Routledge, 2006), 52.

14. Claudia Ghrawi, "Structural and Physical Violence in Saudi Arabian Oil Towns, 1953–1956," in Ulrike Freitag, Nelida Fuccaro, Claudia Ghrawi, and Nora Lafi, eds., *Urban Violence in the Middle East: Changing Cityscapes from Empire to Nation States* (Oxford: Berghahn, 2015), 243–66.

15. Sarah Yizraeli, *Politics and Society in Saudi Arabia: The Crucial Years of Development, 1960–1982* (New York: Columbia University Press, 2012); Vitalis, *America's Kingdom*, 228–64.

16. Vitalis, *America's Kingdom*, 92–110.

17. Thomas F. O'Dea, "Social Change in Saudi Arabia: Problems and Prospects," unpublished report (Special Study Group, February–August 1963), J. Willard Marriot Library, Special Collections. My discussion draws on the comprehensive survey of this report in Vitalis, *America's Kingdom*, 256–62.

18. NARA RG 59 786A.56311/8-2260 HBS, Dhahran to State, Dispatch No. 55, 22 August 1960.

19. Ian Seccombe and Richard Lawless, *Work Camps and Company Towns: Settlement Patterns and the Gulf Oil Industry* (Durham, UK: University of Durham, Centre for Middle Eastern and Islamic Studies, 1987), 75–76.

20. For a thorough analysis of the emerging bureaucratic order under King Faisal, see Steffen Hertog, *Princes, Brokers, and Bureaucrats: Oil and the State in Saudi Arabia* (Ithaca, NY: Cornell University Press, 2010), 61–83.

21. Thamir al-Ahmari, 'Abd al-Rahmān b. 'Abdallah, *Dawr Sharikat al-Zayt al-'Arabiyya al-Amrikiyya (Aramku) fi Tanmiyat al-Mintaqa al-Sharqiyya min al-Mamlaka al-'Arabiyya al-Sa'udiyya* (Riyadh: 'Abd al-Rahman b. 'Abdallah Thamir al-Ahmari, 2007), 180; author interview with Mahdi Asfour, Dammam, 19 May 2013.

22. Author interviews in al-Khobar, Dammam, and Dhahran, May 2013.

23. An Aramco survey of the company's Saudi employees conducted in 1965 shows that nearly 60 percent could read and write in either Arabic or English, 50 percent lived in newly constructed houses, 60 percent of their homes were connected to the electric

grid, and 85 percent had tap water—but only 6.5 percent could afford a gas stove with an oven, and less than 4 percent had an electric air-conditioning system. The average number of persons in a household was estimated at 9.4. NARA RG 59 LAB 2 SAUD, A-133 Dhahran to State, 5 May 1967; author interviews in Dammam and al-Khobar, May 2013.

24. Yizraeli, *Politics and Society in Saudi Arabia*, 164; NARA RG 59 886A.06/9-561, Dispatch No. 61, Dhahran to State, 5 September 1961; author interview in Dhahran, 14 May 2013.

25. The actual share of foreign workers in the local industry is hard to estimate. Statistical data provided by Aramco for the year 1967 on the national composition of its workforce show that more than 80 percent (9,813) of the company's employees were Saudis, while a little more than 10 percent (1,284) were Americans. Not even 10 percent of the Aramco workforce consisted of other Arabs (328), Indians (408), Pakistanis (227), and other nationalities (13) combined. Arabian American Oil Company, *Aramco Handbook: Oil and the Middle East* (Dhahran: Aramco, 1967), 156. No such statistics exist for the numerous foreign contractor firms operating in the area of oil production, but the number of foreign workers in these companies was probably much higher. NARA RG 59 POL 2 SAUD, A-76 Weekly Summary, 8 December 1965.

26. NARA RG 59 POL 2 SAUD, A-76 Weekly Summary, 30 November 1966; ibid., 886A.06/9-561, Dhahran to State, Dispatch No. 61, 5 September 1961; Ghrawi, "Structural and Physical Violence in Saudi Arabian Oil Towns."

27. This was also observed by Aramco management. NARA RG 59 POL 2 SAUD, A-58 Weekly Summary, 14 October 1964. The last strike took place in June 1956, shortly after labor activities had been outlawed by Royal Decree.

28. Ibid., A-286 Weekly Summary, 17 June 1964; A-281 Weekly Summary, 10 June 1964; A-16 Dhahran to State, 22 July 1964; ibid., 886A.062/5-1661 CJ, Jidda to State, 16 May 1961; ibid., POL 2 SAUD, A-4 Weekly Summary, 1 July 1964.

29. NARA RG 59 POL 2 SAUD, A-16 Dhahran to State, 22 July 1964; ibid., A-177 Weekly Summary, 22 June 1966; Georgetown Special Collections Division, William E. Mulligan Papers (hereafter Mulligan Papers), ARD, Chronological Files, "Aramco," Box 7, Folder 2, "Labour relations development," 5 November 1966.

30. Mulligan Papers, ARD, Chronological Files, "Aramco," Box 7, Folder 2, "Labour relations development," 5 November 1966; NARA RG 59 POL 2 SAUD, A-177 Weekly Summary, 22 June 1966.

31. NARA RG 59 POL 2-3 SAUD, A-248 Biweekly Summary, 29 April 1964; ibid., POL 2 SAUD, A-9 Weekly Summary, 8 July 1964; ibid., LAB 6-1 SAUD, Telegram DHAHRAN 18 7-13-64, 13 July 1964; ibid., POL 2 SAUD, A-76 Weekly Summary, 8 December 1965.

32. Toby Matthiesen, "The Shia of Saudi Arabia: Identity Politics, Sectarianism and the Saudi State" (PhD diss., SOAS, University of London, 2011), 170–71.

33. On radical youth organizations in Bahrain, see Nelida Fuccaro, *Histories of City*

and State in the Persian Gulf: Manama since 1800 (Cambridge: Cambridge University Press, 2009), 173–86. A literary account of the politicization of Saudi students in the oil conurbation, probably with autobiographical undertones, is the first book of Turki al-Hamad's trilogy *Al-Karadib*: Turki al-Hamad, *Adama*, trans. Robin Bray (London: Saqi, 2003). See also NARA RG 59 POL 2 SAUD, A-144 Weekly Summary, 8 January 1964; A-148 Weekly Summary, 15 January 1964.

34. NARA RG 59 POL 2 SAUD, A-4 Weekly Summary, 1 July 1964; A-32 Weekly Summary, 26 August 1964; A-1 Weekly Summary, 7 July 1965; ibid., LAB 6-1 SAUD, Telegram DHAHRAN 9 7-7-64, 8 July 1964.

35. Ibid., A-61 Weekly Summary, 21 October 1964; A-160 Weekly Summary, 25 May 1966.

36. Ibid., A-15 Weekly Summary, 10 August 1966.

37. Ibid., A-76 Weekly Summary, 8 December 1965; A-21 Weekly Summary, 18 August 1965; A-36 Weekly Summary, 22 September 1965; A-128 Weekly Summary, 30 March 1966; A-149 Weekly Summary, 11 May 1966; A-160 Weekly Summary, 25 May 1966.

38. Lackner, *House Built on Sand*, 104–5.

39. NARA RG 59 POL 2 SAUD, A-76 Weekly Summary, 7 December 1966; A-88 Weekly Summary, 18 January 1967; A-85 Weekly Summary, 4 January 1967; ibid., POL 23-7 SAUD, Telegram JIDDA 2397 12-21-67, 21 December 1966.

40. Ibid., POL 2 SAUD, A-90 Weekly Summary, 25 January 1967.

41. Mulligan Papers, ARD, Chronological Files, 1967 Riots, Box 16, Folder 8 (hereafter Mulligan Papers, 1967 Riots).

42. NARA RG 59 POL 2 SAUD, A-145 Weekly Summary, 31 May 1967.

43. Ibid., 59 POL 23 SAUD, A-130 Dhahran to State, 3 June 1968; NARA RG 59 886A.50, A-150 Dhahran to State, 14 November 1962.

44. Mulligan Papers, 1967 Riots.

45. Ibid.; NARA RG 59 POL 27 ARAB-ISR, Telegram JIDDA 5095 6-6-67, 6 June 1967.

46. Mulligan Papers, 1967 Riots.

47. Ibid.; Carol Hicke, "Interview with Peter Speers," in Carol Hicke, ed., *American Perspectives of Aramco: The Saudi-Arabian Oil Producing Company, 1930s to 1980s* (Berkeley: University of California Press, 1995), 501–3.

48. NARA RG 59 POL 2 SAUD, A-12 Monthly Review, 10 July 1967.

49. Mulligan Papers, 1967 Riots; NARA RG 59 POL 27 ARAB-ISR, Telegram DHAHRAN 882 6-7-67, 7 June 1967; NARA RG 59 POL 23-8 SAUD, Telegram JIDDA 86 7-6-67, 6 July 1967; A-152 Dhahran to State, 21 June 1967.

50. See Yasser Elsheshtawy's chapter in this volume on the destruction of the Shepheard's Hotel in Cairo by protesters in 1952. This was another episode of political violence that directly targeted the built environment and the symbols and commodities associated with Western/European economic domination and luxurious lifestyles.

51. Mulligan Papers, 1967 Riots; NARA RG 59 POL 23-8 SAUD, A-152 Dhahran to State, 21 June 1967.

52. NARA RG59 POL 27 ARAB-ISR, A-155 Dhahran to State, 28 June 1967; Mulligan Papers, 1967 Riots.

53. Mulligan Papers, 1967 Riots; NARA RG 59 POL 12 SAUD, A-236 Jidda to State, 4 December 1968.

54. NARA RG 59 POL12 SAUD, A-236 Dhahran to State, 11 December 1968.

55. Mulligan Papers, 1967 Riots; NARA RG 59 POL 23-8 SAUD, Telegram DHAH-RAN 883 6-7-67, 7 June 1967; ibid., Telegram DHAHRAN 888 6-7-67, 7 June 1967.

56. Mulligan Papers, 1967 Riots.

57. NARA RG 59 POL 29 SAUD, A-16 Dhahran to State, 2 August 1967.

58. Ibid., POL 23-8 SAUD, Telegram DHAHRAN W 235 10-3-67, 3 October 1967; ibid., POL 18 SAUD, A-25 Dhahran to State, 23 August 1967.

59. On the involvement of Shia Ba'thist activists in the organization of the demonstrations, see Matthiesen, "The Shia of Saudi Arabia," 172. The Saudi political activist and social scientist Tawfiq Alsaif refutes the idea of a sectarian background to the 1967 riots and stresses the involvement of various politicized groups. Author interview with Tawfiq Alsaif, Tarout, 16 May 2013. An American report concludes that the Shia were only "lukewarm participants" in the unrest: NARA RG 59 POL 13-3 SAUD, A-90, Dhahran to State, 9 June 1969. In contrast to what is suggested by some of the historiography, the UPAP did not claim responsibility for the demonstrations. The version that claims the UPAP responsible for the riots stems from Abir, *Saudi Arabia in the Oil Era*, 111; Nasir Al-Sa'id, *Tarikh al-Sa'ud* (Beirut: Manshurat Ittihad Sha'b al-Jazira al-'Arabiyya, 1980), 585. Hamza Hasan mentions that the demonstrations of 5 and 6 June took place in numerous towns and villages in the Eastern Province: Hamza Hasan, *Al-Shi'a fi al-Mamlaka al-'Arabiyya al-Sa'udiyya: Al-Juz' al-Thani* (N.p.: Mu'assasat al-Baqi' li-Ihya' al-Turath, 1993), 305.

60. NARA RG 59 POL 23-8 SAUD, A-17 Dhahran to State, 2 August 1967; Mulligan Papers, 1967 Riots. S.A.S. Al-'Awwami refers to "the demonstration that emanated from the College of Petroleum" (*al-muzahara allati kharajat min jami'at al-bitrul*): Sayyid 'Ali al-Sayyid Baqir Al-'Awwami, *Al-Haraka al-Wataniyya Sharq al-Sa'udiyya 1373-1393 H/1953-1973 M: Al-Juz' Al-Thani* (Beirut: Riyad al-Rayyis al-Kutub wa-'l-Nashr, 2012), 55.

61. NARA RG59 POL 27 ARAB-ISR, Telegram DHAHRAN W 905, 8 June 1967; ibid., POL 29 SAUD, Telegram DHAHRAN 188 2-15-70, 15 February 1970; ibid., POL 2 SAUD, A-120 Monthly Commentary, 1 June 1970; author interview in Dhahran, May 2013.

CHAPTER 8: MAKING AND UNMAKING SPACES OF SECURITY

1. Within the field of Middle East studies, the most sustained engagements between urban history and the history of state violence are those examining colonial and

counterinsurgency policies, particularly in North Africa and Palestine/Israel. On the latter, see, for example, Eyal Weizman, *Hollow Land: Israel's Architecture of Occupation* (New York: Verso, 2007).

2. For World War I Europe, see Jay Winter and Jean-Louis Robert, eds., *Capital Cities at War: Paris, London, Berlin 1914–1919* (Cambridge: Cambridge University Press, 1999).

3. Dina Rizk Khoury, *Iraq in Wartime: Soldiering, Martyrdom and Remembrance* (New York: Cambridge University Press, 2013).

4. Michel Foucault, "Governmentality," in Graham Burchell, Colin Gordon, and Peter Miller, eds., *The Foucault Effect: Studies in Governmentality* (Chicago: University of Chicago Press, 1991), 87–104; Michel Foucault, *Security, Territory and Population*, ed. Michel Senellart (New York: Palgrave Macmillan, 2009); Michel Foucault, *The Birth of Biopolitics*, ed. Michel Senellart (New York: Palgrave Macmillan, 2008).

5. Satish Deshpande, "Hegemonic Spatial Strategies: The Nation-State and Hindu Communalism in Twentieth-Century India," *Public Culture* 10 (1998): 250.

6. Basra (including the city of Basra and the town of Haritha); Umm al-Khasib (including the subdistrict of Seeba); Zubayr (including the town of Zubayr and subdistricts of Safwan and Umm al-Qasr); al-Qurna (including the town of Dayr and subdistrict of Suwayb); Shatt al-'Arab (including subdistricts of 'Ataba and Nashwa); al-Fao (including Fao city and the subdistricts of al-Bahhar and al-Khalij al-'Arabi); and al-Madina (including the city of Madina and the subdistricts of Talha and al-'Izz). Adnan 'Inad al-Ghiyadh and Ussama Isma'il Uthman, "Al-Tawzi' al-Jughrafi li Mudun Muhafazat al-Basra bi hasab Ahjamuha li Muddat 1977–2007" [The geographical distribution of towns in Basra Province according to the density of their populations, 1977–2007], *Majallat Dirasat al-Basra* [Journal of Basra studies] 8 (2006): 1–24.

7. Adill Abdullah Khattab, "Basra City: A Study in Urban Geography" (PhD diss., SOAS, University of London, 1972), 120–59.

8. Ibid., 229.

9. Ali Nuri Hasan, "Tajribat al-Takhtit al-M'uasira fi al-'Iraq" [The experience of modern planning in Iraq], in *Al-Madina wa al-Hayat al-Madaniyya* [The city and urbanity] (Baghdad: Dar al-Huriyya li al-Tiba'a, 1988), 3:171–218.

10. Khattab, "Basra City," 140–49.

11. Abbas 'Ali al-Tamimi, *Al-Numuw al-Sina'i fi Muhafadhatay al-Basra wa Ninawah* [Industrial growth in the provinces of Basra and Ninewah] (Basra: Markaz Dirasat al-Khalij al-'Arabi bi Jami'at al-Basra, 1981), 246–47.

12. Khattab, "Basra City," 180–88.

13. A tourist guide to Iraq, issued by the State Organization of Tourism in 1982 before the cancellation of the meeting of nonaligned states, describes Basra and Iraq generally as attractive tourist destinations. There is no mention of the war. *Iraq: Tourist Guide* (Baghdad: State Organization of Tourism, 1982), 130–32.

14. Khattab, "Basra City," 238.

15. Al-Tamimi, *Al-Numuw al-Sina'i*, 246–47.

16. Ibid., 245.

17. School Registers, Amn 3201 and 3202, Hoover Institution, Stanford University. For the town of al-Qurna, of the 1,335 matriculating students, 1.6 percent had relatives who had belonged either to the Communist or Da'wa Parties, and many were executed. For the town of Zubayr, of the 1,347 students, more than 3 percent had family members who had run afoul of the regime, the majority for belonging to the Da'wa Party.

18. Ba'th Regional Command Council, Hoover Institution (hereafter BRCC), 23-2-030 to 0143.

19. It is telling that the minister of the Region of Autonomous Rule served as an adviser on the committee that planned the displacement in the south.

20. This was not the case in Fao, which was economically closely linked to Basra. Fao's population was moved out early in the war, its landscape mined, and tunnels dug. After the Iranians occupied Fao in February 1986, the landscape could no longer sustain human life. It became a frontline area.

21. BRCC, 01-2062-0001-0254 to 0484. Basra was heavily shelled in December 1986 and January 1987. Beginning in 1985, the Southern Bureau of the Ba'th, based in Basra city, organized the citizenry in several palm grove–cutting campaigns.

22. Ghiyadh and Uthman, "Al-Tawzi' al-Jughrafi," 1–24.

23. Ibid.

24. BRCC, 2140-0003-0132 to 0140.

25. BRCC, 01-3212-0001-0546 to 0550.

26. BRCC, 2219-0004-0195 to 0199.

27. BRCC, 2062-0001-0374 to 0490.

28. There are 1,036 school registers at the Hoover Institution. They are surveys of matriculating male students in middle and secondary schools. It is not clear whether similar surveys were conducted for female students. There are two sets of surveys: those conducted by the Ba'th Party and those by the Directorate of General Security. I have examined the 1987–88 surveys conducted by the party, the first year they are available for the majority of Iraqi provinces, and the 1998–99 surveys, when new categories were included. The data from these surveys can be used for quantitative analysis covering, as an example, population migration and settlement and political affiliation. However, analyzed as text, as I have done, they indicate the ideology of security that undergirds the collection of the data.

29. BRCC, 3212-0001-0546 to 0550.

30. Hazim Najm, author interview, Amman, 3 July 2007.

31. Ibid.

32. Ibid.

33. BRCC, 3212-0001-0549.

34. Najm interview, 3 July 2007.

35. Ibid.

36. BRCC, 01-3212-0001-0546 to 0550.

37. Khoury, *Iraq in Wartime*, 48–160.

38. See Nelida Fuccaro's chapter in this volume on Kirkuk, which also explores the politics of security, but that implemented by the colonial and monarchical regimes between 1924 and 1959, and the extent of its effectiveness to penetrate urban life and contain violent unrest.

39. BRCC, 3212-0001-0503.

40. BRCC, 3212-0001-0667.

41. Author interviews with Haytham Ali, a journalist for the Ba'th Party newspaper, *Al-Thawra*, who covered the war, Amman, 8 August 2007; Hazim Najm, Amman, 15 July 2007; and Waddah Hasan, Amman, 21, 23, and 28 June 2007.

42. Najib al-Salhi, "Al-Zilzal" [The earthquake], *Iraq 4 All News 1998*, Iraq4all.dk/Zlzal/htm (accessed 28 April 2008) [site no longer available].

43. Ibid.

44. Majid al-Majid, *Intifadat al-Sha'b al-'Iraqi* [The uprising of the Iraqi people] (Beirut: Dar al-Wifaq, 1991).

45. Najm interview, 15 July 2007.

46. In addition to the interviews conducted in 2007 and 2009, I draw on al-Salhi's "Al-Zilzal." Al-Salhi, a general in the Iraqi armed forces who defected shortly after the uprising, was stationed in the south and was present at the Safwan negotiations of the Iraqi surrender on 4 and 5 March.

47. Dina Rizk Khoury, "The Intifada in Three Keys: Writing the History of Violence," in Peter Sluglett, Jordi Tejel, and Riccardo Bocco, eds., *History and Historiography of Modern Iraq* (London: World Scientific, 2012), 245–68, and "The Security State and the Practice and Rhetoric of Sectarianism," *International Journal of Contemporary Iraqi Studies* 4 (2011): 325–38.

48. For al-Qurna, 2.8 percent of its 772 matriculating students had relatives executed by the regime, while another 3.6 percent had family members who belonged to the opposition. Of Shatt al 'Arab's 158 matriculating students, 4.5 percent had relatives who had been executed, and an equal percentage belonged to the Communist Party. In al-Madina, nearly 10 percent of students had lost a family member in either the Iran-Iraq War or the First Gulf War. The overall percentage of men executed by the regime in the province of Basra in 1987–88 was 1.6 percent, and the share of men lost in the war was close to 6 percent. These percentages of men lost to the war and to the regime's violence were higher in rural areas and in the poorer areas of the city and the province in general. For 1987–88, see School Registers, Amn 32-01 and Amn 32-02. For 1998–99, see School Registers, Hizb 61-23, 61-23, 61-25.

CHAPTER 9: A PATRIOTIC UPRISING

1. David Semah, "Al-Wathba al-Ula," in *Hatta Yaji' al-Rabi'* (Tel Aviv: al-Matba'a al-Haditha, 1959), 61–66.

2. Marion Farouk-Sluglett and Peter Sluglett, "Some Reflections on the Sunni/Shi'i Question in Iraq," *Bulletin (British Society for Middles Eastern Studies)* 5, no. 2 (1978): 79–87; Hanna Batatu, *The Old Social Classes and the Revolutionary Movements of Iraq* (Princeton, NJ: Princeton University Press, 1978); Samira Haj, *The Making of Iraq, 1900– 1963: Capital, Power and Ideology* (Albany: State University of New York Press, 1997).

3. Orit Bashkin, *The Other Iraq: Pluralism and Culture in Hashemite Iraq* (Stanford, CA: Stanford University Press, 2009), 87–124, 236–43.

4. Ibid., 114–16. On the changing views of the regent and the changes in the views of al-Istiqlal Party, see Batatu, *Old Social Classes*, 552.

5. National Archives of the United Kingdom (hereafter NAUK) FO 371/75125: Sir H. Mack to Mr. Bevin, "Political Review of Iraq for the year 1948," 17 January 1949.

6. NAUK, FO 371/68433: M. Pelhem Baghdad to British Prime Minister Clement Attlee, London, 25 January 1948, "Regarding causes of the riots."

7. NAUK, FO 371/68488: Sir Henry Mack Baghdad to E. Bevin Foreign Secretary London, 29 March 1948, "Political situation in Iraq."

8. "Political Review of Iraq for the Year 1948," Baghdad (Sir H. Mack) to Foreign Office (Bevin), 17 January 1949, FO 371/75125, in Alan de L. Rush and Jane Priestland, eds., *Records of Iraq, 1914–1966*, 15 vols. (Slough, UK: Archive Editions, 2001) 10:6–7; Memo from Embassy Baghdad (M. Pelhem) to British Prime Minister (Clement Attlee) London, 25 January 1948, FO 371/68433, in ibid., 10:232–33; Memo from Ministry of Defence Baghdad to War Office London, 5 February 1948, FO 371/68446, in ibid., 10:249–50; "Political Situation in Iraq," Embassy Baghdad (Henry Mack) to Foreign Secretary London (Bevin), 29 March 1948, FO 371/68488, in ibid., 10:265–68; Report from Consulate-General Basra, May 1948, FO 371/68459, in ibid., 10:272.

9. Orit Bashkin, *New Babylonians: A History of Jews in Modern Iraq* (Stanford, CA: Stanford University Press, 2012), 15–99.

10. Ibid., 183–228.

11. Abraham Twaina, *Golim u-Ge'ulim*, 7 vols. (Ramla: Bet ha-keneset ge'ula, 1979) 7:50–51.

12. Letter from Berman (Baghdad) to Arnon, 20 January 1948; Letter from Yoav Goral to David Ben Gurion, 28 January 1948, both reprinted and annotated in Mordechai Bibi, *Ha-Mahteret ha-zionit ha-haluzit be-iraq*, 4 vols. (Jerusalem: Yad Ben-tzvi, 1988), 4:850–53.

13. Ishaq Bar-Moshe, *Yetziat 'Iraq: zikhronot mi-shenot 1945–1950* (Jerusalem: Va'ad 'adat ha-Sefaradim bi-yerushalayim be-hishtatfut, ha-mahlaka li-kehilot sefaradiyot shel ha-histadrut ha-ziyonit ha-'olamit, 1977), 56–57.

14. Letter from Berman to Arnon, 27 January 1948, reprinted and annotated in Bibi, *Ha-Mahteret*, 4:852.

15. Twaina, *Golim*, 7:50–51.

16. Letter from a Jewish soldier (anonymous) to relatives in Mandatory Palestine, 1 February 1948, reprinted in Bibi, *Ha-Mahteret*, 4:855–58.

17. Ibid.

18. Anonymous letter from Baghdad to Palestine, 4 February 1948, reprinted and annotated in Bibi, *Ha-Mahteret*, 4:858–59.

19. Salim Pattal, *Be Simta'ot Baghdad* (Jerusalem: Carmel, 2003), 296–97.

20. Ya'qub Iliyahu 'Aqabiya, ed., *Al-Ta'ifa al-Isra'iliyya fi Mawakib Shuhada' al-Huriyya* (Baghdad: Matab'at al-Rashid, 1948).

21. Anonymous letter from Baghdad to relatives in Palestine, 4 February 1948, reprinted and annotated in Bibi, *Ha-Mahteret*, 4:858–59.

22. Ibid., 858–59, 852.

23. Twaina, *Golim*, 7:50–51.

24. 'Aqabiya, *Al-Ta'ifa al-Isra'iliyya*, 6.

25. Ibid., 7.

26. Ibid.

27. Ibid., 12, 13.

28. Sasson Somekh, *Baghdad, Etmol*, 3rd ed. (Tel Aviv: Ha-Kibbutz ha-Me'uhad, 2004), 108–9. Translated into English as Sasson Somekh, *Baghdad, Yesterday: The Making of An Arab Jew* (Jerusalem: Ibis, 2007), 136.

29. Somekh, *Baghdad*, 55 (English translation, 70).

30. Twaina, *Golim*, 7:50–51.

31. Peter Wien, "The Long and Intricate Funeral of Yasin Al-Hashimi: Pan-Arabism, Civil Religion and Popular Nationalism in Damascus, 1937," *International Journal of Middle East Studies* 43, no. 2 (2011): 271–92; Avner Ben-Amos, *Funerals, Politics, and Memory in Modern France, 1789–1996* (Oxford: Oxford University Press, 2000).

32. For a critique of the language of pan-Arabism, sacrifice, and how they were manipulated by the Ba'th, see Dina Rizk Khoury, Iraq *in Wartime: Soldiering, Martyrdom, and Remembrance* (New York: Cambridge University Press, 2013); Eric Davis, *Memories of the State: Politics, History and Collective Identity in Modern Iraq* (Berkeley: University of California Press, 2005); Achim Rohde, *State-Society Relations in Ba'thist Iraq: Facing Dictatorship* (London: Routledge, 2010).

33. Dhu Nun Ayyub, *Al-Yad wa'l Ard wa'l Ma'*, in *Al-Athar al-Kamila li-Athar Dhi al-Nun Ayyub*, 3 vols. (1949; repr., Baghdad: Wizarat al-i'lam, 1978) 3:346.

34. Ibid., 347.

35. Baha Al-Din Nuri, *Mudhakkirat Baha' al-Din Nuri: Sikritir al-Lajna al-Markaziyya li'l Hizb al-Shuyu'i al-'Iraqi* (London: Dar al-hikma, 2001), 121–22.

36. Most historians estimate that the number of Baghdadi Jewish members was

between 250 and 400. According to British estimates, one of the communist organizations affiliated with the ICP, the League for Combating Zionism, had 1,000 members. If accounts of the league's membership being at least 50 percent Jewish are correct, then the number of Jews in communist organizations should be adjusted upward. Zionist accounts, however, depict communism as an epidemic overtaking the majority of Jewish youth. It is difficult to ascertain how many of these Jews were actual ICP members and how many were favorably disposed toward the Soviet Union but did not join the party. Bashkin, *New Babylonians*, 145–49.

37. Files on Yehudah Sadiq, Mir Yaqub Cohen, Ammuma Misri, Shafiq Eliyahu Horesh, and Sasson Dallal, in Al-Shurta al-'Amma, *Mawsu'a Siriyya khassa bi'l Hizb al-Shuyu'i al-'Iraqi*, 3 vols. (Baghdad: Matba'at Mudiriyyat al-Tahqiqat al-Jina'iyya, 1949).

38. The statue of General Frederick Stanley Maude, who led the British forces into Iraq, was torn down in 1958 with the rise of 'Abd al-Karim Qasim. For an image of the statue, see http://www.loc.gov/pictures/resource/matpc.13198.

39. Shim'on Ballas, *Be-Guf rishon* (Tel Aviv: Ha-Kibbutz ha-me'uhad, 2009), 29–30.

40. Batatu, *Old Social Classes*, 557–58, 29–30.

41. Interview with Sami Michael no. 7169, interviewer Gidom Lve Ari, 1978, Or Yehuda Archives (Or Yehuda, Israel), cassette number 346.

42. Shoshana Levi, *'Al Em ha-derekh* (Tel Aviv: Sh. Levi, 2001).

43. Avraham Kahila, *Hayinu ke-holmim* (Jerusalem: Research Institute of the Zionist-Pioneer Underground in Iraq, 2007), 65.

44. Upon the establishment of the State of Israel in May 1948, the Iraqi government announced a state of emergency within Iraq, which meant that military rule was in effect nationwide. Military courts were set up in Baghdad, Basra, and Kirkuk, supposedly to safeguard the Iraqi home front.

45. NAUK FO 371/82403: Sir H. Mack to Mr. McNeil, 17 January 1950, "Iraq: Annual Review for 1949."

46. Nissim Kazzaz, *He-Yehudim be-Iraq ba-ma'a he-'esrim* (Jerusalem: Yad Ben-tzvi, 1991), 268–71.

47. On the debates about the meaning of the Wathba among the communists, see Batatu, *Old Social Classes*, 562–66.

48. See article by Jacob Mir Basri in *Al-Thaqafa al-Jadida* 26, no. 162 (March 1985): 55–65.

49. Sasson Dallal, "Message to the Public," 22 January 1949, reprinted in al-'Amma, *Mawsu'a*, 3:560–69.

50. NAUK FO 371/82403: Sir H. Mack to Mr. McNeil, "Iraq: Annual Review for 1949," 17 January 1950. There is a clear correlation between the memorialization of the Wathba as an urban revolutionary event and the harsh repression of the insurgency by the government. This is in contrast with the Kirkuk disturbances of 1959, which became remembered exclusively as acts of ethnic and communal violence in spite of the heavy-

handed intervention of the military in the aftermath. See Nelida Fuccaro's chapter in this volume on the different interpretations and discursive constructions of the 1959 events in Kirkuk. This different memorialization of bloodshed reflects the fundamentally different nature of the Wathba and the Kirkuk disturbances, the former an expression of urban patriotic solidarity and the latter of latent class, ethnic, and socioeconomic friction.

CHAPTER 10: DISSECTING MOMENTS OF UNREST

I thank a number of people for their help with bibliographical materials and suggestions: Arbella Bet Shlimon, Fadi Dawood, Rasmus Elling, Nandini Gooptu, and Peter Sluglett.

1. Liam Anderson and Gareth Stansfield, *Crisis in Kirkuk: The Politics of Conflict and Ethnic Compromise* (Philadelphia: University of Pennsylvania Press, 2009). For a historical and ethnic-centered perspective on Kirkuk's intercommunal conflict, see Arbella Bet Shlimon, "Group Identities, Oil, and the Local Political Domain in Kirkuk. A Historical Perspective," *Urban History* 38, no. 5 (2012): 914–31; and Arbella Bet-Shlimon, "Kirkuk, 1918–1968: Oil and the Politics of Identity in an Iraqi City" (PhD diss., Harvard University, 2012).

2. Jaideep Gupte, *What Is Civil about Intergroup Violence? Five Inadequacies of Communal and Ethnic Constructs of Urban Riots*, MICROCON Research Working Paper 62 (Brighton, UK: MICROCON, 2012), 1–12; Stanley J. Tambiah, *Leveling Crowds: Ethnonationalist Conflicts and Collective Violence in South Asia* (Berkeley: University of California Press, 1996), 20–32, and "Urban Riots and Cricket in South Asia: A Postscript to "Leveling Crowds," *Modern Asian Studies* 39, no. 4 (2005): 897–927, esp. 912–15.

3. On this point see, for instance, the classic Veena Das, "Introduction: Communities, Riots and Survivors—the South Asian Experience," in Veena Das, ed., *Mirrors of Violence: Communities, Riots and Survivors in South Asia* (Delhi: Oxford University Press, 1990), 9–25.

4. For an exception, see the chapters by Dina Khoury and Orit Bashkin in this volume; and Nelida Fuccaro, "Reading Oil as Urban Violence: Kirkuk and Its Oil Conurbation, 1927–1958," in Ulrike Freitag, Nelida Fuccaro, Claudia Ghrawi, and Nora Lafi, eds., *Urban Violence in the Middle East: Changing Cityscapes in the Transition from Empire to Nation State* (Oxford: Berghahn, 2015), 222–42.

5. On the Iraqi Levies, see Robert V. J. Young, "The History of the Iraq Levies, 1915–1932" (PhD diss., SOAS, University of London, 1997). At the time of the disturbance, the 2nd Infantry Battalion and 1st Cavalry Regiment of the Iraqi Levies were stationed in Kirkuk. The former included only Assyrians, while the latter had a majority of Kurdish fighters recruited from Kirkuk's hinterland. The Assyrians belonged to warrior tribes originally from southeastern Turkey, who had left their ancestral home and settled in Iraq during and after World War I. National Archives of the United Kingdom (hereafter NAUK) CO 730/59: "Strength and Distribution of the Iraqi Levies for the Week Ending 10 April 1924," in Intelligence Report, 15 May 1924.

6. Evidence on this disturbance is included in NAUK FO 371/10111, AIR 23/569, CO 730/59, and CO 732/72. For a detailed factual analysis of the 1924 events in the context of local, national, and international politics, see Bet-Shlimon, "Kirkuk, 1918–1968," 95–120.

7. NAUK CO 732/72: Evidence of Captain A. F. Miller, Administrative Inspector, and Testimony of R. A. C. Prevett, 2nd Battalion Assyrian Levies, in "Proceedings of the Court of Enquiry Assembled at Kirkuk on 7 May 1924," included in Residency Baghdad to Secretary of State for the Colonies, 19 February 1925. Quote from Prevett's testimony.

8. NAUK AIR 23/562: "Secret Report on the Recent Disturbances at Kirkuk," 8 May 1924; Kirkuk to Aviation Baghdad, 4 May 1924; Air HQ British Forces in Iraq to Air Ministry, 11 September 1924; CO 730/59: Intelligence Report, 15 May 1924.

9. NAUK FO 371/10111: High Commissioner to Secretary of State for the Colonies, 27 May 1924; CO 730/59: Intelligence Report, 15 May 1924. The surgeon of Kirkuk's hospital gave the commission of inquiry a slightly different figure: forty-three civilians, seven Levies, and three police. Evidence of Dr. F. M. Halley, in CO 732/72: "Proceedings of the Court of Enquiry."

10. NAUK CO 732/72: Evidence of Capt. A. F. Miller, in "Proceedings of the Court of Enquiry."

11. Malik Loko Shlimon d'bit-Badawi, *Assyrian Struggle for National Survival in the 20th and 21st Centuries* (N.p., 2012); John G. Browne, *The Iraq Levies, 1915–1932* (London: Royal United Service Institution, 1932).

12. It seems that, at the beginning of the 1920s, some 150 families of Chaldeans lived in Kirkuk. In contrast to the Chaldeans, the Assyrians followed the Nestorian Church and spoke a neo-Aramaic language. Cecil J. Edmonds, *Kurds, Turks and Arabs: Politics, Travels and Research in North-Eastern Iraq, 1915–1925* (London: Oxford University Press, 1957), 266.

13. NAUK CO 732/72: Evidence by Murad Beg bin Mubarak, Kirkuk's Commandant of Police, by Toma Hindi Effendi and by Khurshid bin Til, in "Proceedings of the Court of Enquiry."

14. NAUK AIR 23/562: "Secret Report on the Recent Disturbances at Kirkuk," 8 May 1924.

15. But British reports are not clear about the ethnic and linguistic affiliation of the civilian casualties. The only ethnic category used in the reports is that of "Kurd," but mostly with reference to the cavalry units of the Iraqi Levies. On the Turkmens of Iraq, see H. Tarik Oğuzlu, "Endangered Community: The Turkoman Identity in Iraq," *Journal of Muslim Minority Affairs* 24, no. 2 (2004): 309–25.

16. On early 1920s Kirkuk and its history, see Edmonds, *Kurds, Turks and Arabs*, 265–67, 280–86. Edmonds estimates that the town's population was approximately twenty-five thousand, of whom one-quarter were Kurds.

17. Fadhil al-Azzawi, *The Last of the Angels*, trans. William M. Hutchins (Cairo: American University in Cairo Press, 2007), 240. On al-Azzawi's fictional representation

of Kirkuk, see Sami Zubaida, "Popular Religion and the Entry into Political Modernity as Seen in *The Last of the Angels*," in Elisabeth Özdalga and Daniella Kuzmanovic, eds., *Novel and Nation in the Muslim World: Literary Contributions and National Identities* (New York: Palgrave Macmillan, 2015), 170–184.

18. The most vivid and well-known account of the event is that of Hanna Batatu, which was written in the 1970s and based on police reports and communist sources. Hanna Batatu, *The Old Social Classes and Revolutionary Movements of Iraq* (Princeton, NJ: Princeton University Press, 1978), 912–21. See also Arshad al-Hirmizi, *The Turkmen Reality in Iraq* (Istanbul: Kerkük Vakfi, 2005), FO 371/140920 to 22 and LAB 13/1307.

19. Batatu, *Old Social Classes*, 915–17.

20. Al-Hirmizi, *Turkmen Reality in Iraq*, 110–12, 118–19; Guldem B. Buyuksarac, "The Politics of Loss and the Poetics of Melancholy: A Case Study on Iraqi Turkmen" (PhD diss., Columbia University, 2010), 207–8.

21. NAUK FO 371/140921: Copeland to Colonel F. T. Davies, 30 July 1959; Batatu, *Old Social Classes*, 915–17.

22. NAUK FO 371/140920: Embassy Baghdad to Foreign Office, 24 July 1959; and FO 371/140921: Copeland to Colonel F. T. Davies, 30 July 1959.

23. NAUK FO 624/1: Confidential Report, Vice-Consulate Kirkuk, 16 April 1933.

24. The first cabaret was opened in 1948. NAUK FO 624/138: "Political Report of Kirkuk and Sulaymaniyya Liwas, August 1948"; Najm al-Din Bayraqdar, *Karkuk bayna al-Haqiqa wa-l Waqi': Dirasa 'an Huquq al-Turkman fi al-'Iraq bayna Haqq al-Wujud wa-al-Sira' hawla Madinat Karkuk* (Beirut: Dar al-'Arabiyya lil Mawsu'at, 2011), 164. In 1939 the Second Division of the Iraqi army included 265 officers and 5,248 soldiers. The presence of the army was one of the factors that contributed to changing the city's demography, as both officers and soldiers were drawn from different areas of Iraq. Appendix A to Quarterly Report n. 26, NAUK FO 371/23127.

25. Bayraqdar, *Karkuk*, 158–59. For a detailed analysis of Kirkuk's demography and oil development, see Bet-Shlimon, "Kirkuk, 1918–1968," 158–71, and "Group Identities, Oil, and the Local Political Domain in Kirkuk," 920–24. According to the census of 1957, which was conducted on the basis of language, 40,047 Kurdish speakers lived in Kirkuk; 45,306 Turkish speakers; and 27,127 Arabic speakers. Yet, as in the 1920s, language continued to be an ambiguous indicator of ethnic affiliation. *Al-Majmu'a al-ihsa'iya li-tasjil 'am 1957* (Mudiriyat al-Nufus al-'Amma: Baghdad, 1962–64).

26. The first post-revolutionary violence occurred in October 1958 in connection with a visit of the Kurdish leader to Kirkuk. Bet Shlimon, "Group Identities, Oil, and the Local Political Domain in Kirkuk," 924. For a firsthand Turkmen account of this event and of the vulnerable position of the community, see Buyuksarac, "Politics of Loss," 193, 206–7.

27. Batatu, *Old Social Classes*, 912. For recent ethnic interpretations of the 1959 disturbances, see Anderson and Stansfield, *Crisis in Kirkuk*, 34; and Bet-Shlimon, "Kirkuk, 1918–1968," 259–70.

28. Paul R. Brass, *The Production of Hindu-Muslim Violence in Contemporary India* (Seattle: University of Washington Press, 2003), esp. 32–33; and Tambiah, "Urban Riots and Cricket," 897–88.

29. Batatu, *Old Social Classes*, 918; NAUK FO 371/140921: Copeland to Colonel F. T. Davies, 30 July 1959.

30. NAUK FO 371/140920: Embassy Baghdad to Foreign Office, 30 July 1959; Buyuksarac, "Politics of Loss," 208–9.

31. For a discussion of the triumphal arch built by Saddam in 1989 to celebrate the Iran-Iraq War, see Samir Khalil, *The Monument: Art, Vulgarity and Responsibility in Iraq* (London: Deutsch, 1991). This discussion focuses primarily on the idea of politics-as-art and the creation of monumental Baghdad as a mirror image of the ugliness of the Ba'thist regime.

32. *Al-Ahali* editorials: "Rasa'il al-Jihat" and "Kayfa Ihtafalat al-Mudun al-'Iraqiyya bi Dhikra Thawra 14 Tammuz al-Khalida," 24 July 1959, Year 1, no. 188, p. 4; "Mahrajanat 14 Tammuz al-Khalid fi Qadha' Afak" and "Ihtifal al-Ta'ifah al Masihiyya fi'l-Mawsil bi Munasabati Dhikra 14 Tammuz al Khalida," 27 July 1959, Year 1, no. 190, p. 3.

33. NAUK FO 371/140920: Embassy Baghdad to Foreign Office, 24 July 1959; al-Hirmizi, *Turkmen Reality in Iraq*, 118–19. Arches are also discussed in Shlimon, "Kirkuk, 1918–1968," 259–60.

34. NAUK FO 371/140920: Embassy Baghdad to Foreign Office, 30 July 1959.

35. "Bayan raqm 104, 107, 108, 109 sadir min al-hakim al-'askari al 'amm," *Al-Ahali*, 20, 23, 26, and 30 July 1959, Year 1, nos. 184, 187, 189, 193.

36. Stathis N. Kalyvas, Ian Shapiro, and Tarek Masoud, "Introduction: Integrating the Study of Order, Conflict and Violence," in Kalyvas, Shapiro, and Masoud, eds., *Order, Conflict and Violence* (Cambridge: Cambridge University Press, 2008), 1.

37. This is one of the underlying arguments of Varshney's study of networks of civic engagement and ethnic violence in contemporary Indian cities. Ashutosh R. Varshney, *Ethnic Conflict and Civic Life: Hindus and Muslims in India* (New Haven, CT: Yale University Press, 2002).

38. See, for instance, NAUK AIR 23/396: SSO Kirkuk to Air Staff Intelligence Baghdad, 27 November 1925.

39. NAUK AIR 23/396: Air Baghdad to SSOs, 22 September 1922. On air power as a regime of terror rooted in imperial epistemologies of intelligence, see Priya Satia, "The Pain of Love: Invention of Aerial Surveillance in British Iraq," in Peter Adey, Mark Whitehead, and Allison J. Williams, eds., *From Above: War, Violence and Verticality* (London: Hurst, 2013), 223–45.

40. Fuccaro, "Reading Oil as Urban Violence," 232–35; NAUK FO 624/117: Political Summary, June 1947, and secret report Vice-Consulate Kirkuk, 29 October 1947; FO 624/138: Political Summary for Kirkuk and Sulaymaniyya Liwas, February 1948; Secret

Report Vice-Consulate Kirkuk, "Political Parties in Kirkuk," 26 January 1948 (quote from here); Vice-Consulate Kirkuk to Embassy Baghdad, 8 and 20 June 1948.

41. Anwar al-Ghassani, "The Rose and Its Fragrance: The Kirkuk Group," http://al-ghassani.net/an-kirkuk-and-kirkuk-group/kirkuk-group-essay-2003.html (accessed 20 March 2014) [site no longer available].

42. Al-Azzawi, *Last of the Angels*, 238–39.

43. As suggested by Paul Brass, identifying the causes of riots leads to the singling out of culprits and generates hegemonic discourses that seek to create consensus. Brass, *Production of Hindu-Muslim Violence*, 22–23. A study conducted in 1978 among Kirkuk's Kurdish, Turkmen, and Arab residents clearly suggests the antagonistic nature of linguistic identity and the role played by language in fostering exclusive community values. Muhammed A. Qadir, "The Linguistic Situation in Kirkuk: A Sociolinguistic Study" (PhD diss., Aston University, 1980).

44. Jonathon Glassman, *War of Words, War of Stones: Racial Thought and Violence in Colonial Zanzibar* (Bloomington: Indiana University Press, 2011), 234–37. Evidence of Capt. W. E. N. Growdown, in "Proceedings of the Court of Enquiry," CO 732/72.

45. On the role of rumors as instigators of violent behavior, see Tambiah, *Leveling Crowds*, 284–90. Quote from evidence of Capt. A. F. Miller, in "Proceedings of the Court of Enquiry," and testimony of David Ben Shimun, CO 730/72. Yusuf Malik, *The British Betrayal of the Assyrians* (Chicago: Assyrian National League of America, 1935), http://www.aina.org/books/bbota.pdf, 7–73.

46. Malik, "British Betrayal," 73; al-Hirmizi, *Turkmen Reality in Iraq*, 120–21. Quote from NAUK FO 371/140924: Embassy Baghdad to Foreign Office, 8 October 1959 (my emphasis).

47. NAUK AIR 23/562: "Secret Report on the Recent Disturbances at Kirkuk," 8 May 1924, and Administrative Inspector Kirkuk to Adviser Interior Baghdad, 20 May 1924; CO 730/72: Testimony of Lieutenant P. Paulet King, in "Proceedings of the Court of Enquiry."

48. NAUK FO 371/140921: Copeland to Colonel F. T. Davies, 30 July 1959; Buyuksarac, "Politics of Loss," 207.

49. NAUK FO 624/1: Confidential Report Vice-Consulate Kirkuk, 16 April 1933; British Petroleum Archive file 162444: Field Headquarters Kirkuk to London, 23 August 1933.

50. Al-Azzawi, *Last of the Angels*, 13.

51. For a discussion of the role of state and communal violence in the making of Turkmen ethnic identity in Iraq, see Buyuksarac, "Politics of Loss," particularly 110–236.

52. See, for example, Mahir Nakip, "The Identity of Kirkuk," Columbia University Turkmen Symposium, November 20, 2004,http://www.turkmen.nl/1A_soitm_e/Kerkuk_identity.pdf; and Şemsettin Küzeci, *Kerkük Soykirimlari (Irak Türklerinin uğradığı katliamlar): 1920–2003* (Ankara: Teknoed Yainlari, 2004).

53. Buyuksarac, "Politics of Loss," 205–10.

54. NAUK AIR 23/562: "Secret Report on the Recent Disturbances at Kirkuk," 8 May

1924; FO 371/140921: Minutes by R. B. M. Chevalier, 14 August 1959; FO 371/140919: Embassy Baghdad to Foreign Office, 24 July 1959.

55. NAUK LAB 13/1307: BBC Summary of World Broadcast no. 95, "Qasim's Statement during a Meeting with Vocational Federations, Trade Unions and Other Organisations," 3 August 1959.

56. NAUK FO 371/140920: Text of Qasim's Press Conference (29 July 1959), in Embassy Baghdad to Foreign Office, 30 July 1959; LAB 13/1307: Embassy Baghdad to Foreign Office, 7 August 1959.

57. This was in contrast to the high-profile court cases presided over by the Special Supreme Military Court convened by the regime to try the "enemies of the revolution" after 1958, which were broadcast on radio and television. See Charles Tripp, "'In the Name of the People': The 'People's Court' and the Iraqi Revolution (1958–1960)," in Julia C. Strauss and Donal B. Cruise O'Brien, eds., *Staging Politics: Power and Performance in Asia and Africa* (London: I. B. Tauris, 2007), 31–48.

58. NAUK FO 371/140923: Embassy Baghdad to Foreign Office, 24 September 1959.

59. NAUK FO 371/140922: *Ittihad al- Sha'b*, 23 August 1959, in Embassy Baghdad to Foreign Office, 10 September 1959.

60. Eric Davis, *Memories of State: Politics, History, and Collective Identity in Modern Iraq* (Berkeley: University of California Press, 2005), 136.

CHAPTER 11: WAR OF CLUBS

1. National Archives of the United Kingdom (hereafter NAUK) FO 248/1435: Tehran to Ahwaz, 30 May 1945.

2. Minorities and ethnicity constitute highly complex and controversial topics in Iran, and only recently have scholars questioned the Persian-centrist bias in Iranian historiography. For comprehensive studies on these topics in post-revolutionary Iran, see Rasmus Christian Elling, *Minorities in Iran: Nationalism and Ethnicity after Khomeini* (New York: Palgrave Macmillan, 2013); Alam Saleh, *Ethnic Identity and the State in Iran* (New York: Palgrave Macmillan, 2013); and Eliz Sanasarian, *Religious Minorities in Iran* (Cambridge: Cambridge University Press, 2007). Apart from ethnography on nomads and tribes, there are only a few studies on ethnic minorities in pre-revolutionary Iran. See Touraj Atabaki, *Azerbaijan: Ethnicity and the Struggle for Power in Iran* (London: I. B. Tauris, 2000); and Abbas Vali, *Kurds and the State in Iran: The Making of Kurdish Identity* (London: I. B. Tauris, 2011).

3. From my knowledge of the English-language literature on Iran, only Abrahamian has dealt with these clashes in more than a passing remark. See Ervand Abrahamian, "Strengths and Weaknesses of the Labour Movement in Iran, 1941–53," in Michael E. Bonnie and Nikki Keddie, eds., *Modern Iran: The Dialectics of Continuity and Change* (Albany: State University of New York Press, 1981); and Ervand Abrahamian, *Iran between Two Revolutions* (Princeton, NJ: Princeton University Press, 1982).

4. Svat Soucek, "Arabistan or Khuzistan," *Iranian Studies* 17, no. 2–3 (1984): 195–213.

5. Adopted, with slight variation, from Kaveh Ehsani, "The Social History of Labor in the Iranian Oil Industry: The Built Environment and the Making of the Industrial Working Class (1908–1941)" (PhD diss., Universiteit Leiden, 2014), 374.

6. Mark Crinson, "Abadan: Planning and Architecture under the Anglo-Iranian Oil Company," *Planning Perspectives* 12 (1997): 341–59; Kaveh Ehsani, "Social Engineering and the Contradictions of Modernization in Khuzestan's Company Towns: A Look at Abadan and Masjed-Soleyman," *International Review of Social History* 48 (2003): 361–99; Ehsani, "Social History of Labor."

7. In this chapter, "Persian" refers broadly to all those Iranians who moved to Abadan in the twentieth century to work in the oil industry. In order to distinguish them from "Arabs," who were also Iranian nationals, they are here called Persians, although most would probably self-identify in regional terms rather than as Persian (*fars*). Thus, the generic Persians in Abadan could include migrants from Tehran, Shiraz, and Esfahan, from Bushehr and Bandar 'Abbas in the south, as well as from other cities in Khuzestan. Non-Arab Iranians in and around Abadan also included large numbers of Lors, Bakhtiyaris, Kurds, and some Turkic-speaking Azeris. In other words, "Persian" in this context does not refer to a particular ethnic group. The Arab community in Abadan, in contrast, was a more or less homogeneous group, tribally structured around kinship traditions, and Arabic speaking. For the sake of simplicity, they will simply be referred to as "Arabs," although the terms "Iranian Arabs" or "Khuzestani Arabs" would arguably be less controversial. It should under all circumstances be stressed that the label "Arab" conceals important social differences between urban Arabs, farmers and seminomadic communities, various tribes, and Arabs from different parts of Khuzestan. Finally, despite a strong tradition of endogamy, the ethnic boundaries between the Arabs and their neighboring communities were permeable.

8. On this strike, see Kaveh Bayat, "With or without Workers in Reza Shah's Iran: Abadan, May 1929," in Touraj Atabaki, ed., *The State and the Subaltern: Modernization, Society and the State in Turkey and Iran* (London: I. B. Tauris, 2007), 111–22; Stephanie Cronin, "Popular Politics, the New State and the Birth of the Iranian Working Class: The 1929 Abadan Oil Refinery Strike," *Middle Eastern Studies* 46, no. 5 (2010): 699–732.

9. See Mona Damluji, "The Oil City in Focus: The Cinematic Spaces of Abadan in the Anglo-Iranian Oil Company's *Persian Story*," *Comparative Studies of South Asia, Africa and the Middle East* 33, no. 1 (2013): 75–88.

10. Yusef Eftekhari, *Khaterat-e dowran-e separi-shodeh, 1299–1329*, ed. Majid Tafreshi and Kaveh Bayat (Tehran: Ferdows, 1991), 31–32. As Ehsani points out in his groundbreaking research, poor Abadanis of all ethnic backgrounds were affected by the Company's "coercive commodification of urban space and everyday life" (Ehsani, "Social History of Labor," 356).

11. Iraj Valizadeh, *Anglo va bungalow dar abadan* (Tehran: Simia Honar, 2003), 55.

12. Brian Mann, "The Khuzistani Arab Movement, 1941–1946: A Case of Nationalism?," in Kamran Aghaie and Afshin Marashi, eds., *Rethinking Iranian Nationalism and Modernity: Histories and Historiographies* (Austin: University of Texas Press, 2013), 113–35.

13. See, for example, NAUK FO 248/1412: Ahwaz to Tehran, 11 September 1943; and FO 248/1436: Ahwaz to Tehran, 11 June 1944.

14. NAUK FO 248/1436: Khuzistan Governor-General to Interpreter, Ahwaz, 17 May 1944.

15. NAUK FO 248/1435-53: Khorramshahr Confidential Diary, 16–18 February 1945.

16. Eftekhari, *Khaterat-e dowran-e.*

17. On intercommunal clashes, see Rasmus Christian Elling, "On Lines and Fences: Labour, Community and Violence in an Oil City," in Ulrike Freitag, Nelida Fuccaro, Claudia Ghrawi, and Nora Lafi, eds., *Urban Violence in the Middle East: Changing Cityscapes in the Transition from Empire to Nation State* (Oxford: Berghahn, 2015), 197–221. On discontented British workers, see Rasmus Christian Elling, "The World's Biggest Refinery and the Second World War: Khuzestan, Oil and Security," paper delivered at the conference "Comparative Histories of Labour in the Oil Industry," Amsterdam, June 2013.

18. Abrahamian, *Iran between Two Revolutions*, 363–64.

19. See, for example, Ali Farrokhmehr, *Abadan, khak-e khuban, yad-e yaran* (Qom: Najaba, 2011); and Valizadeh, *Anglo va bungalow.*

20. For an insight into British culture in Basra and Abadan, see Reidar Visser, "The Gibraltar That Never Was," paper presented at the conference "British World," Bristol, 11–14 July 2007, http://www.historiae.org. For some notes on clubs in Abadan, see Abdolali Lahsaiezadeh, *Jame'e-shenasi-ye abadan* (Tehran: Kianmehr Publications, 2006); and Valizadeh, *Anglo va bungalow*, 62–68.

21. Eftekhari, *Khaterat-e dowran-e separi-shodeh*, 129.

22. Ibid., 127.

23. NAUK FO 248/1435: Ahwaz to Tehran, 14 October 1945 (my emphasis).

24. NAUK FO 248/1468: Khorramshahr to Tehran, 3 May 1946.

25. Abrahamian, *Iran between Two Revolutions*, 361–62.

26. NAUK FO 248/1468: Abadan to Tehran, 16 May 1946.

27. Ibid., 29 May 1946.

28. A similar—albeit smaller-scale—breach of spatial and security lines of demarcation by a labor movement occurred two years later in Iraq when the Iraqi Communist Party took over the K3 oil station along the Kirkuk pipeline for ten days. Nelida Fuccaro, "Reading Oil as Urban Violence: Kirkuk and Its Oil Conurbation, 1927–1958," in Freitag et al., *Urban Violence in the Middle East*, 235–36.

29. NAUK FO 248/1468: Foreign Office to Tehran, 22 June 1946; and FO 248/1468: Khorramshahr to Tehran, 13 May 1946.

30. NAUK FO 248/1468: Secret Report to the AIOC General Manager, Abadan, 7 June 1946; and FO 248/1468: H. J. Underwood to AIOC General Manager, Abadan, 8 June 1946.

31. NAUK FO 248/1468: Tehran Ambassador to Foreign Office, 8 June 1946.

32. NAUK FO 248/1468: Khorramshahr to Tehran, 3 May 1946.

33. Ibid., 15 July 1946.

34. In a report to the US secretary of state the American vice-consul in Basra stated that information "from other sources" confirmed that a Company security officer "gave undercover support" and "at least 'assisted' the Arabs in obtaining arms." The British consul in Khorramshahr is also quoted as admitting that "a few men" from the Company "may have given encouragement to the Arabs." US Consulate in Basra, "Disturbances in Khuzistan," 17 July 1946, collected in F. David Andrews, ed., *The Lost Peoples of the Middle East: Documents of the Struggle for Survival and Independence of the Kurds, Assyrians, and Other Minority Races in the Middle East* (Salisbury, NC: Documentary Publications, 1982).

35. NAUK FO 248/1468: Abadan to Tehran, 16 May 1946.

36. NAUK FO 248/1468: Underwood to General Manager, 11 July 1946.

37. Ibid., 12 June 1946.

38. NAUK FO 371/72700: Consul-General Diary, Ahwaz, June 1946.

39. NAUK FO 248/1468: Secret Memorandum No. 36/B, 16 June 1946.

40. NAUK FO 248/1468: Secret Report to General Manager, 24 June 1946; US Consulate in Basra, "Disturbances in Khuzistan."

41. NAUK FO 371/72700: Consul-General Diary, Ahwaz, June 1946. It is unclear how the union itself named its facilities in Khorramshahr. However, the Abadan facilities were known locally as *kolub-e 'ashayer* (the Tribal Club).

42. NAUK FO 248/1468: Secret Report to AIOC General Manager, 24 June 1946. Indeed, the club was housed in a building owned by Jaseb's sister. US Consulate in Basra, "Disturbances in Khuzistan."

43. NAUK FO 248/1468: Khorramshahr to General Manager, 22 June 1946.

44. NAUK FO 248/1468: Underwood to Tehran, 4 July 1946.

45. NAUK FO 248/1468: Tehran to Foreign Office, 16 July 1946.

46. NAUK FO 248/1468: Khorramshahr to Tehran, Ahwaz to Tehran and Tehran to Foreign Office, 14 July 1946.

47. British Petroleum Archives (hereafter BP) 130264: "Abadan General Strike Report," 19 July 1946.

48. Farajollah Mizani Javanshir, *Hamase-ye 23-e tir. Gushe'i az mobarezat-e kargaran-e naft-e khuzestan* (N.p., 1980), reprinted as PDF file by Chawoshan Nowzai Kabir, http://chawoshan.mihanblog.com, n.d., 60.

49. NAUK FO 248/1468: Ahwaz to Tehran, 17 July 1946.

50. Javanshir, *Hamase-ye 23-e tir*, 60. The US Consulate in Basra put the number

"conservatively" at forty but admitted that numbers were probably higher. US Consulate, "Disturbances in Khuzestan."

51. BP 130264, "Abadan General Strike Report," 19 July 1946.

52. NAUK FO 248/1468: Khorramshahr to Tehran, Skrine's report, 17 July 1946.

53. Ibid., 23 July 1946.

54. Ibid., 17 July 1946.

55. BP 130264: Secret Report to General Manager, 19 July 1946.

56. Javanshir, *Hamase-ye 23-e tir.*

57. Ibid., 54.

58. Ibid., 57–58.

59. The theme of violent irrational riff-raff descending on the city from its treacherous hinterland also emerges in British accounts of the 1933 riots in Jaffa. See Lauren Banko's chapter in this volume. For another example of the construction of ethnic difference operated by violent progressive politics in an oil city, see Nelida Fuccaro's chapter in this volume on the 1959 disturbances in Kirkuk.

60. Najaf Daryabandari, "E'tesab-e bozorg-e kargaran dar abadan," interviewed by Hossein Mirzai (*Feydus* online magazine, www.feydus.ir, 2 January 2014).

61. NAUK FO 248/1468: Foreign Office to Tehran, 18 July 1946.

62. NAUK FO 248/1468: Khorramshahr to Tehran, 21 August 1946.

63. Javanshir, *Hamase-ye 23-e tir*, 67.

64. Karl E. Meyer and Shareen Blair Brysac, *Kingmakers: The Invention of the Modern Middle East* (New York: W. W. Norton), 330.

65. NAUK FO 371/52711: Underwood to Foreign Office, 31 July 1946.

66. NAUK FO 248/1468: Underwood to General Manager, 22 August 1946.

CHAPTER 12: URBAN RUPTURE

1. "Shepheard's Hotel: British Base in Cairo," *Life* magazine, December 1942.

2. My methodology relies on an archival investigation of news records at the time. I also make use of one key source in Arabic, which can be considered a primary source for the Cairo fire. It was written in 1976 under the provocative title "The Cairo Fire: A New Indictment" by Gamal el-Sharqawy. It cites eyewitness accounts and provides an extensive and definitive record of these events. Another primary source is a report by a retired RAF officer who was a resident of Cairo at the time of the fire. Written in harrowing detail, it provides a useful personalization of the events. My brief overview of Cairo's modern history is based on a number of sources, chief among which is Janet Abu-Lughod's seminal *Cairo: 1001 Years of the City Victorious* (Princeton, NJ: Princeton University Press, 1971). Complementing these texts is a visual analysis of archival photographs, newsreels, and historical maps showing the city's changing morphology. The brief Nile Hilton analysis is based on previous work of mine concerning the hotel's history. This chapter is intended as complementary to other research and should be seen as

both a precursor and prelude to Yasser Elsheshtawy, "City Interrupted: Modernity and Architecture in Nasser's Post-1952 Cairo," *Planning Perspectives* 28, no. 3 (2013): 347–71, http://dx.doi.org/10.1080/02665433.2013.739827.

3. Radwa Ashur, *Qit'a min Uruba* (Cairo: Dar Al Shoruq, 2003), 50. All passages cited from this text are my own translations.

4. David Harvey, "The City as a Body Politic," in Janet Schneider and Ida Susser, eds., *Wounded Cities: Destruction and Reconstruction in a Globalized World* (Oxford: Berg, 2003), 25–44, 53.

5. Christine Rosen, *The Limits of Power: Great Fires and the Process of City Growth in America* (Cambridge: Cambridge University Press, 1986).

6. M. Baur and Colonel Szultz, "Plan general de la VILLE du KAIRE et des environs, topographie medical du Caire, Munich, 1847."

7. Yasser Elsheshtawy, "Nineteenth Century Globalization: Transforming the Historic Center of Cairo," IASTE Working Paper Series, vol. 125, *Preservation, Transformation and the Making of Place* (Berkeley: International Association for the Study of Traditional Environments, 2000); Yasser Elsheshtawy, "Learning from the Past: Globalization in 19th-Century Cairo, Egypt," in *Proceedings of the 17th Conference of the International Association for People-Environment Studies (IAPS)* (Coruna, Spain: IAPS, 23–27 July 2002), 504–5.

8. The 1874 map is archived at http://web.archive.org/web/20100609230428/http://cmes.berkeley.edu/outreach/icmc_files/icmc/images/MAPS/1874-grand-bay-down.jpg.

9. Timothy Mitchell, *Colonizing Egypt* (Berkeley: University of California Press, 1991).

10. Mara Naaman, *Urban Space in Contemporary Egyptian Literature: Portraits of Cairo* (New York: Palgrave Macmillan, 2011).

11. Nina Nelson, *Shepheard's Hotel* (1960; repr., Bath, UK: Cedric Chivers Portway, 1974), 25.

12. Naaman, *Urban Space*, 20.

13. Trevor Mostyn, *Egypt's Belle Epoque: Cairo and the Age of the Hedonists* (1986; repr., New York: Palgrave Macmillan, 2006).

14. Anne-Claire Kerboeuf, "The Cairo Fire of 26 January 1952 and the Interpretations of History," in Arthur Goldschmidt, Amy Johnson, and Barak Salmoni, eds., *Re-envisioning Egypt, 1919–1952* (Cairo: American University in Cairo Press, 2005), 194–217, 195.

15. Ashur, *Qit'a min Uruba*.

16. Naaman, *Urban Space*, 18.

17. For more details, see Alan Moorehead, *Desert War: The North African Campaign 1940–43* (1959; repr., London: Penguin, 2001); James Aldridge, *Cairo: Biography of a City* (London: Macmillan, 1970).

18. Nancy Y. Reynolds, *A City Consumed: Urban Commerce, the Cairo Fire, and the Politics of Decolonization in Egypt* (Stanford, CA: Stanford University Press, 2012).

19. Galila Kadi and Dalila Elkerdany, "Belle-Epoque Cairo: The Politics of Refurbishing the Downtown Business District," in Diane Singerman and Paul Ammar, eds., *Cairo Cosmopolitan: Politics, Culture and Urban Space in the New Globalized Middle East* (Cairo: American University in Cairo Press, 2006), 345–74.

20. Samia Mehrez, *The Literary Atlas of Cairo: One Hundred Years on the Streets of the City* (Cairo: American University in Cairo Press, 2011).

21. "Doors Open in Cairo: Roosevelt Gets the Warmest Welcome in Present Generation," *Toledo Weekly Blade*, 31 March 1910.

22. "Shepheard's Hotel Stands as Symbol of East's Era of British Colonialism," *Associated Press*, 22 September 1958.

23. Rosemary Pitcher, "Shepheard's Hotel: Glorious Cairo Institution Recalled," *Toronto Star*, 2 January 1988, B11.

24. Mostyn, *Egypt's Belle Epoque*, 149.

25. "King of Mixers: Joe, Lately Barman of Shepheard's Hotel, Cairo, Pours Out Some Bubbling Anecdotes," *New York Times*, 27 April 1952.

26. Allan Berube, *Coming Out under Fire: The History of Gay Men and Women in World War Two* (New York: Free Press, 1990), 192.

27. Nelson, *Shepheard's Hotel*, 100–101.

28. Gamal el-Sharqawy, *Hariq al-Qahira: Qarar Itiham Gadid* [The Cairo fire: A new indictment] (Cairo: Dar Al-Thaqafa Al-Gadida, 1976).

29. Ashur, *Qit'a min Uruba*, 175.

30. Reynolds, *A City Consumed*, 7.

31. "British Soldiers Fire on Egyptian Demonstrators," *Associated Press*, 21 February 1946.

32. This is a brief sample of headlines that were reported at the time: "5 More Bodies Found in Cairo, Death Toll 67," *Associated Press*, 29 January 1952; "Shepheard's Hotel Is Reported Ruined: Americans, Escaping through Mob, Tell of a Flaming Up, Possibly from Grenade," *New York Times*, 27 January 1952 ; "Break-Off of British Tie Nears," *Sunday Herald*, 27 January 1952.

33. As quoted in Reynolds, *A City Consumed*, 189.

34. El-Sharqawy interviewing Ahmed Hussein, chairman of the leftist Young Egypt Party; el-Sharqawy, *Hariq al-Qahira*, 68.

35. Ashur, *Qit'a min Uruba*, 170.

36. El-Sharqawy, *Hariq al-Qahira*, 105.

37. Ashur, *Qit'a min Uruba*, 173.

38. Jacques Berque, *Imperialism and Revolution* (New York: Faber & Faber, 1972). For further discussion, see Fayza Hassan's review of the Cairo fire in "Burning Down the House," *Al-Ahram Weekly*, 24–30 January 2002, http://weekly.ahram.org.eg/2002/570/sc3 .htm. For eyewitness accounts, see "The Burning of Cairo," Memories of Egypt, 26 January 1952, http://www.rootsweb.ancestry.com/~nafrica/EGYPT/BurningOfCairo.html;

and Maurice Guindi, "Arson and Upheaval," *Al-Ahram Weekly*, 24–30 January 2002, http://weekly.ahram.org.eg/2002/570/sc2.htm. Also see Harold Hindle James, *Personal Report on Riots in Cairo, 26 Jan 1952*, report written for the British embassy in Cairo, 1952, transcribed and annotated by John Barnard, May 2009, http://www.johnbarnard.me.uk/docs/HHJ_Docs/HHJ-18-1%20Cairo%20Riots%201952%20Transcript.pdf.

39. James, *Personal Report on Riots in Cairo*.

40. El-Sharqawy, *Hariq al-Qahira*, 468.

41. Quoted in Reynolds, *A City Consumed*, 185.

42. Naaman, *Urban Space in Contemporary Egyptian Literature*, 16.

43. Ashur, *Qit'a min Uruba*, 202.

44. Reynolds, *A City Consumed*; el-Sharqawy, *Hariq al-Qahira*.

45. For a detailed account of these events, see Reynolds, *A City Consumed*; Abu Lughod, *Cairo*; Ashur, *Qit'a min Uruba*. See also Nezar AlSayyad, *Cairo: Histories of a City* (Cambridge, MA: Belknap Press of Harvard University Press, 2011); Samir Raafat, *Cairo: The Glory Years* (Alexandria: Harpocrates, 2003).

46. Abu-Lughod, *Cairo*; Naaman, *Urban Space in Contemporary Egyptian Literature*.

47. Ashur, *Qit'a min Uruba*, 202.

48. Reynolds, *A City Consumed*, 219.

49. Ashur, *Qit'a min Uruba*, 202.

50. Abu-Lughod, *Cairo*.

51. Drawings presented by architect Muhammad Dhul-Faqqar in *al-Musawar*, an Egyptian journal, showed plans for the site of the current Hilton used for the Egyptian parliament, while the entire area was converted into some sort of government center. None of this materialized, of course.

52. Nelson, *Shepheard's Hotel*.

53. Osgood Caruthers, "New Shepheard's Opened in Cairo," *New York Times*, 21 July 1957.

54. "'New Egypt' Gets Off to Slow Start," *Associated Press*, 21 July 1956.

55. Ashur, *Qit 'a min Uruba*.

56. "Cairo Nationalizes Two Famed Hotels," *New York Times*, 4 December 1960.

57. For a full analysis of Cairo's Nile Hilton Hotel, see Elsheshtawy, "City Interrupted."

58. "Map of Cairo," drawn by Alexander Nicohosoff after 1933, http://commons.wiki media.org/wiki/File:Cairo_map1933_Nicohosoff.jpg.

59. "Tito and Nasser See New Hotel in Cairo," *New York Times*, 23 February 1959.

60. Anabelle Wharton, *Building the Cold War: Hilton International Hotels and Modern Architecture* (Chicago: University of Chicago Press, 2001).

61. Yasser Elsheshtawy and Bechir Kenzari, "The Ambiguous Veil: On Transparency, Mashrabiyas and Architecture," *Journal of Architectural Education* 56, no. 4 (2003): 17–25.

62. Jay Waltz, "A Top Cairo Hotel Awaits Top Arabs; 12-Country Parley on Israel Will Dislodge Tourists," *New York Times*, 5 January 1964.

63. Raymond Anderson, "Hussein and Arafat Sign Arab Pact to End Clashes," *New York Times*, 28 September 1970.

64. Ashur, *Qit'a min Uruba*, 203.

65. Andrew Humphreys, *Grand Hotels of Egypt: In the Golden Age of Travel* (Cairo: American University in Cairo Press, 2011).

66. For a full Dubai account, see Yasser Elsheshtawy, *Dubai: Behind an Urban Spectacle* (London: Routledge, 2010). At the time of writing, the Nile Hilton was undergoing renovations and was slated to open under a new management (Ritz-Carlton). Events related to the revolution of 25 January 2011 have put this on hold for a while. Recent reports seem to suggest that it will open in the late summer of 2015 ("A Legend Rises Again with the Nile Ritz-Carlton, Cairo," 6 May 2015, http://news.ritzcarlton.com/2015/05/a-legend -rises-again-with-the-nile-ritz-carlton-cairo/). During the revolution the building was inaccessible, surrounded by construction boards, and acted as a curious backdrop to popular mobilization when demonstrations were permitted to take place there. For a discussion of the impact of Gulf- and Dubai-based architecture on the region, see the blog dubaization.com.

67. Naaman, *Urban Space*.

INDEX